Making Memories

Program Guide For Public T.V. Series – 600

By Martha Campbell Pullen, Ph. D.

May God Bless You
Martha Pullen

Book Team

Book Design: Ann Le Roy
Contributing Sewing Designers: Louise Baird, Jena Blair, Margaret Boyles, Elda Bratager,
Kris Broom, Joyce Catoir, Charlotte Gallaher, Brenda Jones, Camela Nitschke, Donna
Marcum, Sue Pennington, Charlotte Potter, Roberta Przybylski, Gail Settle, Beverly Sheldrick,
Patty Smith, Margaret Taylor, Children's Corner and Lydia's
Construction Consultants and Editors: Kathy McMakin, Claudia Newton and Charlotte Potter
Illustrated by: Kris Broom, Angela Pullen and Wendy Schoen
Photography: Jack Cooper Photography, and Jennifer & Company Photography,
Huntsville, AL
Photo Stylists: Marie Hendon, Claudia Newton and Margaret Taylor

Printed By

The C. J. Krehbiel Company
Cincinnati, Ohio

Published And Distributed By

Martha Pullen Company, Inc.
518 Madison Street
Huntsville, Alabama 35801-4286
Phone 205-533-9586
Fax 205-533-9630

Library of Congress Catalog Card Number 96-71614

ISBN 1-878048-11-2

Dedication

To Sue Pennington

Meeting Sue Pennington for the first time was through a garment bag of dresses in Missouri. A friend of hers came to a class that I was teaching and told me she wanted me to look at some garments that a friend of hers had made. That friend was Sue Pennington. The dresses were spectacular and I asked her if this lady would like to sew for me. She answered that she would relay the message to Sue. A few days later I talked with Sue on the telephone and she began the first seams of a long journey we have taken together. If I recall correctly, I sent a box of fabric, laces and trims and Sue returned some fabulous creations very quickly. She is a designer with elegant ideas in her head; her sewing is beyond incredible as well as very fast. The first box of garments arrived in Huntsville and I was absolutely amazed. Not only were the designs creative and unusual, the sewing was as beautiful on the inside as it was on the outside. Her stitching details were as beautiful as the ones on my turn of the century white clothes which are my passion. I quickly began to see that new techniques were about to be written for the magazine and the books using her creativity in sewing, designing, and embroidering. By the way, she can do hand embroidery as well as she sews by machine. Now, that is an unusual talent indeed. Many people sew with perfection. Sue's work is so much more than gorgeous perfection in the stitching. She has a creative dimension that is like no other and it is a pure thrill to see what Sue has designed and made for the next book, magazine or television show.

As many of you know, not everybody can teach. Many people who do beautiful work, don't have the same skills in teaching. Sue is the exception. After she began to teach at our Martha Pullen School of Art Fashion here in Huntsville, her evaluations by our students read like, "Unbelievable teacher; I really understood her technique." "She made things seem so easy." "Sue is such a nice person that I wish I could study with her every week." "I never dreamed that someone who would be such a top notch designer could be such a loving and caring teacher also." Her pre-day classes fill so fast that many people are disappointed when they call too late to get one of Sue's classes. We have some students that just say for the pre-day, "I don't care what Sue is teaching, just sign me up in her class." That is such a compliment and one that Sue Pennington deserves.

When we started the television series, we contacted Sue about sewing many parts of the television series garments and doll clothes. With only a description of the technique to be taught on the show, Sue would design doll clothes and garments with the most joy you can imagine. Her clothes make me happy. Her ideas make me happy. Her doll clothes make me giggle and I love her sewing. She has designed christening dresses for *Grandmother's Hope Chest*, blouses for *Heirloom Sewing For Women*, many projects for our other books and *Sew Beautiful* magazine, and ever so many projects for all of our television series.

She is not only a talented seamstress but also a devoted wife and mother to her husband, Steve and her two precious children, David and Annie. She loves the Lord and her actions and words indicate that completely. She is the author of a fabulous book, *Easy Elegance* published by Albright and Company. Everywhere we go, women are so happy to have Sue's book finally ready for them to buy. God sent Sue into my life to help me guide the business in bringing joy to women who love to sew. Sue Pennington has brought so much joy and sewing happiness to thousands of people through her designs in our television series, *Martha's Sewing Room*. For all the hours of sewing for all of our television series as well as our other books and magazine, thank you. For all you mean to me personally and to my family, thank you. For always having new and innovative ideas and for being willing to share them with our viewers and readers, thank you. For shark's teeth which has probably been the most beloved new technique in heirloom sewing in many years, thank you. For doll dresses, blouses, pillows, little girl dresses, little boy suits, women's clothing, and much more, thank you. It is with much love and appreciation that I dedicate this book to Sue Pennington. We love you and appreciate you more than you will ever know. You are precious to me, my staff and my family.

Acknowledgments

Delight yourself in the Lord and he will give you the desires of your heart. Psalms 37:4

Developing a television series for public television has been a dream of mine for many years, and without the help of God, my family, friends and staff, it would never have happened. I am forever grateful to the following people:

My mother and father, Anna Ruth Dicus Campbell and the late Paul Jones Campbell were my first and greatest teachers. Their example of living a Godly, decent, and hard-working life certainly formed my attitude toward life and what should and could be accomplished. I love them and I thank them.

My children, Camp and Charisse, John and Suzanne, Mark and Sherry Ann, Jeff and Angela and Joanna have always loved me and believed in me. I love them all, and I am so proud of them.

My grandchildren have to be the most beautiful, the smartest, the cutest, and the most creative in the world! Isn't that spoken like a true grandmother? To Campbell, Morgan Ross, Sarah Joy, Rebekah, Marshall, Bradley and Christopher—I love you dearly, and I thank you for coming into my life bringing such pure joy!

My sisters and brothers-Mary, Dottie, Cliff, and Robin-and their families are beautiful individuals whom I love very much. Brothers and sisters are gifts from God who grow more precious with every year.

The University of Alabama has been a real cornerstone in my educational life. My first degree was awarded from this institution in 1965. In 1972, the College of Education offered me enough money for an assistantship, making it possible for me to return to my alma mater to attend graduate school full time. I received my Ph.D. in 1977. To have "my" university as my partner in this television series demonstrates that once more, this great institution was there to help me achieve my goals. I am grateful for all that the University of Alabama means to me and my family. I might add that my husband received both his undergraduate and dental degrees from Alabama, our son Mark received his dental degree from there and my mother received her undergraduate degree from Alabama.

Tom Rieland, Director, Center for Public Television, Alabama Public Television at the University of Alabama, returned my call very quickly when I contacted several states about the possibility of filming a public television series about sewing! Without his vision, this series and this book would not have been possible. Tom, you certainly started this dream on the track of possibilities. Throughout the first two years, Tom has offered excellent advice on promoting the program to PBS stations throughout the US.

Dwight Cameron, Program Director, University of Alabama Center For Public Television, was there to hear my ideas when we first visited Tuscaloosa with two suitcases full of clothing, quilts, and projects. Dwight is unshakable and very creative. Dwight is a perfectionist; the quality of our shows are brought to you under the able and most exacting direction of Dwight. Sometimes I think, "that shot surely was good enough," and Dwight says, "Shoot again." Dwight, thanks for believing in me and in creative sewing.

Mike Letcher, Production Manager, University of Alabama, Center For Public Television, has been uplifting and helpful in the meticulous planning of this series. He carefully explained the necessity of sitting down and planning every minute of 26 shows two months before filming. Mike quietly offers suggestions and sometimes directs from the control room.

Brent Davis, public relations director for The University of Alabama Center For Public Television, has worked diligently helping to open doors to our getting aired on stations all over the country. He prepares excellent promotional packages including computerized breakdowns of each show so the local stations don't have to do much work in order to be ready to air our show. He was instrumental in developing a poster of Martha's Sewing Room to send to each station in the US.

Bill Teague of the University of Alabama Theatre Department has worked long and hard building the wonderful set which houses Martha's Sewing Room. I love the stairs which lead to Martha's Attic. I've been talking about Martha's Attic all these years; now I even have one on my television show.

Dawn Leach and Vince Pruitt, graphics designers with the University of Alabama Center for Public Television, have captured the essence of Martha's Sewing Room with their graphics to introduce and close each show and to divide the sections of the show. Their research into the "feel" of heirloom sewing is greatly appreciated.

I am appreciative to the Southern Educational Communications Association (SECA) for choosing to air Martha's Sewing Room on their satellite. I am especially grateful to the SECA President, Skip Hinton and to the SECA Program Director, Chuck McConnell. Because of Chuck's advice to me a couple of years ago, I believe my performance on this television series is much better than it would have been if he hadn't taken the time to give me an honest evaluation.

Judy Stone and Henry Bonner of Alabama Public Television have offered nothing but encouragement about Martha's Sewing Room. They have done everything possible to share the joy of Martha's Sewing Room with other television networks. APT was the first television network in the U.S. to air the series and I thank them for being great partners.

I want to thank every television station throughout the whole country which has run Martha's Sewing Room. The program directors make decisions concerning which shows will air and which ones do not. We are grateful for every program director who chose us!

My business could not be a reality without the talents of many people. I have dedicated staff who have helped me produce this show and write this book. I love them and I appreciate them.

Kathy Pearce, Toni Duggar, Lakanjala Campbell, Angie Daniel, Amy Duggar, Patsy Vaughan, Camp Crocker, Charisse Crocker, Kathy Brower, Leighann Simmons, Amber Bagsby and Susan Baker have kept the business running while others worked on this book!

Camp Crocker, my son who is in business with me, dreamed of this television show first. He believed that we could do it and insisted that we begin the process several years ago when I didn't think it could possibly happen. I thank him for his vision for not only this television show but for many other creative endeavors in this business. It was also his vision that we put our catalogue on the internet so that people can pull up information not only about our television show but also about our other publications and products.

Patty Smith has always been available to sew clothing for all of our publications. She works with great creativity, speed and enthusiasm even when we ask her to sew 40 things in two days.

Louise Baird creates such gorgeous things with a sewing machine. She always helps us sew and plan, never complaining about deadlines.

Seeley's Doll Company gave us permission to use their doll bodies for the pattern drafting section of this book. They have been wonderful to work with.

Elda Bratager made some of the gorgeous dolls which you see on Martha's Sewing Room. Of course, they have a Seeley's body! Elda's doll clothing is absolutely fabulous, too. She designs, cuts, sews with the greatest of ease, it seems.

The Bernina, Elna, Pfaff, Singer, Baby Lock, and Viking sewing machine companies have been such a support in my business endeavors. They have invited me to teach at their national and international conventions, they have always advertised in the magazine, they have sent in hundreds of sewing machines for my schools here in Huntsville, they have sent educators to teach with us, they have planned for our traveling schools with their dealers over the world, and they have opened many doors for me. We appreciate their willingness to allow us to use their machines alternately on this television series. I consider this to be the ultimate in cooperation among companies. Each one of these companies is as wonderful as their machines, and I am very grateful not only to the corporate offices but also to the wonderful dealers around the world who have supported me and my business. We appreciate each company's sending in educators for this 500 and 600 series. They have added so much as guest celebrities.

Donna Marcum, Jena Blair, Joyce Catoir, Susan York, Patty Smith, Laura Jenkins Thompson, Mary Soltice, Louise Baird, Mary Penton, Gail Settle, Charlotte Gallaher, Sue Pennington, The Children's Corner, Claudia Newton and Margaret Taylor loaned us garment after garment for our beautiful clothing for the introductory section of each show. Each of them have helped this endeavor in so many different ways.

My daughter, Joanna Pullen, was the original inspiration for this whole business and she has been a vital part of all aspects.

Gail Settle designed and made pillows and crafts with such flair. Her work is so exciting and fresh.

Charlotte Gallaher has such creative ability. She made some of our boxes and crafts.

Marie Hendon has helped us in so many aspects of our business for many years. Her sewing is wonderful.

Camela Nitschke does beautiful ribbon work and it is a pleasure to have her as a guest on some of our shows.

Brenda Jones is a wonderful seamstress and designer. She sews beautifully and with great precision.

Charlotte Potter has helped with sewing and in getting ready for the taping of the shows. Her willingness to help is a valuable asset to us, as well as her talent for designing and sewing.

Claudia Newton's work at a sewing machine is unbelievable. She's made clothing and pillows that take my breath away. She is an excellent television star and teaches with precision.

Louise Baird has become a great little television star and demonstrates techniques like no one else can.

Margaret Boyles has been teaching with me for over 13 years. It is such a pleasure to have her demonstrate embroidery for the viewing audience.

Sue Pennington designed doll dresses, pillows, garments and "story boards" for the series. She stitched until all hours of the night helping us meet deadlines. I truly don't know what I would do in this business without her.

Donna Marcum, Joyce Catoir and Jena Blair are always willing to create and stitch designs for doll dresses, girls dresses and home decorating projects with a moments notice. Their work is beyond beautiful.

Jack Cooper's photography is professional and creative. He has such patience in working with little people.

Cynthia Handy-Quintella is much appreciated for the lovely illustrations on lace shaping.

Angela Pullen's drawings add life and magic to all of our books. Her illustrations have great depth, detail, and creativity. She always meets deadlines and never complains about the boxes of work that we send her.

Beverly Sheldrick came into my life at one of my courses in Australia years ago. Her designs fascinated me then and they still do. I appreciate her coming from New Zealand to teach silk ribbon stitches for this series. I love her silk ribbon projects which she created just for our television series and this book.

Ann Le Roy's book design is creative and lends a professional touch to all of the sections. It is not an easy task to take hundreds of drawings and computer disks of information and create a book out of it. To have an element of style and beauty in addition to correctness of directions and pictures is quite a feat. It overwhelms me to think of all the decisions which she had to make concerning the layout of this book.

Margaret Taylor stitched the heirloom quilt, wrote directions on several sections, prepared items for the television show "how-to" portions and in general helped with everything. Margaret is always there with her talent in many different areas. I also think she is a great television teacher.

Kris Broom's designing and drawing ability for the "how-to" sections absolutely amaze me. Not only are her illustrations gorgeous, she knows how to draw everything in the construction sequence by just looking at the item.

Wendy Schoen also did beautiful illustrations showing how-to steps for some sections. I have known Wendy for several years and she is a very talented designer and artist.

Kathy McMakin's pattern drafting, construction ideas, technical writing skills and designing/sewing ability make her invaluable to every aspect of this business. She literally helped with every part of this book from direction writing to sewing and serging. Her contributions to this television series program guide are vast. Now her talents include television teaching and she does a great job of it all.

There is one person to whom I am especially grateful. Next to God, he has been my faithful advisor, my financial partner, my idea person, and my mentor. My husband, Joe Ross Pullen, has always believed in me more than I believe in myself. I can truthfully tell each of you who enjoys this television show as well as all of our books and the magazine, Sew Beautiful, that none of these things would be available for you today if Joe hadn't paid the bills many times to keep my business going for the first ten years. He is a wonderful dentist and has been one of the worldwide pioneers in implant dentistry. It is so exciting to me to see him still traveling to take new courses in new areas of dentistry. He is a wonderful Christian husband and father, and God blessed me beyond my wildest imaginations the day that Joe asked me to marry him twenty-two years ago. He is my best friend and my partner. I love him, and I thank him.

A number of years ago, I gave this whole business to God. He took it, figured out what to do next, and has given the guidance for moving in the directions in which we are moving. All the credit and glory for any success that we have had in the sewing industry go to Him and Him alone. The path has not been nor is it now an easy one. I don't think He promised us an easy trip through life. He did promise to be with us always and I can testify that He has never failed me. ▨

Special Thanks To Our Underwriters

It is so exciting to have completed the 500 and 600 series of Martha's Sewing Room! Dreaming of producing a television series for PBS had been in my mind for many years. Having that dream come true is a blessing from God! Your response to this television series has been greatly appreciated and we are running on all or part of the public television stations in at least 44 states of this great United States of America! Many people helped this dream come true. Six of those "people" are actually companies who believed in this series enough to underwrite with great generosity! I thank them, and I believe in their products or I wouldn't have asked them to be the underwriters.

When you need notions please give consideration to calling Clotilde! Her catalogue is all inclusive for heirloom sewing and other types of sewing also! When you stitch with silk ribbon, wool thread or other types of decorative threads, please give consideration to choosing YLI brands! You won't be sorry! When you need to purchase a sewing machine cabinet, please look for the Parsons name! You will love the Martha Pullen cabinet! When you need scissors or rotary cutters, please look for the Fiskars name! You will love the quality and the price! When you need heirloom sewing supplies, please call Linda's Silver Needle! She has it all for heirloom sewing! When you are in the market for a new automobile, truck or van, please give consideration to buying a Ford! My family loves our Ford vehicles!

I have known Clotilde nearly as long as I have been in this business. Her catalogue will forever be a boost to the sewing industry and her enthusiasm is unending. She helped me spread the word about Sew Beautiful magazine to millions of people through her catalogue. She has sold thousands of books from us, and I have bought lots of notions from her. She even has an heirloom/Martha Pullen Suggests section in her catalogue! She has always been there for me for friendship and for business advice. She and Don even furnished the place for my son Camp and his bride Charisse to go for their honeymoon. Thanks Clotilde!

Esther and Dan Randall of YLI have been good friends for ever so long. My first trip to Utah was to teach for them in one of our traveling schools. I have enjoyed a long and exciting relationship with both them and their children, Nancy, Scott, Dana, and Esther. Esther Randall is responsible for reviving the art of silk ribbon embroidery and spreading it to the world. Esther and Dan have opened many doors for me in this sewing industry and they are truly close friends. Everyone has enjoyed the silk ribbon sections on Martha's Sewing Room. She is now importing the lovely New Zealand wools to bring back the art of wool embroidery. Thanks Esther and Dan!

Barbara Parsons Massey loves heirloom sewing and is a new shop owner in Arkansas. When I first told my school in February about the new television series, she came to me immediately

and said, "Martha, who are your underwriters going to be?" After I replied that I didn't know yet, she said, "Well, I want Parsons Cabinets to be one." I am so excited about the first Martha Pullen Designer Cabinet made by Parsons! It is everything I ever wanted in a sewing machine cabinet to go in my den! Thanks Barbara and Bud! And Jessie, too! (Jessie is their granddaughter who has traveled to Huntsville many times with her grandparents!)

My relationship with Fiskars Scissors company first came about when I purchased a pair of their "arthritis" scissors. After seeing the absolutely perfect quality of these lightweight scissors, I had to have several more pairs. I found out about the kindergarten scissors with the blunt point and I found my dream scissors for trimming fabric from behind laces! Another thing I enjoy about Fiskars is their reasonable price for the absolute best quality! I have enjoyed working with Kevin Phays and Sandra Cashman in telling them about our dreams and in sharing with them how completely sold I was on Fiskars.

Linda's Silver Needle has been one of the most dynamic mail order companies in the heirloom sewing industry! Linda has sold thousands of my books and offers quick service all over the United States. When I called Linda to see if she would like to underwrite the 300 and 400 series, she absolutely squealed and said, "I am so thrilled that you have called me. We love the series and would be honored to help bring it to our friends out across the United States." Linda Steffens is a true friend and conscientious supplier for loads of heirloom sewing supplies which are sometimes hard to find locally. Thanks, Linda!

To my friends at the Ford Motor Company in Detroit I must say thank you. I believe this is the first time that one of the largest companies in the world has chosen to fund a sewing show and I think that speaks to me in letting me know that Ford truly cares about women's interests and women. I can vouch for the fact that my immediate family has bought 3 Ford vehicles in the last two years and we have loved each one of them! Joe loves his big Ford truck (the biggest Ford makes) and says he would never drive another truck again because this one is so comfortable! Ford, thanks for believing in women who love to sew! Thanks for putting this woman's show as a top priority in your advertising plan!

To Clotilde, YLI, Parsons Cabinets, Fiskars, Linda's Silver Needle and Ford, I hope you love the programs as much as we do. Since your products are the very best, I know our viewers will be anxious to purchase them. I also know the readers and viewers who love Sew Beautiful magazine and Martha's Sewing Room will also appreciate your making this program possible, in part. Our readers and viewers tend to be very loyal individuals, and I feel assured that they will give your products every consideration. ▨

Table of Contents

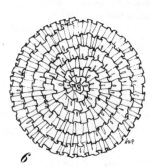

Show Index

Foreword To This Program Guide

It thrills me beyond words to know that our television show is being played somewhere in 47 of the states of this great United States. You, our viewers, have been instrumental in getting our show on the air since the PBS stations really do want to hear from their viewers. Thank you so very much and I certainly must thank each and every television station who has played our series, *Martha's Sewing Room*. We have loved making every series of *Martha's Sewing Room* and this 600 series is no exception. I really believe that this series is better than ever and we have many new and exciting things in this show guide!

We have had so many wonderful comments about *Martha's Sewing Room*. Some viewers enjoy the broad range of subjects that are covered, while others particularly appreciate the antiques in the attic and the volunteer sewing ideas. Others say that even the non-sewing members of their families enjoy the show just for the beauty of the projects, including doll dresses and children's clothing, adult clothing, home decorating ideas, crafts and quilts. There truly is something for everyone and we thank you for your enthusiasm.

After all of the projects come in from all of our designers, we start the real process of final show evaluation. We have to find out if the project is really exciting enough and beautiful enough or different enough to be included. Asking many questions about each project enables us to evaluate if you will really love having the show guide with the patterns and the directions. Being "not wonderful or not interesting enough" means that certain projects get pulled out of the schedule even after they are finished. That doesn't happen often, but it does happen. We evaluate until the final couple of weeks before we go to film. Everything is discussed and re-discussed.

Margaret Boyles has once again added her special touch with hand embroidery. Our hand silk ribbon teacher for this series is Beverly Sheldrick from New Zealand. Beverly has authored a book on this topic and she was delighted to fly in to appear on the 600 series. Her stitches as well as her

projects designed especially for this show are most exciting and different.

Knowing that lots of you make gifts, we have again included some beautiful craft and home decorating ideas perfect for anyone on your gift list. There is a wonderful angel quilt designed by Angela Pullen that will make quilters of those who thought they would never try it; Margaret Taylor gives great construction tips. Camela Nitschke, from Perrysburg, Ohio, also starred in an exciting ribbon show with her elegant ribbon shaping techniques used to make beautiful lamp shades for home decoration.

Since the antique clothing section in the series 500 show guide was so well received, we decided to include artist's illustrations and complete descriptions of the antique clothing in this show guide as well. This is something you have loved about many of our other books.

We have many brand new techniques included in this book as well as an overview of basic French Sewing Techniques and Lace Shaping Techniques. These great techniques are used on the doll dresses and the girl's dresses. The doll dresses are the prettiest we have ever had and include basic dresses with gorgeous pinafore variations. Notice how full all of the skirts are! The child's dress is absolutely elegant and one that so many little girls will love to wear. The pattern is for a pinafore or sundress and was adapted from an antique garment.

The wonderful joy of heirloom sewing is celebrated in this television series as well as this book with the instructions and projects. Please enjoy this book and know that we are very happy with its contents. Please send us any suggestions you may have for improvements to the shows or the show guides, or suggestions for future projects. Thank you again for believing in us and our television series; it was produced with love for your pleasure. Without your excitement and loyalty we wouldn't have the privilege of coming into your home with this series and/or this book. ▨

Antique Clothing

I am so glad that you have enjoyed my attic presentation at the end of each *Martha's Sewing Room* show. My husband has always accused me of having an unnatural attraction to antique clothing, especially the white garments from the end of the last century and the beginning of this one. I believe we have some very beautiful ones for this 600 series and you will find lots of creative ideas to adapt for your own garments, home decoration pieces and doll clothing.

The French Pinafore shown at the right was the inspiration for the pinafore variations shown throughout this series. The Tucks and Lace Dress is a good choice for duplication, from the elegant simplicity of the sleeves, to the beautiful bodice of the dress to the simple paneled skirt with the three tucks on the bottom. Can you imagine wearing drawers as elaborate as the Lace Butterfly Drawers? Even more interesting, can you imagine putting that much work into underwear? The Lace Rectangles Dress is simple and beautiful. This dress falls more in the tailored category for those of you with little girls who like tailored clothing. Using silk ribbon on clothing isn't a thing just for the late 1900s; it was used in the early part of this century also. I love the details on the Batiste, Netting and Silk Ribbon Dress. I love the sleeves on the Pintucks and Galloon Lace Blouse. It would be so easy to make this sleeve with a double needle.

Oh, how I love that Massachusetts Vintage Clothing Show in Sturbridge. The Massachusetts Little Girl's Dress is a masterpiece with details from the double lace edging gathered at the bottom of the sleeves to the tucks holding in the fullness of the skirt. These are such traditional details for us to use on something we make. Using a dish towel purchased in Albertville, Alabama, we helped inspire the peek-a-boo technique used so eloquently on a white pinafore. I think you will also love the peek-a-boo technique on the Triangular Ruffle Christening Dress.

Finding printed voile fabrics used in vintage heirlooms is so unusual that I jumped up and down when I found the Pink Flowered Blouse. It is very delicate; however, it held up for the television show and for the artist to illustrate it for you to see. Finding shadow work embroidery on antique clothing is also difficult at best. I was elated to find the White Shadow Work Blouse, which even has white shadow work on the sleeves.

Feeling like a kid in a candy shop, I couldn't believe my eyes when I spotted the Victorian Picture Transfer Pillow. The Wedding Blouse and Skirt in white organdy is gorgeous and has the most creative ruffles over the sleeve caps. Mrs. Crocker's Bow Dress thrilled me to pieces since my boys' name is Crocker. I don't think I have ever bought a dress which was in a box addressed to someone. I think this dress would be wonderful to copy using today's fabulous embroidery stitches on the machines. I certainly wouldn't do it by hand. I also love the bows on the skirt of this glorious dress. Once again, the Linen Four Leaf Flower Blouse would be so easily adapted for today's wearing by using the embroidery features on your sewing machine or embroidery machine. Have fun if you are so fortunate as to own one of these beauties.

Enjoy this section and enjoy looking at these clothes on the 600 series of Martha's Sewing Room. Maybe you will be inspired to create a special garment of your own!

Mrs. Crocker's Bow Dress

French Pinafore

Lace Butterfly Drawers

French Pinafore Used as Inspiration for the 600 Series Pinafore Pattern

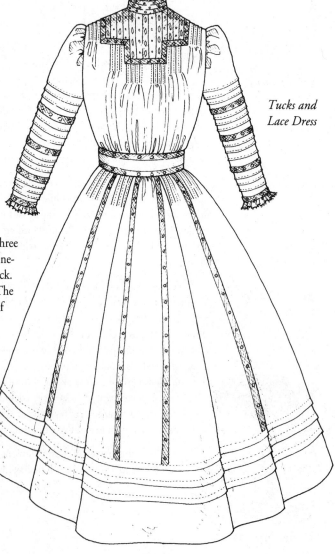

It was at the Paris Flea Market in an elegant little antique clothing shop that I spotted this beautiful pinafore. Made of white Swiss batiste and featuring white on white Swiss embroideries, it demanded my attention. One of the main reasons for our trip to Paris was to purchase antique garments for the 600 series of *Martha's Sewing Room*. After examining the details of this classic pinafore, I thought I might have found the garment to use as inspiration for the pattern for the series.

Using the fold-back miter method which we have enjoyed for several years now, this French mother was probably very excited as she made this adorable pinafore for her cute little girl. The mitered neck piece is composed of four straight strips of narrow fabric and three strips of Swiss quadruple entredeux with little squares in-between. Flat Swiss edging finishes the neckline. Two rows of wider eyelet trim finish the bodice; one is around the armscye and one travels over the shoulder. A placket opens the back and two pearl buttons close the top of the bodice. Eighteen tiny released tucks are found on the middy waistline section of the bodice. Three rows of fabric with two rows of Swiss quadruple entredeux finish the midsection. The gathered skirt is very pretty with three ¼" tucks on the bottom and a deep hem. It is from this pinafore that we present the pinafores for this series. Enjoy! ▨

French Pinafore

Tucks and Lace Dress

Prim and prissy is what I almost named this white dress because of its delicate daisy maline laces. Using tucks in four different places is very unusual in a dress and I especially like the use of tucks on this dress. The mitered lace on the bodice surrounds lace strips stitched together. Three strips of lace make the high collar with gathered lace finishing the top. One-eighth-inch released tucks are found on the bodice front as well as the back. The sleeves have four sets of three tucks between the strips of insertion. The bottom is finished with straight insertion and gathered lace. Two strips of insertion circle the waistline with a strip of plain white batiste in the center. One-fourth-inch tucks are used to gather in the fullness between the strips of lace running vertically down the skirt.

The three tucks on the skirt bottom are three-fourths-inch wide and the hem is nearly five inches deep. The back is closed with ten buttons and buttonholes and there are hooks and eyes at the waistline, with one button and buttonhole between the two hooks and eyes. Hooks and eyes also close the placket found below the waistline of the dress. ▨

Tucks and Lace Dress

Peek–A–Boo Strips Dish Towel

Who would ever imagine that a pinafore as elegant as the one in this series would be inspired by a 1930 vintage dish towel? Sometimes when I examine closely the amount of embroidery on dish towels, I cannot possibly imagine putting that kind of work into a towel for such utilitarian purposes. I found this towel at an antique store in Albertville, Alabama and it has such fascinating work. The butterfly is orange and has the most gorgeous buttonhole stitches around the outside of the butterfly. There are orange flowers and brown trims on both the flowers and on the butterfly. Bright green leaves and stems finish the picture. Bright orange featherstitch surrounds each of the diamonds on the bottom and a lovely purchased trim which looks very much like tatting is found on the bottom.

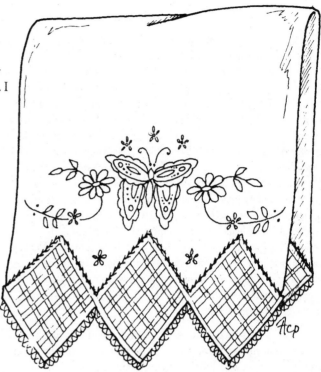

The strips on the elegant diamonds are bias strips which have been doubled. They are crossed and each cross section is stitched with a tiny square. These same crossed diamonds are found on the back of the towel without the butterfly embroidery motif. Tiny little orange stitches tack the bottom trim in place. I would like to know if women really used these dish towels or if they just hung them in the kitchen for beauty? ▨

Peek–A–Boo Strips Dish Towel

Pink Flowered Blouse

Rarely do I find anything of a Victorian vintage which has printed fabric. This fabric is so beautiful and it looks as if pink roses have been water colored on the fabric. Actually there are six little lines woven into the fabric which appear to be double needle pintucks. Of course they couldn't be since double needles weren't invented at the time this fabric was woven. A really beautiful panel goes over the shoulders on this blouse and three rows of French edging have been stitched together to form the outline trim for these panels. Two rows of French edging are stitched at the top of the blouse neckline on both the front and back. A wider row of French edging is gathered and stitched at the bottom of the puffed sleeve.

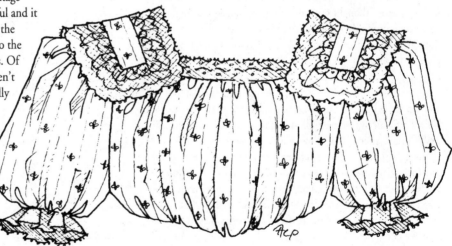

The blouse has a lining as was typical of pigeon breast garments; the lining was closed with hooks and eyes. I would be willing to bet that the blouse closed with tiny beauty pins. This blouse is really different and I found it in an antique store in Huntsville, AL. ▨

Pink Flowered Blouse

White Shadow Work Blouse

Flea markets all over the world are absolute passions of mine. I would love to think that white Victorian clothing is found in major antique stores; however, I don't think that is true. My finds are usually at flea markets and this blouse is no exception. Joe and I had discovered one final flea market in Paris. We hopped a cab and went tearing to the other side of Paris, of course knowing that we couldn't speak a word of French after we got there. Not too many French speak English and certainly not at a flea market on the wrong side of Paris. This blouse caught my eye immediately and upon examining the embroidery I found my very favorite, shadow work. Very few of my antique pieces have shadow work embroidery so needless to say, I purchased it. This particular antique dealer was a very friendly man who was most anxious to sell us everything he had. He went immediately to another booth and brought back a man who spoke a little English. We purchased lots of things from him and he said he would bring more to our hotel for us to look at later. Getting this message across was interesting to say the least; however, he did show up on Thursday morning with several garbage bags of goodies.

The flowers are beautiful on this blouse and each petal has tiny French knots running down the center. Stem stitches make the stems connecting the flowers. Six tiny released pintucks are on either side of the shoulder area and more beautiful shadow work is found on each cuff. A really sweet tuck is at the top of the flowers on the sleeve and two tiny pintucks are on the bottom. Gathered lace is found on the bottom of the sleeve. More flowers and gathered lace are found on the collar. The back is beautiful also with its three sets of three released tucks. The back is closed with buttons and buttonholes; a placket covers the button treatment. ▣

*White Shadow
Work Blouse*

Victorian Picture Transfer Pillow

Upon first viewing the modern version of picture transfer a few years ago, I thought we had certainly come upon something very new indeed. Wrong was I! Apparently this method of transferring favorite pictures of family, places and friends was popular many years ago also. This dark ecru piece came out of a Massachusetts estate and probably dates around 1910. The photo transfer is chocolate brown. Actually, I'm just guessing on the date since the picture could have been older than the pillow. Silk is the fabric on this picture pillow and it is lovely. Measuring 18" by 18", the center of the pillow is almost covered by a picture featuring a family of thirteen children of varying ages. A very full five-inch wide ruffle is gathered around the pillow. This ruffle has a one-fourth-inch tuck and a one-fourth-inch hem on the very edge; this appears to be two tucks on the edge of the ruffle. Pillows like this would be the perfect way to use your old photos to make permanent memories for each of your family members. With today's technology, it would also be appropriate to use color photographs for a collage. Please get a permanent marking pen to write whose photograph it is on the front and the date and place it was taken. I am amazed at how many photographs that my grandmother had kept, but I have no idea who is in the photographs. Of course, you could also stitch the information on the back of the pillow using the alphabet capability on your sewing machine. Either way, this photo transfer pillow is a great idea. ▣

*Victorian Picture
Transfer Pillow*

Massachusetts Little Girl's Dress

Searching each stall at a Massachusetts show, my friend Ann Sullivan alerted me that she had found a few things in a booth that I hadn't yet discovered. This stunning little girl's white batiste dress she had tucked in her arms. The dealer apologized that the dress was torn in the back and that she hadn't had time to properly repair the dress. The price was very reasonable, which is certainly unusual in antique shopping these days. I immediately took the dress and only when I got it home did I realize the full extent of the wonderful details on this masterpiece. Needless to say, it isn't too hard for me to repair a dress as long as the fabric isn't too rotten.

Forming the high yoke of the dress is a beautiful piece of round thread lace about 2¹/₂" wide. The scalloped edge is used for the neckline finish. The shoulder piece is stitched straight and the center pieces of both the front and back are inserted straight also. Many dresses made like this are mitered at the corners of the front and back. Two beautiful lace edging rosettes have been rolled on either side of the front bodice. Tiny silk ribbon flowers in pink, blue and green have been stitched in the center of each of these rosettes. It is very rare to see rosettes made of lace.

The sleeves are probably the fullest puffs that I have seen in a turn-of-the-century sleeve and they are gorgeous. They are finished with a little bias band on the bottom and the most unusual lace treatment is found. Two rows of French round thread insertion are gathered very full and stitched on; one is at the top of the tiny bias binding and one is at the bottom.

The skirt has sixty-two inches of fullness and is made of the most beautiful Swiss embroidered border eyelet. Released tucks and gathers are featured on the front bodice as well as the back. There are two sets of four tucks and two sets of seven tucks on the front of the dress. The tucks are five inches in length. In the back of the dress there are sets of eight tucks close to the placket. It would be my guess that this mother needed to take in a little extra fullness in the back and just put in another tuck. The eyelet has deep, large scallops composed of smaller scallops; the embroidery design looks like roses and leaves. The machine-embroidered eyelet has been made of a course thread to make it resemble true embroidery. I had to check the back of the eyelet very carefully to be sure that it was machine embroidery rather than by hand.

I love the bottom of the dress. French edging lace has been added below the eyelet; a strip of Swiss batiste is next. Next comes French gallooning, which has two finished sides, and a fabulous French edging nearly three inches wide is slightly gathered at the bottom of this gallooning. The back of the dress is as beautiful as the front and even has the little French edging rolled rosettes near the center back where one finds the buttons and handmade loops. The back top yoke made of lace has four pearl buttons for its closing. ▨

Massachusetts Little Girl's Dress

Wedding Blouse and Skirt

Made of white organdy and lace, this has to be one of the most elegant wedding ensembles that I have ever seen. After shopping at a Massachusetts show for hours, I walked by a booth and saw a dress on a mannequin that hadn't been there just hours before. I thought, "That dress just winked at me and I had promised myself that I was through buying and ready to go back to the hotel room." What beautiful sleeves with their three bias organdy and lace ruffles. The top two pointed ruffles have three points; the bottom one has five. The bottom of the sleeve is finished with a bias organdy ruffle trimmed with narrow lace. The bias ruffle around the neck goes all the way around the bodice and two rows of lace insertion finish the upper bodice of the dress. There is a boned and fitted under-bodice with looser organdy on the top.

The skirt is cut on the straight of grain, but all of the ruffles are cut on the bias and trimmed with very narrow lace matching the lace ruffles on the bodice. The three narrow bias ruffles on the skirt are three inches wide; the bottom ruffle is eight inches wide. The train is beautiful and this skirt would make a gorgeous skirt for a wedding dress today. ▨

Wedding Blouse

Wedding Skirt

Mrs. Crocker's Bow Dress

This is probably one of the most fabulous dresses that I have ever purchased. Once again, my friend Ann Sullivan found this white Swiss batiste, embroidered, lace shaped dress in the booth next to the one where I was browsing. It was in a box addressed to Mrs. Crocker which contained this dress plus a petticoat. Many times I can't be sure if a garment were intended for a graduation dress or a wedding dress. Surely this was a wedding dress because it is one of the most elaborate that I have ever seen. The details on this dress are breathtaking. At first I thought the embroidery was done by hand. Upon closer study, I can truly say that it might be Swiss embroidery done probably 100 years ago. During that era, Swiss embroidery was done in an almost coarse thread, sometimes, to give the look of hand embroidery. To tell if an antique embroidery is Swiss or hand, turn the garment over to the back and see where the threads cross on a pattern. If the threads cross at exactly the same places on all of the other patterns, it is machine made. If the threads don't match on the back, then most likely the embroidery was done by hand.

The bodice of the dress features so many details it is hard to describe them. Finding lace shaped bows is almost an impossibility. This dress has flip-flopped bows on the bodice and the skirt. The streamers of the bows are flip-flopped down to the lace insertion on the skirt. The back bodice of the dress has more flip-flopped bows; however, the back skirt panels only have the beautiful white on white embroidery. The round yoke bodice has a row of lace insertion around the neckline with a row of lace edging meeting the embroidery on the bodice of the dress. The sleeves have a beautifully embroidered panel in the middle and Irish crocheted lace on both sides of this embroidered panel. The bottom of sleeves finds rows of lace insertion with lace edging gathered at the top and bottom of this insertion cuff.

The front and back bodices of this dress feature flip-flopped bows of French round thread lace insertion, shaped Irish crocheted lace insertion and beautiful, heavy Swiss embroidery. The seamstress even cut out pieces of the heavy embroidery and stitched it on top of the lace to appear as if the embroidery is handmade. Tiny released pintucks are found at the top of the bodice on both the front and the back. I might add that the back bodice of this dress is as beautiful as the front. This is typically the case with Victorian garments.

The skirt has a total of six panels and there are seven 1¹/₂" released pintucks at the top of each panel. Two rows of Irish crocheted lace form the waistband. The panels on the skirt are separated by either a single row of French round thread lace insertion or two rows of the same. The skirt panels in the front have large flip-flopped bows made of French round thread insertion. Each bow has four streamers flowing from the bow. On the front two panels, the flip-flopped bow is found higher on the skirt; on the two side panels the bows are found much lower. All of the skirt flip-flopped bows have four streamers. The bottom of the skirt features lace insertion stitched horizontally and there is a double hem on the bottom. The panels on the back of the dress have embroidery only, but it stretches from the hip area to the top of the horizontal lace pieces on the bottom. The back of the dress is closed with covered lace buttons and tiny loops.

Finding a dress like this one thrills me to the very depths of my heart. This dress might be reproduced today if one could find embroidery similar to this or if one were willing to do this much hand-stitched embroidery. I certainly wish dresses could speak so this one could tell me her story. Please, when you make heirloom garments, stitch in the information for your family members to know about in the next generation. ▨

Lace Butterfly Drawers

I believe this is the fanciest underwear that I have ever seen! Split drawers were the style around the turn of the century and what drawers these were. The lace shaping is so unusual that we have included it in this book. The French lace butterfly motifs were made at the factory; however, I believe it would be very easy to copy these motifs in lace today if one adds a little bit of hand embroidery. Perhaps one of your embroidery machines would stitch in a butterfly outline around lace pieces; then you could embroider the veins in the wings. The lace shaping makes little boxes with its crosses and the main lace is flat on the bottom with miters at the top to make a little house-like effect. This lace shaping would be beautiful on the bottom of any garment that you might want to make. This particular butterfly would be gorgeous in many places on many garments. It would be especially appropriate if you cut a large serger hole in your French dresses somewhere.

Seven rows of lace and Swiss beading complete the waistline treatment. The waist measures twenty-four inches around. There are two rows of beading with ribbon run through. The top ribbon ties to close the drawers. There are also four pearl buttons with buttonholes for closing down the stomach area. What gorgeous drawers! ▨

Lace Butterfly Drawers

Lace Butterfly Drawers Template

Triangular Ruffle Christening Dress
(Antique Peek-a-Boo Technique)

Sometimes I find something so wonderful that I am practically squealing. I purchased this dress on my first trip to England after opening my business. Made of white batiste, it has two very unusual design features. The first is a beautiful ruffle which has three points of batiste with lace edging around the points. The second is a beautiful detail of lace with bias tubing in-between the design points. To reproduce this technique see our technique section (Antique Peek-a-Boo). We have used this technique on a doll dress as well as a pinafore. To reproduce the lace technique on this dress, it is necessary to have a heavy, round thread lace with a large single pattern. This pattern needs to have space in-between each design so there will be room for the bias tubing.

The bodice of the dress is composed of $^3/_4$ inch wide lace insertion strips zigzagged

together. To reproduce the antique, any width insertion can be used in place of the $^3/_4$ inch width. The zigzagged lace piece should measure about $8^1/_2$ inches by 11 inches in order to be placed at the proper angle to go into any size christening dress. Bias tubing $^1/_8$ inch wide is double-stitched using a double needle right on top of the zigzagged lines. For a slightly different method of working this same technique, refer to Antique Peek-a-Boo in the new technique section of this book.

On the skirt there are three pintucks on either side of the single row of insertion which travels around the bottom of the dress. The double hem goes up to the insertion and strips of bias tubing have been stitched in between each rose design in the dress. The total length of this christening dress is forty-two inches. ▨

Triangular Ruffle
Christening Dress

Batiste, Netting And Silk Ribbon Dress

Loving silk ribbon trims isn't just a passion for the late 1990's; the late 1890's had the same love of silk ribbon trims. This batiste dress has a very unusual silk ribbon trim at the top of the belt. The basic dress is relatively simple with its stitched-down pleated skirt and released pleats in the bodice. There is a bodice lining of netting which has three pintucks underneath the netting/scalloped edging pieces on either side of the front buttons. These buttons are there for looks only since the dress opens to the side and has snaps in the left side of the netting lining. A little peach silk ribbon bow is found at the center neckline at the top of the pearl buttons. A sweet netting collar which is square in the back finishes off the neckline. The square collar has a $1^1/2$" wide row of edging made of the same netting with scallops finishing the edge. A row of entredeux is used to join the square netting collar and the netting/scalloped edge ruffle. The sleeves have a $3/4$" tuck at the top and at the bottom, and a little netting undersleeve peeks out; entredeux once again joins a netting/scalloped edge ruffle to the netting lining of the sleeve. The $2^1/2$" wide batiste cummerbund is absolutely beautiful; it is stitched into the dress at the waistline except for the center front which must be loose in order to open the dress. There is a 2" wide folded peach silk ribbon gathered and stitched onto the top of the cummerbund. The back of the dress has 10 released pleats which are stitched down about 4" and then tied off. The skirt has a simple $4^1/2$" hem which has been stitched using a straight stitch on a sewing machine. The whole bodice of the dress has been lined with cotton netting. ▨

Batiste,
Netting And
Silk Ribbon
Dress

Linen Four Leaf Flower Blouse

I always get excited when I find a garment which is truly unusual. Of course hand embroidery always gets my attention, also. This blouse is made of a heavy linen and has the most elegant heavy embroidery on the front. Four $3/8$" tucks are on each shoulder. Heavy embroidered four leaf flowers have heavy buttonhole stitching on the outside around French knots filling in each leaf. There are six beautifully worked eyelets in the center of each flower. Satin stitches make loops around the flowers and the stems are stem stitched. There is a matching but smaller flower on the cuffs with gathered heavy round thread lace on the bottom.

The back of the blouse is beautiful with sixteen buttons and buttonholes for closing. Four tucks are found on either side of the back placket. Looking at this blouse, I can envision making a heavy linen blouse using our wonderful embroidery machines with white on white or ecru on ecru. I truly think sixteen buttons and buttonholes would be beautiful also. With today's machines making small buttonholes perfectly, it wouldn't be such a chore. You might want to be sure that you have someone to button your blouse if you put this many buttonholes in! ▨

Linen Four Leaf Flower Blouse

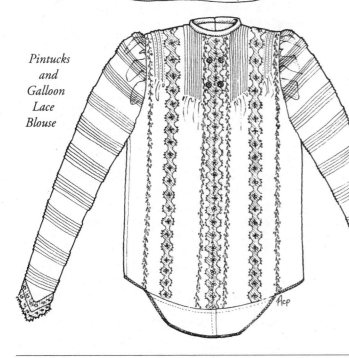

*Lace
Rectangles Dress*

Lace Rectangles Dress

Featuring a beautiful Swiss fabric with tiny daisy-like embroidered clusters scattered about, this gorgeous dress has wonderful rectangular shapes of lace on both the bodice and the skirt. The bodice features $1/8$" tucks on the front and the back. The laces are crossed and mitered in a beautiful way and the center bodice has four layers of French lace insertion. The sleeves are tailored and pretty, ending with two rows of insertion plus gathered lace edging. Two rows of lace insertion are found around the waistline. There is a double row of fabric behind these waistline lace insertions. The bust of this dress measures forty inches around and the waistline is twenty-four inches. Maybe I have found one dress without a twenty-inch waist!

The skirt has 102 inches of fullness, which is very unusual for Victorian dresses. The laces are very pretty in their horizontal placement with the miters at each corner. I simply like the skirt design on this garment. The back of the dress, as usual, is as beautiful as the front with its almost matching designs and ten buttons and buttonholes for closing. The waistline is closed with hooks and eyes and there is a placket in the skirt. The back skirt has not only gathers, but also tucks to gather in the fullness. That is such a pretty way to gather a skirt so it doesn't have so much fullness at the waistline seam. ▣

*Pintucks
and
Galloon
Lace
Blouse*

Pintucks and Galloon Lace Blouse

Using several types of lace, this blouse has beautiful details. Galloons resembling crochet are found in the center and on either side of the blouse front. Tiny pintucks, nine on each side of the center lace, are about six inches long. Three $1/4$" pintucks are on each side of the second strip of gallooning. A curved embroidered stem with what appears to be little white satin stitched grapes travels from the shoulder to the bottom of the front of the blouse. The sleeves are really beautiful and have a lovely pintuck treatment which would be beautiful on a sleeve for a blouse for today. Ten sets of six pintucks are found horizontally on the sleeve and the pointed cuff has two rows of a crochet-like trim on it. The back of the blouse has three sets of five pintucks on each side of the buttons and there are beautiful round pearl buttons to close the garment. There is entredeux in-between the shoulder seams. The neck is finished with a fabric binding about $3/4$" wide. There are so many beautiful ideas from this blouse which could be used on many garments. ▣

Introduction To Doll Dresses

Making doll dresses has been a passion of mine since I was five years old. I always think about Alice in Wonderland when I think of pinafores and the pinafores in this 600 series are the cutest doll dresses I have ever seen. There is such variety and there are so many cute techniques you will love doing or studying; you will learn all types of new techniques while dressing your doll. Scalloped skirts are fabulous on dolls or on children or pillowcases or wedding dresses; our white dotted Swiss one will make you very happy. I love the ribbons pinafore which has blue bow trim to decorate it. You could use blue bows or any color of bow to celebrate any occasion. If you love to embroider and the French knot is your area of mastery, there is the cutest little French knot lamb pinafore for your special doll. And if your doll doesn't have a shadow sandwich pinafore, shame on you!

Copying antique Victorian clothing is possibly my greatest sewing passion. I travel, literally, all over the world searching for beautiful white garments to share with you, our television audience, as well as our audience for *Sew Beautiful* magazine. The antique peek-a-boo pinafore uses one of my all-time favorite antique techniques. Pintucks, scallops, corded appliqué, serger ruffles, couched ribbon and many other techniques can be added to your doll pinafores.

There are four basic dress variations given in these instructions so that you may choose the one that you feel is most appropriate for the pinafore you have chosen to make. All of the dresses feature a waisted bodice, full skirt and short, puffed sleeves. The sleeves may be finished with entredeux and gathered edging, a sleeve binding with entredeux and gathered edging, or sleeve binding alone. Necklines are finished with entredeux and gathered lace or a stand-up binding. The hem variations included are plain, plain with decorative stitching, and a hem variation with an attached underslip. These variations may all be used in any combination. By customizing the fabric type and color, a one-of-a-kind designer outfit will be yours for your doll.

One of the best things about beautiful doll dresses is that the ideas can be adapted very easily to other sewing projects. A long time ago in *Sew Beautiful* magazine, we had a pattern called Grace's Easter Dress. The skirt featured a double scalloped skirt filled with double needle pintucks. The skirt was so popular that creative women all over the world used it for women's clothing, wedding clothing, a pillowcase, christening dresses and even a pillow for a bedroom. That is the beauty of heirloom sewing. One shares an idea which inspires more ideas from the original. Perhaps this is the most fun of sewing for me. I love sharing ideas and waiting for the creativity to flow from our readers and viewers. Please let us know about the doll dresses you make from these beautiful pinafore and under-dress patterns included in this series of *Martha's Sewing Room*.

Thank you for your letters and comments telling us what you enjoy the most on our television series and from our books. Please let us know what types of doll dresses you most want us to feature next. Most of all please enjoy these gorgeous pinafore patterns we have for you. I think pinafores on dolls seem to be a rather unique idea. For the next doll competition you enter, you might just want to dress your baby using one of these patterns. ▨

Doll Dress and Pinafores Directions

The Seeley body types and sizes given in the charts below, French (FB), Modern (MB) and German (GB), are the most popular composition child bodies. Size charts will be referred to in each set of doll dress directions to create the proper lengths and/or widths for the size of the doll being dressed. The doll bodies are also divided into small, medium and large bodies. After determining the doll body style and size being used, refer to the measurements on the charts for that specific body size to create any one of these beautiful dresses. General directions are given for the mid-waist dress construction and three different pinafore styles; 1) Basic, 2) Bib and 3) Apron. The doll dresses and pinafores also have specific directions for the special details of each dress and/or pinafore.

FB - French Child Bodies
MB - Modern Child Bodies
GB - German Child Bodies
Small Bodies Include: FB12, FB14, GB11, GB13
Medium Bodies Include: MB140, MB160, GB15, GB16
Large Bodies Include: FB17, FB19, MB190, MB21.5, GB21

Dress Skirt Measurements

These measurements are cutting measurements including seam allowances and ruffles (if any). If a hem is desired, add 1" to 3" to these lengths for a hem allowance (refer to the specific dress directions for any alterations to these measurements). Note: For the dresses requiring a 61" width when 45" fabric is used, cut two pieces $15^3/4$" and one piece $30^1/2$" by the length given. Stitch the shorter pieces to each side of the longer piece to create a 61" width. The seams in the fabric will fall at the sides of the dress.

FB12	8" x 45"	MB140	$9^3/4$" x 45"	GB11	8" x 45"
FB14	9" x 45"	MB160	11" x 45"	GB13	$9^1/2$" x 45"
FB17	12" x 61"	MB190	$12^1/2$" x 61"	GB15	$9^3/4$" x 45"
FB19	13" x 61"	MB21.5	15" x 61"	GB16	11" x 45"
				GB21	$14^1/2$" x 61"

Pinafore Skirt Measurements

* The smocked pinafore and the apron pinafore are open on the sides requiring a skirt front piece and a back skirt piece.

* For the apron pinafore cut a skirt to the measurement below, then cut the width in half to create a front skirt and a back skirt. For 61" width, cut two skirt pieces 30" wide by the length below.

* For the pinafores requiring a 61" width when 45" fabric is used, cut two pieces $15^3/4$" and one piece $30^1/2$" by the length given. Stitch the shorter pieces to each side of the longer piece to create a 61" width. The seams in the fabric will fall at the sides of the dress.

FB12	$7^1/2$" x 45"	MB140	$8^3/4$" x 45"	GB11	7" x 45"
FB14	8" x 45"	MB160	10" x 45"	GB13	$8^1/2$" x 45"
FB17	11" x 61"	MB190	$11^1/2$" x 61"	GB15	$8^3/4$" x 45"
FB19	12" x 61"	MB21.5	14" x 61"	GB16	10" x 45"
				GB21	$13^1/2$" x 61"

Neck Band Measurements (unfinished)

FB12	6"	MB140	$6^1/2$"	GB11	5"
FB14	$6^3/4$"	MB160	$7^1/2$"	GB13	$6^1/2$"
FB17	$7^1/2$"	MB190	$7^1/2$"	GB15	$6^3/4$"
FB19	$7^3/8$"	MB 21.5	$8^1/2$"	GB16	$6^3/4$"
				GB21	$8^1/2$"

Sleeve Band Measurements (unfinished)

FB12	4"	MB140	$4^1/2$"	GB11	$3^1/2$"
FB14	$4^1/2$"	MB160	$4^1/2$"	GB13	4"
FB17	$5^1/2$"	MB190	5"	GB15	$4^1/2$"
FB19	$5^1/2$"	MB 21.5	$5^1/2$"	GB16	$4^1/2$"
				GB21	$6^1/2$"

General Doll Dress Directions

> All pattern pieces are found on the pattern pull-out section of this book. Specific pattern pieces required for the dresses and pinafores can be found in the specific directions.
>
> All seams are ¹/₄". Overcast the seam allowance using a zigzag or serger.

I. Cutting

1. Refer to the specific directions for decorating the front bodice. Cut out the front bodice from decorated fabric or plain fabric.

2. If selvage fabric is available, cut two back dress bodices from the selvage. If the selvage is not available, cut the back bodices from the fabric and serge or zigzag the back edges of the dress bodice pieces. Mark the fold lines and dart lines (if required).

3. Refer to the specific directions for the sleeve length (short or long) and decorating the sleeves. Cut out two sleeves.

4. The skirt will be cut out later. Finished measurements are given in the chart (pg. 21). Specific directions for each skirt are given under each dress title.

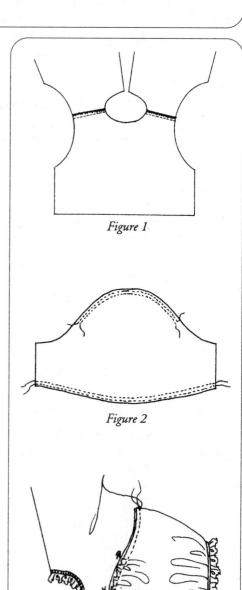

Figure 1

Figure 2

Figure 3

II. Dress Construction

1. Place the shoulders of the front bodice and back bodice, right sides together and stitch (**fig. 1**). If back darts are indicated on the pattern piece, stitch darts in place.

2. Finish the neck of the dress (refer to the section on Neck Finishes).

3. Decorate the sleeve as desired (refer to specific directions for each dress). Run gathering rows in the top and bottom of the sleeve at ¹/₈" and ¹/₄" (**fig. 2**).

4. Finish the ends of the sleeve using the trims and instructions for each specific dress (refer to Sleeve Finishes).

5. Gather the top of the sleeve to fit the arm opening of the dress. Match the center of the sleeve with the shoulder seam of the dress. The gathers should fall ³/₄" to 1¹/₂" on each side of the shoulder seam. The gathers of the sleeve should not extend past the yoke to skirt seam on the dresses with yokes. Pin the right side of the sleeve to the right side of the arm opening.

6. Stitch the sleeve to the dress using a ¹/₄" seam (**fig. 3**). Overcast.

7. Using the skirt chart found on page 21 find the measurement required for the doll you are dressing. The chart gives the total length around the skirt and the finished length. Refer to the specific dress directions for any additions to the length, such as a hem allowance or any embellishments. Embellish the skirt as desired referring the specific directions for each dress. Cut out skirt.

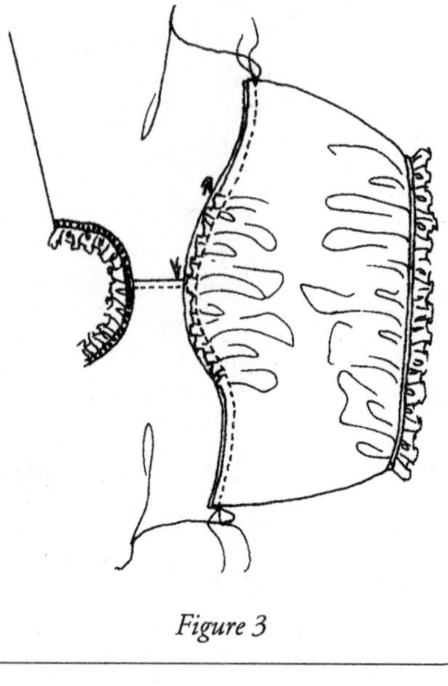

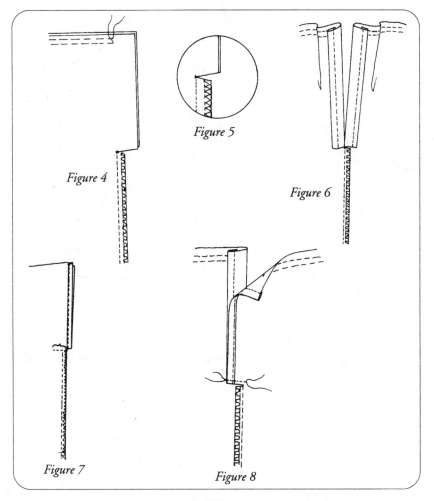

Figure 4

Figure 5

Figure 6

Figure 7

Figure 8

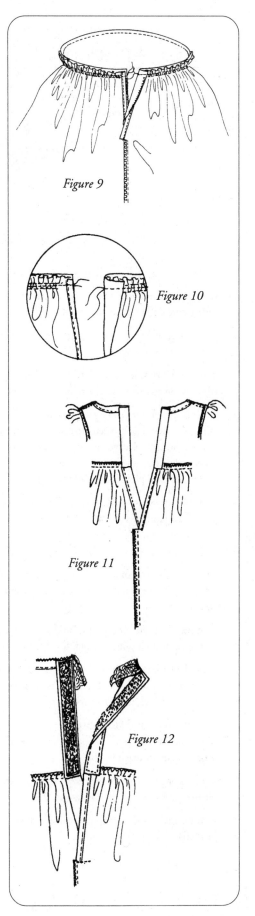

Figure 9

Figure 10

Figure 11

Figure 12

8. Create a placket in the skirt by placing the back edges of the skirt right sides together. Start stitching from the bottom of the skirt using a $^1/_2$" seam. Stop the seam 3" from the top on a small doll and 4" from the top on a medium or large doll. Clip across the seam allowance at the end of the stitching. Trim the seam allowance along the stitching line to $^1/_8$". Overcast the edge (**figs. 4 and 5**).

9. Turn each side of the remaining upper seam allowance to the inside $^1/_8$" and stitch in place (**fig. 6**). Place the seam allowances right sides together and stitch $^3/_8$" across the skirt at the end of the opening. This stitching will be made from the inside of the skirt (**fig. 7**). Press to the left side of the skirt.

10. From the top of the skirt, fold the right hand side of the opening $^3/_8$" to the inside (**fig. 8**). Press in place.

11. Mark the center and quarter points of the skirt. Place the skirt to the bodice, right sides together, matching the quarter points to the side seam and the center front to the center. Gather the top edge of the skirt to fit the bodice. Place the left side of the skirt opening $^3/_8$" from the left edge of the bodice and wrap the bodice over the edge of the skirt. Place the right edge of the skirt opening even with the edge of the bodice (**figs. 9 and 10**). Pin.

12. Stitch the bodice to the skirt using a $^1/_4$" seam. Overcast or serge the seam allowance. Pull the bodice up and away from the skirt, allowing the back placket to flip to the inside of the bodice (**fig. 11**).

13. Attach Velcro™, snaps or buttons and buttonholes along the folds of the back bodices to close the dress (**fig. 12**).

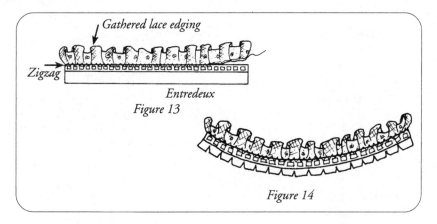

Gathered lace edging

Zigzag

Entredeux

Figure 13

Figure 14

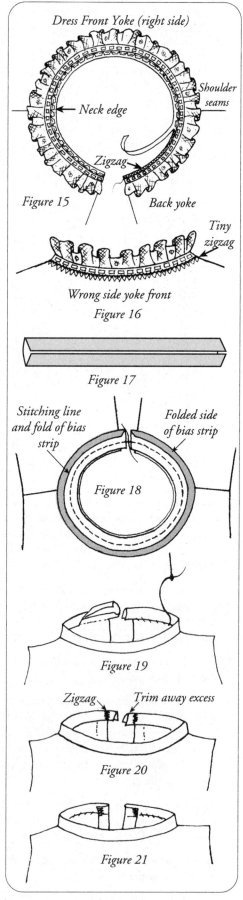

Dress Front Yoke (right side)

Shoulder seams

Neck edge

Zigzag

Figure 15   Back yoke

Tiny zigzag

Wrong side yoke front

Figure 16

Figure 17

Stitching line and fold of bias strip

Folded side of bias strip

Figure 18

Figure 19

Zigzag   Trim away excess

Figure 20

Figure 21

A. Neck Finishes

a. Entredeux to Gathered Edging Lace

1. Cut a strip of entredeux to the neck band measurement given in the chart (pg. 21) for the specific doll body to be dressed.

2. Cut a piece of edging lace two times the length of the entredeux and gather the lace to fit the entredeux strip.

3. Trim away one side of the entredeux and attach the gathered edging lace to the trimmed entredeux using the technique entredeux to gathered lace (**fig. 13**).

4. If the fabric edge remaining on the entredeux is not already ¹/₄", trim to ¹/₄". Clip this fabric allowing the entredeux to curve along the neck edge of the dress (**fig. 14**). Unfold the back placket edges of the bodice and place this strip to the neck of the dress, right sides together. Attach using the technique entredeux to fabric (**fig. 15**). Refold the back placket edges of the bodice to the inside along the fold lines.

5. Using a tiny zigzag, tack the seam allowance to the dress. This stitching will keep the entredeux/gathered lace standing up at the neck (**fig. 16**).

b. Stand-Up Collar

1. Cut a straight strip of fabric 1" wide for small dolls or 1¹/₄" wide for medium and large dolls by the length given on the neck band chart (pg. 21) for the specific doll body to be dressed.

2. Fold each long side of the fabric to the wrong side ¹/₄", press. This will create two creases along each side ¹/₄" from the edge (**fig. 17**).

3. With the back bodice placket edges extended, place the strip to the neck edge, right sides together. Stitch the strip to the neck using a ¹/₄" seam. You will be stitching in one of the creases. Clip the curve along the seam allowance (**fig. 18**).

4. With the top edge folded, place the top fold just past the seam enclosing the seam allowance. Pin the folded strip in place and stitch the lower edge of the strip to the neck by hand or machine (**fig. 19**).

5. Zigzag along the ends of the neck strip even with the edges of the back bodices. Trim off any excess beyond the zigzags (**fig. 20**).

6. Fold the bodices/neck strip to the inside of the bodice along the back fold lines and press (**fig. 21**).

B. Sleeve Bands and Ruffles

The sleeve patterns are cut in two lengths: short - to the elbow or long - to the wrist. Refer to specific directions for decorating the sleeves.

a. Entredeux and Gathered Edging Lace

1. Cut two strips of entredeux to the measurement for the specific doll body given on the sleeve band chart. Cut two pieces of edging lace twice the length of the entredeux.

2. Gather the edging lace to fit the entredeux. Stitch together using the technique entredeux to gathered lace (**refer to fig. 13**).

3. Gather the bottom of the sleeve to fit the entredeux/edging lace band. Stitch the band to the sleeve, right sides together, using the technique entredeux to gathered fabric (**fig. 22**).

b. Sleeve Cuff Bindings

1. Cut two strips of fabric 1" wide for small dolls or 1¼" wide for medium and large dolls by the measurement given on the sleeve band chart (pg. 21) for your specific doll body.

2. Gather the bottom of the sleeve to fit the band. Stitch the band to the sleeve, right sides together, using a ¼" seam. Fold the lower edge of the band to the inside ¼". Place the folded edge just over the seam line on the inside of the sleeve creating a ¼" band. Hand stitch or machine stitch in place (**fig. 23**). This will finish the end of the sleeve.

c. Sleeve Cuff Binding with Entredeux and Gathered Edging Lace

1. Cut two strips of fabric 1" wide for small dolls or 1¼" wide for medium and large dolls by the measurement given on the sleeve band chart (pg. 21) for your specific doll body.

2. Gather the bottom of the sleeve to fit the band. Stitch the band to the sleeve, right sides together, using a ¼" seam. Fold the lower edge of the band to the inside ¼". Place the folded edge just over the seam line on the inside of the sleeve creating a ¼" band. Hand stitch or machine stitch in place (**refer to fig. 23**).

3. Cut two strips of entredeux to the measurement for the specific doll body given on the sleeve band chart. Cut two pieces of edging lace twice the length of the entredeux.

4. Gather the edging lace to fit the entredeux. Stitch together using the technique entredeux to gathered lace (**refer to fig. 13**).

5. Trim the other side of the entredeux. Butt the entredeux against the lower edge of the sleeve binding and zigzag in place (**fig. 24**).

C. Hems

a. Plain Hem

1. Cut the skirt 3" longer than the measurement found on the skirt chart (pg. 21).

2. Finish the lower edge of the skirt using a serger or machine zigzag (**fig. 25**). This edge can also be finished by turning the lower edge to the inside ⅛" and pressing.

3. Refer to the General Dress Directions steps 8 - 12 to attach the skirt to the bodice.

4. Turn the finished edge of the skirt to the inside 3" creating a hem. Press. Pin in place.

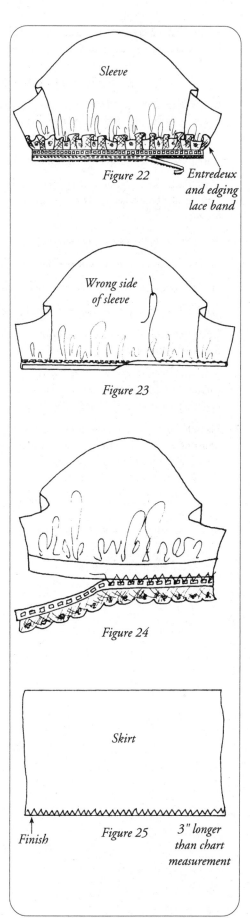

Figure 22 Entredeux and edging lace band

Sleeve

Figure 23 Wrong side of sleeve

Figure 24

Skirt

Finish *Figure 25* 3" longer than chart measurement

5. Stitch the finished edge of the hem in place by hand or machine creating a hem. The hem can also be stitched in place using a decorative machine stitch (**fig. 26**).

b. Plain Hem with Underslip

1. Cut the skirt 2" longer than the measurement found on the skirt chart (pg. 21). Finish the lower edge of the skirt using a serger or machine zigzag. This edge can also be finished by turning the lower edge to the inside $^1/_8$" and pressing.

2. Turn the finished edge of the skirt to the inside 3" and press. Pin in place.

3. Stitch the finished edge in place by hand or machine creating a hem (**fig. 27**). The hem can also be stitched in place using a decorative machine stitch (**refer to fig. 26**). Set aside.

4. To create the upper panel of the underslip use the following directions:

    small dolls - cut a strip of fabric $4^1/_2$" long by the width found on the skirt chart

    medium dolls - cut a strip of fabric 6" long by the width found on the skirt chart

    large dolls - create a strip of fabric 9" long by the width found on the skirt chart

5. Cut the embroidered edging to the following measurements: small and medium dolls - $1^2/_3$ yds.; large dolls - $2^1/_2$ yds.

6. Run two gathering rows along the top edge of the embroidered edging. Gather the embroidered edging to fit the upper slip panel. Attach the gathered edging to the upper slip panel using a $^1/_4$" seam (**fig. 28**). Press.

7. Place the right side of the underslip to the wrong side of the skirt piece so that the underslip extends 1" past the hem of the skirt. Trim any excess upper slip fabric that extends above the top edge of the skirt. Pin together along the sides and top edge (**fig. 29**). Treat as one layer of fabric.

8. Refer to the General Dress Directions steps 8 - 12 to attach the skirt to the bodice. ▨

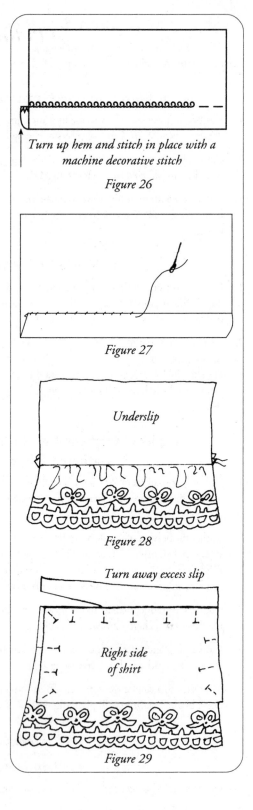

Turn up hem and stitch in place with a machine decorative stitch

Figure 26

Figure 27

Underslip

Figure 28

Turn away excess slip

Right side of shirt

Figure 29

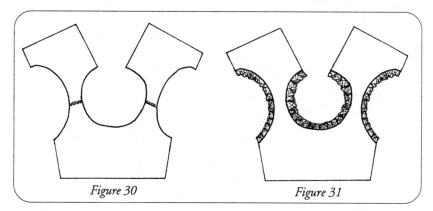

Figure 30

Figure 31

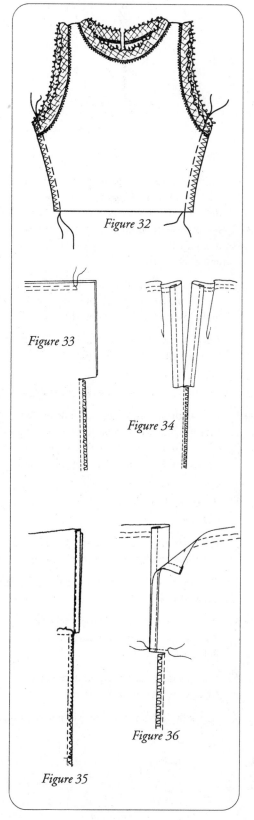

Figure 32

Figure 33

Figure 34

Figure 36

Figure 35

Basic Pinafore (unlined)

1. Refer to the specific directions for decorating the pinafore front and back. Cut one basic pinafore bodice front from the fold and two basic pinafore backs from the selvage.

2. Stitch the pinafore front and the pinafore back right sides together at the shoulders (**fig. 30**). If darts are required on the back bodice, stitch in place at this time.

3. Finish the neck and the arm openings using general pinafore neck finishes and general pinafore sleeve finishes (**fig. 31**).

4. Place the side of the pinafore bodice, right sides together and stitch using a $^1/_4$" seam (**fig. 32**).

5. Using the pinafore skirt chart found on page 21, find the measurement required for the doll you are dressing. The chart gives the total length around the skirt and the finished length. Refer to the specific pinafore directions for any additions to the length, such as a hem allowance or any embellishments. Embellish the pinafore skirt as desired referring to the specific directions for each pinafore. Cut out the pinafore skirt.

6. Create a placket in the skirt by placing the back edges of the skirt right sides together. Start stitching from the bottom of the skirt using a $^1/_2$" seam. Stop the seam 3" from the top on a small doll and 4" from the top on a medium or large doll. Clip across the seam allowance at the end of the stitching (**fig. 33**). Trim the seam allowance along the stitching line to $^1/_8$". Overcast the edge.

7. Turn each side of the remaining upper seam allowance to the inside $^1/_8$" and stitch in place (**fig. 34**). Place the seam allowances right sides together and stitch $^3/_8$" across the skirt at the end of the opening (**fig. 35**). This stitching will be made from the inside of the skirt. Press to the left side of the skirt (**fig. 36**).

8. From the top of the skirt, fold the right hand side of the opening $^3/_8$" to the inside. Press in place.

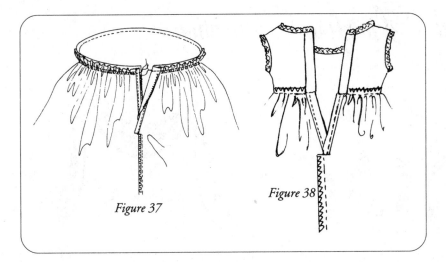

Figure 37

Figure 38

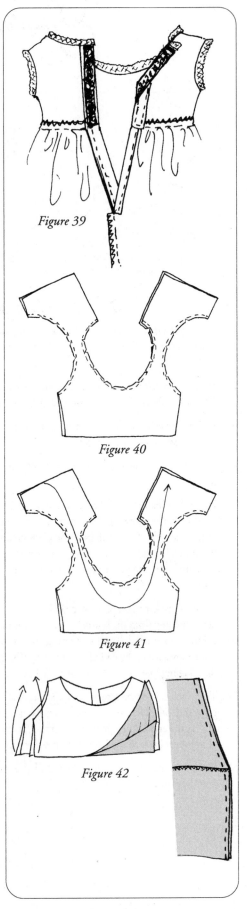

Figure 39

Figure 40

Figure 41

Figure 42

9. Mark the center and quarter points of the skirt. Place the skirt to the bodice, right sides together, matching the quarter points to the side seams and the center front to the center. Gather the top edge of the skirt to fit the pinafore bodice. Place the left side of the skirt opening ³/₈" from the left edge of the bodice and wrap the bodice over the edge of the skirt. Place the right edge of the skirt opening even with the edge of the bodice (**fig. 37**). Pin.

10. Stitch the bodice to the skirt using a ¹/₄" seam. Overcast or serge the seam allowance. Pull the pinafore bodice up and away from the skirt, allowing the back placket to flip to the inside of the bodice (**fig. 38**).

11. Attach Velcro™, snaps or buttons and buttonholes along the folds of the back bodices to close the pinafore (**fig. 39**).

Basic Pinafore (lined)

1. Refer to the specific directions for decorating the pinafore front and back. Cut one basic pinafore bodice front from the fold and two basic pinafore backs from the selvage. For the lining cut one basic pinafore bodice front on the fold and two basic pinafore backs on the selvage from plain fabric.

2. Stitch the pinafore front and the pinafore back right sides together at the shoulders. Repeat for the lining pieces. If darts are required on the back bodice, stitch in place at this time.

3. Place the lining to the pinafore, right sides together. Stitch, ¹/₄" from the neck edge and arm openings. Clip all curves (**fig. 40**).

4. Turn the bodice to the right side pulling through the shoulders (Follow the arrow.)(**fig. 41**).

5. Pull the pinafore front and back, right sides together, away from the lining pieces. The lining front and lining back will be right sides together. Stitch in place (**fig. 42**). Pull pinafore over lining.

6. Place the lower edge of the pinafore and lining together and press. Treat the lower edges and back edges as one layer.

7. Attach the skirt and finish the pinafore referring to Basic Pinafore (unlined) step 5 - step 11.

Bib Pinafore

1. Refer to the specific directions for decorating the bib pinafore front. Cut one bib pinafore front from the fold. Cut one waist band $1^1/4$" wide to the measurement on the chart below. Cut two straps $1^1/4$" wide to the measurement on the chart below. *Ruffle and Sash Option*: Cut two bib ruffles. Cut two sash pieces 16" long by $1^3/4$" wide. Refer to the specific directions for other options.

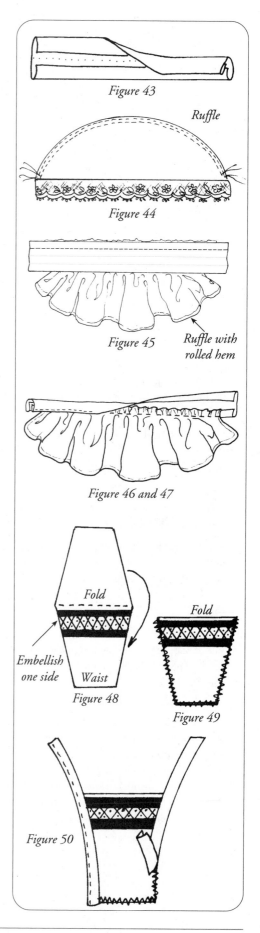

Figure 43

Ruffle

Figure 44

Waist Band Measurement - cut one $1^1/4$" wide by the length below.

FB12	9"	MB140	$10^1/4$"	GB11	$8^1/4$"
FB14	$10^1/2$"	MB160	12"	GB13	10"
FB17	$13^7/8$"	MB190	$13^1/2$"	GB15	$10^1/2$"
FB19	$13^1/2$"	MB21.5	$15^3/4$"	GB16	11"
				GB21	$14^1/2$"

Strap Measurement - cut two $1^1/4$" wide by the length below.

FB12	$6^3/8$"	MB140	$8^1/8$"	GB11	$6^1/4$"
FB14	$6^1/2$"	MB160	$9^7/8$"	GB13	7"
FB17	$10^1/4$"	MB190	11"	GB15	$7^3/4$"
FB19	$10^1/4$"	MB21.5	13"	GB16	$8^5/8$"
				GB21	$12^3/4$"

Figure 45

Ruffle with rolled hem

2. Fold each long edge of the waist band to the inside $1/4$". Fold in half again with the folded edges meeting (**fig. 43**). Press. Repeat this folding process on the two strap pieces. Set the folded waist band and strap pieces aside.

3. Ruffle Option: (Refer to the specific pinafore directions for details.)

    a. Finish the outer edge of the ruffle (straight side) with edging lace or a rolled hem by serger. Run two gathering rows in the remaining edge of the ruffle at $1/8$" and $1/4$" (**fig. 44**).

    b. Unfold the strap pieces. Gather the ruffle to fit the strap with each end of the strap extending past the ruffle $1/2$". Pin in place, right sides together.

    c. Sew the ruffle to the strap along the crease using a $1/4$" seam (**fig. 45**).

    d. Refold the strap along the creased lines to sandwich the seam allowance of the ruffle between the folds of the strap (**fig. 46**). Topstitch along the outer folded edge to complete the strap/ruffle piece (**fig. 47**). Set aside.

Figure 46 and 47

4. Embellish the bib starting at the fold line and working toward the waist (**fig. 48**). Fold the bib in half wrong sides together to create a lining. Zigzag or serge around the sides and lower edge of the bib (**fig. 49**).

Fold

Embellish one side

Waist

Figure 48

Fold

Figure 49

5. Attach the straps to the bib by placing the zigzagged or serged side edges of the bib sides under the straps. The lower edge of the straps should be even with the lower edge of the bib. Top stitch the bib in place $1/8$" from each edge of the strap. If no strap ruffle is used, continue stitching along the strap to close the edge (**fig. 50**). Refer to the specific directions for other options.

Figure 50

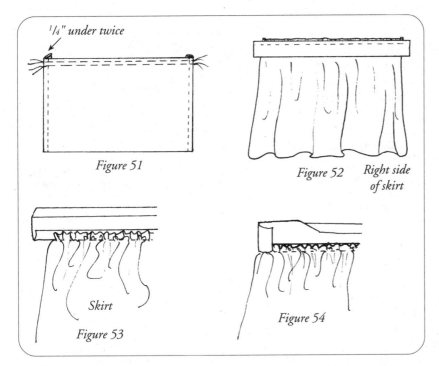

Figure 51

Figure 52 Right side of skirt

Skirt

Figure 53

Figure 54

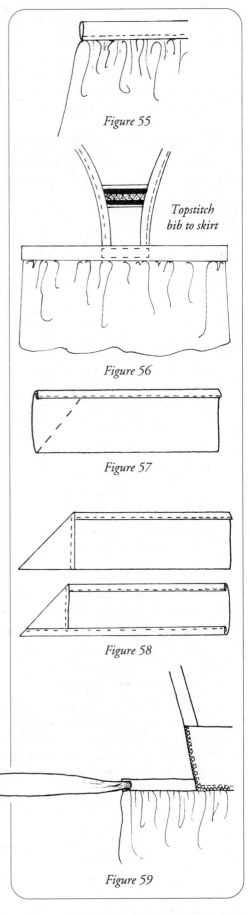

Figure 55

Topstitch bib to skirt

Figure 56

Figure 57

Figure 58

Figure 59

6. Refer to the specific directions for embellishing the skirt. Cut the skirt, referring to the specific directions for any changes to the length given on the pinafore skirt chart (pg. 21).

7. Finish the backs of the skirt by turning the edges to the inside $^1/_4$" and $^1/_4$" again. Press and stitch in place. Run two gathering rows in the top edge of the skirt at $^1/_8$"and $^1/_4$" (**fig. 51**).

8. Unfold the waist band. Place the waist band to the skirt piece, right sides together. Allow $^1/_4$" of the waist band to extend on either side of the finished back edges. Gather the skirt to fit the waist band. Stitch in place using a $^1/_4$" seam (**fig. 52**).

9. Flip the waist band away from the skirt (**fig. 53**). Fold the $^1/_4$" extensions to the inside of the waist band. Fold the top edge of the waist band to the inside $^1/_4$" along the crease (**fig. 54**). Place this folded edge just over the seam line on the inside of the skirt creating a $^3/_8$" band at the top of the skirt. Hand stitch or machine stitch in place (**fig. 55**).

10. Place the center of the bib to the center of the waist band, right side of bib to wrong side of waist band. The lower edge of the bib should meet the lower edge of the waist band. Top stitch the bib in place along the top and bottom edges of the waist band (**fig. 56**).

11. Finish **one** long side of each sash piece by turning under $^1/_4$" and $^1/_4$" again and stitching in place (**fig. 57**). Fold the end of the sash to the unfinished edge, wrong sides together. Finish the second side by turning under $^1/_4$" and $^1/_4$" again and stitching in place (**fig. 58**). The sash can be finished by serging around two long sides and one short side of each sash piece. Run two gathering rows in the unfinished edge of the sash at $^1/_4$" and $^1/_8$". Gather to about $^3/_8$". Pin along the back edges of the waist band. Stitch in place by machine $^1/_4$" from the edge of the waist band (**fig. 59**). The unfinished edge of the sash will be covered by the bib strap.

12. Place the pinafore on the doll and fit the straps to the doll's body by pinning the straps to the back edge of the waist band covering the ends of the sash. The straps should fit securely across the dolls shoulders. Remove the pinafore from the doll and stitch the strap in place using a zigzag (**fig. 60**). Trim off any excess fabric beyond the zigzag.

Apron Pinafore

1. Refer to the specific directions for decorating the pinafore front and back bodices. Cut one basic pinafore bodice front from the fold and two basic pinafore backs from the selvage. For the lining cut one basic pinafore bodice front on the fold and two basic pinafore backs on the selvage from plain fabric.

2. Stitch the pinafore front and the pinafore back right sides together at the shoulders. Repeat for the lining pieces. If darts are required, stitch darts.

3. Place the lining to the pinafore, right sides together. Stitch, $1/4$" from the neck edge, arm openings and the sides. Clip all curves (**fig. 61**).

4. Turn the bodice to the right side, pulling one of the backs through the shoulders and out the other back (follow the arrow) (**fig. 62**).

5. Place the lower edges of the pinafore and lining together and press. Treat the lower edges of the bodices as one layer of fabric.

6. Refer to the pinafore skirt chart (pg. 21). This skirt is open on the sides, therefore requiring a skirt front and a skirt back. Cut two skirt pieces to the length given on the chart by 21" for small and medium dolls and 33" for large dolls. Refer to the specific directions for any additional changes in the length and width of the skirt pieces. Embellish the skirt pieces referring to the specific pinafore directions.

7. Cut a slit down the center back of the skirt for the back placket to the following measurement: small bodies = 2", medium bodies = 3", large bodies = 4" (**fig. 63**).

8. Cut a strip of fabric from the selvage $3/4$" wide by twice the length given above, plus 1". For example, the small doll placket will be figured as follows: 2 x 2 = 4" and 4 + 1 = 5". The strip would be cut $3/4$" by 5".

9. Pull the slit in the skirt apart to form a "V". Place right side of the strip to right side of the skirt slit. The stitching will be made from the wrong side with the skirt on top and the placket strip on the bottom. The placket strip will be straight and the skirt will form a "V" with the point of the "V" $1/4$" from the edge of the placket. Stitch, using a $1/4$" seam. As you stitch, you will just catch the tip (a few fibers) at the point of the "V" (**fig. 64**).

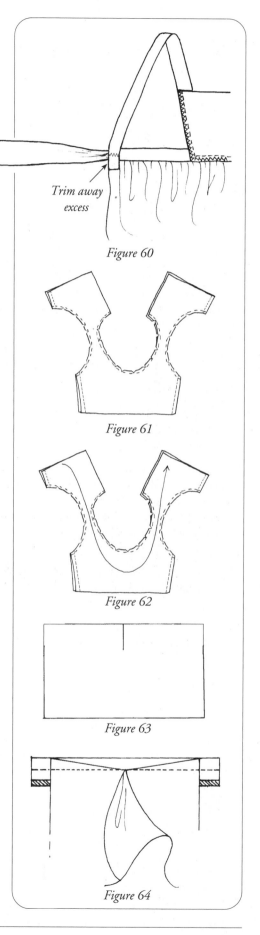

Trim away excess

Figure 60

Figure 61

Figure 62

Figure 63

Figure 64

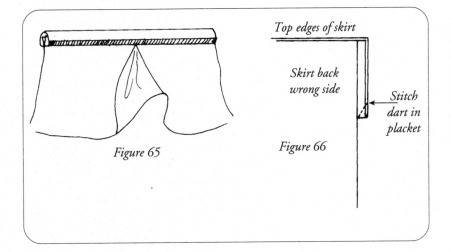

Top edges of skirt

Skirt back
wrong side

Stitch
dart in
placket

Figure 65

Figure 66

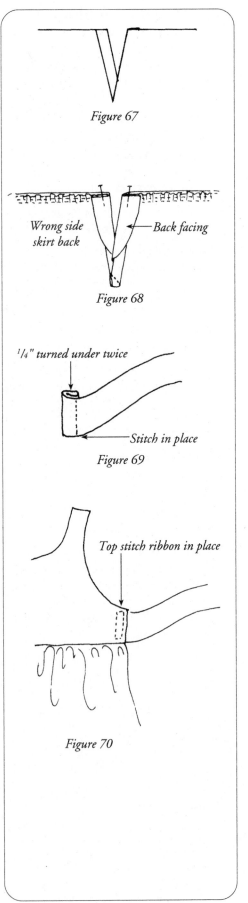

Figure 67

Wrong side
skirt back

Back facing

Figure 68

¹/₄" turned under twice

Stitch in place

Figure 69

Top stitch ribbon in place

Figure 70

10. Pull the placket away from the skirt. Press the seam toward the selvage edge of the placket strip. Turn the selvage edge to the inside of the dress, enclosing the seam allowance. Whip by hand or stitch in place by machine (**fig. 65**). Fold the placket in half and stitch a dart (**fig. 66**).

11. The back of the pinafore will lap right over left. Fold the right side of the placket to the inside of the skirt and pin. Leave the left back placket open (**fig. 67**).

12. Run two rows of gathering in the top edges of the skirt front and each side of the skirt back at ¹/₈" and ¹/₄".

13. Gather the front skirt to fit the pinafore front bodice/lining. Place right sides together and stitch using a ¹/₄" seam.

14. Place the pinafore/lining back bodice to the back skirt, right sides together. Gather the skirt to fit the back bodices. The placket edge will come to the fold line on the left back bodice. The folded edge of the placket will come to the fold line on the right back bodice. Wrap the back edge of the bodice to the inside along the fold lines. Stitch using a ¹/₄" seam (**fig. 68**). Press.

15. Cut four pieces of ribbon 4" by 14". Fold one end of the ribbon to the inside ¹/₄" and ¹/₄" again. Stitch the folded edge in place (**fig. 69**). Repeat for each ribbon piece. Place the folded edge of the ribbon to the sides of the pinafore and top stitch in place (**fig. 70**).

16. Attach Velcro™, snaps or buttons and buttonholes along the folds of the back bodices to close the pinafore. ▨

Specific Doll Dress Directions

All Seams ¼" unless otherwise indicated.

Please read through both the General Dress Directions and the Specific Dress Directions before starting the dress. The General Dress Directions can be found on pages 22 - 26 and give generic instructions for the basic dress. The Specific Directions give instructions for the special details concerning each particular dress and the sequence of the construction.

The following pattern pieces are needed for these dresses: dress front bodice, dress back bodice and short sleeve. These patterns are found on the center pull-out section.

Basic Dress—Neckline and Sleeve Finished with Entredeux and Gathered Edging, Plain Hem

Fabric Requirements

	Small Body	Medium Body	Large Body
Fabric	½ yd.	⅔ yd.	1¼ yds.
Entredeux	½ yd.	½ yd.	⅔ yd.
Edging Lace (³/₈")	1 yd.	1 yd.	1⅓ yds.

Notions: Lightweight sewing thread, Velcro™, snaps or tiny buttons

Directions

1. Cut the bodice front from the fold. If selvage fabric is available, cut the back bodices from the selvage. If the selvage is not available, cut two back bodices from the fabric and serge or zigzag the back edges of the bodice pieces. Refer to the chart on pg. 21 for the dress skirt measurement. Cut the dress skirt 3" longer than the length given on the chart to be used for the hem.

2. Refer to the General Dress Directions, section II. for dress construction.

3. To finish the neck of the dress, refer to the General Dress Directions - A. Neck Finishes - a. Entredeux to Gathered Edging Lace.

4. To finish the ends of the sleeves, refer to the General Dress Directions - B. Sleeve and Ruffles - a. Entredeux and Gathered Edging Lace.

5. To finish the dress bottom, refer to the General Dress Directions - C. Hems - a. Plain Hems. ▨

Basic Dress—Neckline and Sleeve Binding with Entredeux and Gathered Edging, Plain Hem

Fabric Requirements–Same As Above

Directions

Follow directions for Basic Dress—Neckline and Sleeve Finished with Entredeux and Gathered Edging, Plain Hem; except step 4 see below.

4. To finish the ends of the sleeves, refer to the General Dress Directions - B. Sleeve and Ruffles - c. Sleeve Cuff Binding with Entredeux and Gathered Edging Lace. ▨

Basic Dress – Neckline and Sleeve Finished with Entredeux and Gathered Edging, Plain Hem

Basic Dress – Neckline and Sleeve Binding with Entredeux and Gathered Edging, Plain Hem

Basic Dress—Stand-Up Neckline, Sleeve Binding and Hem with Underslip

Fabric Requirements

	Small Body	Medium Body	Large Body
Fabric	$^1/_2$ yd.	$^2/_3$ yd.	$1^1/_4$ yds.
Fabric (Slip Upper Panel)	$^1/_8$ yd.	$^3/_{16}$ yd.	$^1/_2$ yd.
Embroidered Edging for Slip (6")	$1^2/_3$ yds.	$1^2/_3$ yds.	$2^1/_2$ yds.

Notions: Lightweight sewing thread, Velcro™, snaps or tiny buttons

Directions

1. Cut the bodice front from the fold. If selvage fabric is available, cut the back bodices from the selvage. If the selvage is not available, cut two back bodices from the fabric and serge or zigzag the back edges of the bodice pieces. Refer to the chart on pg. 21 for the dress skirt measurement. Cut the dress skirt 3" longer than the length given on the chart to be used for the hem.

2. Refer to the General Dress Directions, section II. for dress construction.

3. To finish the neck of the dress, refer to the General Dress Directions - A. Neck Finishes - b. Stand-Up Collar.

4. To finish the ends of the sleeves, refer to the General Dress Directions - B. Sleeve and Ruffles - b. Sleeve Cuff Bindings.

5. To finish the dress bottom, refer to the General Dress Directions - C. Hems - b. Plain Hem with Underslip. ▨

Basic Dress—Stand-Up Neckline, Sleeve Binding and Hem with Underslip

Basic Dress—Stand-Up Neckline, Sleeve Binding and Plain Hem

Fabric Requirements

	Small Body	Medium Body	Large Body
Fabric	$^1/_2$ yd.	$^2/_3$ yd.	$1^1/_4$ yds.

Notions: Lightweight sewing thread, Velcro™, snaps or tiny buttons

Directions

1. Cut the bodice front from the fold. If selvage fabric is available, cut the back bodices from the selvage. If the selvage is not available, cut two back bodices from the fabric and serge or zigzag the back edges of the bodice pieces. Refer to the chart on pg. 21 for the dress skirt measurement. Cut the dress skirt 3" longer than the length given on the chart to be used for the hem.

2. Refer to the General Dress Directions, section II. for dress construction.

3. To finish the neck of the dress, refer to the General Dress Directions - A. Neck Finishes - b. Stand-Up Collar.

4. To finish the ends of the sleeves, refer to the General Dress Directions - B. Sleeve and Ruffles - b. Sleeve Cuff Bindings.

5. To finish the dress bottom, refer to the General Dress Directions - C. Hems - c. Plain Hem. ▨

Basic Dress—Stand-Up Neckline, Sleeve Binding and Plain Hem

Show 1

Lace Scallops On Lace Pinafore

Yummy is the word to describe this white dotted Swiss pinafore with the scalloped lace treatment on the bottom. The neckline and armholes are finished with flat lace. The back closes with buttons and buttonholes. The skirt is simply glorious with the scalloped lace insertion at both the top and the bottom. Actually this is a double scalloped skirt with strips of insertion butted together and stitched in-between the double scalloped lace. Gathered white French lace is zigzagged onto the bottom of this magnificent skirt. Can you even imagine this skirt treatment on the bottom of a christening dress or an Easter dress? You might even win the grand prize in a doll show with this pinafore!

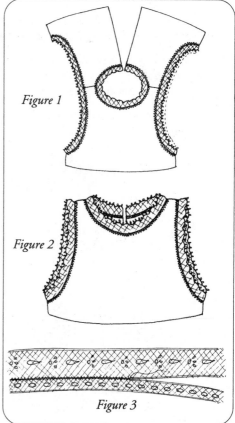

Lace Scallops On Lace Pinafore

Fabric Requirements

Fabric - Dotted Swiss	Small Body	Medium Body	Large Body
Fabric - Dotted Swiss	$^3/_8$ yd.	$^5/_8$ yd.	$^7/_8$ yd.
Edging Lace ($^3/_8$")	$^2/_3$ yd.	1 yd.	$1^1/_8$ yds.
Edging Lace ($^3/_4$")	$3^3/_4$ yds.	$3^3/_4$ yds.	5 yds.
Lace Insertion ($^1/_2$")	7 yds.	7 yds.	$9^1/_2$ yds.
Lace Insertion (1")	$3^1/_2$ yds.	$3^1/_2$ yds.	$4^1/_2$ yds.

Notions: Lightweight sewing thread, Velcro™, snaps or tiny buttons.

All Seams $^1/_4$" unless otherwise indicated.

Please read through both the General Pinafore Directions (Basic Pinafore) and the Specific Pinafore Directions before starting the pinafore. The General Directions for the Basic Pinafore can be found on pages 27 to 32 and give generic instructions for the pinafore. These Specific Directions give instructions for the special details concerning this particular pinafore and the sequence of the construction.

The following pattern pieces are needed for this pinafore: basic pinafore front bodice, basic pinafore back bodice. These patterns are found on the center pull-out section.

Template Needed: double scallop template found on page 268.

Figure 1

Figure 2

Figure 3

Directions

1. Cut one pinafore front from the fold. If selvage fabric is available, cut two pinafore back bodices from the selvage. If the selvage is not available, cut the back bodices from the fabric and serge or zigzag the back edges of the bodice pieces. Stitch the pinafore front to the pinafore back, right sides together, at the shoulders.

2. Attach $^3/_8$" lace edging to the neck and arm openings using the technique extra stable lace finishing (pg. 237). The scalloped edge of the lace should be placed on the seam line which is $^1/_4$" from the cut edge of the bodice (**fig. 1**).

3. Place the sides of the bodice right sides together and stitch (**fig. 2**).

4. Cut one piece of $^1/_2$" insertion lace and one piece of 1" insertion lace to $3^1/_2$ yds. for small and medium dolls and $4^1/_2$ yds. for large dolls. Zigzag the 1" lace to the $^1/_2$" lace using the technique lace to lace (**fig. 3**).

5. Cut the lace strip into 11¹/₂" pieces and zigzag the 1" lace of one strip to the ¹/₂" lace of the other strip. Now cut the 11¹/₂" strips into three equal pieces and zigzag the 1" lace of one strip to the ¹/₂" lace of the other strip until a 45" strip is achieved for the small and medium dolls and a 60" strip is achieved for the large dolls (**fig. 4**).

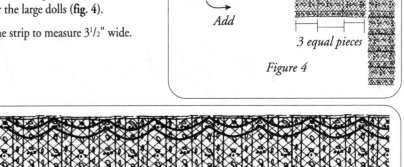

11¹/₂"   11¹/₂"   11¹/₂"

Add

3 equal pieces

Figure 4

6. Starch and press until the lace strip is very stiff. Cut the strip to measure 3¹/₂" wide.

7. For the upper row of scallops, fold the lace strip in half and trace the center of the scalloped template to the center of the lace strip with the top points of the scallop even with the top of the lace strip. Continue tracing the scallops on either side of the center scallop keeping the top points of the scallops even with the top of the lace strip (**fig. 5**).

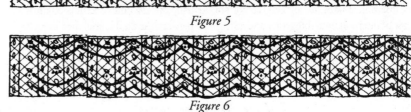

Figure 5

8. Trace the lower row of scallops along the lower edge of the lace strip keeping the scallops of the lower row in line with the scallops of the upper row (**fig. 6**).

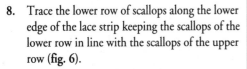

Figure 6

9. Shape lace insertion along the traced lines of the scallops, referring to the technique for scalloped skirts. Using a small tight zigzag, stitch along the inside of the top and lower scallops. Do not stitch along the outer edges. Trim away the excess lace from behind the scallops. Zigzag along the folds of the miters and trim away any excess lace at the miters (**fig. 7**).

10. Gather the ³/₄" edging to fit the lower scallops and zigzag in place using the technique lace to lace (**fig. 8**).

11. Refer to the chart on pg. 21 for the pinafore skirt measurement. Cut the pinafore skirt 3" shorter than the length given on the chart.

12. Place the scalloped lace panel along the skirt with the lower edge of the top lace scallop overlapping the edge of the skirt by ¹/₂". Zigzag the lace panel to the skirt along the top edge of the scallops. Trim the excess fabric from behind (**fig. 9**).

13. To finish the pinafore refer to the General Pinafore Directions - A. Basic Pinafore (unlined) - steps 6 to 11. ▣

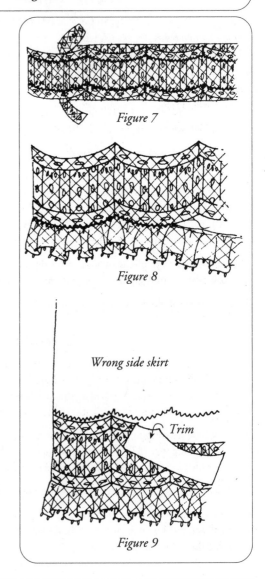

Figure 7

Figure 8

Wrong side skirt

Trim

Figure 9

Pintucks and Gathered Lace Scallops

Creamy organdy has to be one of the most elegant treatments for a pinafore. The front bodice has machine embroidery in the center with sets of three pintucks on either side. A beautiful hand-scalloped stitch finishes the neckline and the sleeves. What a beautiful scalloped skirt! Pintucks have been placed vertically to make the skirt look as if has been stitched in gores. Scallops are stitched between these pintucks and finished with gathered ecru lace stitched on with wing needle pinstitching. A beautiful ecru machine embroidery has been stitched between the scallops in a scalloped shape. The back is closed with buttons and buttonholes. This pinafore is beautiful worn over any number of the dresses in this book.

Pintucks and Gathered Lace Scallops

Fabric Requirements

	Small Body	Medium Body	Large Body
Fabric - Organdy	³/₈ yd.	⁵/₈ yd.	⁷/₈ yd.
Edging Lace (³/₄")	3³/₄ yds.	3³/₄ yds.	5 yds.

Notions: Two spools of lightweight sewing thread, #100 wing needle, 1.6/70 or 2.0/80 double needle, 7 or 9 groove pintuck foot (optional), tear away stabilizer for hemstitching and Velcro™, snaps or tiny buttons.

All Seams ¹/₄" unless otherwise indicated.

Please read through both the General Pinafore Directions (Basic Pinafore) and the Specific Pinafore Directions before starting the pinafore. The General Directions for the Basic Pinafore can be found on pages 27 to 32 and give generic instructions for the pinafore. These Specific Directions give instructions for the special details concerning this particular pinafore and the sequence of the construction.

The following pattern pieces are needed for this pinafore: basic pinafore front bodice, basic pinafore back bodice. These patterns are found on the center pull-out section.

Template Needed: 4" scallop template found on page 44.

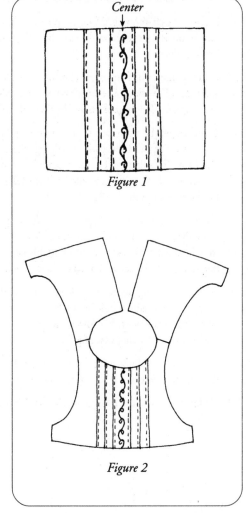

Center

Figure 1

Figure 2

Directions

1. Cut a piece of fabric 1" wider and 1" longer than the pinafore front bodice pattern. Fold the fabric in half and finger press. Choose a small built-in decorative stitch from your sewing machine that looks like a vine. Stitch the vine along the creased line (see **fig. 1**).

2. Using a double needle and pintuck foot (optional) stitch double needle pintucks ³/₈" on either side of the decorative stitch. Add two more double needle pintuck ³/₈" and ³/₈" again outside the first pintucks for a total of three double needle pintucks on each side of the center decorative stitch (**fig. 1**).

3. Fold the decorated fabric in half along the decorative stitch and cut the pinafore bodice front from the fold. If selvage fabric is available, cut two pinafore back bodices from the selvage. If the selvage is not available, cut the back bodices from the fabric and serge or zigzag the back edges of the bodice pieces. Stitch the pinafore front to the pinafore back, right sides together, at the shoulders (**fig. 2**).

4. Turn the neck edge to the inside ¹/₈" and ¹/₈" again, finger press. Work a shell stitch hem along the folded edges by hand in the following manner: a) starting at the back edge take several small stitches through the hem. b) slide the needle through the lower

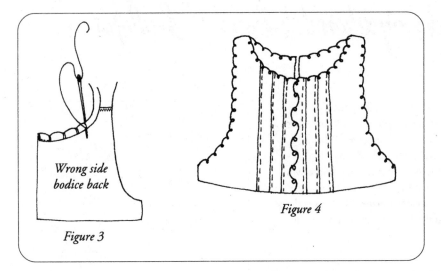

Figure 3

Wrong side bodice back

Figure 4

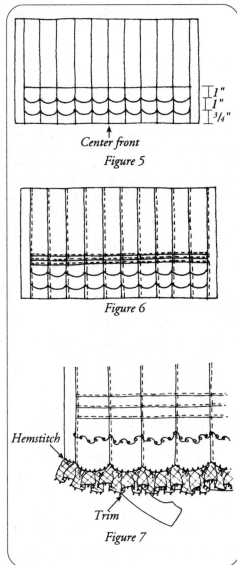

Figure 5

Center front

Figure 6

Hemstitch

Trim

Figure 7

fold about ³/₈" and out the lower folded edge. c) wrap the thread over the top edge of the bodice and back into the fabric just below the hem, keeping the stitches straight. Pull the thread to form an indention in the hem. d) repeat this wrap one more time. There should be two strands of floss at each indention. e) repeat steps b to e across the hem to form a scalloped or shell effect (**fig. 3**).

5. Repeat step 4 to finish the arm openings.

6. Place the bodice backs and front right sides together and stitch side seams (**fig. 4**).

7. Refer to the chart on pg. 21 for the pinafore skirt measurement. Cut the pinafore skirt to the length given on the chart by 41" for small and medium dolls and by 57" for large dolls.

8. Fold the skirt in half and draw a line down the fold (center front). Repeat lines 4" apart, across the skirt. The small and medium doll skirts will be divided into 10 four inch sections. The large skirts will be divided into 14 four inch sections (**see fig. 5**).

9. Trace scallops between each section starting ³/₄" from the edge of the skirt. This line will be used to attach the gathered edging. Trace a second row of scallops 1" from the lower row. This line will be used as a guide for the decorative stitching. Draw a straight line 1" from the top points of the scallops. This line will be used as a guide for the straight pintucks (**fig. 5**).

10. Using a double needle and pintuck foot (optional) stitch double needle pintucks along the vertical lines drawn in step 8. Also stitch a double needle pintuck along the straight line drawn in step 9. Add a double needle pintuck ³/₈" above and ³/₈" below the horizontal pintuck for a total of three double needle pintucks (**fig. 6**).

11. Gather the edging lace to fit the lower drawn scallops. Pin or baste the lace in place. Using a wing needle, a built-in machine hem stitch and tear away stabilizer under the fabric, stitch the lace to the lower scalloped line. Trim the excess fabric from behind the hemstitched scallops (**see fig. 7**).

12. Choose the same built-in decorative vine stitch in step 1, replace the wing needle with the regular needle and stitch the vine along the upper scallop line (**fig. 7**).

13. To finish the pinafore refer to the General Pinafore Direction - A. Basic Pinafore (unlined) - steps 6 to 11. ▨

Ribbons and Lace Pinafore

This little white batiste pinafore I would call a bib pinafore. The front section stands alone and the straps make the back pinafore. Purchased ribbon trim with blue bows on it is very, very sweet. This purchased white and blue trim is used for the waistline, the shoulder straps, the center front of the pinafore and for two strips along the skirt. Sweet machine embroidery travels across the front pinafore as well as around the skirt. Blue featherstitch is at the top and bottom of the ribbon trim on the skirt and the flat white French lace has been wing needle honeycomb stitched onto the bottom of the skirt. A beautiful white satin ribbon sash closes the back of the pinafore. This pinafore would be beautiful on any of the dresses in this book. On doll clothing, many purchased ribbon-type trims are beautiful. I love the idea of using a separate color, based on the type trim on the white ribbon which has been stitched onto the pinafore.

Fabric Requirements

	Small Body	Medium Body	Large Body
Fabric - Swiss Batiste	⅓ yd.	½ yd.	⅞ yd.
Decorative Satin Ribbon (³⁄₈")	3½ yds.	4 yds.	4¾ yds.
Satin Ribbon (³⁄₈")	⅜ yd.	⅓ yd.	½ yd.
Edging Lace (1")	1¼ yds.	1¼ yds.	1¾ yds.
Satin Ribbon (1")	1 yd.	1 yd.	1 yd.

Ribbons and Lace Pinafore

Notions: Lightweight sewing thread, decorative thread, #100 wing needle, stabilizer, seam sealant, Velcro™, snaps or tiny buttons.

All Seams ¼" unless otherwise indicated.

Please read through both the General Pinafore Directions (Bib Pinafore) and the Specific Pinafore Directions before starting the pinafore. The General Directions for the Bib Pinafore can be found on pages 27 to 32 and give generic instructions for the pinafore. These Specific Directions give instructions for the special details concerning this particular pinafore and the sequence of the construction.

The following pattern pieces are needed for this pinafore: bib pinafore front. This pattern piece can be found on the center pull-out section.

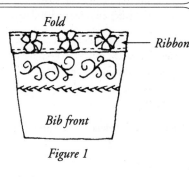

Fold

Ribbon

Bib front

Figure 1

Directions

1. Cut one bib front from the fold. Mark the fold on the bib. Refer to the length measurements given in the bib pinafore general directions (pg. 29) and cut one piece of decorative ribbon to the waist band measurement and two strap pieces. Also cut one plain piece of ribbon ½" shorter than the waist band measurement to use as a lining. Use seam sealant on the cut edges of the ribbon to keep them from fraying.

2. Starting ⅜" below the fold, decorate the bib front using decorative built-in machine stitches. Refer to the general bib pinafore directions - step 4, to finish the bib. Place a piece of decorative ribbon at the top of the bib with the top edge of the ribbon to the fold. Stitch in place along each edge of the ribbon (**fig. 1**).

3. Stitch the ribbon straps on each side of the bib with the strap overlapping the bib sides and the ends of the strap even with the end of the bib (**fig. 2**).

4. Cut a skirt to the measurement on the pinafore skirt chart (pg. 21).

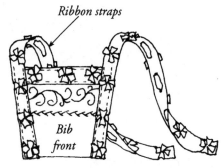

Ribbon straps

Bib front

Figure 2

5. Place the wrong side of the lace to the right side of the skirt with the scalloped edge of the lace to the edge of the skirt. Stitch in place along the straight side of the lace using a wing needle and a machine honeycomb stitch (refer to Machine Entredeux - pg. 216). Stabilizer may be used behind the fabric if needed. Tear away stabilizer and trim away the excess fabric from behind (**fig. 3**).

6. Stitch decorative ribbon 1¹/₄" above the lace. Stitch another piece of decorative ribbon 1¹/₄" above the first ribbon (**see fig. 4**).

7. Stitch a decorative stitch in-between the two pieces of ribbon. Stitch a feather stitch ¹/₄" above the upper ribbon and ¹/₄" below the lower ribbon (**fig. 4**).

8. Refer to the general pinafore directions - step 7 to finish the sides of the skirt and to run gathering rows in the skirt top.

9. Gather the skirt to fit the plain piece of ribbon. Place the ribbon ¹/₈" above the top edge of the skirt on the wrong side. Stitch in place along the lower edge of the ribbon (**fig. 5**).

10. Place the center of the bib to the center of the skirt waist band with the wrong side of bib to the right side of the skirt. The lower edge of the bib should overlap the skirt by ¹/₄". Stitch in place along the lower edge of the bib (**fig. 6**).

11. Place the decorative waist ribbon on the right side of the skirt with the top edge of the decorative ribbon even with the plain ribbon. The skirt seam allowance and the lower edge of the bib will be sandwiched between the two ribbon pieces. The decorative ribbon should extend beyond the back skirt edges ¹/₄". Stitch the ribbon in place along the top and bottom edges. Fold the ¹/₄" ribbon tabs to the inside of the waist band and stitch in place by hand or machine (**see fig. 7**).

12. Cut the 1" ribbon in half at an angle for the two sash pieces. Use seam sealant on the cut edges of the ribbon to keep them from fraying. Run two gathering rows in the short straight sides of the ribbon at ¹/₈" and ¹/₄". Gather to ³/₈". Pin along the back edges of the waist band. Stitch in place by machine ¹/₄" from the edge of the waist band (**fig. 7**).

13. Refer to the general bib pinafore directions - step 12 to finish the pinafore. ▨

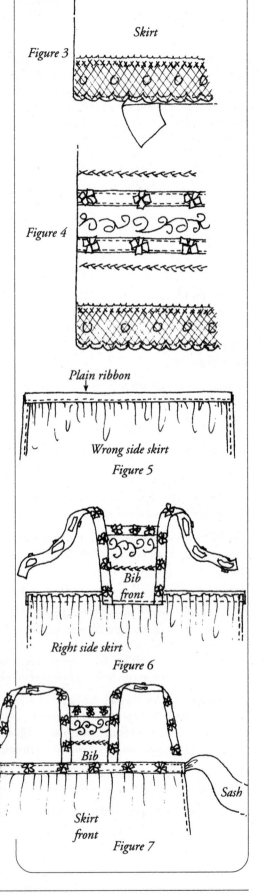

Figure 3

Figure 4

Plain ribbon

Wrong side skirt

Figure 5

Bib front

Right side skirt

Figure 6

Bib

Sash

Sash

Skirt front

Figure 7

French Knot Lamb Pinafore

French Knot
Lamb
Pinafore

This has to be one of my favorite doll garments which I have ever seen. A tiny little lamb has been stitched by using primarily ecru French knots. The face, the ears and the feet are gray embroidery floss done in a satin stitch and there are two tiny peach rosebuds with green stems beside the lamb. Beautiful geometric smocking is underneath the front bodice of the pinafore in the front and ecru satin sashes tie the pinafore on both sides. Flat ecru English lace is stitched onto both the front and back of this pinafore and it closes in the back with buttons and buttonholes. This type of pinafore is sometimes called a tabard pinafore and the dress pictured with it in the color section of the book has little lambs printed on it. What a sweet combination!

Fabric Requirements

Fabric - Swiss Batiste	Small Body	Medium Body	Large Body
Fabric - Swiss Batiste	$^3/_8$ yd.	$^5/_8$ yd.	$^7/_8$ yd.
Satin Ribbon (1")	$1^3/_4$ yds.	$1^3/_4$ yds.	$1^3/_4$ yds.
Edging Lace ($^3/_4$")	$1^1/_4$ yds.	$1^1/_4$ yds.	2 yds.

Notions: Lightweight sewing thread, floss for smocking and embroidery (DMC - ecru #712, gray #414, light green #955 and peach #224), Velcro™, snaps or tiny buttons.

All Seams $^1/_4$" unless otherwise indicated.

Please read through both the General Pinafore Directions (Apron Pinafore) and the Specific Pinafore Directions before starting the pinafore. The General Directions for the Apron Pinafore can be found on pages 27 to 32 and give generic instructions for the pinafore. These Specific Directions give instructions for the special details concerning this particular pinafore and the sequence of the construction.

The following pattern pieces are needed for this pinafore: basic pinafore front bodice, basic pinafore back bodice. These patterns are found on the center pull-out section.

Templates Needed: lamb template, smocking graph found on page 42.

Directions

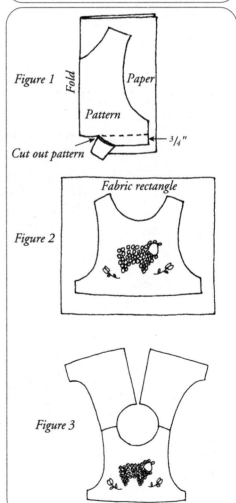

Figure 1

Fold   Paper

Pattern

Cut out pattern $^3/_4$"

Fabric rectangle

Figure 2

Figure 3

1. Trace the bodice front on a folded piece of paper. Cut $^3/_4$" from the lower edge of the pattern piece (**fig. 1**). Cut a fabric rectangle a little larger than the shortened front bodice pattern or large enough to fit into an embroidery hoop. Trace the shortened front bodice pattern onto the rectangle. Center the lamb template on the drawn bodice front (**fig. 2**).

2. Embroider the lamb using gray satin stitches for the lamb's face and feet, ecru French knots for the body, and gray bullion stitches for the ears. Use peach bullion stitches for the flowers, green straight stitches for the stems and green lazy daisy stitches for the leaves.

3. Cut one front bodice from the embroidered fabric along the drawn lines. Cut one front bodice lining using the shortened pattern on the fold. If selvage fabric is available, cut four pinafore back bodices (two bodice backs and two bodice linings) from the selvage. If the selvage is not available, cut the back bodices from the fabric and serge or zigzag the back edges of the bodice pieces. Stitch the pinafore front to the pinafore back, right sides together, at the shoulders (**fig. 3**).

4. Refer to the General Pinafore Directions, Apron Pinafore, steps 2 - 5 to complete the bodice. Set aside.

5.   Refer to the pinafore skirt chart (pg. 21). Cut one back skirt piece $^3/_4$" shorter than the length given on the chart by 21" for small and medium dolls and 33" for large dolls. Cut one front skirt piece to the length given on the chart by 21" for small and medium dolls and 33" for large dolls. Attach $^3/_4$" edging lace along one long edge of each skirt piece using the technique lace to fabric (**see fig. 4**).

6.   Pleat the top edge of the skirt front with 6 half-space rows. The first row of pleating should fall $^1/_8$" from the top edge of the skirt. This row will be #1 and will not be smocked but will be used as a holding row for construction. The half space rows will be numbered 1 through 6. Remove $^1/_4$" of the pleating threads from each side. Gather the skirt front to fit the lower edge of the front bodice. Tie the pleating threads to this measurement (**fig. 4**).

7.   Smocking Directions: (all smocking is stitched using ecru floss)

Refer to *Martha's Attic* or *The Joy of Smocking* for smocking instructions.

   Step 1: Cable across Row 2.

   Step 2: Between Rows 2 and 3 work baby waves. Refer to graph.

   Step 3: Between Rows 3 and 4 work baby waves forming diamonds. Refer to graph.

   Step 4: Between Rows 4 and 5 work baby waves forming diamonds between every other diamond of the row above. Refer to graph.

   Step 5: Between Rows $3^1/_2$ and $5^1/_2$ work 3-step waves. Refer to graph.

8.   Finish the sides of the skirt by turning the cut edges to the back side $^1/_8$" and $^1/_8$" again. Stitch in place (**fig. 5**).

9.   Complete the pinafore referring to the General Pinafore Directions, Apron Pinafore, steps 7 - 15. ▣

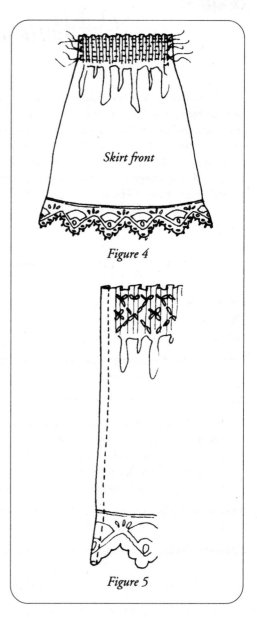

Skirt front

Figure 4

Figure 5

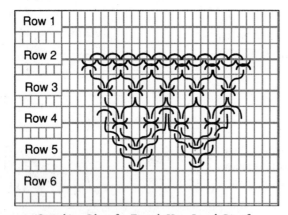

Smocking Plate for French Knot Lamb Pinafore

Stitch Guide and template

⌀ Bullion – for flowers and ears   Satin Stitch – Face and feet

◖ Lazy Daisy – leaves   French Knots – Body

╱ Straight Stitch – stems

Shadow Sandwich Pinafore

Using a brand new technique taught in this book for the first time, this white batiste pinafore features precious purple shadow sandwich bows. Of course, they are made by machine and you will love this fast and easy technique which looks just like shadow work embroidery by hand. The front bodice has one of the bows on it and the pinafore closes in the back with Velcro. Machine wing needle entredeux attaches the scalloped hem in a very easy technique also. The little bows are on the front of the pinafore skirt also. This hem treatment would be just as pretty on a little girl's dress as it is on this doll pinafore. As a matter of fact, this is one of my favorite hem treatments not only for doll clothing and little girl clothing, but also as a hem for a ladies' skirt. This pinafore will be precious over any number of the basic dresses given in this book.

Shadow Sandwich Pinafore

Fabric Requirements

	Small Body	Medium Body	Large Body
Fabric - Batiste	$3/8$ yd.	$5/8$ yd.	$7/8$ yd.
Shadow Fabric - Burgundy	$1/8$ yd.	$1/8$ yd.	$1/8$ yd.

Notions: Lightweight sewing thread, colored thread for shadow sandwich, lightweight fusible web, #100 wing needle, Velcro™, snaps or tiny buttons

All Seams $1/4$" unless otherwise indicated.

Please read through both the General Pinafore Directions (Basic Pinafore - lined) and the Specific Pinafore Directions before starting the pinafore. The General Directions for the Basic Pinafore (lined) can be found on pages 27 to 32 and give generic instructions for the pinafore. These Specific Directions give instructions for the special details concerning this particular pinafore and the sequence of the construction.

The following pattern pieces are needed for this pinafore: basic pinafore front bodice, basic pinafore back bodice. These patterns are found on the center pull-out section.

Templates Needed: bow shadow sandwich template for bodice, hem and 4" scallop template found on page 44.

Shadow Sandwich Pinafore with dress

Directions

1. Refer to the technique Shadow Sandwich (pg. 254) to create one bow for the pinafore bodice and 5 bows (small and medium dolls) or 7 bows (large doll) for the skirt. Set aside.

2. Cut two front bodices from the fold (one lining and one bodice). If selvage fabric is available, cut four back pinafore bodices from the selvage (two linings and two back bodices). If the selvage is not available, cut the back bodices from the fabric and serge or zigzag the back edges of each pinafore bodice piece.

3. Remove the paper backing from the bodice bow and center the design on the wrong side of the front bodice lining. Press in place. Set aside (**fig. 1**).

4. Refer to General Pinafore Directions, Basic Pinafore (lined), steps 2 - 5.

5. Stitch along the bow of the shadow sandwich bodice (refer to the technique Shadow Sandwich, pg. 254). Set aside.

6. Refer to the chart on pg. 21 for the pinafore skirt measurement. Cut the pinafore skirt 3" longer than the length given on the chart.

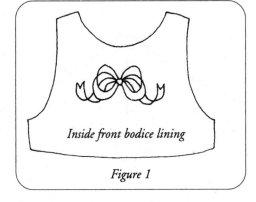

Inside front bodice lining

Figure 1

7. Using a fabric marker, trace the scallops on the wrong side of the skirt with the points ¹/₂" from the edge, upside down, with a point of the scallop in the center of the skirt. With the paper backing removed from the skirt bows, place the bows at each point along the front skirt, starting at the point in the center front. Place the remaining bows on each side of center bow, two on each side of center for small and medium dolls and three on each side of center for large dolls. The center of the bow should fall 1" from each drawn point. Press in place (**fig. 2**). Turn 3" of the lower edge of the skirt to the wrong side and press the hem in place. Pin (**fig. 3**).

8. The scalloped line of the hem can be seen through the skirt. Stitch along the drawn scalloped line using a wing needle (refer to the technique Hemstitching a Scalloped Hem, pg. 250)(**fig. 4**).

9. Stitch along the bows of the shadow sandwich hem (refer to the technique Shadow Sandwich, pg. 250).

10. To finish the pinafore refer to General Pinafore Directions, Basic Pinafore (unlined), steps 6 - 11. ▨

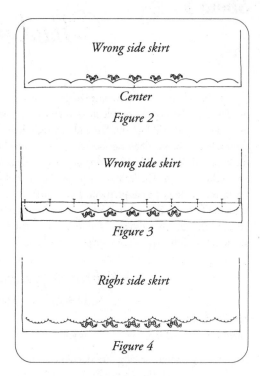

Wrong side skirt

Center

Figure 2

Wrong side skirt

Figure 3

Right side skirt

Figure 4

Bodice Template for bow on Shadow Sandwich Pinafore

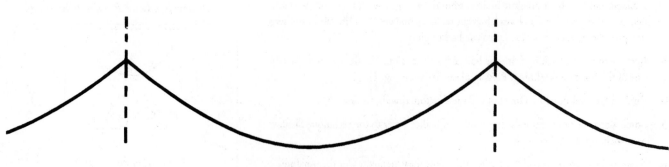

4" scallop template

Antique Peek-A-Boo Pinafore

Using an idea from an antique christening dress, this pinafore is a masterful delight of beautiful techniques. The front-only pinafore has the peek-a-boo technique on the front, with fabric pieces extending from the front waistline to the back waistline of the bodice. Entredeux is on the outside of these pieces with gathered ecru French laces making the finishing touch. Ecru satin ribbon ties the pinafore together at the back. A beautiful peek-a-boo heart is found on the front of the pinafore skirt. This new technique is found in this book. The skirt treatment is interesting in that it dips up in the front and down, following the general shape of the bottom of the heart. The gathered ecru French lace has been wing needle entredeux stitched onto the bottom of the pinafore. This pinafore will be beautiful over any of the basic dresses given in this book.

Antique Peek – A – Boo Pinafore

Fabric Requirements

	Small Body	Medium Body	Large Body
Fabric - Swiss Batiste	$^1/_2$ yd.	$^3/_4$ yd.	$1^1/_8$ yds.
Edging Lace (1")	$3^1/_2$ yds.	4 yds.	5 yds.
Lace Insertion ($^3/_4$")	$1^1/_2$ yds.	$1^1/_2$ yds.	$2^1/_2$ yds.
Entredeux	$^1/_2$ yd.	$^5/_8$ yd.	$^3/_4$ yd.
Satin Ribbon (1")	1 yd.	1 yd.	1 yd.

Notions: Lightweight sewing thread, $^1/_2$" bias tape maker, water soluble stabilizer, liquid pins or fabric glue, #100 wing needle, stabilizer, seam sealant, Velcro™, snaps or tiny buttons.

All Seams $^1/_4$" unless otherwise indicated.

Please read through both the General Pinafore Directions (Bib Pinafore) and the Specific Pinafore Directions before starting the pinafore. The General Directions for the Bib Pinafore can be found on pages 27 to 32 and give generic instructions for the pinafore. These Specific Directions give instructions for the special details concerning this particular pinafore and the sequence of the construction.

The following pattern pieces are needed for this pinafore: bib pinafore front. This pattern piece can be found on the center pull-out section.

Template: Antique peek-a-boo heart template found on page 269.

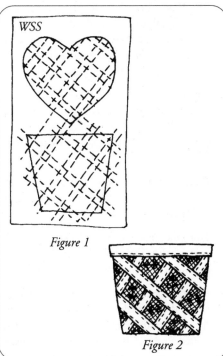

Figure 1

Figure 2

Directions

1. Trace one bib front on a folded piece of tissue paper to make a whole bib pattern. Trace the whole bib pattern on water soluble stabilizer. Also trace the heart template on the water soluble. Use the grid lines on the heart for the bib extending the lines as needed (**fig. 1**).

2. Refer to the directions on Antique Peek-a-Boo (pg. 251). Cut strips of lace to cover the pattern of the bib and heart following the grid lines. Cut bias strips 1" wide for the double fold bias tape strips needed for the antique peek-a-boo technique. An extra piece of double fold bias tape, about 20", will be needed for the top edge of the bib and outlining the heart. Attach lace strips and double fold bias pieces to the traced patterns using the antique peek-a-boo directions.

3. Cut the bib front and the heart along the template lines. Set the heart aside. Using another piece of double fold bias tape, sandwich the top edge of the bib between the folds of the tape. Stitch in place (**fig. 2**).

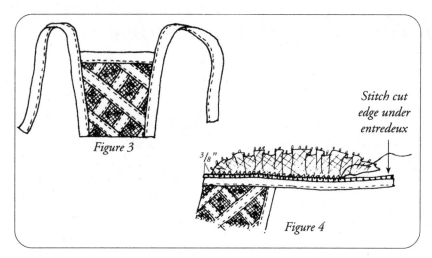

Figure 3

Figure 4

Stitch cut edge under entredeux

Skirt — *Heart & hem template lines*

Center
Figure 5

Skirt (wrong side) — Trim

Center
Figure 6

Figure 7

Wrong side skirt

Trim

Figure 8

Stitch ¹/₄" from edge of waist band

Skirt (wrong side)

Sash

Figure 9

4. Refer to the General Bib Directions (pg. 29) to cut the straps and the waist band. Follow the General Bib Directions - steps 2 to fold the waist band and the straps.

5. Sandwich the sides of the bib between the folds of the straps. The ends of the straps should be even with the lower edge of the bib. Stitch in place (**fig. 3**).

6. Cut two pieces of entredeux the length of the strap measurement. Cut two pieces of lace edging twice the length of the strap measurement. Trim away one fabric side of the entredeux. Butt the trimmed side of the entredeux to the outer edge of the strap. Zigzag in place. Trim the remaining side of the entredeux. Gather the edging lace 2¹/₂" shorter than the strap. Place the cut edges of the lace just under the entredeux with the scalloped side of the lace ³/₈" from the ends of the strap. Pin in place. Butt the remaining gathered edging to the entredeux. Zigzag along the outer bar of the entredeux catching the cut ends of the lace. Attach the gathered edging to the entredeux using the technique lace to entredeux (**fig. 4**).

7. Cut a skirt piece to the measurement on the pinafore skirt chart (pg. 21). Fold the skirt in half to find the center front. Trace the heart and hem template lines along the lower edge of the skirt with the lower point of the hem template 1" above the cut edge of the skirt. Continue the hem template line 1" from the bottom edge of the skirt (**fig. 5**).

8. Place the antique peek-a-boo heart on the heart template lines of the skirt. Using a medium zigzag, stitch along the template lines. Trim the fabric from behind the heart and zigzag again (**fig. 6**).

9. Using the remaining piece of bias tape, shape the tape along the heart template lines covering the zigzag. Fold the cut edge under at the bottom point of the heart. Trim off the excess. "Glue" the tape in place. Stitch along each side of the tape (**fig. 7**).

10. Gather the remaining lace to fit the hem template line. Place the wrong side of the lace to the right side of the skirt along the template lines. Stitch the lace in place along the straight side using a wing needle and a machine entredeux stitch (refer to Machine Entredeux - pg. 216). Stabilizer may be used behind the fabric if needed. Tear away stabilizer and trim away the excess fabric from behind (**fig. 8**).

11. Refer to the general pinafore directions - steps 7 to 10 to finish the skirt.

12. Cut the 1" ribbon in half at an angle for the two sash pieces. Use seam sealant on the cut edges of the ribbon to keep them from fraying. Run two gathering rows in the short straight sides of the ribbon at ¹/₈" and ¹/₄". Gather to ³/₈". Pin along the back edges of the waist band. Stitch in place by machine ¹/₄" from the edge of the waist band (**fig. 9**).

13. Refer to the general bib pinafore directions - step 12 to finish the pinafore. ▣

Scalloped Lace Pinafore

So very elegant is this white Swiss batiste tabard style pinafore with the sides joined only with white ribbon sashes. The bodices of the front and back are lined and the front bodice has machine-embroidered flowers in lavender with green stems. This same machine-embroidered flower design is repeated in the scallops on the front of the pinafore. The back bodice is closed with buttons and buttonholes. The front and back skirt portions have three scallops each. At the bottom of each scallop is white lace insertion which has been stitched down with wing needle entredeux; gathered white French lace finishes the skirt sections from the waistline all the way around the scallops on the bottom and back up to each waistline section. Details make the difference in all heirloom clothing and this doll pinafore is the perfect way to illustrate wonderful details. You could choose any of the basic dresses to wear underneath this pinafore.

Fabric Requirements

	Small Body	Medium Body	Large Body
Fabric - Swiss Batiste	$^3/_8$ yd.	$^5/_8$ yd.	$^7/_8$ yd.
Lace Insertion ($^1/_2$")	$2^1/_2$ yds.	$2^3/_4$ yds.	4 yds.
Satin Ribbon (1")	$1^3/_4$ yds.	$1^3/_4$ yds.	$1^3/_4$ yds.
Edging Lace ($^3/_4$")	5 yds.	$5^1/_2$ yds.	8 yds.

Notions: Lightweight sewing thread, colored thread for machine embroidery or lavender and green floss for hand embroidery, #100 wing needle, tear away stabilizer, Velcro™, snaps or tiny buttons.

All Seams $^1/_4$" unless otherwise indicated.

Please read through both the General Pinafore Directions (Basic Pinafore - lined) and the Specific Pinafore Directions before starting the pinafore. The General Directions for the Basic Pinafore (lined) can be found on pages 27 to 32 and give generic instructions for the pinafore. These Specific Directions give instructions for the special details concerning this particular pinafore and the sequence of the construction.

The following pattern pieces are needed for this pinafore: basic pinafore front bodice, basic pinafore back bodice. These patterns are found on the center pull-out section.

Templates Needed: $6^1/_2$" scallop found on pull-out section, embroidery template for neck and skirt found on page 48.

Directions

1. Cut one front bodice lining from the fold. If selvage fabric is available, cut four back pinafore bodices from the selvage (two linings and two back bodices). If the selvage is not available, cut the back bodices from the fabric and serge or zigzag the back edges of each pinafore bodice piece.

2. Trace the bodice front on a rectangle of fabric. Stitch the embroidery design on the front bodice with hand embroidery or with built-in machine stitches. This design should be placed about $^1/_2$" from the drawn line of the neck edge (**fig. 1**).

3. Refer to the General Pinafore Directions, Apron Pinafore, steps 2 - 5 to complete the bodice. Set aside.

4. Refer to the pinafore skirt chart (pg. 21). Cut two skirt pieces to the length given on the chart by 21" for small and medium dolls and 33" for large dolls. One piece will be for the front and one piece will be for the back.

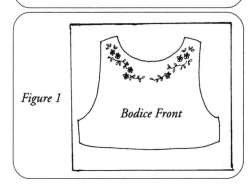

Scalloped Lace Pinafore

Scalloped Lace Pinafore with Dress

Figure 1

Bodice Front

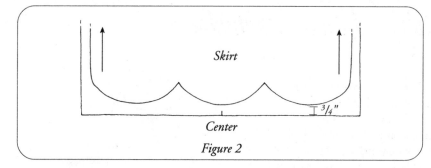

Figure 2

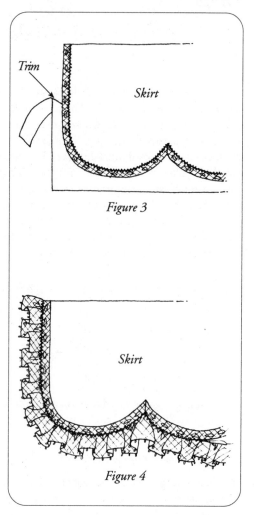

Figure 3

Figure 4

5. Fold the skirt front in half to find the center front. Center the scallop template in the center of the skirt with the lower edge of the scallop $^3/_4$" from the edge of the skirt. For the small and medium dolls, trace one scallop on each side of the center scallop. For the large dolls, trace two scallops on each side of the center scallop. Extend the lines at the outer points of the scallops to the top edge of the skirt. Repeat for the back skirt piece (**fig. 2**).

6. Shape lace along the template lines of the front and back skirt pieces referring to the technique for scalloped skirts. Stitch along the inside edge of the lace using a small tight zigzag or wing needle hem stitch (refer to pg. 225). Trim away any excess fabric from behind the scallops (**fig. 3**).

7. Cut the piece of edging lace in half and gather the edging to fit the outer edge of the lace insertion. Stitch the gathered lace to the lace insertion using the technique lace to lace. Set the back skirt piece aside (**fig. 4**).

8. Complete the pinafore referring to the General Pinafore Directions, Apron Pinafore, steps 7 - 15.

9. The embroidery design should be worked $^1/_2$" above the lace scallops of the skirt front. Stitch the embroidery using either built-in stitches from your sewing machine or hand embroidery using the embroidery template. ▨

Embroidery Template For Bodice
Medium and Large -use template twice

Embroidery Template For Scallops

Pintucked Dress with Embellished Pinafore

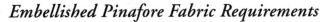

This dress and pinafore are spectacular as a pair or by themselves. The pink Nelona batiste dress features double needle pintucks running vertically on the bodice. The long puffed sleeves have three pintucks on either side of the middle section which has entredeux, white French insertion, white French beading, insertion, and entredeux again. Pink silk ribbon has been run through the beading. The bottom of the sleeve is finished with entredeux, beading, and flat lace edging. The neckline is finished with entredeux and gathered white French edging. The dress closes in the back with snaps. The pretty skirt has three pintucks at the bottom and the fancy band consists of entredeux, insertion, beading, insertion and flat edging on the bottom. Pink silk ribbon is run through the beading.

The super-elegant white batiste pinafore has a scooped neckline which is finished with entredeux and gathered white edging. The armholes are finished the same way. The back of the pinafore is closed with snaps and silk ribbon which has been run through the Swiss triple-entredeux which is used for the waistline. The skirt has been divided into sections and each section features insertion on each side with beading in the middle. Silk ribbon has been run through the beading. White entredeux is on the bottom of the pinafore and wide white French edging finishes the bottom as well as traveling up the back of the pinafore to the waistline.

Embellished Pinafore

Embellished Pinafore Fabric Requirements

	Small Body	Medium Body	Large Body
Fabric - Swiss Batiste	3/8 yd.	5/8 yd.	7/8 yd.
Edging Lace (3/8")	1 1/3 yds.	2 yds.	2 1/4 yds.
Edging Lace (1 1/2")	4 yds.	4 1/2 yds.	6 yds.
Swiss Beading (1/4")	1/3 yd.	1/3 yd.	1/2 yd.
Entredeux	2 2/3 yds.	3 yds.	3 1/4 yds.
Lace Beading (3/8")	2 3/4 yds.	3 1/4 yds.	4 1/2 yds.
Lace Insertion (1/2")	5 1/2 yds.	6 1/2 yds.	9 yds.
Silk Ribbon (4mm)	4 yds.	5 yds.	6 yds.

Notions: Lightweight sewing thread, #100 wing needle (optional), Velcro™, snaps or tiny buttons.

Template Needed: Skirt curve found on page 272.

All Seams 1/4" unless otherwise indicated.

Please read through both the General Pinafore Directions (Basic Pinafore) and the Specific Pinafore Directions before starting the pinafore. The General Directions for the Basic Pinafore can be found on pages 27 to 32 and give generic instructions for the pinafore. These Specific Directions give instructions for the special details concerning this particular pinafore and the sequence of the construction.

The following pattern pieces are needed for this pinafore: basic pinafore front bodice, basic pinafore back bodice. These patterns are found on the center pull-out section.

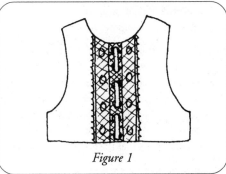

Figure 1

Directions

1. Cut the 1/2" lace insertion in half. Attach the lace insertion to each side of the lace beading using the technique lace to lace. This long lace strip will be used to decorate the bodice and the skirt.

2. Cut the pinafore front bodice from the fold. If selvage fabric is available, cut two pinafore back bodices from the selvage. If the selvage is not available, cut the back bodices from the fabric and serge or zigzag the back edges of the bodice pieces. Center a piece of the lace strip to fit the center of the bodice. Stitch in place along the sides of the lace strip using a zigzag or a wing needle and a pin stitch (refer to Machine Entredeux - pg. 216). Trim the lace strip to fit the neck edge and lower edge of the bodice. Trim the fabric from behind the lace. Weave a piece of ribbon through the holes of the beading (**fig. 1**).

3. Stitch the pinafore front to the pinafore backs, right sides together, at the shoulders.

4. Attach entredeux around the neck and arm openings using the technique entredeux to fabric. Trim the remaining fabric edge from the entredeux. Gather the $^3/_8$" edging to fit the entredeux at the neck and arm openings. Attach the gathered edging to the entredeux using the technique lace to entredeux (**fig. 2**).

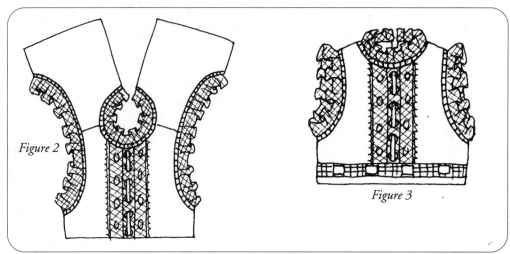

Figure 2

Figure 3

5. Place the sides of the bodice right sides together and stitch (**see fig. 3**).

6. Attach a piece of Swiss beading along the waist of the bodice using the technique entredeux to fabric. Trim off the excess beading at the back edges of the bodice (**fig. 3**).

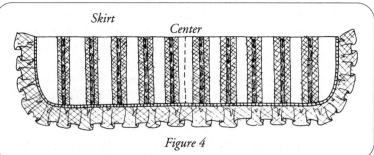

Skirt *Center*

Figure 4

7. Refer to the chart on pg. 21 for the pinafore skirt measurement. Cut the pinafore skirt $1^1/_2$" shorter than the length given on the chart.

8. Fold the skirt fabric in half and crease the fold. Measure 2" from each side of the crease and draw lines vertically. Continue making lines 4" apart to total 5 lines on each side of the center crease. Cut 10 lace strips from the long lace strip created in step 1 the length of the skirt. Place each strip in the center of the drawn line, pin in place. Stitch the strips to the fabric using the same stitch used in step 2, attaching the lace to the bodice. Trim the fabric from behind the lace. Weave a pieces of ribbon through the holes of the beading (**see fig. 4**).

9. Curve the lower corners of the skirt back by placing the template along the edges of the fabric and trimming away the designated area (**see fig. 4**).

10. Place entredeux down the back edge of the skirt, across the bottom and up the other back edge using the technique entredeux to fabric (**see fig. 4**).

11. Trim the remaining fabric edge from the entredeux. Gather the $1^1/_2$" lace edging to fit the entredeux and attach using the technique entredeux to lace (**fig. 4**).

12. Run two gathering rows in the top edge of the skirt/lace at $^1/_8$" and $^1/_4$". Gather the skirt to fit the pinafore bodice with the edges of the lace $^1/_4$" from the back folds of the bodice. Pin in place, right sides together.

13. Wrap the back edges of the bodice to the front side of the skirt, folding along the fold lines. Stitch the bodice to the skirt using a $^1/_4$" seam and the technique entredeux to fabric. Overcast with a zigzag or serger (**fig. 5**).

14. Attach Velcro™, snaps or buttons and buttonholes along the folds of the back bodices to close the pinafore.

15. Weave the remaining ribbon through the beading at the waist. Tie the excess into a bow (**fig. 6**).

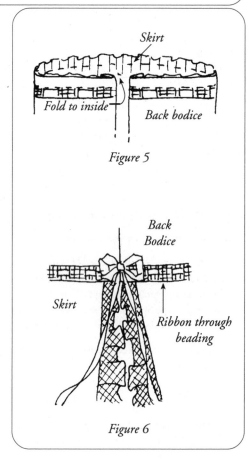

Skirt

Fold to inside

Back bodice

Figure 5

Back Bodice

Skirt

Ribbon through beading

Figure 6

Pintucked Dress Fabric Requirements

	Small Body	Medium Body	Large Body
Fabric - Swiss Batiste	$5/8$ yd.	$3/4$ yd.	$1^1/8$ yds.
Edging Lace ($3/8$")	1 yd.	1 yd.	$1^1/4$ yds.
Edging Lace ($1^1/2$")	$1^1/3$ yds.	$1^1/3$ yds.	$1^3/4$ yds.
Entredeux	$2^3/4$ yds.	3 yds.	$3^3/4$ yds.
Lace Beading ($3/8$")	$2^1/8$ yds.	2-$1/4$ yds.	3 yds.
Lace Insertion ($1/2$")	$3^1/2$ yds.	$3^1/2$ yds.	$4^3/4$ yds.
Silk Ribbon (4mm)	3 yds.	3 yds.	$3^1/2$ yds.

Notions: Two spools of lightweight sewing thread, double needle (1.6/70 or 2.0/80), 7 or 9 groove pintuck foot (optional), ribbon rosebud, Velcro™, snaps or tiny buttons.

All Seams $1/4$" unless otherwise indicated.

Please read through both the General Dress Directions and the Specific Dress Directions before starting the dress. The General Dress Directions can be found on page 22 - 26 and give generic instructions for the basic dress. These Specific Directions give instructions for the special details concerning this particular dress and the sequence of the construction.

The following pattern pieces are needed for this dress: dress front bodice, dress back bodice and long sleeve. These patterns are found on the center pull-out section.

Pintucked Dress

Directions

1. Cut a piece of fabric to be pintucked for the bodice to the following measurement:

   (length and width) Small Dolls = 5" by 10", Medium Dolls = $6^1/2$" by 12", Large Dolls = $8^1/2$" by 16"

2. Using a double needle and two spools of thread, stitch pintucks about $1/4$" apart parallel to the short side of the rectangle. Refer to basic pintucking (pg. 220) for specific directions on pintucking. Stitch enough pintucks on the rectangle to fit the bodice front. Starch and press. Cut the front bodice from the pintucked fabric. Cut two bodice backs from the selvage.

3. Place the front bodice to the back bodice, right sides together at the shoulders and stitch in place (**fig. 7**).

4. Using $3/8$" lace edging, finish the neck using the instructions found under General Dress Directions, A. Neck Finishes, a. Entredeux to Gathered Edging.

5. Cut a piece of $3/8$" edging lace, a piece of entredeux and a piece of beading to the following measurement: Small Dolls = 16", Medium Dolls = 20", Large Dolls = 24". Attach the lace edging to the lace beading using the technique lace to lace. Attach the entredeux to the lace beading using the technique entredeux to lace. These pieces are for the ends of the sleeves. Set aside (**fig. 8**).

6. Cut two pieces of lace insertion to fit the remaining lace beading. Attach the insertion to each side of the beading using the technique lace to lace. This lace strip will be used for decorating the sleeves and for the decorating on the skirt bottom (**fig. 9**).

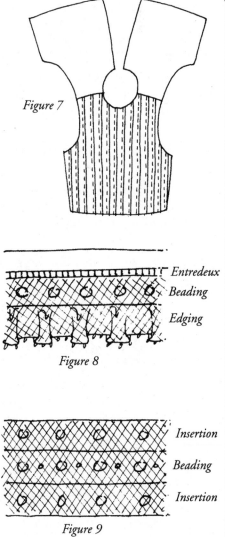

Figure 7

Entredeux
Beading
Edging

Figure 8

Insertion
Beading
Insertion

Figure 9

7. Cut a piece from the lace strip to the following measurement: Small Dolls = 12", Medium Dolls = 14", Large Dolls = 18". Cut two pieces of entredeux to fit each side of the lace strip. Attach the entredeux to the lace strip using the technique lace to entredeux. Cut the lace/beading/entredeux strip in half. These will be used in the center of each sleeve. Set aside (**fig. 10**).

8. Cut two fabric rectangles for the sleeves to the following measurements: (length and width) Small Dolls = 5^1/$_2$" by 8", Medium Dolls = 7" by 10", Large Dolls = 9" by 12". Fold each fabric rectangle in half (width wise). Cut along the fold. Attach the fabric pieces to each side of the lace/beading/entredeux strips created in step 6 using the technique entredeux to fabric (**see fig. 11**).

9. Using a double needle and two spools of thread, stitch pintucks on each side of the lace strip about ^{3}/$_8$" from the lace/beading/entredeux strip. Stitch two pintucks ^{1}/$_4$" apart on each side of the first pintucks to total three pintucks on each side of the lace/beading/entredeux strip. Starch and press the decorated fabric. Weave ribbon through the beading in the sleeves. Place the decorated fabric right sides together and cut out the sleeves. Attach the sleeve bands (created in step 5) to the ends of the sleeve using the technique entredeux to fabric. Set the sleeves aside (**fig. 11**).

10. Refer to the chart (pg. 21) dress skirt measurements. Cut a skirt piece 2^1/$_2$" shorter than the measurement given on the chart. Cut the remaining lace strip created in step 4 to 46" for small and medium dolls and 62" for large dolls. Attach the 1^1/$_2$" edging lace to one side of the lace strip. Cut one strip of entredeux to fit the other side of the lace strip. Attach the entredeux to the lace strip using the technique entredeux to lace. Attach the entredeux/lace strip to the skirt piece using the technique entredeux to fabric (**see fig. 12**).

11. Using a double needle and two spools of thread, stitch a pintuck ^{3}/$_8$" above the lace strip. Stitch two more pintucks ^{1}/$_4$" apart the first pintucks to total three pintucks. Starch and press the skirt decorated fabric. Weave ribbon through the beading in the skirt. Set skirt aside (**fig. 12**).

12. Finish the dress using the instructions found under General Dress Directions, steps 5 - 6 and steps 8 - 13.

13. Cut the remaining ribbon in half. Weave each piece through beading in the sleeves tying the excess ribbon into a bow. Stitch the tiny rose in the center of the bodice at the neck (see finished drawing).

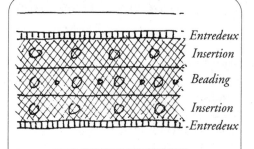

Entredeux
Insertion
Beading
Insertion
Entredeux

Figure 10

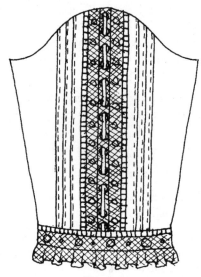

Figure 11

Skirt

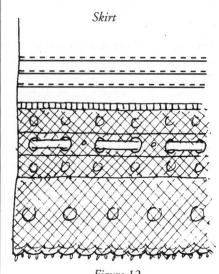

Figure 12

Corded Appliqué Pinafore

Having pretty baby French white edging lace stitched on flat, the neck and armholes of this white Swiss batiste pinafore form the perfect background for the elegant machine treatment on the bodice and skirt. Peach thread is used for the corded petals on the bodice and the skirt. Peach fabric is used behind the corded loops and it barely shows through as a hint of color from the back. This pinafore would be pretty over any of the basic dresses given in this book. Used as a child's dress treatment, this corded design would be beautiful done in white on white and used over several different colors of dresses. This pinafore is a more tailored use of French sewing by machine and would be great for the older girl also.

Fabric Requirements

	Small Body	Medium Body	Large Body
Fabric - Swiss Batiste	3/8 yd.	5/8 yd.	7/8 yd.
Colored Appliqué Fabric - Peach	1/3 yd.	1/2 yd.	5/8 yd.
Edging Lace (3/8")	2/3 yd.	1 yd.	1 1/8 yd.

Notions: Lightweight sewing thread, colored thread for appliqué, tear away stabilizer, gimp cord, Velcro™, snaps or tiny buttons

All Seams 1/4" unless otherwise indicated.

Please read through both the General Pinafore Directions (Basic Pinafore) and the Specific Pinafore Directions before starting the pinafore. The General Directions for the Basic Pinafore can be found on pages 27 to 32 and give generic instructions for the pinafore. These Specific Directions give instructions for the special details concerning this particular pinafore and the sequence of the construction.

The following pattern pieces are needed for this pinafore: basic pinafore front bodice, basic pinafore back bodice. These patterns are found on the center pull-out section.

Templates Needed: corded appliqué bodice template and corded appliqué skirt template found on page 272.

Directions

1. Cut a square of white fabric and one square of colored appliqué fabric 1" wider and 1" longer than the pinafore bodice front pattern. Trace the pattern onto the white fabric. Center the appliqué design on the drawn bodice and trace. Place the colored appliqué fabric behind the white fabric and stitch, trim and cord along the appliqué lines referring to the Corded Shadow Appliqué directions (pg. 244) (**fig. 1**).

2. Cut the front bodice from the decorated fabric treating the two layers (bodice fabric and appliqué fabric) as one. If selvage fabric is available, cut two back pinafore bodices from the selvage. If the selvage is not available, cut the back bodices from the fabric and serge or zigzag the back edges of the pinafore bodice pieces.

3. Stitch the pinafore front to the pinafore backs, right sides together, at the shoulders (**fig. 2**).

4. Attach 3/8" lace edging to the neck and arm openings using the technique Extra Stable Lace Finishing (pg. 237). The scalloped edge of the lace should be placed on the seam line, 1/4" from the cut edge of the bodice.

Corded Appliqué Pinafore

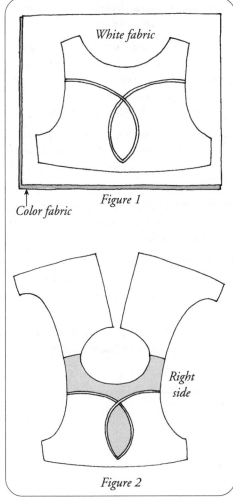

White fabric

Color fabric

Figure 1

Right side

Figure 2

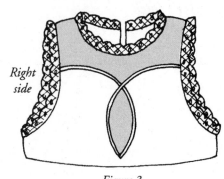

Right side

Figure 3

Skirt

Center

Figure 4

5. Place the sides of the bodice right sides together and stitch (**fig. 3**).

6. Refer to the chart on pg. 21 for the pinafore skirt measurement. Cut the pinafore skirt $^1/_4$" longer than the length given on the chart.

7. Trace the corded appliqué skirt template $1^3/_4$" from the cut edge of the skirt for medium and large dolls and $1^1/_4$" from the cut edge for large dolls, centering the loop of the template to the center of the skirt. Continue tracing the template across the skirt to each side of the center loop (**fig. 4**).

8. For small and medium dolls, cut one strip of colored appliqué fabric 7" by 45". For large dolls cut two strips 7" wide by $15^3/_4$" and one strip 7" by $30^1/_2$". Attach the shorter pieces to each side of the longer piece, right sides together taking a $^1/_4$" seam.

9. Place the wrong side of the colored appliqué fabric strip to the right side of the skirt. Stitch in place across the bottom edge of the skirt using a $^1/_4$" seam (**fig. 5**).

10. Turn the colored appliqué fabric to the wrong side of the skirt and press. This will hem the bottom of the skirt (**see fig. 6**).

11. Following the directions for Corded Shadow Appliqué (pg. 244) stitch, trim and cord the colored appliqué fabric to the skirt along the template lines (**fig. 6**).

12. To finish the pinafore refer to the General Pinafore Directions - A. Basic Pinafore (unlined) - steps 6 to 11.

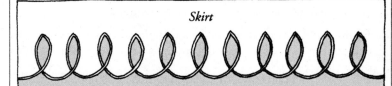

Skirt – right side

Color appliqué fabric – right side

Figure 5

Skirt

Figure 6

Show 10
Organdy Pinafore with Serger Ruffles

Using decorative stitches on one's sewing machine is so much fun in heirloom sewing. I believe heirloom sewing is the type of sewing that the new embroidery machines were made for. What fun to use the cross stitch stitches on any sewing machine to embellish the center bib, the waistline and the over-the-shoulder pieces of this white organdy pinafore. Pink is the color of both the machine cross stitch as well as the serger trimmed ruffles. The ruffles on the sleeves of this pinafore, as well as the three ruffles on the skirt, have a pink serger treatment on the edges. I like the fact that serger pink trim is on both the top and the bottom of the organdy skirt ruffles. The ruffles are stitched down to the pinafore skirt using pink machine featherstitch. Wonderful organdy sashes close the back of this pinafore and, you guessed it, pink organdy serger stitching finishes the edges of the sash. Any of the dresses featured in the book would be the perfect dress to go under this pinafore.

Organdy Pinafore with Serger Ruffles

Fabric Requirements

	Small Body	Medium Body	Large Body
Fabric - Organdy	³/₄ yd.	1 yd.	1⁵/₈ yds.

Notions: Lightweight sewing thread, decorative thread for embellishing, one spool of woolly nylon to be used in the serger to match decorative thread (optional), Velcro™, snaps or tiny buttons.

All Seams ¹/₄" unless otherwise indicated.

Please read through both the General Pinafore Directions (Bib Pinafore) and the Specific Pinafore Directions before starting the pinafore. The General Directions for the Bib Pinafore can be found on pages 27 to 32 and give generic instructions for the pinafore. These Specific Directions give instructions for the special details concerning this particular pinafore and the sequence of the construction.

The following pattern pieces are needed for this pinafore: bib pinafore front and bib ruffle. These pattern pieces can be found on the center pull-out section.

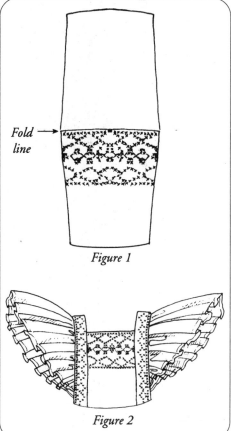

Figure 1

Figure 2

Directions

1. Cut one bib front from the fold. Mark the fold on the bib. Cut two bib ruffles. Refer to the measurements given in the bib pinafore general directions (pg. 29) to cut one waist band piece and two strap pieces. Cut a skirt piece ¹/₄" longer than the measurement given on the pinafore skirt chart (pg. 21). Cut two sash pieces 16" long by 1³/₄" wide. Cut strips for the ruffles as follows: small and medium dolls - cut six fabric strips 2" wide by 45" long; large dolls - cut nine fabric strips 2" long by 40" wide.

2. Follow the bib pinafore general directions steps 2 - 5 using the information below:

   The bib is embellished with a cross-stitch sewing machine design but any decorative stitch can be used (**fig. 1**). The edges of each bib ruffle are finished using a serger rolled hem with decorative thread in the upper looper or a satin stitch zigzag. After the straps are attached to the ruffles and bib, a decorative stitch can be used to embellish the straps (**fig. 2**).

3. Turn one long edge of the skirt to the inside ¼" and then ¾". Press. Stitch the hem in place along the upper folded edge (**fig. 3**).

4. Stitch the ruffle pieces together in the following manner: for the small and medium dolls cut three of the 45" fabric strips in half and stitch a smaller piece to each side of the remaining long strips creating three ruffle strips each measuring about 90" in length; for large dolls stitch three fabric strips together to create three 120" ruffle strips (**see fig. 4**).

5. Finish each long side of the ruffle strips using a serger rolled hem with decorative thread in the upper looper or a satin stitch zigzag (**see fig. 4**).

6. Stitch a gathering row ½" from one long side of each ruffle piece (**fig. 4**). Gather each ruffle strip to the width of the skirt. Place the first ruffle strip on the right side of the skirt matching the gathering row with the stitching line of the hem. The ruffle will extend beyond the folded edge of the skirt. Stitch the second ruffle strip just above the first and the third ruffle just above the second. If desired, stitch a machine feather stitch with decorative thread along the stitching line of each ruffle (**fig. 5**).

7. Refer to the bib pinafore general directions steps 7 - 12 to finish the pinafore. The sash pieces of the pinafore are finished using a serger rolled hem with decorative thread in the upper looper or a satin stitch zigzag. ■

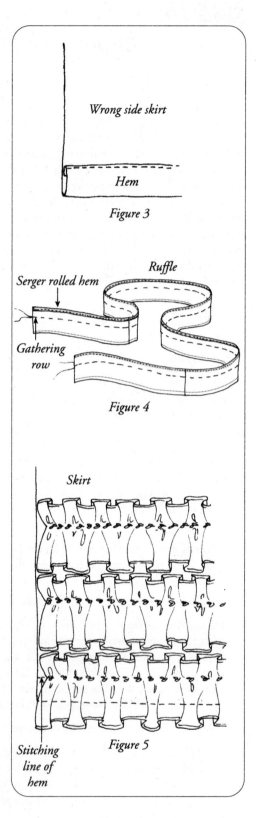

Wrong side skirt

Hem

Figure 3

Serger rolled hem

Ruffle

Gathering row

Figure 4

Skirt

Stitching line of hem

Figure 5

Oval Lace Picture Transfer Pinafore

Perfectly elegant is the way I would describe this tabard-style pinafore. Pintucks are one of the most versatile heirloom techniques, and they are used to their best advantage on the entire pinafore bodice and in oval lace shapes on the skirt. The bottom curves of the skirt ovals are echoed in the lace scallops that run across the skirt bottom. Ruffled white edging lace finishes the skirt edges. The final touch of elegance is the sweet picture transfer in the center oval, which shows a precious little girl with an armful of roses.

Fabric Requirements

	Small Body	Medium Body	Large Body
Fabric - Swiss Batiste	$^1/_2$ yd.	1 yd.	$1^1/_8$ yds.
Lace Insertion ($^1/_2$")	$3^3/_4$ yds.	4 yds.	$5^1/_4$ yds.
Satin Ribbon (1")	$1^3/_4$ yds.	$1^3/_4$ yds.	$1^3/_4$ yds.
Edging Lace ($^3/_4$")	5 yds.	$5^1/_2$ yds.	8 yds.

Notions: Lightweight sewing thread, picture for picture transfer to fit lace oval, 1.6/70 or 2.0/80 double needle, 7 or 9 groove pintuck foot (optional), Velcro™, snaps or tiny buttons.

All Seams $^1/_4$" unless otherwise indicated.

Please read through both the General Pinafore Directions (Apron Pinafore) and the Specific Pinafore Directions before starting the pinafore. The General Directions for the Apron Pinafore can be found on pages 27 to 32 and give generic instructions for the pinafore. These Specific Directions give instructions for the special details concerning this particular pinafore and the sequence of the construction.

The following pattern pieces are needed for this pinafore: basic pinafore front bodice, basic pinafore back bodice. These patterns are found on the center pull-out section.

Templates Needed: $6^1/_2$" scallop on pull-out section and lace oval found on page 58.

Directions

1. Cut a piece of fabric to be pintucked for the bodices and lace ovals to the following measurement: Small Dolls = 5" by 36", Medium Dolls = $6^1/_2$" by 40", Large Dolls = $8^1/_2$" by 45".

2. Using a double needle and two spools of thread, stitch pintucks about $^1/_4$" apart, parallel to the short side of the strip. Refer to basic pintucking (pg. 220) for specific directions on pintucking. Starch and press the strip. Cut one front bodice from the fold and two back bodices from the pintucked fabric. Save the remaining pintucked fabric for the center of the two outer lace ovals (**fig. 1**).

3. Cut one front bodice lining from plain fabric on the fold and two back bodices from plain fabric. Refer to the General Pinafore Directions, Apron Pinafore, steps 2 - 5 to complete the bodice. Set aside.

4. Refer to the pinafore skirt chart (pg. 21). Cut two skirt pieces to the length given on the chart by 21" for small and medium dolls and 33" for large dolls. One piece will be for the front and one piece will be for the back.

5. Fold the skirt front in half to find the center front. Center the scallop template in the center of the skirt with the lower edge of the scallop $^3/_4$" from the edge of the skirt. For the small and medium dolls, trace one scallop on each side of the center scallop. For the large dolls, trace two scallops on each side of the center scallop. Extend the

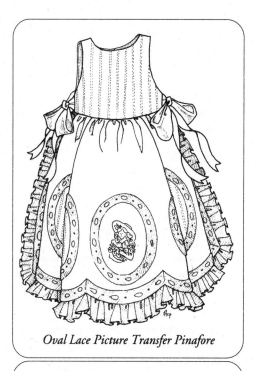

Oval Lace Picture Transfer Pinafore

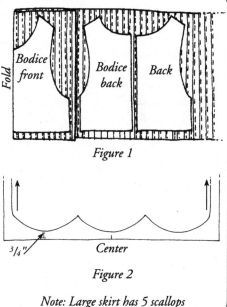

Bodice front | *Bodice back* | *Back*

Fold

Figure 1

$^3/_4$" | *Center*

Figure 2

Note: Large skirt has 5 scallops

lines at the outer points of the scallops to the top edge of the skirt. Repeat for the back skirt piece (**fig. 2**).

6. Shape lace along the template lines of the front and back skirt pieces referring to the technique for scalloped skirts. Stitch along the inside edge of the lace using a small tight zigzag. Trim away any excess fabric from behind the scallops (**fig. 3**).

7. Cut the piece of edging lace in half and gather the edging to fit the outer edge of the lace insertion. Stitch the gathered lace to the lace insertion using the technique lace to lace. Set the back skirt piece aside (**fig. 4**).

8. On the skirt front, trace a lace oval template ¹/₂" above the three center lace scallops. Shape insertion lace along the template lines referring to the technique for lace circles. Stitch along the outer edge of the lace oval using a small tight zigzag. Trim the fabric from inside the outer two lace ovals (**fig. 5**).

9. Place the pintucked fabric in the center of the outer ovals and stitch in place along the inside edge of the lace oval using a small tight zigzag. Trim away the excess pintucked fabric (**fig. 6**).

10. Transfer the picture into the center of the center oval. This completes the embellishment of the skirt front.

11. Complete the pinafore referring to the General Pinafore Directions, Apron Pinafore, steps 7 - 15. ▣

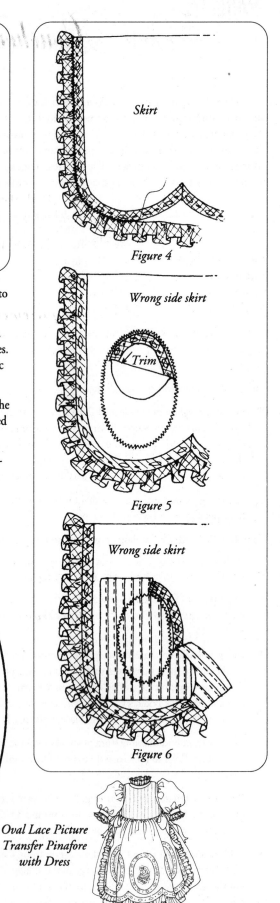

Trim

Skirt

Figure 3

Skirt

Figure 4

Wrong side skirt

Trim

Figure 5

Wrong side skirt

Figure 6

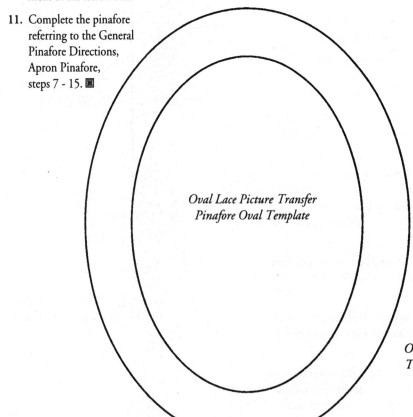

Oval Lace Picture Transfer Pinafore Oval Template

Oval Lace Picture Transfer Pinafore with Dress

Couched Ribbon Pinafore

Everybody loves a Christmas dress! I have such fond memories of my Mama's making me a Christmas dress every year. I did the same for Joanna and the grandchildren always have something wonderful also. Dolls love Christmas dresses, and what a Christmas pinafore this one is. Using the wonderful decorative stitches on your sewing machine, stitch in a beautiful forest green over a beautiful burgundy red silk ribbon on both the hem of the skirt and vertically on the skirt and bib of the pinafore. The fabric is white organdy and the ruffle on the sleeve is trimmed with white French edging lace. Machine or hand-worked silk ribbon poinsettias are filled with gold beads in the center. Machine-embroidery makes the leaves around the silk ribbon lazy daisy poinsettias. A beautiful white organdy sash trims this pinafore. Any of the beautiful dresses in this book would be perfect underneath this pinafore. This pinafore would be just as beautiful on a child as on a doll.

Couched Ribbon Pinafore

Fabric Requirements

	Small Body	Medium Body	Large Body
Fabric - Organdy	$1/2$ yd.	$3/4$ yd.	$1^1/8$ yds.
Lace Edging ($3/4$")	$1^1/4$ yds.	$1^1/4$ yds.	$1^3/4$ yds.
Silk Ribbon (4mm)	5 yds.	7 yds.	9 yds.

Notions: Lightweight sewing thread, gold beads for the flower centers, decorative thread for couching silk ribbon in place, Velcro™, snaps or tiny buttons.

All Seams $1/4$" unless otherwise indicated.

Please read through both the General Pinafore Directions (Bib Pinafore) and the Specific Pinafore Directions before starting the pinafore. The General Directions for the Bib Pinafore can be found on pages 27 to 32 and give generic instructions for the pinafore. These Specific Directions give instructions for the special details concerning this particular pinafore and the sequence of the construction.

The following pattern pieces are needed for this pinafore: bib pinafore front and bib ruffle. These pattern pieces can be found on the center pull-out section.

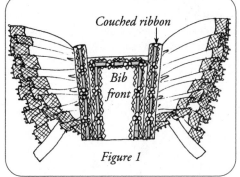

Couched ribbon

Bib front

Figure 1

Directions

1. Cut one bib front from the fold. Mark the fold on the bib. Cut two bib ruffles. Refer to the measurements given in the bib pinafore general directions (pg. 29) to cut one waist band piece and two strap pieces. Cut a skirt piece $2^1/4$" longer than the measurement given on the pinafore skirt chart (pg. 21). Cut two sash pieces 16" long by $1^3/4$" wide.

2. This pinafore is embellished with silk ribbon, stitched in place with an open decorative stitch. This technique is called couching. Choose an open decorative stitch on your machine that allows the ribbon to show through the stitching for all couching work.

3. Follow the bib pinafore general directions steps 2 - 3. The ruffles have edging lace attached to the straight side of the ruffle using the technique lace to fabric.

4. Follow the bib pinafore general directions steps 4 - 5. To embellish the bib - couch ribbon just below the fold line of the bib and $1/2$" from each edge of the bib sides. After the straps are attached to the ruffles and bib, couch ribbon in the center of each strap (**fig. 1**).

Couched Ribbon Pinafore with Dress

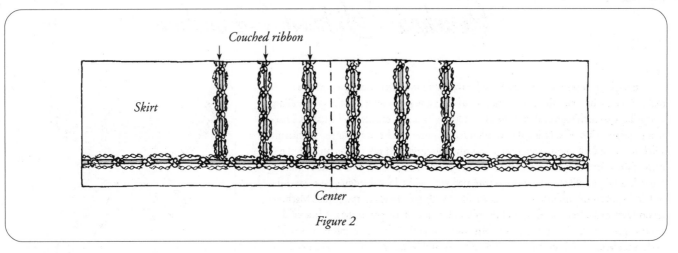

Couched ribbon

Skirt

Center

Figure 2

5. Turn one long edge of the skirt to the inside ¼" and then 2". Press. Stitch the hem in place along the upper folded edge.

6. Fold the skirt piece in half to find the center front. Using a fabric marker draw lines 2" from the center front stopping at the stitching line of the hem. Draw lines 4" from each drawn line to total six lines, three lines on each side of center. Couch ribbon along each of the drawn lines stopping at the stitching line of the hem. Couch ribbon on top of the stitching line of the hem (**fig. 2**).

7. Stitch by hand or machine, flowers and leaves in the center of each panel. The embroidery on this pinafore has been stitched in the following manner: the leaves are a machine decorative stitch and the flowers have been added by hand using silk ribbon lazy daisy stitches. Stitch beads to the center of each flower (**fig. 3**).

8. Refer to the bib pinafore general directions steps 7 - 12 to finish the pinafore. ▧

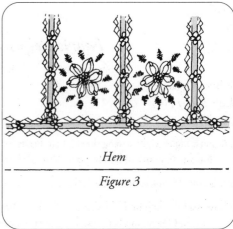

Hem

Figure 3

Embroidery Template

  Lazy Daisy – 4mm silk ribbon burgundy

🌿 *Feather Stitch – floss green*

❀ *Beads or French Knot gold*

Show 13
Antique Pinafore Dress and Antique Bonnet

This bonnet is an exact copy of an antique doll bonnet I purchased at a very exclusive doll shop in Paris. The bonnet is composed of ecru laces, beading and insertion, zigzagged together to form the fabric from which the bonnet is cut. A circular crown in the back is encircled by gathered ecru French edging. Two rows of ecru French edging are slightly gathered to one row of ecru insertion for the ruffle around the bonnet. A beautiful scalloped treatment of gathered French ecru lace insertion and edging trims the top of the bonnet and four robin's egg blue silk ribbon rosettes add such a pretty touch. Robin's egg blue silk ribbons are run through the beading areas on the bonnet and the same ribbon is used for tying the bonnet under the chin. What a lucky doll to have this bonnet!

The dress and pinafore are as magnificent as the bonnet. The dress is so wonderful, you may not want to cover it up! The bodice of the dress has two sets of three pintucks running vertically down the front, with featherstitching in the middle. A sweet ribbon rose is at the neck, which is finished with entredeux and gathered lace edging. The sleeves and cuffs have the same pintucks and featherstitching. The skirt is glorious, featuring the same pintucks and featherstitching, but with fancy bands added. The fancy bands include lace insertion, lace beading, and entredeux. The same robin's egg silk ribbon that was used on the bonnet is run through the beading of the dress.

The pinafore adds the final magnificent touch to this ensemble. The entire front bodice, over-the-shoulder ruffles and the skirt pockets are made of the same laces as the skirt fancy bands. Ruffled lace edging finishes the edges of the neckline, ruffles and pockets. The hem is embellished with a sweet, vertically-pieced lace band with robin's egg silk ribbon through the beading. The lace band is edged with entredeux across the top and bottom, and wide flat lace edging finishes the hem.

Embellished Pinafore Fabric Requirements

	Small Body	Medium Body	Large Body
Fabric - Swiss Batiste	$3/8$ yd.	$5/8$ yd.	$7/8$ yd.
Edging Lace ($5/8$")	5 yds.	6 yds.	7 yds.
Edging Lace (1")	$1^1/4$ yds.	$1^1/4$ yds.	$1^3/4$ yds.
Entredeux	6 yds.	6 yds.	7-1/2 yds.
Lace Beading ($1/2$")	6 yds.	7 yds.	9 yds.
Lace Insertion ($1/2$")	7 yds.	8 yds.	10 yds.
Silk Ribbon (4 mm)	9 yds.	11 yds.	13 yds.

Notions: Lightweight sewing thread, #100 wing needle (optional), Velcro™, snaps or tiny buttons.

All Seams $1/4$" unless otherwise indicated.

Please read through both the General Pinafore Directions (Basic Pinafore) and the Specific Pinafore Directions before starting the pinafore. The General Directions for the Basic Pinafore can be found on pages 27 to 32 and give generic instructions for the pinafore. These Specific Directions give instructions for the special details concerning this particular pinafore and the sequence of the construction.

The following pattern pieces are needed for this pinafore: basic pinafore front bodice, basic pinafore back bodice, bib ruffle. These patterns are found on the center pull-out section.

Antique Pinafore

Antique Dress

Antique Bonnet

Directions

1. Cut a piece of fabric larger than the front pinafore bodice pattern. Trace the front bodice on the fabric piece. If selvage fabric is available, cut two pinafore back bodices from the selvage. If the selvage is not available, cut the back bodices from the fabric and serge or zigzag the back edges of the bodice pieces.

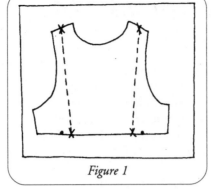

Figure 1

2. Place an X in the center of each shoulder line of the traced front bodice. Place dots at the waistline of the pinafore bodice straight down from the X's at the shoulder. Place an X, $^1/_2$" to the inside of each dot. Draw lines joining the X's of the shoulders to the X's at the waist (**fig.** 1). Repeat this process on each back bodice.

3. Cut laces as described below:

Doll Sizes	Beading	Insertion
Small 5"	5 pieces	4 pieces
Medium 7"	5 pieces	6 pieces
Large 8"	6 pieces	8 pieces

4. Stitch the laces pieces together using the technique lace to lace alternating beading and lace. Run ribbon through the beading. Place the created rectangle on top of the pinafore front bodice with the center piece of beading along the center front of the bodice. Using a small, tight zigzag, stitch the lace panel to the bodice along the lines drawn in step 2 and just inside the bodice lines inside the drawn lines. Cut out the front bodice and trim the excess lace from the sides of the drawn lines (**fig.** 2).

5. Stitch the pinafore front to the pinafore backs, right sides together, at the shoulders (**see fig.** 3).

6. Attach entredeux around the arm openings using the technique entredeux to fabric. Trim the remaining fabric edge from the entredeux. Gather the $^3/_8$" edging to fit the entredeux at the arm openings. Attach the gathered edging to the entredeux using the technique lace to entredeux (**fig.** 3).

7. Bodice ruffle - Cut two pieces of insertion and one piece each of beading, entredeux and $^5/_8$" edging to the following measurements: Small dolls 32", Medium 44", Large 56". Also cut two strips of fabric 1" wide by the length above.

8. Attach the laces together in the following order using the technique lace to lace: edging, insertion, beading and insertion. Attach entredeux to the insertion lace using the technique lace to entredeux. Attach the fabric to the entredeux using the technique entredeux to fabric. Place the scalloped edge of the edging on the straight side of the pattern and cut two ruffles. Run two gathering rows $^1/_4$" and $^1/_8$" in the curved side of each ruffle (**fig.** 4).

9. Gather the ruffle to fit the lines drawn in step 2. Pin in place with the right side of the ruffles to the right side of the bodice, starting and stopping the ruffle $^1/_4$" from the cut edges of the bodice waistline. Stitch in place along the $^1/_4$" gathering row. Trim the ruffle seam allowance down to $^1/_8$" being careful not to cut the bodice fabric. Zigzag the seam allowance of the ruffle to the bodice. Flip the ruffle toward the arm opening. Top stitch along the seam of the ruffle with a small zigzag (**fig.** 5).

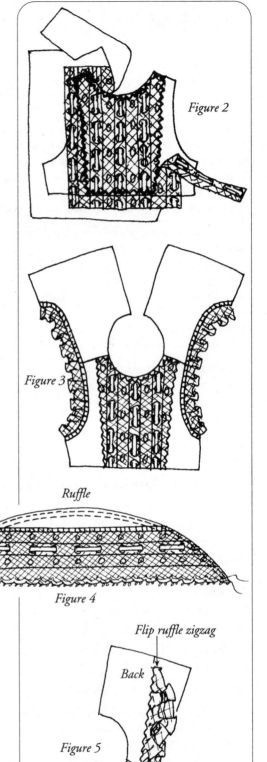

Figure 2

Figure 3

Ruffle

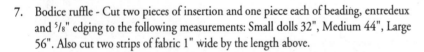

Figure 4

Flip ruffle zigzag

Back

Figure 5

Front bodice

Trim

Ruffle right side down and zigzag

10. Neck edge - Measure around the neck edge of the pinafore with the back folds extended. Cut a piece of entredeux $^{1}/_{2}$" longer than the measurement. Cut a piece of $^{5}/_{8}$" edging lace twice the length of the entredeux. Gather the lace to fit the entredeux. Attach the gathered lace to the entredeux using the technique lace to entredeux.

11. Place the right side of the entredeux/lace strip to the wrong side of the neck edge. Stitch in place using the technique entredeux to fabric. Flip the entredeux/lace piece to the right side of the bodice. Stitch the entredeux/lace piece to the bodice using a tiny zigzag along the lower edge of the entredeux. This will enclose the seam allowance (see fig. 6).

12. Place the sides of the bodice right sides together and stitch (fig. 6).

13. Refer to the chart on pg. 21 for the pinafore skirt measurement. Cut the pinafore skirt 2" shorter than the length given on the chart.

14. Cut five pieces each of beading and insertion 18" long for small and medium dolls and seven pieces each of beading and insertion 18" long for large dolls. Stitch the laces pieces together using the technique lace to lace, alternating beading and lace. Run ribbon through the beading. Cut the 18" rectangle into three equal pieces, about 6" each. Stitch these pieces together keeping the pattern of alternating beading and lace. Now cut the 6" rectangle into three equal pieces, about 2" each. Stitch these pieces together keeping the pattern of alternating beading and lace. Continue adding 2" strips of lace insertion and beading until the strip measures 45" for small and medium dolls and 60" for large dolls. Starch and press (see fig. 7).

15. Cut two pieces of entredeux 45" for small and medium dolls and 60" for large dolls. Stitch the entredeux to each side of the lace strip using the technique entredeux to fabric. Attach the 1" lace edging to one of the entredeux pieces using the technique lace to entredeux. Attach the skirt fabric to the other entredeux piece using the technique entredeux to fabric (fig. 7).

16. Pockets - Cut laces as described below:

Doll Sizes	Insertion	Beading
Small 7"	6 pieces	5 pieces
Medium 8"	7 pieces	6 pieces
Large 9"	8 pieces	7 pieces

17. Stitch the lace pieces together using the technique lace to lace, alternating beading and lace. Starch and press. Run ribbon through the beading. Trace two pocket patterns on the created lace rectangle. Stitch along the drawn lines of each pocket using a straight stitch. Cut out the pockets (fig. 8).

18. Cut one piece of beading and one piece of entredeux to 10" for small dolls, 12" for medium dolls, and 14" for large dolls. Cut one piece of $^{5}/_{8}$" edging twice the length of the beading and gather to fit the beading. Stitch the beading to the gathered lace using the technique lace to lace. Attach the beading to the entredeux using the technique entredeux to lace. Cut the strip in half. Place the right side of the strip to the wrong side of the pocket with the entredeux along the top edge of the pocket. Stitch in place using the technique entredeux to fabric. Flip the strip to the right side of the pocket and stitch in place along lower edge of the entredeux. Cut four pieces of ribbon 9" long. Weave each piece through the top of the pocket beading from the outside edge of the pocket to the pocket center. Pin the ribbon in place along the outside edge and tie the excess into a bow at the center of the pocket (fig. 9).

19. Measure around the unfinished edge of the pocket. Cut two pieces of entredeux, each 1" larger than this measurement. Cut two pieces of lace edging twice the length of the entredeux. Gather the lace to fit the entredeux and attach together using the technique lace to entredeux. Clip the remaining fabric edge of the entredeux so that the entredeux will curve. Place the entredeux/gathered lace to the pocket edge, right

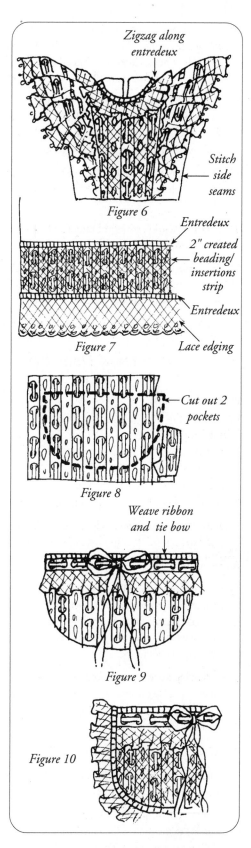

Zigzag along entredeux

Stitch side seams

Figure 6

Entredeux

2" created beading/insertions strip

Entredeux

Lace edging

Figure 7

Cut out 2 pockets

Figure 8

Weave ribbon and tie bow

Figure 9

Figure 10

sides together with a $^{1}/_{2}$" tab extending at the top edges. Stitch in place using the technique lace to fabric. Flip the entredeux/gathered lace away from the pocket and press (fig. 10).

20. For pocket placement, fold the skirt in half to find the center front, fold again to find the quarter points. The pockets should be centered between the center front fold and the quarter folds, about 1¹/₂" from the top edge of the skirt. Stitch each pocket in place along the outer edge of the entredeux (fig. 11).

21. Fold the back edges of the skirt to the inside ¹/₄" and ¹/₄" again. Stitch in place. Run two gathering rows in the top edge of the skirt/lace at ¹/₈" and ¹/₄". Gather the skirt to fit the pinafore bodice with the edges of the skirt ¹/₄" from the back folds of the bodice. Pin in place, right sides together.

22. Wrap the back edges of the bodice to the inside of the skirt, folding along the fold lines. Stitch the bodice to the skirt using a ¹/₄" seam. Overcast with a zigzag or serger (fig. 12).

23. Attach Velcro™, snaps or buttons and buttonholes along the folds of the back bodices to close the pinafore.

24. Cut a piece of silk ribbon 1¹/₂ yards long. Place dots with a fabric marker about 2" apart starting and stopping 7" from each end. To make the rosette refer to "rosettes" in the technique section, pg. 239.

25. Tack the rosette at the center front of the pinafore (fig. 13).

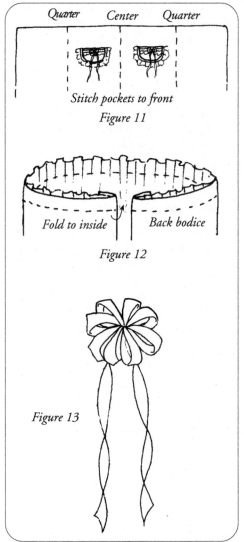

Stitch pockets to front
Figure 11

Fold to inside   Back bodice
Figure 12

Figure 13

Pintucked Dress Fabric Requirements

	Small Body	Medium Body	Large Body
Fabric - Swiss Batiste	⁵/₈ yd.	³/₄ yd.	1¹/₈ yds.
Edging Lace (⁵/₈")	1¹/₂ yds.	2 yds.	2 yds.
Edging Lace (1")	1¹/₄ yds.	1¹/₄ yds.	1³/₄ yds.
Entredeux	5 yds.	5 yds.	6 yds.
Lace Beading (¹/₂")	3 yds.	3 yds.	4 yds.
Lace Insertion (¹/₂")	5 yds.	5 yds.	7 yds.
Silk Ribbon (4 mm)	3 yds.	3 yds.	4 yds.

Notions: Two spools of lightweight sewing thread, double needle (1.6/70 or 2.0/80), 7 or 9 groove pintuck foot (optional), ribbon rosebud, Velcro™, snaps or tiny buttons.

All Seams ¹/₄" unless otherwise indicated.

Please read through both the General Dress Directions and the Specific Dress Directions before starting the dress. The General Dress Directions can be found on page 22 - 26 and give generic instructions for the basic dress. These Specific Directions give instructions for the special details concerning this particular dress and the sequence of the construction.

The following pattern pieces are needed for this dress: dress front bodice, dress back bodice and long sleeve. These patterns are found on the center pull-out section.

Directions

1. Cut a piece of fabric to be pintucked for the bodice to the following measurement:

   (length and width) Small Dolls = 5" by 10", Medium Dolls = 6¹/₂" by 12", Large Dolls = 8¹/₂" by 16".

2. Using a double needle and two spools of thread, stitch six pintucks about ¹/₄" apart parallel to the short sides, in the center of the fabric. Refer to basic pintucking (pg. 220) for specific directions on pintucking. Starch and press the pintucks away from the center of the fabric (three pressed to the left and three pressed to the right). Using a machine decorative stitch, like a feather stitch, stitch down the center of the fabric between the sets of pintucks. Cut the front bodice from the pintucked fabric. Cut two bodice backs from the selvage.

Antique Pintucked Dress

3. Place the front bodice to the back bodice, right sides together at the shoulders and stitch in place (**fig. 14**).

4. Using ⁵/₈" lace edging, finish the neck using the instructions found under General Dress Directions, A. Neck Finishes, a. Entredeux to Gathered Edging.

5. Cut two pieces of entredeux and a piece of fabric 1¹/₂" wide by the following measurement: Small Dolls = 16", Medium Dolls = 20", Large Dolls = 24". Stitch a double needle pintuck ¹/₂" from each long side of the fabric. Press the pintucks away from each other. Using a machine decorative stitch, like a feather stitch, stitch down the center of the fabric between the two pintucks. Attach entredeux to each side of the fabric band using the technique entredeux to fabric. Cut a piece of lace twice the length of the band and gather to fit the entredeux. Stitch in place using the technique entredeux to gathered lace. Cut the band in half. Set aside (**fig. 15**).

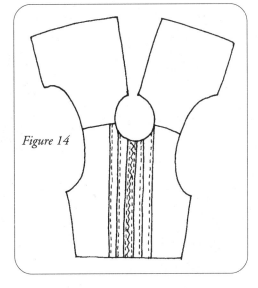

Figure 14

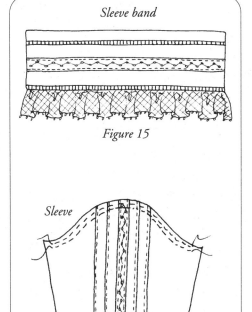

Sleeve band

Figure 15

Sleeve

Figure 16

6. Cut out two long sleeves. Stitch six pintucks about ¹/₄" apart in the center of the sleeve, starting with the two center tucks about ¹/₈" from the center of the sleeve. Starch and press the pintucks away from the center of the fabric (three pressed to the left and three pressed to the right). Using a machine decorative stitch, like a feather stitch, stitch down the center of the sleeve between the sets of pintucks (**see fig. 16**).

7. Run two gathering rows in the top and lower edge of the sleeve at ¹/₄" and ¹/₂" and gather the bottom of each sleeve to fit a sleeve band. Stitch the sleeve band to each sleeve using the technique entredeux to gathered fabric. Set aside (**fig. 16**).

8. Refer to the chart (pg. 21) for dress skirt measurements. Cut a skirt piece 5¹/₂" shorter than the measurement given on the chart. Cut four pieces of insertion lace, two pieces of beading, three pieces of entredeux, one piece of 1" wide edging lace and a strip of fabric 3" wide to the following measurements: 46" for small and medium dolls and 62" for large dolls. Note: to achieve a 62" length for the large dolls, cut one strip 30¹/₂" and two strips 15³/₄". Attach the shorter strips to each end of the longer strip.

9. Using a machine decorative stitch, like a feather stitch, stitch down the center of the fabric. Place three double needle pintucks about ¹/₄" apart on each side of the decorative stitch. The two center pintucks are ¹/₄" apart. Press (**see fig. 17**).

10. Create two lace bands by attaching lace insertion to each side of the beading. On one of the lace bands attach entredeux on each side of the insertion lace. On the other lace band attach entredeux on one side on the band and attach edging lace on the other side (**see fig. 17**).

11. Attach the lace bands to each side of the pintucked fabric strip using the technique entredeux to lace. Attach the entredeux of the band to the skirt piece. Weave ribbon through the beading. This completes the skirt (**fig. 17**).

12. Finish the dress using the instructions found under General Dress Directions, steps 5 - 6 and steps 8 - 13.

13. Stitch the tiny rose in the center of the bodice at the neck.

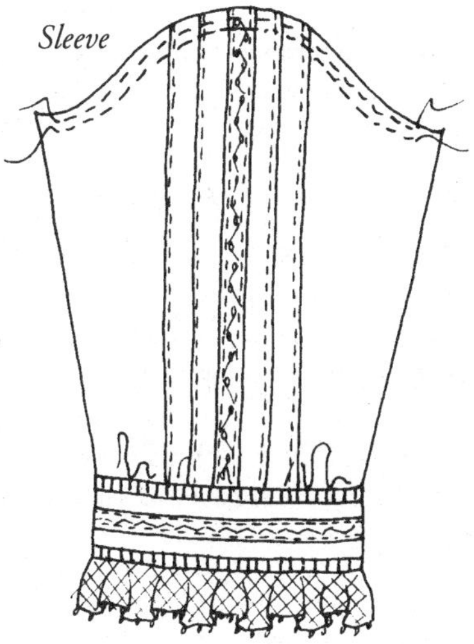

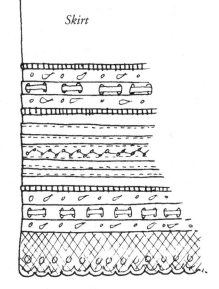

Skirt

Figure 17

Bonnet Fabric Requirements

	8/9 &10/11	12/13	14/15
Edging Lace (⁵/₈")	4⁵/₈ yds.	5 yds.	5 yds.
Lace Insertion (³/₄")	2¹/₂ yds.	2¹/₂ yds.	2³/₄ yds.
Lace Beading (¹/₂")	3 yds.	3¹/₂ yds.	4 yds.
Lace Insertion (¹/₂")	3 yds.	3¹/₂ yds.	4 yds.
Silk Ribbon (4 mm)	6 yds.	6 yds.	6 yds.
Medium Wt. Interfacing	¹/₈ yd.	¹/₈ yd.	¹/₈ yd.

Notions: Lightweight sewing thread, #100 wing needle (optional), Velcro™, snaps or tiny buttons.

All Seams ¹/₄" unless otherwise indicated.

The following pattern pieces are needed for this bonnet: antique bonnet, antique bonnet back circle, antique bonnet facing. These patterns are found on pages 265-266.

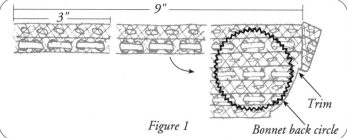

Antique Bonnet

Directions

1. Cut 9" of beading and 9" of ¹/₂" insertion. Stitch the two pieces together using the technique lace to lace. Weave ribbon through the beading. Cut the lace strip into 3" pieces. Zigzag the lace pieces together with the beading attached to the lace. Starch and press. Trace the bonnet back circle on to this lace piece. Stitch with a tiny zigzag along the outline of the circle. Cut the bonnet back circle along the outside edge of zigzag stitching (**fig. 1**).

2. Attach the remaining beading to the ¹/₂" lace insertion. Cut the piece in half and zigzag the lace pieces together with the beading attached to the lace. Continue cutting and stitching until the following measurement is achieved: 8/9 & 10/11 - 16" long by 5" wide, 12/13 - 17" long by 6" wide and 14/15 - 18" long by 7" wide. Starch and press. Trace the bonnet onto this created lace piece. Weave ribbon through the beading (**fig. 2**).

3. Cut the bonnet facing from the interfacing and zigzag along the back edge. Trace the dotted lines onto the facing piece (**fig. 3**). Place the right side of the facing to the wrong side of the bonnet, lining up the lines on the bonnet with the front edge of the facing. Place a tuck at the tuck line so that the center back edges line up. Using a zigzag (1.0 length and 2.0 width) stitch the facing to the bonnet. Zigzag along the other drawn lines. Cut just outside the zigzags. Trace the dotted lines of the facing on the bonnet using a fabric marker or pencil. Run two gathering rows in the back of the bonnet at ¹/₈" and ¹/₄", starting and stopping ³/₈" from the ends (**fig. 4**).

4. Cut one piece of lace edging and one piece of ³/₄" lace insertion to the following measurement: 35" for 8/9 & 10/11, 38" for 12/13 and 45" for 14/15. Stitch the laces together using the technique lace to lace (**fig. 5**).

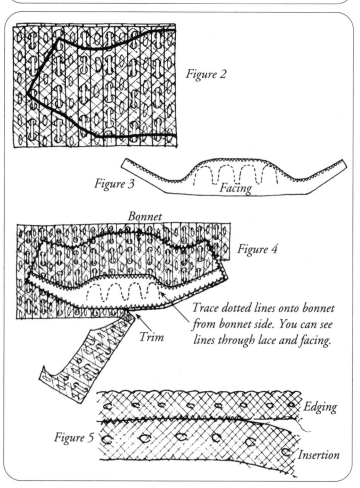

Figure 1

3" 9" Trim Bonnet back circle

Figure 2

Figure 3 Facing

Bonnet *Figure 4*

Trim

Trace dotted lines onto bonnet from bonnet side. You can see lines through lace and facing.

Figure 5 Edging Insertion

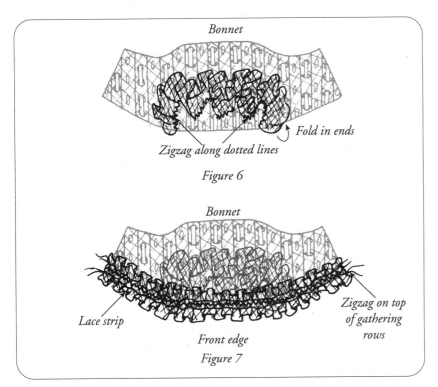

Bonnet

Fold in ends

Zigzag along dotted lines

Figure 6

Bonnet

Lace strip

Zigzag on top of gathering rows

Front edge
Figure 7

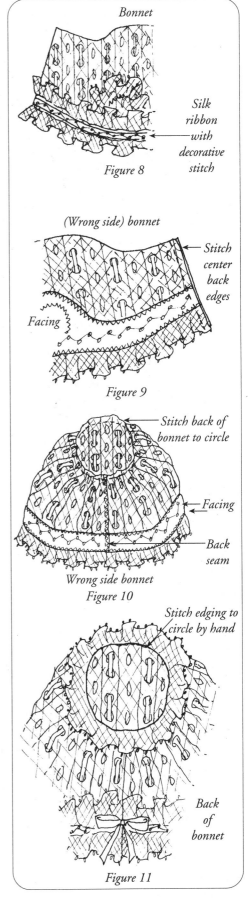

Bonnet

Silk ribbon with decorative stitch

Figure 8

(Wrong side) bonnet

Stitch center back edges

Facing

Figure 9

Stitch back of bonnet to circle

Facing

Back seam

Wrong side bonnet
Figure 10

Stitch edging to circle by hand

Back of bonnet

Figure 11

5. Gather the insertion side of the lace strip to fit the dotted lines of the bonnet. Fold the ends of the lace to the inside $^1/_8$" and $^1/_8$" again. Stitch the gathered lace in place along the dotted lines using a zigzag. Curl and tack each folded end of the lace to the bonnet by hand or with a zigzag (**fig. 6**).

6. Cut two pieces of lace edging and one piece of $^3/_4$" lace insertion to 52". Stitch edging lace to each side of the insertion using the technique lace to lace. Run two gathering rows about $^1/_{16}$" from the center of the insertion lace. Gather the lace $^1/_4$" from the front edge of the bonnet (**fig. 7**).

7. Place silk ribbon along the gathering lines and stitch in place with a feather stitch or other decorative stitch (**fig. 8**).

8. Make four 12 loop ribbon rosettes each from 26" of ribbon placing the dots about 2" apart. (Refer to Ribbon Rosette - Page 239.) Tack each ribbon rosette in place at each X along the front of the bonnet (see finished drawing).

9. Create two more ribbon rosettes with streamers, using 18" of ribbon for each. Place dots in ribbons 1" apart, starting 12" from the end. This will create a rosette with a long ribbon streamer for the bonnet tie. Tack the ties to the silk ribbon at each front corner of the bonnet (see finished drawing).

10. Place the center back edges right sides together and stitch using a $^1/_4$" seam (**fig. 9**).

11. Tie a bow using about 6" of silk ribbon. Tack at the center back seam (see finished drawing).

12. Gather the back of the bonnet to fit the back bonnet circle. Place the circle to the bonnet, right sides together and stitch in place using a $^1/_4$" seam (**fig. 10**).

13. Gather 24" of edging lace to fit the seam line of the bonnet circle. Stitch in place on the right side by hand (**fig. 11**). ▨

Introduction To Home Decorating

Right now, it seems to be more important than ever before in my life to have home as a haven. With my fabulous travels taking me out around the world nearly once a week, I need to walk into my home and see things that I love and that make me feel happy. Victorian bedrooms, chintz, pictures of my family, lace, needlepoint, magazines, books, flowered wallpaper, and a bed full of handmade pillows are things that make my heart say, "Martha, you are home." A return to yesterday for me is back to Kyle Street in Scottsboro, Alabama where my white wallpaper had little lavender flowers dancing all over it. My bedspread was white lace and I had beautiful pillows on my bed. My furniture was mohagany and our furniture was classic and well worn. In the dining room Mama had pink Spode china and beige china from Lenox with a pink rose in the middle. No wonder I love pink and lavender so much. At my grandparents' home we had gray wallpaper with big pink roses on it and little tiny flowers on the walls of their bedroom. Once again mohagany furniture with lace doilies were everpresent. Fried chicken, sugar cookies, and homemade biscuits are further memories of home from my grandparents' home.

With such happy memories, it isn't too hard to decide that I love traditional, rather Victorian home decorating items such as the pillows you find on *Martha's Sewing Room*. With this sixth set of shows, the six hundred series, I believe you will find some of our most beautiful projects yet. Not only do we have beautiful pillows such as the Rose Pillow and the Ribbon Thread Pillow, we also have silk ribbon manipulated flowers on tiny lampshades and a silk ribbon embelllished manne-quin to stand gracefully on the corner of your dresser.

I love the shoe bag which you can use to store treasures rather than shoes if you like. I remember a neighbor of mine in Charlotte, NC who had a beautiful box in her living room. She kept in this box letters from her grandmother who had died years before. I had thought this gorgeous shoe bag would be the perfect place in which to tuck old letters which have a lot of memory for you. The heart door hanger would be so nice not only on a door but also on a wall in your bedroom or bath. Just a touch of the romantic to remind you of the lovely times of rest and relaxation at home. Other projects include absolutely wonderful pillows as well as a cute gift item of a baby powder cover. This cover isn't limited to baby powder; you could adapt it to any tall container of any type of bath powder.

Whatever your fancy, I think these home decorating projects will be interest-ing and inviting to you. Please make pillows for special occasions for your little girls who have outgrown fancy dresses. Each year I made a special pillow for Joanna's bedroom; this was in the years of the bluejean stage. She always loved dolls and gorgeous pillows. She still does. Have fun sewing for your home or for your daughter's or son's home. Several of our mothers are having the time of their lives making Victorian pieces for their daughter's first apartment or house. Whatever use you intend to make of this section, know how much we loved planning and sewing it for you. ▣

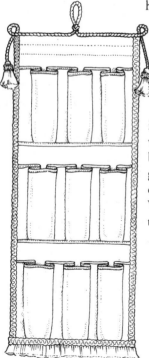

Rose Pillow

Looking ever so much like a real rose, this unusual pillow is made of hot pink silk dupioni. The petals of the rose are composed of a folded fabric ruffle which is stitched down to the round pillow to form the base of the rose. The center section of fabric folds around to look like the center of a rose. The idea for this pillow was taken from an antique one in my collection; I estimate the date to be in the 1930's since I have seen pillows like this in my old magazines. I would love to see this pillow in almost any fabric in almost any room. Done in this lovely hot pink, I think of a bedroom with pink and green chintz. Done in calico, a family room comes to mind. This would be a wonderful gift for Mother's Day done in white or red. That way, your mother's corsage would last forever. If made for a gift, please write the occasion and the date on the back of the pillow with a permanent marking pen or with letters from your sewing machine.

Rose Pillow

Materials

❖ 1¼ yds. of crinkled fabric
❖ ⅞ yd. of woven fusible interfacing
❖ Polyfil for stuffing pillow
❖ All-purpose thread to match fabric
❖ Tiny cording or heavy thread (such as crochet cotton)

I. Cutting (refer to fig. 1)

1. Cut two 14" circles from the interfacing and from the fabric. Iron interfacing to the wrong side of the circles. Mark the center of the circle on the right side of one piece and mark an "X" 2" from the edge of the circle. Set the pieces aside.

2. Cut enough 4" strips of fabric to total 7 yards. Note: These strips are not cut on the bias. They are cut across the fabric.

3. Cut a bias strip 4" by 10".

II. Construction

1. Using the strips cut across the fabric in step 2 above, stitch the strips together at the 4" ends using a ¼" seam allowance. Finish the seams with either a zigzag or serger.

2. Fold the long strip in half so that you have a strip 2" wide by seven yards long. Press lightly. Fold the bias strip in half lengthwise and press, so that it measures 2" x 10".

3. Loosen the tension on your machine and stitch two rows of gathering stitches along the raw edge (both layers) of the 10" bias strip, tapering the stitching off the edge at each end (**fig. 2**).

4. Pull up the gathering stitches on the 10" strip and coil the fabric around to create a rosebud shape. Whip stitch the raw end to the coil. Set aside (**fig. 3**).

5. Place one end of the cording along the ¼" seam line at the raw edge of the long folded strip; taper off at the ends as before. Zigzag over the cording with a medium zigzag through both layers of fabric, going over the cording and not stitching into the cording. The cord must be left free to slide, forming the gathers in the ruffle (**fig. 4**).

6. Pull up the gathers on the seven yard strip and pin the gathered strip to the circle at the "X" near the outside edge of the circle. Your stitching will begin at the "X" and continue around the circle, spiraling towards the center. You may want to pin one row of the ruffle at a time to make the stitching easier (**see fig. 5**).

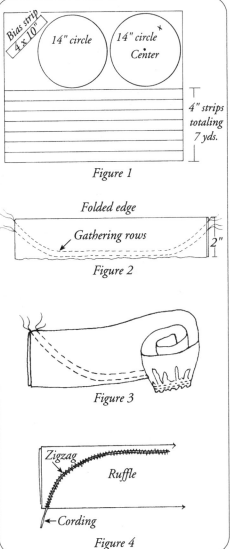

Figure 1

Folded edge

Gathering rows

2"

Figure 2

Figure 3

Zigzag

Ruffle

Cording

Figure 4

7. Stitch the ruffle to the circle with a zigzag stitch, stitching over the gathers to encase the raw edges (**fig. 5**).

8. When you reach the center of the circle with the ruffle, continue spiraling the ruffle around. Gathering stitches will need to be pulled up tighter as your circle gets smaller towards the center of the pillow. If you have too much ruffle, you may trim some off at the end but be sure the center is full.

9 Whip stitch the raw end of the ruffle to the center of the circle so the edges will not show beneath the rose bud.

10. Place the rosebud in the center of the circle so that it stands up straight and whip stitch it in place.

11. Stitch the pillow back to the front, right sides together, using a $^{1}/_{2}$" seam and leaving about 3" unstitched for turning and stuffing the pillow. Clip the seam allowance. Note: You may need to fold the ruffles toward the center of the pillow and pin them in place to keep from stitching the ruffle into the seam of the pillow (**fig. 6**).

12. Turn the pillow right side out and stuff with polyfil to the desired firmness. Whip stitch the opening.

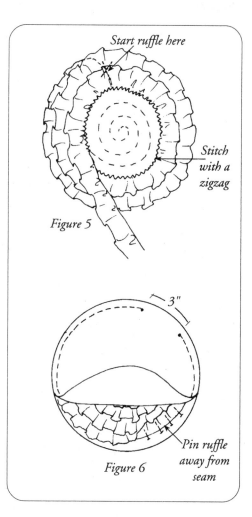

Start ruffle here

Stitch with a zigzag

Figure 5

3"

Pin ruffle away from seam

Figure 6

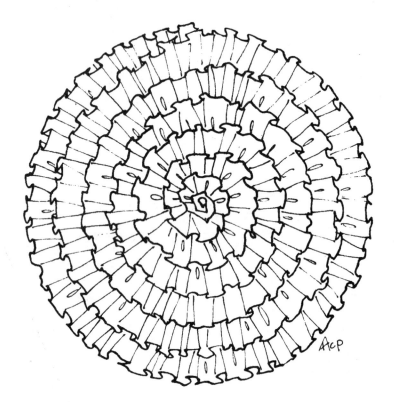

Ribbon Thread Pillow

Having a reversible pillow has to be a wonderful idea for any room in your house. Since linen is one of my favorite home decorating fabrics and since ribbon thread is one of my favorite trims, this pillow makes me very happy. The technique used is ribbon thread in the bobbin for the embellishment. On the ecru side, a beautiful blue ribbon thread has been used for a very sophisticated crisscross design on the back with a cluster of blue French knots, by machine of course, in the center of each square. On the blue linen side of the pillow, four swirls have been stitched using the feather stitch in ecru ribbon thread. The square pillow has a most unusual flange treatment going around the outside. This is a very tailored pillow for any room in your house.

This project was contributed by Jane Burbach of Elna, Inc.

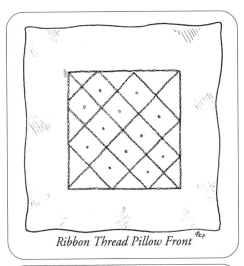

Ribbon Thread Pillow Front

Materials

✦ One 18" square of ecru linen
✦ One 18" square of blue linen
✦ One spool of ecru ribbon thread
✦ One spool of blue ribbon thread to match fabric
✦ Ecru and blue all-purpose sewing thread
✦ Lightweight fusible fleece, two 11" squares
✦ Polyfil for stuffing pillow
✦ **Templates Required:** Blue Thread Template and Ecru Thread Template, found on pull-out section

A. Cutting and Preparation

1. Cut a 17" x 17" square on the straight of grain from the ecru and the blue linen.

2. Use a washout marker to draw a line 3" from each side edge on the wrong side of the fabric, creating an 11" square in the center of both pieces of the linen (**fig. 1**).

3. Fuse the fleece to the wrong side of the fabric squares, inside the drawn lines (**see fig. 2**).

4. Transfer the designs from the templates onto the fleece squares (**fig. 2**).

B. Construction

1. Wind two bobbins, one with ecru ribbon thread and one with blue ribbon thread.

2. Using matching all-purpose thread in the needle, stitch the designs onto the pillow pieces from the wrong side (refer to Ribbon Thread Bobbin Technique on page 243 in the new technique section). Stitch the ecru fabric with blue thread, using a straight stitch for the lines and a star stitch for the centers; stitch the blue fabric with ecru thread, using a feather stitch. Stitch only the diamond and star design on the ecru fabric and the swirls on the blue fabric; the squares will be stitched later (**fig. 3**).

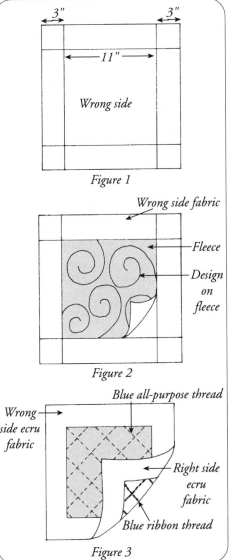

Figure 1

Figure 2

Figure 3

3. Place the pillow pieces right sides together, making sure that the squares of the designs are matched together. Stitch with a ¹/₂" seam and all-purpose thread around three sides of the pillow; stitch only 2" past the corners on the fourth side, leaving it open for turning the pillow (**fig. 4**).

4. Turn the pillow right side out and press. Pin the layers together so they do not shift.

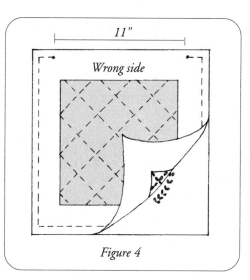

Figure 4

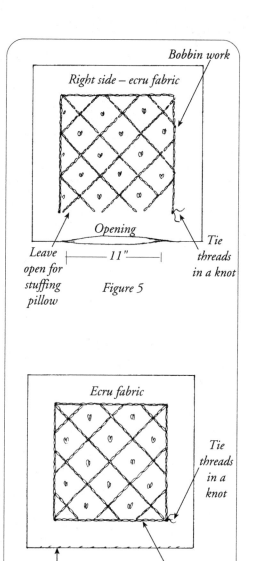

Figure 5

Figure 6

5. Straight stitch the layers together with blue sewing thread and blue ribbon thread along the square of the design, using the bobbin work technique and sewing with the blue fabric on top. Stitch on the same three sides that were stitched around the outer edge. Leave the fourth side open for stuffing the pillow. Pull the thread ends to the ecru fabric side and tie in a small, tight knot, then trim the ends close to the fabric (**fig. 5**).

6. Stuff the pillow with polyfil and finish by machine stitching the fourth side of the design square, using the bobbin work technique and blue thread as before. A zipper foot may be helpful for this last stitching. Pull the thread ends to the ecru fabric side and tie in a small, tight knot, then trim the ends close to the fabric (**fig. 6**).

7. Slip-stitch the opening along the outer edge by hand. ▨

Ribbon Thread Pillow Back

Ribbon Embellished Lamp Shades

4" Lamp Shade

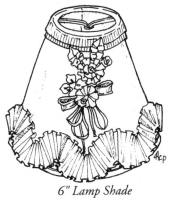

6" Lamp Shade
Ribbon Embellished Lamp Shades

8" Lamp Shade

In so many European countries, lamp shade embellishment is quite the vogue now and in the years gone past. For the white and blue lamp shade, a beautiful white lamp shade was purchased, then lace trim was attached around the top and a knotted cording was glued on top of the lace. Little stems of beaded white trims were used at the bottom. Beautiful blue and white ribbons were folded to make seven flowers running vertically; green leaves are used in three places. On one flower little French knots in yellow are in the center and purchased yellow stems peek out of the bottom of the blue flowers. Lamps similar to this beauty sell for $100! One small ecru lamp shade is embellished in shades of ecru with pleated ribbon running from the top to the bottom of the shade. The ribbons are glued onto the shade. Little clusters of silk and grosgrain ribbon flowers are found at the top and bottom of the ribbon points. Little streamers of tiny ecru ribbon make loops at the bottom of each flower cluster. The darker ecru lamp shade has serpentine grosgrain ribbon on the bottom of the shade. The flower clusters are in wonderful shades of dusty peach, white, ecru, dusty rose and greenish/brown. Again, little ribbon loops are attached at the bottom of the flower cluster. Small lamps like these sell for $50 in the decorator shops. What an elegant gift any of these lamp shades would be for almost any occasion. They would be so pretty used on an antique lamp or on a brass lamp. Have fun creating your own for a fraction of the cost!

4" Lamp Shade

Materials

❖ 4" diameter tapered lamp shade
❖ $^1/_4$ yd. of textured satin fabric or taffeta for covering shade
❖ 1 yd. of 2" wide wired-edged pre-pleated ribbon to match shade
❖ Assorted ribbons for making roses: $1^1/_4$ yds. of $^5/_8$" wide satin-edged chiffon ribbon, 2 yds. of $^1/_2$" grosgrain ribbon
❖ 2 yds. of $^1/_8$" satin ribbon for bows beneath roses
❖ Hot glue or craft glue
❖ Placement diagram found on page 74

Instructions

1. Cover the lamp shade with fabric and glue in place at the back seam. Lap $^1/_4$" to $^1/_2$" to the inside of the shade and glue in place (**fig. 1**). The top edge can be covered with flat braid (optional).

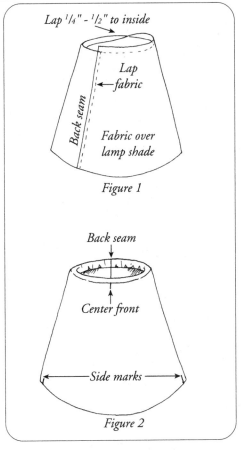

Lap $^1/_4$" - $^1/_2$" to inside

Lap fabric

Back seam

Fabric over lamp shade

Figure 1

Back seam

Center front

Side marks

Figure 2

2. Using the back seam as the first mark, divide the top edge of the shade in half and place a mark at the center front, opposite the back seam. Place two marks at the bottom edge of the shade, halfway between the top marks, at the sides of the shade (**fig. 2**).

2. Arrange the ribbon in a serpentine shape by pinching the wire together at the inside of the curves, matching the outer edges of the curves to the marks at the top and bottom edges of the shade. Refer to the instructions for serpentine ribbon manipulation on page 209 (**fig. 3**).

3. Make four medium and eight small roses out of the ribbon. Refer to Cabachon Roses on page 209.

4. Tie multi-looped bows and glue in place at the inner edge of the curves, shown by X's on the diagram. Glue the roses in place at the tops of the ribbon loops (**fig. 4**). Place one rose in the center and a small rose on each side.

6" Shade

— Materials —

❧ 6" diameter ecru lamp shade
❧ 1¹/₂ yds. of 1" wide ribbon for serpentine design
❧ Assorted peach and ecru shades of ribbon for flowers and leaves: 12" for leaves, 12" each of two colors for flowers, 16" of one color for flower and bud
❧ 6" of ¹/₂" wide textured ribbon for bow loops
❧ 1 yd. of ¹/₁₆" satin ribbon
❧ Hot glue or craft glue
❧ Placement diagram found on page 75

— Instructions —

1. Cut a piece of 1" ribbon long enough to go around the top outside edge of the lamp shade. Fold the ribbon according to the diagram (**fig. 5**). Press. Glue the ribbon together so it does not come unfolded. Glue the folded ribbon along the top of the lamp shade, overlapping the ends at the seam on the lamp shade.

2. Make serpentine ribbon according to the instructions on page 209. Arrange the ribbon along the bottom edge of the lamp shade and glue it in place, lapping the cut ends at the back seam.

3. Make the flowers and leaves according to the specific instructions for Cabachon Roses (page 209) and Ribbon Leaves (page 210).

4. Tie a knot in each end of the ¹/₁₆" ribbon. Loop the ribbon back and forth as if you were going to tie a bow and secure it in the center. The bow needs to be approximately 4" wide (**fig. 6**). Glue the bow about three-fourths of the way down on the front of the lamp shade. The loops will hang out underneath the flowers.

5. Using the 6" piece of ¹/₂" wide ribbon, fold both ends to the middle to look like two bow loops. Glue the loops to the shade, covering the top edge of the ribbon loops attached in step 4. Arrange the leaves and flowers and glue in place (**fig. 7**).

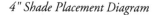

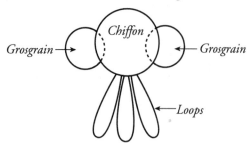

4" Shade Placement Diagram

Chiffon

Grosgrain →   ← Grosgrain

← Loops

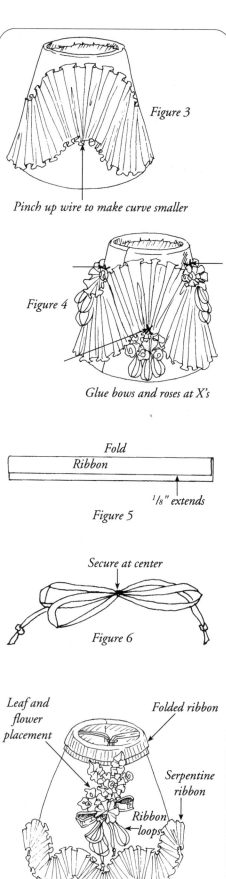

Figure 3

Pinch up wire to make curve smaller

Figure 4

Glue bows and roses at X's

Fold

Ribbon

¹/₈" extends

Figure 5

Secure at center

Figure 6

Leaf and flower placement

Folded ribbon

Serpentine ribbon

Ribbon loops

Figure 7

8" Shade

Materials

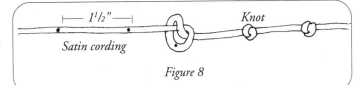

Figure 8

- ❧ 8" diameter white lamp shade
- ❧ ³/₄ yd. of scalloped bridal edging
- ❧ 1 yd. of satin cording
- ❧ Assorted blue shades of ribbon for flowers
- ❧ Green ribbon for leaves
- ❧ Scraps of bridal beaded sprays for embellishment
- ❧ Hot glue or craft glue

Instructions

1. Glue the top edge of the bridal edging along the top of the lamp shade so that the edging lies flat.

2. Mark the satin cording every 1¹/₂" and tie a knot at each mark (**fig. 8**). Glue the cording in place along the top edge of the lamp shade on top of the heading of the bridal edging.

3. Make four cabachon roses, three rosebuds, one pansy, three flower buds and three ribbon leaves according to specific instructions for these flowers and leaves, found in the technique section.

4. Arrange the flowers (**fig. 9**) with the beaded sprays extending from below the flowers. Glue in place (refer also to the finished drawing). ▨

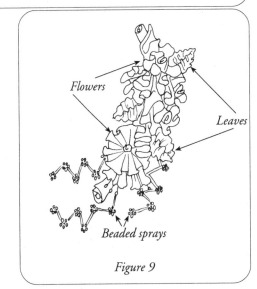

Figure 9

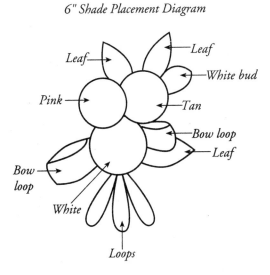

6" Shade Placement Diagram

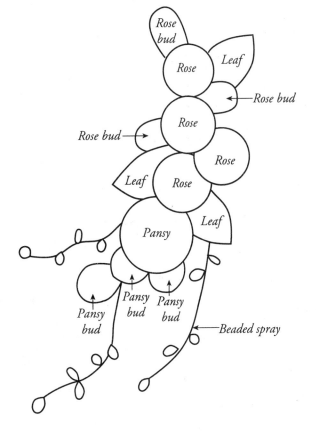

8" Shade Placement Diagram

Baby Powder Cover

Making several of these and having them ready for new baby presents would be a fun idea since they are so easy and quick to make. Made of pink broadcloth, white ribbon beading and wide Swiss edging pieces, this is a very beautiful and practical gift for any new mother. The little cover ties in the back with pink and blue ribbons run through the beading. Those same ribbons are attached on the bottom so the powder box won't fall out. Of course it is completely washable. Be sure to find out the nursery colors and make one to match! You might also machine stitch the baby's name and birth date!

NOTE: These instructions are for a small container of baby powder. The base of the container measures 2³/₄" by 2¹/₄" and has straight sides. If you use another size container, adjustments will need to be made to the measurements below.

Baby Powder Cover

Materials

❖ ¹/₃ yd. of Swiss embroidered edging (edging needs to be at least 4¹/₂" wide)
Note: Pick an edging that does not have anything that cannot be turned sideways. For example: Birds flying would not be a good choice.
❖ ¹/₄ yd. of batiste for lining to complement embroidery (we used pink)
❖ ²/₃ yd. of ³/₄" wide Swiss beading
❖ 1¹/₂ yds. of ribbon, width to fit openings in beading (suggested—pink)
❖ 1¹/₂ yds. of ribbon narrower than above ribbon (suggested—blue)
❖ Thread to match fabric of Swiss edging and beading

I. Cutting

1. Cut two pieces of batiste measuring 9¹/₄" by 5¹/₂" for the lining.

2. Cut two pieces of Swiss edging 5¹/₂" wide.

3. Cut the beading piece in half to give two 12" pieces.

4. Cut two pieces of ribbon, each 24" long, from each width of ribbon. You will have approximately 6" left of each ribbon.

II. Construction

1. Place one piece of lining on a flat surface. Place the two pieces of Swiss edging on top of the lining right sides up. The scallops of the edging will be touching at the center of the rectangle (**fig. 1**).

2. If any fabric from the Swiss edging extends beyond the lining, trim it away. Baste around the edge of the Swiss edging, stitching it to the lining. These two layers will now be considered one layer.

3. Place the second piece of lining on top of the layered Swiss piece with right sides together. Stitch the pieces together using a ¹/₄" seam and leaving 2" open in the center of one long side for turning (**fig. 2**).

4. Turn and press. Place the 6" pieces of ribbon, with the narrower one on top of the other, exactly 2" from one short side of the cover (**see fig. 3**). Pin in place. Mark an "X" on the lining side 2" from the other short side of the cover.

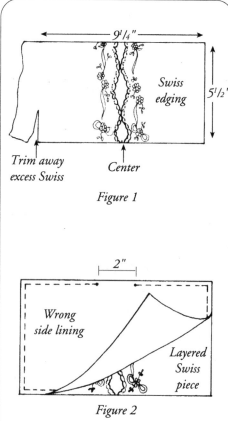

9¹/₄"

Swiss edging

5¹/₂"

Trim away excess Swiss

Center

Figure 1

2"

Wrong side lining

Layered Swiss piece

Figure 2

5. Place Swiss beading at the top and bottom edges of the cover on top of the Swiss edging, positioning the eyelet holes evenly from each end. Pin in place, turning under approximately $^{1}/_{4}$" on each end to make the trim flush with the sides of the cover. Trim away the excess beading (**see fig. 3**).

6. Topstitch the beading trim in place along both edges. When stitching the outermost edge of the trim, continue stitching down the sides of the cover and be sure to stitch through the ribbon pieces shown in figure 2. Measure $2^{3}/_{4}$" down the ribbon and pin (**fig. 3**).

7. With a large tapestry needle or bodkin, run the wider ribbon through the eyelet trim at the top edge of the cover. Run the narrower ribbon through the eyelets on top of the wider ribbon. Repeat for the other trim (**fig. 4**).

8. Fit the cover around the powder container and tie at the back.

9. Place the loose ribbon pieces across the bottom of the container and pin the ribbons to the other side at the "X". Remove the cover from the container and stitch the ribbons in place. Trim away the excess ribbon. ▣

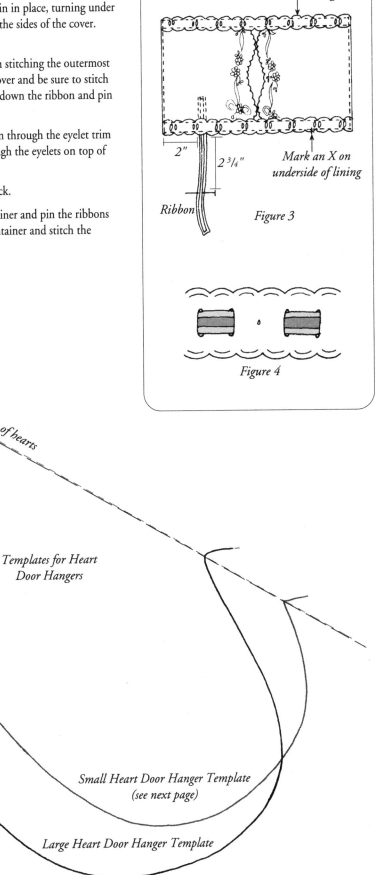

Swiss beading

2"

$2^{3}/_{4}$"

Mark an X on underside of lining

Ribbon

Figure 3

Figure 4

Center of hearts

Templates for Heart Door Hangers

Small Heart Door Hanger Template
(see next page)

Large Heart Door Hanger Template

Heart Door Hangers

Although we call these door hangers, they can certainly be used as a wall hanging or on a dresser knob in the bedroom. Using a basic heart pattern, the base fabric on our two are pink taffeta and pink linen. With the embellished corner of a handkerchief, the bottom or the top of the heart can be decorated. We stitched little beads and pearls following the designs on the handkerchiefs. On the pink heart a little lace trim finishes the outside. On the linen one, the outside of the heart is plain. These would be precious used as a pin cushion in your sewing room. Since they are so quick and easy to make, they would be wonderful teacher presents or hostess gifts!

Materials

❧ ¼ yd. of any fabric you wish for pillow
❧ 1 handkerchief with embroidery in one corner
❧ 10" of ¼" ribbon
❧ polyfil for stuffing
❧ 1 yd. of ½" wide lace edging (optional)
❧ Beads (optional)
❧ Embroidery floss to complement color of pillow (optional)
❧ Fabric glue
❧ **Pattern piece needed:** Heart Door Hanger Pattern (small or large) found on page 77

I. Cutting and Construction

1. Draw the heart pattern onto one end of the fabric for the pillow. Mark the dots for the ribbon hanger placement.

2. Place the decorative corner of the handkerchief on the heart at any angle you wish (see fig. 1). Baste the layers together along the edge of the heart where it is covered with the handkerchief. The handkerchief may be glued down to the fabric or left loose.

3. Embellish the handkerchief with beads or embroidery if desired.

4. Cut out the embellished heart. Also use the heart pattern to cut a second heart from the fabric.

5. Position the ribbon hanger on the heart (fig. 1).

6. Place the hearts with right sides together and stitch using a ¼" seam, leaving approximately 2" open along side for turning. Be sure to stitch through the ribbon several times to secure it. Clip the seam at the curves if necessary (fig. 2).

7. Turn the pillow and stuff it with polyfil. Whip stitch the opening closed.

8. Gathered lace may be hand-stitched at the seam around the pillow if you wish (see the finished drawing). ▨

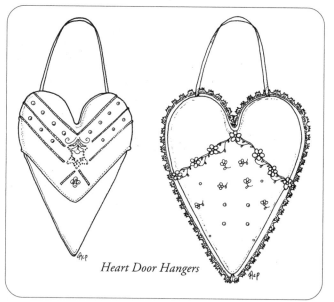

Heart Door Hangers

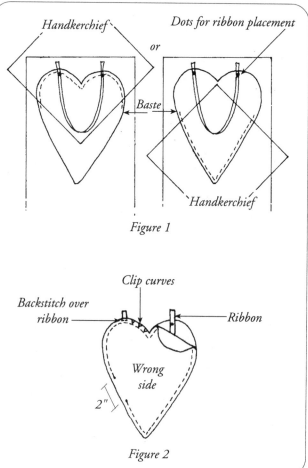

Figure 1

Figure 2

Lace Fan Pillow

Spectacular would be my word to describe this museum quality decorative pillow. With cotton netting as the base netting, lace shaping with ecru narrow insertions, Swiss embroidered motifs and tatting complete the whole picture. A Swiss motif is found at the base of the lace fan; insertions weave over and under for the next area. Five lace hearts surround the Swiss motifs across the top of the fan. The whole fan is made on a dark brown tapestry base. Tatting and a tassel finish the outside of the pillow. Perfect for most rooms in the house, this is a pillow to cherish.

Lace Fan Pillow

Materials

❖ ³/₈ yd. of fabric for pillow
❖ ¹/₄ yd. of cotton netting
❖ ¹/₄ yd. of water-soluble stabilizer (WSS)
❖ 5 motifs for centers of hearts
❖ 1 semicircular motif for base of fan
❖ 2 yds. of ³/₈" lace insertion for spokes of fan
❖ 2 yds. of ¹/₂" lace insertion for hearts
❖ 2¹/₄ yds. of tatting
❖ 1 tassel
❖ Lightweight machine thread to match lace
❖ Polyfil
❖ **Pattern piece needed:** Lace Fan Pillow Pattern found on pull-out section
❖ **Template needed:** Lace Template for Lace Fan Pillow found on pull-out section

A. Making the Lace Fan

1. Trace the lace shaping design onto paper with a permanent marker. Place the paper onto a lace shaping board.

2. Cut a rectangle of the netting larger than the fan shape. Place the cotton netting over the design on the paper.

3. Place a piece of WSS over the netting (**fig. 1**).

(Refer to **figure 2** while shaping lace, steps 4 through 12.)

4. Begin shaping the lace with the spokes of the fan first. Refer to lace shaping instructions in the technique section.

5. Place the centers of the hearts onto the netting, then shape the hearts over the centers. Refer to lace-shaped hearts in the technique section.

6. Place the semicircular motif at the base of the spokes. Pin the motif in place.

7. When the shaping is completed, re-pin the lace so that the pins are flat through the lace and netting, and not pinned into the lace shaping board or paper.

8. Zigzag the lace through the WSS onto the netting, beginning with the spokes of the fan.

9. Zigzag the lace at the centers of the hearts. Trim away any excess of the lace motif from between the WSS and the lace which was shaped around the heart.

10. Zigzag around the outside edge of the heart.

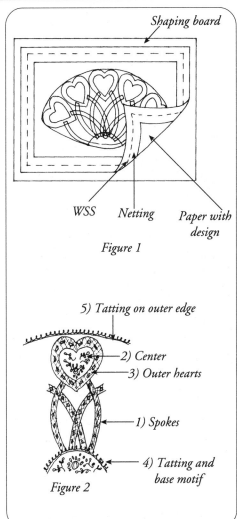

Shaping board

WSS   Netting   *Paper with design*

Figure 1

5) *Tatting on outer edge*

2) *Center*

3) *Outer hearts*

1) *Spokes*

4) *Tatting and base motif*

Figure 2

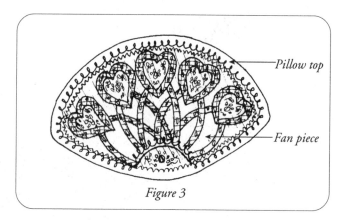

Pillow top

Fan piece

Figure 3

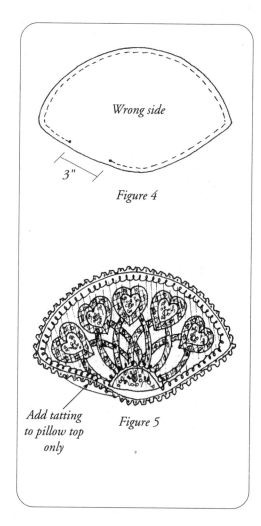

Wrong side

3"

Figure 4

Add tatting to pillow top only

Figure 5

11. Zigzag the motif in place at the base of the spokes, attaching tatting at the top curve of the motif as you zigzag.

12. Begin at one corner of the motif at the base of the spokes and zigzag across the bottom edge of the motif. Continue to zigzag around the fan shape, attaching the tatting as you stitch.

13. Be sure that all of the lace is stitched in place.

14. Carefully trim the lace ends and cotton netting from behind the lace motif and the tatting, cutting out the fan shape.

15. Dissolve the WSS and allow the lace piece to dry. Be very careful not to stretch the lace out of shape. Press.

B. Constructing the Pillow

1. Cut out the pillow front and back from the fabric.

2. Place the lace fan piece on the right side of the pillow top, centering the lace on the fabric. Stitch over the previous zigzag around the lace shape, attaching the lace fan to the fabric (**fig. 3**).

3. Place the pillow pieces with right sides together and stitch, using a $^1/_2$" seam. Leave a 3" opening along the bottom edge of the pillow (**fig. 4**).

4. Turn the pillow right side out and press. Zigzag tatting to the outer edge of the pillow before stuffing. When stitching across the opening, stitch the tatting to only the pillow top, so that the opening is not stitched shut (**fig. 5**).

5. Stuff the pillow with polyfil and whipstitch the opening closed.

6. Hand-stitch the tassel to the bottom edge of the pillow, below the center of the motif at the base of the fan (see the finished drawing). ▨

Shoe Bag

You might use this shoe bag to store shoes in a closet area. But perhaps, you might want to put it on the wall in your bedroom to display treasures such as dried roses, letters, jewelry, or other wonderful things. It is made of a beautiful rust and ecru fabric and is trimmed with ecru braid. Ecru cording is found at the top and the bottom and a dowel stick is run through the top to make a convenient hanging device. The back is lined with ecru tapestry. What a wonderful gift for either a woman or a man.

Materials

❧ 1¹/₄ yds. of 45" wide decorator fabric
❧ ¹/₂ yd. of 45" wide decorator fabric without nap (or 1 yd. of 45" wide decorator fabric with nap) for lining
❧ 1¹/₄ yds. of heavyweight fusible interfacing
❧ 2¹/₂ yds. of gimp trim
❧ ¹/₂ yd. of decorator fringe
❧ 1 yd. of cording with tassel at each end (a tasseled curtain tieback will work)
❧ 15" piece of ¹/₂" diameter wooden dowel
❧ Thread

A. Cutting (fig. 1) and Preparation

1. Cut one piece of fabric for the shoe bag, one piece of the interfacing and one piece for the lining, each 15¹/₂" by 36¹/₂". If the decorator fabric has a nap or a definite pattern, the 36¹/₂" length needs to go with the nap or design.

2. Draw a line across the bag piece 2¹/₂" from the top edge of the fabric; this is the top facing line (see fig. 2).

3. Draw a line across the shoe bag front 10¹/₂" from the bottom edge; this is the bottom placement line for the middle pocket (see fig. 2).

4. Draw another line 10¹/₂" above the line drawn in step 2. This is the bottom placement line for the top pocket (fig. 2).

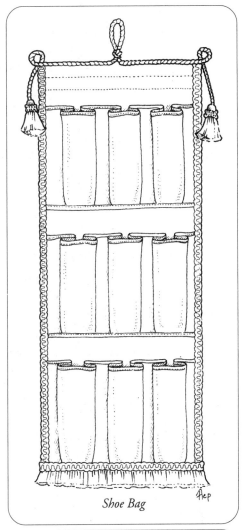

Shoe Bag

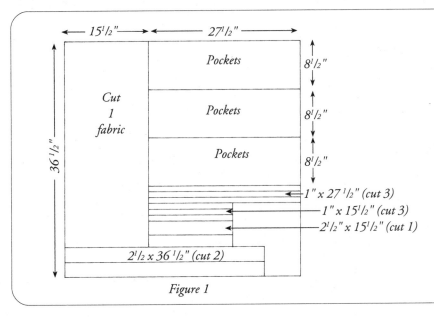

Figure 1

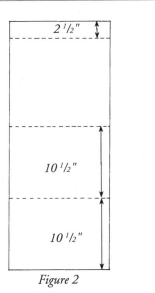

Figure 2

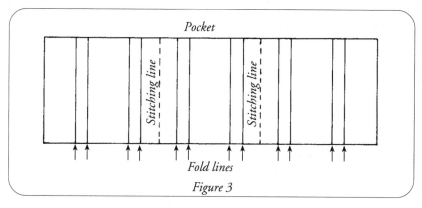

Pocket

Stitching line   *Stitching line*

Fold lines

Figure 3

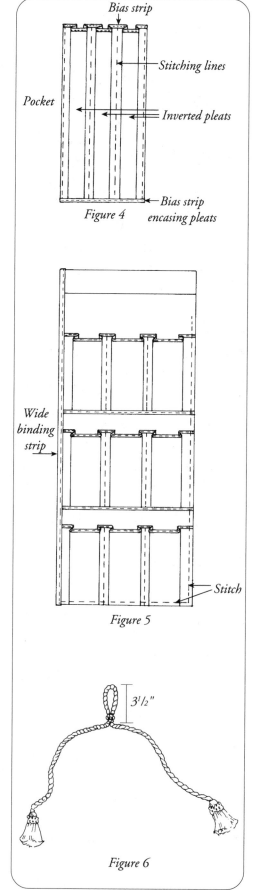

Bias strip

Stitching lines

Pocket

Inverted pleats

Figure 4

Bias strip
encasing pleats

*Wide
binding
strip*

Stitch

Figure 5

3¹/₂"

Figure 6

5. Cut three pieces by the pattern for the shoe bag pockets, making sure that the fabric design runs the same way as on the shoe bag piece. The pockets are not lined. Draw fold lines and stitching lines with a disappearing pen (**fig. 3**).

6. Cut strips for making double fold fabric binding: cut three strips, each 1" wide and 27¹/₂" long; cut three strips 1" wide and 15¹/₂" long; cut two strips, each 2¹/₂" wide and 36¹/₂" long; cut one strip 2¹/₂" wide and 15¹/₂" long.

7. Fuse the interfacing to the wrong side of the lining piece.

B. Construction

1. Place the shoe bag fabric and lining wrong sides together and stitch ¹/₄" from the edge around the piece, through both layers.

2. Make fabric binding out of the 1" and 2¹/₂" pieces of fabric following the instructions for making double fold bias binding in the technique section. These strips are not cut from bias since there are no curves to stitch. NOTE: The 1" strips will be used for the pockets and the 2¹/₂" strips will be used for the outside edge of the shoe bag.

3. Attach a binding strip to the top edge of each pocket piece, encasing the cut edge of the fabric according to C. Double-Fold Bias Tape on page 248. Top stitch in place.

4. Fold one pocket piece along the fold lines, making inverted pleats (**see fig. 4**). Press well. Stitch close to the edge along the bottom of the pocket to hold the folds in place. Attach a binding strip, encasing the bottom edge of the pocket piece (**fig. 4**).

5. Repeat steps 3 and 4 for the other two pockets, except omit the binding strip at the bottom edge of one pocket piece. This will be the bottom pocket on the shoe bag and will be encased with the trim around the bag.

6. Place the pockets with the bottom edges along the lines drawn on the shoe bag. The bottom pocket is placed flush with the bottom edge of the bag.

7. Stitch the pockets in place at the sides and across the bottom edge. Stitch along the stitching lines between the pockets on each strip, being sure to secure the stitching well at the top edge (**see fig. 5**).

8. Stitch the wide binding strips down the sides and across the bottom of the bag, encasing the edges (**fig. 5**).

9. Fold the cording (tieback) in half and tie a knot approximately 3¹/₂" from the fold to make a loop (**fig. 6**).

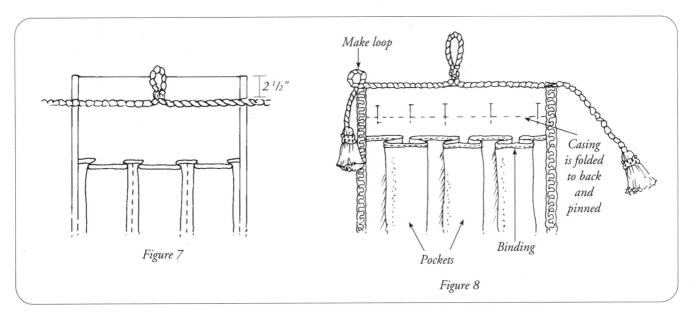

Figure 7

Make loop

2 ¹/₂"

Casing
is folded
to back
and
pinned

Pockets

Binding

Figure 8

10. Find the center of the line drawn in Step 1, Cutting. Place the knot at the center point and let the cording extend to each side along the line. Zigzag the cording in place, securing the stitching at both sides of the knot (**fig.** 7).

11. Place the gimp trim along the side edges of the bag on the right side, letting the gimp lie over the fabric strip and cording on the front of the bag; zigzag the gimp in place along both edges (see the finished drawing).

12. Attach fringe to the bottom edge of the gimp trim and attach both to the bottom edge of the bag on top of the fabric strip. Let ¹/₂" of the trim extend on each side to be folded to the back of the bag (see the finished drawing).

13. Fold the casing at the top of the bag to the back along the line where the cording was stitched and pin the casing in place.

14. Make a small loop in the cording at the top corners and lay the remaining cording against the sides of the bag (**fig.** 8). The cording will be caught in the stitching in steps 15 and 16.

15. Fold under ¹/₄" at the raw edge of the casing and stitch across the bag through all layers.

16. Stitch across the bag again 1¹/₂" above the stitching in step 15. This will make a casing for the dowel. Be sure to secure the stitching well at the sides. Insert the dowel into the casing. ▧

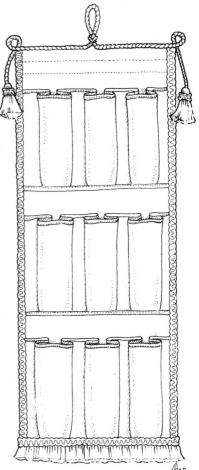

Machine Embroidery Tatting Pillow

I adore the new embroidery features of today's spectacular sewing machines! This elegant dusty lavender linen pillow has gorgeous built-in designs stitched in a wonderful medium beige. The designs travel all the way around this square pillow. The very full ruffle has a machine-made tatting which looks just like handmade tatting! You'll have to see it to believe it! What a beautiful pillow for many rooms of your house. This would make a spectacular gift. Please use your creativity along with the lovely designs in your embroidery machines, if you are so fortunate as to have one. If you haven't seen these machines which do the embroidery completely by themselves, please go to your sewing machine dealer and enjoy a demonstration.

This project was contributed by Sue Hausmann, host of *America Sews*.

Machine Embroidery Tatting Pillow

Materials

❖ ³/₄ yd. of solid fabric for pillow
❖ Rayon thread for machine embroidery, in a color to complement pillow
❖ Silk or cotton buttonhole twist for machine tatting, to match the rayon thread
❖ Heat-Away stabilizer
❖ 10" square pillow form
❖ **Template Required:** Machine Embroidery Template for Viking Embroidery Card/disc 15, design #21, embroidery template found in pull-out section

A. Cutting and Preparation

1. Cut the backs, front and ruffle pieces (**fig. 1**).

2. On the back piece WITHOUT the selvage press under ¹/₄" along one 12" side then press under another ³/₄" to form a hem. Topstitch the hem in place close to the edge, using a hemstitch or straight stitch (**fig. 2**).

3. Trace the embroidery design onto the pillow front, or mark the placement for a machine-embroidered design (refer to your machine manual for machine-embroidering directions).

4. Seam the ruffle pieces together at the short ends to make a long strip. Press the seams open. Fold the ruffle strip in half along the length, making a ruffle 3¹/₂" wide. Press the ruffle well. Do not stitch the ends of the ruffle together into a tube; leave the ruffle in a long strip (**fig. 3**).

B. Construction

1. Complete the embroidery design on the pillow front. Refer to Machine Embroidery on page 255 for general instructions.

2. On the folded edge of the ruffle, create machine tatting. Refer to Machine Tatting on page 252.

3. Stitch the ruffle strip together using a French seam, referring to the technique section for directions if needed.

4. Divide the ruffle into fourths, placing the marks so that they <u>do not</u> fall at the seams. Run two rows of gathering stitches along the raw edge of the ruffle strip.

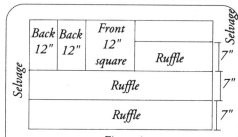

Back 12"	Back 12"	Front 12" square		
			Ruffle	7"
		Ruffle		7"
		Ruffle		7"

Figure 1

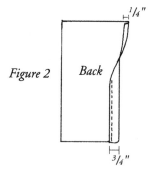

Figure 2

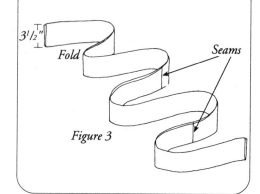

Figure 3

5. Pull up the ruffle to fit the pillow top and pin in place. NOTE: Do not place a seam at any corner of the pillow; the seams need to be along the sides. Match the quarter marks on the ruffle to the corners of the pillow top (**fig. 4**).

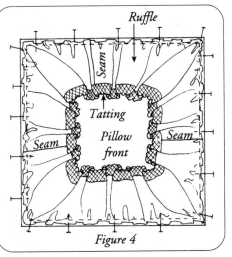
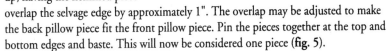
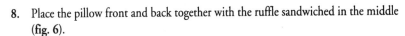

Ruffle

Seam

Tatting Pillow front

Seam

Seam

Figure 4

6. Stitch the ruffle to the pillow top with a $^{1}/_{2}$" seam.

7. Place the hemmed back piece over the back piece with the selvage edge, both right side up, having the hemmed piece overlap the selvage edge by approximately 1". The overlap may be adjusted to make the back pillow piece fit the front pillow piece. Pin the pieces together at the top and bottom edges and baste. This will now be considered one piece (**fig. 5**).

8. Place the pillow front and back together with the ruffle sandwiched in the middle (**fig. 6**).

9. Stitch all the way around the pillow with a $^{1}/_{2}$" seam. Trim and finish the raw edges of the seam.

10. Turn the pillow through the opening in the back.

11. Insert the pillow form. 🔳

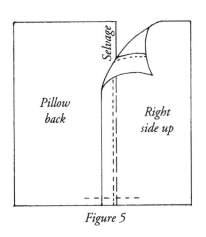

Pillow back

Selvage

Right side up

Figure 5

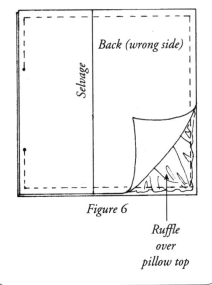

Back (wrong side)

Selvage

Figure 6

Ruffle over pillow top

Pillow/Lap Quilt

This is such a clever and practical idea that you will find yourself making more than one. This pretty lap quilt folds into a built-in pocket to become a pillow for easy storage, and no one would guess that the pillow hides a quilt inside. Keep one in the den for cozy winter evenings and one in the car for those sleepy little heads. This is a great gift idea for a new mom - no more getting caught away from home without a nap blanket! With today's wonderful fabric choices, you can create a pillow/lap quilt to fit any occasion and match any decor.

This project was contributed by Sue Hausmann, host of America Sews.

Note before purchasing fabric: The pillow pocket is placed on the back of the quilt. To make this pocket less noticeable you may want your pillow pocket back to match your quilt back.

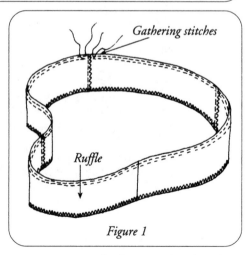
Pillow

Materials Needed

★ Two 18" squares of printed fabric for the pillow pocket top and back
★ $1^7/8$ yds. of fabric for quilt top
★ $1^7/8$ yds. of fabric for quilt back
★ $1/2$ yd. of fabric for ruffle <u>or</u> 5 yds. of flat 2" wide eyelet edging
★ 45" by 66" batting for quilt
★ 18" square of batting for pillow
★ Thread to match quilt
★ Transparent thread for quilting
★ Cellophane tape
★ Large safety pins

I. Cutting

1. Cut one piece of calico 45" by 63" for the quilt top.

2. Cut one piece of calico 45" by 63" for the quilt back.

3. Cut one piece of batting 45" by 63".

4. Trim the pillow pocket top and back to measure 18" square.

5. Cut a piece of batting 18" square.

6. If you are using fabric to make the ruffle, cut 4 strips 4" by 45". Seam the short ends together, making a continuous strip. Finish the seams neatly with a zigzag or serge. Hem one long side with a serger rolled hem, a shirt tail hem or turn under $1/4$" and $1/4$" again and stitch. Machine-made tatting may be added to the ruffle edge (see page 252 for instructions).

II. Construction

A. Pillow Pocket

1. Place the 18" square of batting on the wrong side of the pillow pocket top. Pin in place. If you wish to have only the pillow pocket top quilted and the back un-quilted, quilt the design now using transparent thread. If you wish to quilt through all layers, wait until the pillow pocket is complete and quilt through all layers.

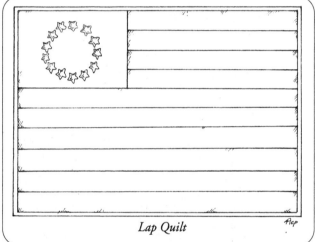
Lap Quilt

Gathering stitches

Ruffle

Figure 1

2. Run two rows of gathering stitches along the raw edge of the ruffle or eyelet $1/4$" and $1/2$" from the raw edge (**fig. 1**).

3. Placing the seams at the corners of the pillow top and having more gathers at the corners, gather the ruffle to fit the pillow top, right sides together. Stitch the ruffle to the pillow top with a $^1/_2$" seam. Tape the ruffle down to keep it from getting caught in future stitching (**fig. 2**).

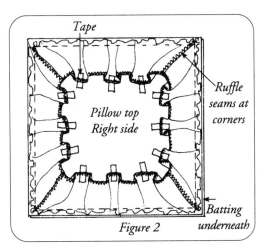

Figure 2

4. Place the pillow pocket bottom to the pillow pocket top, right sides together. The batting is underneath the pillow top and the ruffle is sandwiched between the two layers of the pillow. Pin in place. Stitch all layers together using a $^1/_2$" seam, leaving about 6" along one side unstitched. Note: Stitching from the batting side will allow you to follow the previous stitching of the ruffle (**fig. 3**).

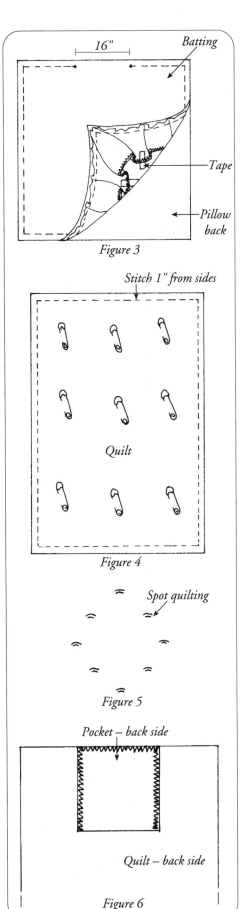

5. Turn the pillow pocket through the opening. Close the opening using a slip stitch by hand. Note: You may quilt the pillow pocket top now if you chose to have the design quilted through all layers.

B. Quilt

1. Place the two quilt pieces right sides together. Place the batting on top of the two fabric pieces. Pin in place. Stitch around the edges with a $^1/_2$" seam, leaving a 10" opening along one short side of the quilt. Instead of having sharp turns at the corners of the quilt, round the corners slightly. Clip the corners. Turn the quilt with the batting in the center and close the opening by hand.

2. Spread the quilt on a hard surface. Pin through all layers with large safety pins so that the layers do not shift when quilting. Stitch 1" from the sides, creating a binding look (**fig. 4**).

3. Quilt inside the 1" border as desired using transparent thread.

   Note from Viking: Using a dual-feed foot will make quilting easier. An easy quilting method is to "spot quilt" by using a narrow zigzag with a "0" length. You can measure and place your spots in an even pattern or spot quilt around a design (**fig. 5**).

III. Finishing

1. Tape the ruffle to the pillow top.

2. Place the quilt right side down on a hard surface.

3. Place the pillow pocket, top side down, to the center top edge at the back of the quilt. You will not be able to see the ruffle. Pin the pocket in place (**see fig. 6**).

4. With transparent thread, zigzag (Length-4, Width-6) the pillow pocket top to the quilt along three sides. The side of the pillow pocket opposite the side against the quilt edge will be left open. Be sure to stitch the sides near the opening very well. Just like pockets, this is a stress point (**fig. 6**).

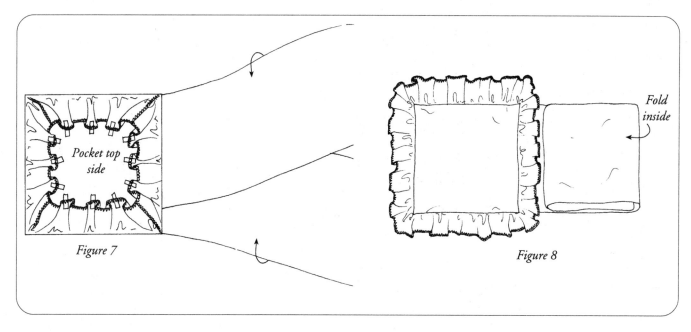

Figure 7 — Pocket top side

Figure 8 — Fold inside

IV. Folding The Quilt Into a Pillow

1. Turn the pillow pocket to the right side, the quilt will fold into thirds lengthwise (**fig.** 7).

2. Then fold in half crosswise and turn the quilt into the pillow pocket. This will stuff the pillow. Remove the tape holding the ruffles to the pillow pocket top (**fig.** 8).

ENJOY!!!!!

Sue's Keep America Sewing Pillow/Quilt featured a flag quilt made from red and white striped fabric with a starred field of blue and a bound edge. The pillow top has an American theme and the ruffle is edged with machine–made tatting (see page 252 for instructions). 🞖

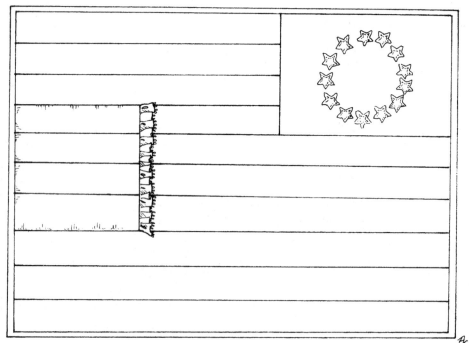

Pillow/Lap Quilt showing pocket that quilt folds into to make pillow

Mannequin

What fun to make these precious mannequins! This is the ultimate answer to the sewing question, "What's new?" Used as a decoration in either your bedroom, sewing room, or sun porch, they are sure to be a conversation maker. The robin's egg blue mannequin is embellished with several bright shades of silk ribbon embroidery. These ribbons are in shades of purple, pink, blue, dusty purple, green, white, and brownish burgundy. What yummy shades! The mannequin has a wide ombre burgundy ribbon tied at the lower waistline and there are tassels of silk ribbon flowers along with a gold charm bow at the top of the tassels. Around the neck of the mannequin is wrapped gold lace braid and little gathers of pink and gold organza ribbon. Tiny gold beads are stitched in several places and a gold belt of gold lace is found around the waist. There is the sweetest silk ribbon flower on the back waistline of the mannequin. The base is dark green wood with gold braid glued in place around the scalloped edges of the base. A delight to make for yourself or to give, you might want to try several variations of this craft.

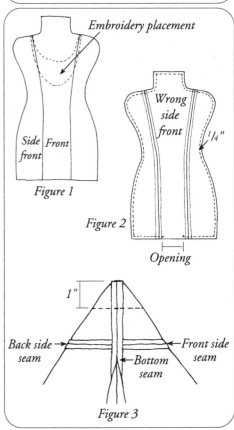

Mannequin

Materials

❖ 24" by 18" piece of fabric

❖ Polyfil

❖ Wooden base, painted to complement colors used

❖ Wooden turned dowel, painted to match base

❖ Various ribbons, charms, lace and flowers for embellishing

❖ Optional: floss or silk ribbon for embroidery

❖ **Pattern pieces needed:** Mannequin Center Front, Center Back, Side Front and Side Back found on pull-out section

❖ **Template needed:** Mannequin Embroidery Template found on page 90.

Directions

1. Cut out one center front, two side fronts, one center back and two side back pieces.

2. Stitch the side fronts to the center front, right sides together, using ¼" seams; press the seams open (**fig. 1**).

3. Stitch the side backs to the center back, right sides together, using ¼" seams; press the seams open.

4. Optional: Any embroidery you choose to do should be done at this point, before stitching the front and back together (**see fig. 1 for placement**).

5. Stitch the front and back with right sides together, using a ¼" seam; leave an opening at the bottom for turning and stuffing (**fig. 2**).

6. To make the bottom flat, place the side and bottom seams together and stitch 1" from the point (**fig. 3**).

7. Trim the seams and clip all curves. Turn the body right side out and stuff the upper portion of the mannequin with polyfil.

Embroidery placement

Side front | Front

Figure 1

Wrong side front

¼"

Figure 2

Opening

1"

Back side seam

Front side seam

Bottom seam

Figure 3

8. Drill a hole in the center of the base to fit the dowel. Insert the dowel in hole and glue in place (**fig. 4**).

9. Glue polyfil to the top end of the dowel and insert it into the mannequin. Finish stuffing the mannequin tightly with polyfil (**fig. 5**).

10. Whip stitch the opening in the bottom of the mannequin.

11. Embellish as desired with ribbons, flowers, trims, and charms (see the finished drawing). ▣

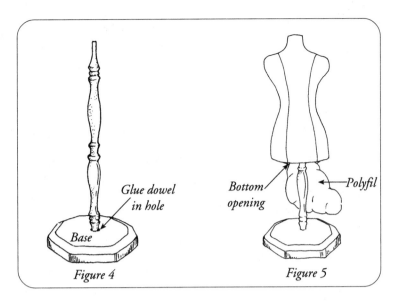

Glue dowel
in hole

Base

Figure 4

Bottom
opening

Polyfil

Figure 5

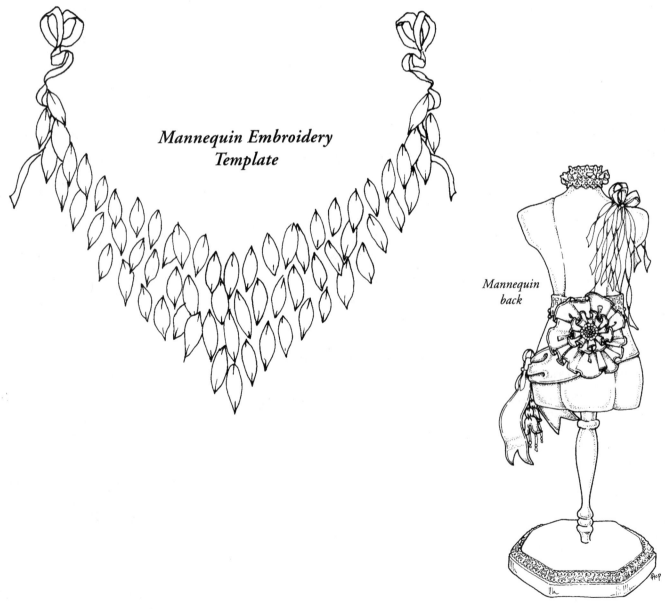

*Mannequin Embroidery
Template*

Mannequin
back

Metallic Gimp Shadow Pillow

Unusual fabrics are so much fun to work with. This is a crushed organza fabric in a lovely shade of beige. The unusual shape is intriguing as well as the double ruffle which follows the outline on the outside. Shadow shapes of the crinkle fabric over a darker brown linen are found on the outside and another unusual shape is in the middle. Using variegated thread, gimp has been zigzagged down; two rows of this gimp trim are on the outside design and three rows are on the inside. This unusual pillow could go in a lot of places in your home because of the metallic crushed fabric. It almost has a contemporary feel.

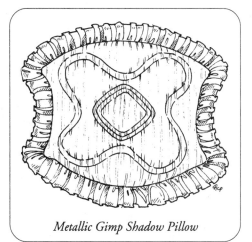

Metallic Gimp Shadow Pillow

Materials

♣ ³/₄ yd. of white silk dupioni
♣ 15" square of dark brown linen or silk for shadow design
♣ 1¹/₄ yds. of crinkled silk for pillow
♣ Gimp cording
♣ Variegated rayon thread (Sulky #2116 was used for the pillow shown)
♣ Polyfil
♣ Other Requirements: #70 machine needle, tear-away stabilizer, white embroidery thread for bobbin, blue washout marker
♣ **Pattern piece needed:** Crinkled Silk Pillow Pattern, found in pull-out section

A. Cutting and Preparation

1. From the pillow pattern piece, cut two pieces from the white dupioni and two pieces from the crinkled silk. Trace the shadow design onto the crinkled silk with the washout marker.

2. Spray starch the dark brown fabric and place it beneath the crinkled pillow top.

3. Place the stabilizer under the two pieces and pin in place.

4. Cut enough 4" wide strips of the crinkled fabric to make 72".

B. Construction

1. Using the rayon thread in the needle of the machine and white in the bobbin, satin stitch over the gimp cording around the center diamond design (refer to the instructions for corded appliqué on page 244). Use the open toe foot as a guide for placing the second and third gimp rows to the outside of the first row (**fig. 1**).

2. Stitch the gimp on the outside design. Using the foot as a guide, stitch a second row of gimp on the outside of the design, next to the first row (**fig. 2**).

3. When all of the satin stitching is done, tear away the stabilizer from the back.

4. With appliqué scissors or embroidery scissors, carefully cut away the excess brown fabric from behind the design (**fig. 3**).

5. Baste the white dupioni pieces behind the pillow front and back.

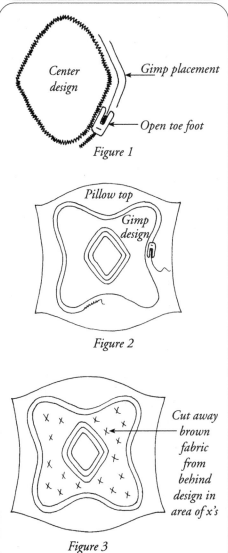

Center design

Gimp placement

Open toe foot

Figure 1

Pillow top

Gimp design

Figure 2

Cut away brown fabric from behind design in area of x's

Figure 3

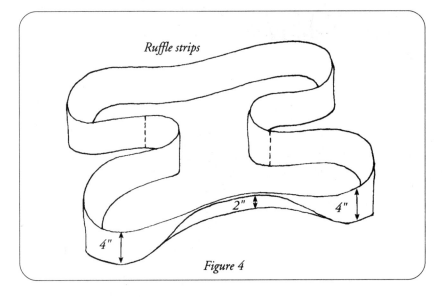

Ruffle strips

2"

4"

4"

Figure 4

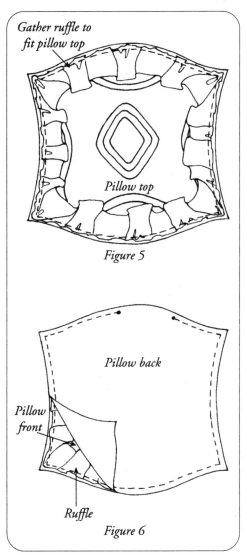

Gather ruffle to
fit pillow top

Pillow top

Figure 5

Pillow back

Pillow
front

Ruffle

Figure 6

6. Seam the 4" strips for the ruffle together with a $1/4$" seam. Seam the ends of the ruffle strip together to form a circle. Fold the ruffle strips in half along the length to form a 2" ruffle (**fig. 4**).

7. Run two rows of gathering stitches along the raw edge of the ruffle. Pull up the gathers and adjust the ruffle to fit the pillow top (**fig. 5**).

8. Stitch the ruffle to the pillow top with a $1/2$" seam.

9. Place the pillow front and back with right sides together and stitch, leaving an opening for stuffing (**fig. 6**).

10. Turn the pillow right side out and stuff with polyfil.

11. Whip stitch the opening closed by hand. ▨

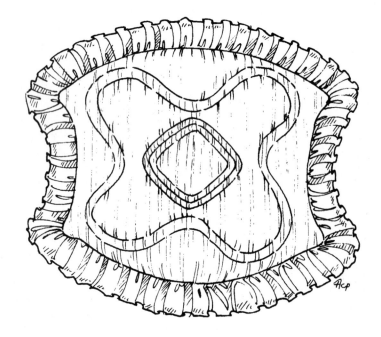

Corded Shadow Appliqué Neckroll

What an elegant accent for a bedroom or sunroom! This beautiful pillow features the corded shadow appliqué technique. Pastel flowers in pink and blue have yellow centers and green leaves. The corded edges add elegance and sophistication. Pretty lace-edged ruffles and tied satin ribbon bows finish the ends of this beautiful and functional pillow.

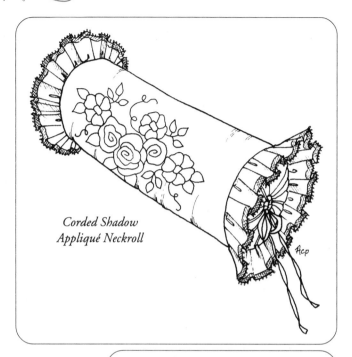

*Corded Shadow
Appliqué Neckroll*

Supplies

♣ ⁷/₈ yd. of white batiste
♣ 2⁵/₈ yds. of 1" wide lace edging
♣ 1 yd. of ¹/₄" wide double-faced satin ribbon
♣ ¹/₄ yd. each of green, blue and pink broadcloth
♣ 9" square of yellow broadcloth
♣ ³/₄ yd. of white batiste or broadcloth (for lining)
♣ machine embroidery thread to match broadcloth colors
♣ gimp for cording
♣ crib size quilt batting
♣ tear-away paper stabilizer
♣ **Template Required:** Flower Template for Corded Appliqué Neckroll found on center pull-out section

I. Cutting and Preparation

1. Cut or tear the following pieces from the white batiste:

    a. One rectangle, 18" x 24", with the 24" side on the long grain of the fabric.

    b. Two rectangles, 4¹/₂" x 24", with the 24" side on the long grain of the fabric.

    c. Two ruffle strips torn across the width of the fabric, 3" x 45".

2. Lightly starch and press the fabric dry. Fold the 18" x 24" rectangle in half in both directions. Press a light crease to mark the center.

3. Trace the flower template onto the rectangle, matching the center of the fabric to the center of the template. The length of the template should run along the 18" direction of the fabric.

4. Refer to the directions for corded shadow appliqué on page 244 and work the appliqué design onto the fabric.

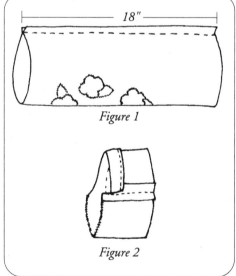

Figure 1

Figure 2

II. Making the Neckroll Cover

1. Fold the fabric right sides together with the 18" sides meeting; stitch with a ¹/₄" seam allowance. Finish the seam with a zigzag or serged edge (**fig. 1**).

2. Finish one long edge of each 4¹/₂" x 24" rectangle.

3. Fold one of the rectangles in half with the 4¹/₂" edges meeting. Sew the short ends together, using a ¹/₄" seam allowance and stopping the stitching ⁷/₈" from the finished edges. Press the seam open. Repeat for the other piece (**see fig. 2**).

4. Turn the finished edge of each circular piece to the inside by ¹/₂", leaving the seam allowances pressed in the turned-under area (**see fig. 2**).

5. Topstitch ³/₈" from the folded edge to form a casing, leaving the pressed edges of the seam unstitched (**fig. 2**).

6. Attach lace edging to one long side of each ruffle piece, using the technique lace to fabric. Mark the center of the ruffle on the unfinished long edge (**see fig. 3**).

7. Meet the short ends of one ruffle piece with right sides together. Stitch with a $1/4$" seam and finish the seam allowance as above. Repeat for the other ruffle piece (**see fig. 3**).

8. Run two gathering rows across the unfinished edge of the ruffle strips, at $1/4$" and $1/8$" from the raw edge (**fig. 3**).

9. Turn the pillow tube right side out. Place the ruffle to the ends of the pillow tube, right sides together, with the ruffle on the outside and having the raw edges meet. Let the ruffle seam match the pillow back seam and match the ruffle center to the pillow center front (**see fig. 4**).

10. Pull up the ruffle gathers to fit the end of the pillow. Pin or baste in place.

11. Place the casing section over the end of the pillow tube, right sides together and raw edges meeting. Let the seam fall at the center front of the pillow tube (**see fig. 4**).

12. Stitch around the ends of the tube, through all layers. Be careful not to catch the lace edge of the ruffles in the seams. Finish the seam with a zigzag or serge (**fig. 4**).

13. If the batting measures about 18" long and 24" around in the package, use it as is. If not, fold it to 18" wide and roll the batting until it is 24" around. Slide the batting roll into the pillow.

14. Cut the $1/4$" ribbon in half and thread the ribbon through the casings at each end of the pillow. Pull up the ribbons to close the ends tightly, then tie the ribbon ends into a bow (**fig. 5**).

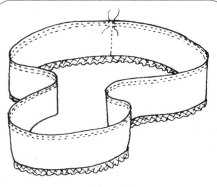

Figure 3

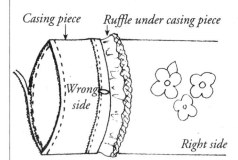

Casing piece   Ruffle under casing piece

Wrong side

Right side

Figure 4

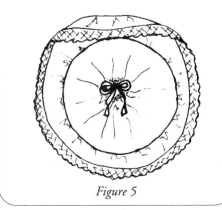

Figure 5

Acp

Show 10

Metallic Trim Neck Roll Pillow

Made entirely on the serger using metallic gold threads, this fabulous pillow has many different types of home decorating braids in shades of ecru, blue, peach, black, pink, and gold. Several strips of lace are used also. The ends of the pillow are of white satin and they tie for ease of construction. Gold serger trim is found on the end of each pillow. This is quite a snazzy pillow and I love gold in home decorating. You could use any colors to fit your living room, family room or bedroom color scheme.

Metallic Trim Neck Roll Pillow Design by E. Ann Reigel for Baby Lock®.

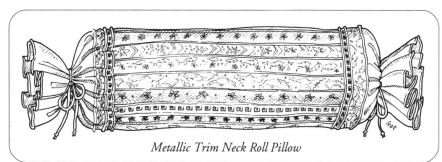
Metallic Trim Neck Roll Pillow

Materials

❧ 12 yds. of assorted widths of lace insertion, metallic trims, and ribbons, in 18" or 36" lengths; width needs to be at least 1"
❧ 1³/₄ yds. each of two ribbons, at least 1" wide
❧ ⁷/₈ yd. of satin fabric for ends of pillow
❧ Gold metallic thread
❧ Serger thread to match fabric
❧ 3 yds. of satin cording
❧ 18" long by 24" round neck roll pillow form

A. Cutting

1. Cut 4 strips of satin fabric, each 7" by 45".

2. Cut several 18" pieces of trim. Lay the strips side by side, in the order they will be sewn. Continue cutting trims and laces, arranging them into a section 24" by 18" (**fig.1**).

B. Construction

Note: This pillow was constructed using a serger and a conventional machine. If a serger will not be used, substitute a satin-stitch zigzag for the directions which say "flatlock" or "rolled hem".

1. Thread the serger with metallic thread in the upper looper. Refer to the serger manual for flatlocking with metallic thread, and refer to the instructions in this book on page 256.

2. Flatlock (zigzag) the trims together, with wrong sides together (the decorative seams will be on the outside).

3. After all of the pieces have been flatlocked together, re-measure the piece. If needed, add more strips to make the length measure 24", as some of the length will be taken up in the seams.

4. When the block of trims measures 18" x 24", trim the ends even (**fig. 2**).

5. Flatlock (zigzag) the two long sides together (with wrong sides together) creating a tube (**fig. 3**).

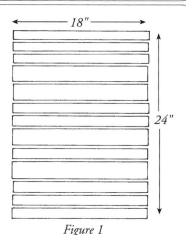
Figure 1

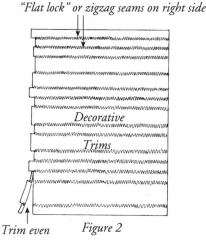
Figure 2

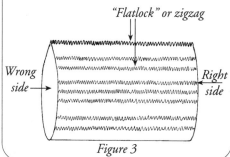
Figure 3

6. Cut two pieces of one trim, each 24¹/₂" long. Seam each strip into a circle, taking a ¹/₄" seam across the short ends (**fig. 4**).

7. Repeat for a second trim, making a total of four circles, two of each kind.

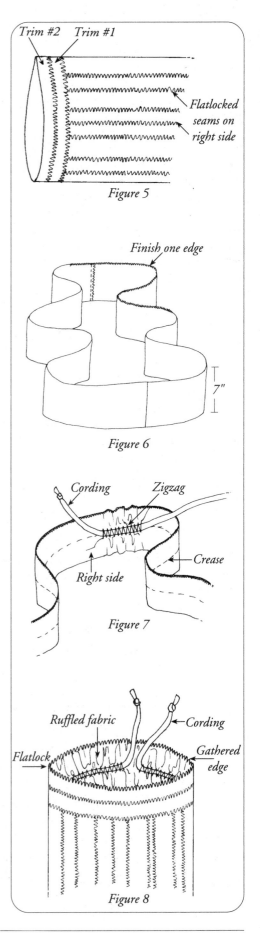

Figure 4

8. Flatlock (zigzag) one piece of the first trim to one end of the pieced ribbon tube. Flatlock one piece of the second trim to the edge of the first trim, forming a band around one end of the pieced ribbon tube (**fig. 5**).

9. Repeat step 8 on the other end of the tube.

10. Seam two of the 7" x 45" fabric pieces together at one short end, with right sides together and using a ¹/₂" seam. Seam the other end together making a circle of fabric 88" around and 7" wide (**see fig. 6**).

11. Hem one edge of the circle using metallic thread and the rolled hem (zigzag) stitch on the serger (**fig. 6**).

12. Fold the edges of the circle together to create a 3¹/₂" wide tube. Press a light crease. Open the fabric back out flat. There will be a crease down the middle of the 7" wide tube.

13. Cut the satin cording into two pieces. Tie a knot in each end of one piece.

14. Place the cording on the right side of the fabric along the crease line and zigzag over (not into) the cording, so that the cording is encased under the stitches, but the fabric will slide freely over the cording. You will need to slide the fabric up onto the cording as you stitch, because the 54" piece of cording will not be long enough to go the whole length of the ruffle (**fig. 7**).

15. Run two rows of gathering stitches along the unfinished edge of the ruffle. Pull up the gathers to fit the end of the ribbon tube.

16. Place the wrong side of the ruffle to the wrong side of the ribbon tube and flatlock the two pieces together (**fig. 8**).

17. Repeat steps 7 through 13 for the other end of the pillow.

18. Slide the pillow form into the pillow and pull up the cording at each end to close the pillow. Tie the cording into a bow (see the finished drawing). ▣

Dainty Photo Pillow

Searching through antique shops is one of my favorite activities. You have probably guessed as such over the last years that some of you have been purchasing my books. I happened upon a little torn up pillow in France with a photograph printed in black and white. Little gathered lace ran around the pillow and it had a tattered ribbon in one corner. We used that idea on this little pillow which has a square base pillow of pink silk dupioni, ecru lace, and the black and white photograph of me surrounded by two of my grandchildren and four other gorgeous children. There is a little heart-shaped gold charm with a "P" in the corner and little pink ribbons tied in a beautiful bow. This is a great present for anyone who loves pictures and I believe that is just about everyone, especially mothers and grandmothers. Please have your favorite photograph transferred onto fabric at your local photocopy place and make as many of these treasures as your sewing time allows. What joy!

Dainty Photo Pillow

Materials

- ❖ NOTE: These measurements are for a 5" by 6" photo. Adjust measurements according to the size photo you have.
- ❖ One 5" x 6" photo
- ❖ Two pieces of fabric cut 9" x 10" for pillow
- ❖ One piece of white satin, cut 6" x 7"
- ❖ 3$^1/_2$ yds. of $^3/_4$" wide lace edging
- ❖ $^3/_4$ yd. of tiny satin cording to go around picture
- ❖ 1 yd. of $^1/_8$" wide satin ribbon for bow
- ❖ One charm
- ❖ Polyfil

Instructions

1. Take the photo to a copy service and have it transferred to a piece of transfer paper. Iron the transfer onto the piece of satin (refer to the picture transfer instructions on page 247).

2. Fold under the edges of the transferred photo, so that only the picture shows. Press. Center the photo on one square of the pillow fabric and stitch around the edges of the photo with a straight stitch or tiny zigzag (**fig. 1**).

3. Gather 1$^1/_2$ yds. of lace edging by pulling the top thread in the heading.

4. Zigzag the lace in place around the edge of the picture. Turn the raw ends to the back and lap $^1/_2$" where the ends meet (**fig. 2**).

5. Gather the remaining lace edging and zigzag this piece just under the scalloped edge of the previous row, being careful not to catch the first row of lace in the stitching (**see fig. 3**).

6. Place the tiny cord around the edge of the picture where the lace is joined and stitch the cord in place with a tiny zigzag (**fig. 3**).

7. Place the pillow top to the back with right sides together and stitch, being careful not to catch the lace in the seam. Leave a small opening for turning.

8. Turn the pillow and stuff it with polyfil. Slip stitch the opening closed.

9. Make a multi-looped bow from the $^1/_8$" wide ribbon. Attach the charm and multi-looped bow in one top corner of the picture (see the finished drawing). ▦

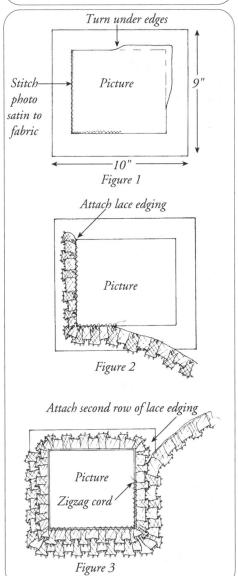

Turn under edges

Stitch photo satin to fabric

Picture

9"

10"

Figure 1

Attach lace edging

Picture

Figure 2

Attach second row of lace edging

Picture

Zigzag cord

Figure 3

Triangular Pillow

I love crazy patch and everything which resembles it! Using antique linens, scraps of laces and such, little charms, motifs, ribbons, old handkerchiefs, silk ribbon roses, and braid, this pillow shaped into a triangle is wonderful. Lace is gathered and stitched around the outside of the pillow. The basic color of the pillow is white and the trims are in wonderful shades of lavender, yellow, green, and dusty pink. The back of the pillow is plain white batiste. This just has to be a fancy bedroom pillow. When I was a little girl, I had lavender flowers on white wallpaper in my bedroom. Joanna always loved lavender clothing. Lavender is simply one of my favorite colors and it has such happy memories. You can use any color scheme you love and have quite an elegant way to use your scraps.

Triangular Pillow

Materials

❖ ¹/₃ yd. of white batiste
❖ 3 handkerchiefs or napkins
❖ Assorted scraps of lace, ribbons, doilies and other trims to complement the handkerchiefs
❖ Lightweight machine embroidery thread
❖ 2³/₄ yds. of 1" wide lace edging
❖ 2³/₄ yds. of 2" wide lace edging
❖ Polyfil
❖ **Pattern piece needed:** Triangular Pillow Pattern found in pull-out section

A. Cutting

1. Cut 3 triangles from the pattern (**fig. 1**).

2. Place two triangles with wrong sides together and stitch around the edges with a ¹/₄" seam. These two layers will be treated as one piece for the back of the pillow.

3. Arrange each handkerchief in a corner of the pillow top with the handkerchief corners pointing toward the center of the pillow top; pin in place. Cut away the excess handkerchief fabric (**fig. 2**).

4. Place the laces and trims in a crazy patch style on the pillow top, overlapping the edges to look neat. Make sure that any raw edges are covered by finished edges (refer to the finished drawing).

B. Construction

1. Using a narrow zigzag and matching thread, stitch along the edges of the pieces being attached to the pillow top.

2. Gather the 1" lace edging and attach it to the pillow top with right sides together, ¹/₂" from the edge. Turn the raw ends to the back and lap over ¹/₂" where the ends meet (**fig. 3**).

3. Repeat step 2 with the 2" lace edging. This wider lace edging will lay on top of the narrower one during construction (**fig. 4**).

4. Place the pillow back to the pillow front (right sides together) and stitch around the pillow with a ¹/₂" seam. Leave a 5" opening along one straight side for turning the pillow. Be careful not to catch the scalloped edge of the lace in the stitching (**fig. 5**).

5. Turn the pillow and stuff with polyfil. Whip stitch the opening closed. ▨

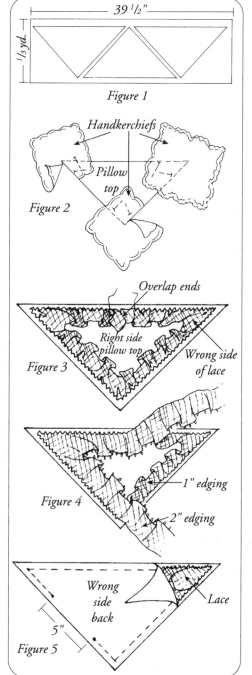

Figure 1

Handkerchiefs

Pillow top

Figure 2

Overlap ends

Right side pillow top

Wrong side of lace

Figure 3

1" edging

2" edging

Figure 4

Wrong side back

5"

Lace

Figure 5

Introduction To Girl Dresses

$\mathcal{L}$ooking back through history in the area of little girl's clothing, I seem to sense an overwhelming emphasis on the pinafore. Long ago, white pinafores, which could be washed, were worn over nearly everything. Can you imagine days when wool clothing was put on children and there were no dry cleaners nearby? Pinafores served a very practical purpose and they still can. This section has beautiful pinafores inspired by some antique pinafores and dresses which I purchased at a French flea market. I loved pinafores on Joanna when she was little and I especially enjoyed the fact that I could use one pinafore over several dresses. One pinafore with lots of beautiful needle-work or lace work can go over a pink broadcloth dress for spring, a yellow batiste for summer, a plaid silk dupioni for fall and a dark velveteen for Christmas. What value for your sewing time and money!

These pinafores are beyond magnificent. The patterns for the different variations are included in this book. The dress, included in this book also, is Heirloom Party Dress made up in all sorts of fabric variations. I love the embellishments used on each of these child's pinafores; they are so varied and interesting. If you are so fortunate as to have a new sewing machine which does machine embroidery, you are going to have the time of your life embellishing these pinafores. Machine embroidery is so elegant and so quick. Many times it looks just like hand work and it is ever so easy to do! Some of the pinafores are very fancy; some are a little plainer. I think you will find a pinafore for every little girl that you love to sew for. Our pinafore fabrics are varied from Swiss Nelona to handkerchief linen, to silk organza, to organdy and Victorian batiste. The dresses underneath use a large fabric variety also: linen, batiste, broadcloth, wool challis and silk dupioni. Combine the two ideas - pinafore over elegant dress - and you will be sure to please your little girl.

Corded shadow appliqué is used on the scalloped white organdy pinafore over navy blue wool. I love the ecru machine embroidery on the baby blue Swiss Nelona batiste pinafore. For a completely different look we used silver lamé machine embroidery on silk organza fabric for a pinafore; the dress underneath is off-white silk dupioni and even the sleeves on this dress have silver machine embroidery.

I believe your imagination will take over when you study the pinafore variations found in this section. You might want to put cross stitch or other types of embroidery on your pinafore. I remember one cross stitch pinafore that Joanna wore over many different dresses. It had different colors of beautiful bows running vertically on the pinafore. Whatever embellishment you choose, I think you will love the patterns in this section. I also believe that you might love using these ideas on dresses, pillows and, in a smaller version, on doll dresses. Enjoy these patterns as much as we enjoyed making them for you. On a final note, pinafores are still great protection for dresses! Maybe your little one can get two wearings out of the underdress if you put a pretty pinafore on top!

Girl's Dress General Instructions

General Information

* Yardage given in this section is for the basic dress. Any additional requirements will be found in the specific directions for each dress (lace, entredeux, trims, notions, etc.).

* Pattern pieces and templates required are listed in the specific instructions for each dress, along with their location.

* All seam allowances are given on the pattern pieces and seams are sewn with right sides together unless otherwise noted.

Fabric Requirements

*Amounts given are for 45" fabric.

Size	Fabric
4	2 yds.
6	$2^1/4$ yds.
8	$2^1/2$ yds.
10	$2^3/4$ yds.
12	3 yds.

Skirt and Sleeve Band Chart

Size	*Skirt Length	**Sleeve Band
4	$25^1/2$"	$9^3/4$"
6	29"	$10^3/8$"
8	35"	$10^3/4$"
10	$36^3/4$"	11"
12	$39^1/2$"	$11^1/4$"

* Cut two $36^1/2$" widths to the following measurements unless the specific directions say otherwise. Lengths given include a 4" hem allowance and $^1/2$" waist seam allowance. More accurate measurements may be obtained by measuring the individual child.

** Use these measurements as cutting lengths for bias strips or lace/entredeux strips; $^1/2$" seam allowances are included in the length. More accurate measurements may be obtained by measuring the individual child. The width for bias strips is 1", which includes $^1/4$" seam allowances.

I. Cutting

1. Cut one front yoke on the fold.

2. Cut out two yoke backs from the selvage. Mark the fold lines along the backs.

3. Cut out two sleeves.

4. The skirt will be cut out later. Cutting measurements are given in the chart on this page. Specific directions for any skirt alterations are given under each dress title. Trace the armhole guide onto stiff paper and cut the armholes from the sides of the skirt front and back.

II. Construction of the Yokes and Skirt

1. Place the shoulders of the front yoke and back yokes with right sides together and stitch (**fig. 1**).

2. Finish the neck of the dress, referring to the specific directions for each dress.

3. Cut front and back skirt pieces using the skirt chart found on this page.

4. Place the armhole guide along the sides of the skirt. Cut armholes from the sides of both skirt pieces (**see fig. 2**).

5. Cut a $4^1/2$" slit down the center back of the skirt for the back placket (**fig. 2**).

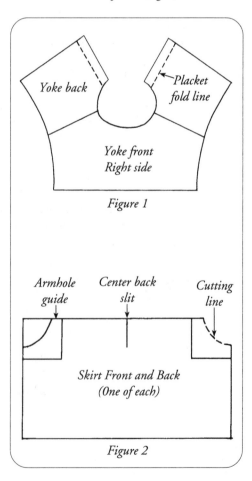

Figure 1

Figure 2

6. Back Placket –

   a. Cut a strip of fabric from the selvage ³/₄" wide by 10".

   b. Pull the slit in the skirt apart to form a "V". Place the right side of the strip to the right side of the skirt slit. The stitching will be made from the wrong side with the skirt on top and the placket strip on the

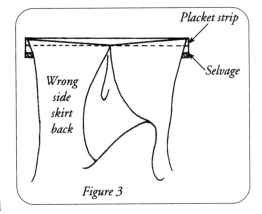

Figure 3

   bottom. The placket strip will be straight and the skirt will form a "V" with the point of the "V" ¹/₄" from the edge of the placket. Stitch, using a ¹/₄" seam. As you stitch, you will just catch the tip (a few fibers) at the point of the "V" (**fig. 3**).

   c. Press the seam toward the selvage edge of the placket strip. Turn the selvage edge to the inside of the dress, enclosing the seam allowance. Whip by hand or stitch in place by machine (**fig. 4**).

   d. From the wrong side, fold the placket in half so that the top edges of the skirt are even. Stitch a small dart across the bottom fold of the placket, being careful not to catch the skirt in the stitching (**fig. 5**).

7. The back of the dress will lap right over left. Fold the right side of the skirt placket to the inside of the skirt and pin. Leave the left skirt placket open (**see fig. 6**).

8. Run two rows of gathering threads in the top edges of each skirt piece at ¹/₄" and ¹/₂" (**fig. 6**).

9. Open up the fold back on each side of the back yoke pieces (fold line is clearly marked).

10. Place the back yokes to the back skirt piece, right sides together. Pull up the gathered skirt backs to fit the back yokes. The placket edge will come to the fold line on the left back yoke. The folded edge of the placket will come to the fold line on the right back yoke. Wrap the back yoke facings over the placket. Stitch the skirt to the yokes with a ¹/₂" seam (**fig. 7**). Overcast with a zigzag or serge the seam.

11. Place the front skirt to the front yoke, right sides together. Stitch using a ¹/₂" seam. Overcast or serge the seam.

12. Pull the back yokes away from the skirt, folding the back yoke facings to the inside along the fold lines (**fig. 8**).

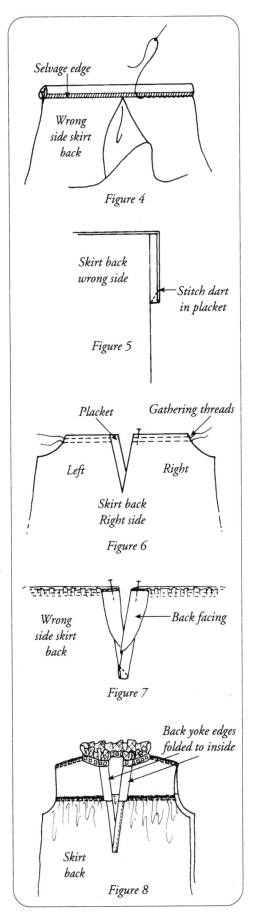

Figure 4

Figure 5

Figure 6

Figure 7

Figure 8

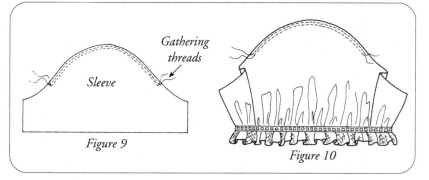

Figure 9

Figure 10

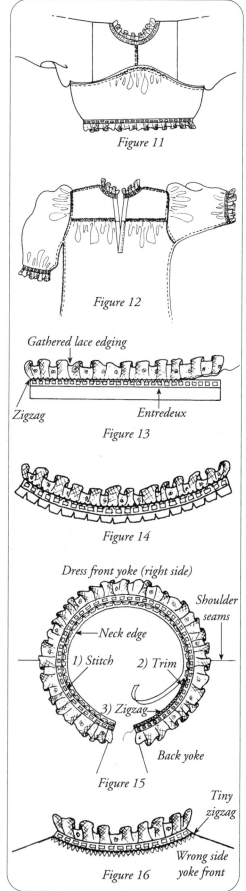

Figure 11

Figure 12

Gathered lace edging

Zigzag   *Entredeux*

Figure 13

Figure 14

Dress front yoke (right side)

Shoulder seams

Neck edge

1) *Stitch*   2) *Trim*

3) *Zigzag*

Back yoke

Figure 15

Tiny zigzag

Wrong side yoke front

Figure 16

III. Constructing the Sleeves

1. Decorate the sleeve if desired (refer to specific directions for each dress).

2. Run gathering rows across the top of the sleeve at $^1/_4$" and $^3/_8$" (**fig. 9**).

3. Finish the ends of the sleeves using the trims and instructions for each specific dress (**fig. 10**).

4. Gather the top of the sleeve to fit the arm opening of the dress. Match the center of the sleeve with the shoulder seam of the dress. The gathers of the sleeve should not extend past the bodice seam of the yoke. Pin the right side of the sleeve to the right side of the arm opening.

5. Stitch the sleeve to the dress using a $^3/_8$" seam (**fig. 11**). Overcast the seam.

6. Place the sleeve/side seams with right sides together and stitch a $^1/_2$" seam from the bottom edge of the sleeve to the bottom edge of the skirt (**fig. 12**). Overcast the seam.

IV. Finishing the Dress

1. Finish the bottom edge of the skirt with a zigzag or serged edge, or press $^1/_2$" to the inside. Turn the hem allowance to the inside and press in place.

2. Hem the dress by hand or machine.

3. Work buttonholes in the right back yoke.

4. Attach buttons to the left back yoke.

V. Neck Finishes

A. Entredeux to Gathered Edging

1. Measure the neck edge of the dress with the facings opened out flat. Cut a strip of entredeux to that measurement.

2. Cut a piece of edging lace two times this length and gather it to fit the entredeux strip.

3. Trim away one side of the entredeux and attach the gathered edging lace to the trimmed entredeux using the technique entredeux to gathered lace (**fig. 13**).

4. If the fabric edge remaining on the entredeux is not already $^1/_4$", trim it to $^1/_4$". Clip this fabric so that it will curve along the neck edge of the dress (**fig. 14**). Place this strip to the neck (back facings extended - not folded) of the dress, right sides together. Attach using the technique entredeux to fabric (**fig. 15**).

5. Using a tiny zigzag, tack the seam allowance to the dress. This stitching will keep the entredeux/gathered lace standing up at the neck (**fig. 16**).

B. Bias Neck Facing

1. Cut a bias strip 1" wide and
   $^1/_2$" longer than the length of
   the neck edge measurement.
   Fold the bias strip in half and
   press. Place the cut edges of the
   strip to the neck of the dress.
   Cut the ends of the strip off
   $^3/_8$" from each side of the back
   bodice edges (**see fig. 17**).

2. Flip the back yoke edges to the
   outside along the fold lines.
   Place these folds under the bias
   strip. Stitch the bias strip to the
   neck edge using a $^1/_4$" seam.

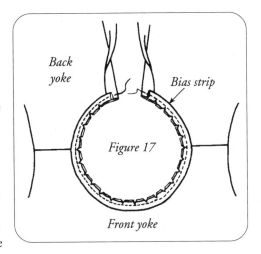

Figure 17

   Trim the seam allowance to $^1/_8$". Clip the curves (**fig. 17**). Flip the bias strip and the
   back bodice edges to the inside of the bodice. Hand stitch the bias strip in place,
   finishing the neck edge (**fig. 18**).

C. Bias Neck Binding

1. Trim off the edge of the neck $^1/_4$". Fold the back edges of the back bodice to the
   inside along the fold lines. Press.

2. Measure around the neck with the back folds in place and add $^1/_2$" to this measurement. Cut a bias strip 1" wide by this measurement. Fold each long side of the bias
   strip to the inside $^1/_4$". Press in place (**fig. 19**). Open out one side of the bias strip and
   stitch to the neck using a $^1/_4$" seam (stitch in the fold) (**fig. 20**). The bias strip will
   extend $^1/_4$" beyond the folded edges of the back. Flip the bias up, away from the neck,
   fold the ends to the inside and pull the upper folded edge of the bias strip over the
   seam allowance (**fig. 21**). Press. Hand stitch or machine stitch in place.

VI. Sleeve Bands and Ruffles

Refer to specific directions for decorating the sleeves.

A. Entredeux, Insertion and Gathered Edging Lace

1. Cut four strips of entredeux and two strips of insertion lace to the measurement given
   on the sleeve band chart on page 100. Cut two pieces of edging lace twice the length
   of the entredeux.

2. Gather the edging lace to fit the entredeux. Stitch together using the technique
   entredeux to gathered lace (**refer to fig. 13**).

3. Attach a strip of lace insertion to the free edge of each edging/entredeux strip, then
   attach entredeux to the free edge of each lace insertion strip, using the technique
   entredeux to lace each time. This completes a sleeve band consisting of entredeux/
   insertion/entredeux/edging (**fig. 22**).

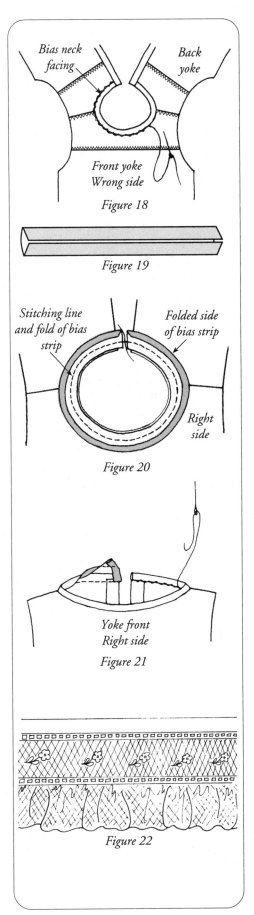

Bias neck facing   Back yoke

Front yoke
Wrong side

Figure 18

Figure 19

Stitching line
and fold of bias
strip

Folded side
of bias strip

Right
side

Figure 20

Yoke front
Right side

Figure 21

Figure 22

4. Run gathering rows across the bottom of the sleeve at $^1/_8$" and $^1/_4$", then gather the bottom of the sleeve to fit the free edge of the entredeux on the sleeve band. Stitch the band to the sleeve, right sides together, using the technique entredeux to gathered fabric (**fig. 23**).

5. Attach the sleeve to the bodice (**refer to fig. 11**).

B. Bias Sleeve Bindings

1. Cut two bias strips of fabric 1" wide by the measurement given on the sleeve band chart on page 100.

2. Run two gathering rows across the bottom of the sleeve at $^1/_8$" and $^1/_4$", then gather the bottom of the sleeve to fit the bias band.

3. Stitch the band to the sleeve, right sides together, using a $^1/_4$" seam. Press the seam toward the band.

4. Refer to section III. Constructing the Sleeves steps 4-6. Attach the sleeve to the dress and sew the side seam before hemming the band edge in place.

5. Fold the lower edge of the band to the inside $^1/_4$". Place the folded edge just over the seam line on the inside of the sleeve creating a $^1/_4$" band. Hand stitch or machine stitch in place (**fig. 24**). This will finish the end of the sleeve. ▨

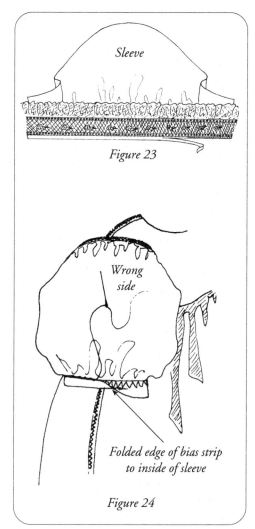

Sleeve

Figure 23

Wrong side

Folded edge of bias strip to inside of sleeve

Figure 24

Specific Instructions

Pink and Blue Silk Dresses with Bias Bindings

Supplies

✪ Refer to the supply chart on page 100. No additional supplies are needed.

✪ **Pattern Pieces Needed:** Front Yoke, Back Yoke, Armhole Guide and Sleeve found on the pattern pull-out section

I. Cutting and Preparation

Refer to section I. Cutting on page 100, steps 1-4. No additions or alterations are needed.

II. Construction

1. Follow the steps in section II. Construction of the Yokes and Skirts on page 100, steps 1 - 12.

2. Refer to section III. Constructing the Sleeves on page 102, beginning with step 2. For step 3, see page 102, section VI. Sleeve Bands and Ruffles, B. Bias Sleeve Bindings to finish the sleeve ends. Continue the sleeve construction with steps 4 - 6.

3. Finish the neck edge, using the instructions in section V. Neck Finishes, C. Bias Neck Binding on page 103.

4. Refer to section IV. Finishing the Dress. ▨

Pink and Blue Silk Dresses with Bias Bindings

Navy Dress with Neck Ruffle

Supplies

✿ Refer to the supply chart on page 100. No additional supplies are needed.

✿ **Pattern Pieces Needed:** Front Yoke, Back Yoke, Armhole Guide and Sleeve found on the pattern pull-out

I. Cutting and Preparation

Refer to section I. Cutting on page 100, steps 1-4. No additions or alterations are needed.

II. Construction

1. Follow the steps in section II. Construction of the Yokes and Skirts on page 101, steps 1 - 12.

2. Refer to section III. Constructing the Sleeves on page 102, beginning with step 2. For step 3, see page 102, section VI. Sleeve Bands and Ruffles, B. Bias Sleeve Bindings to finish the sleeve ends. Continue the sleeve construction with steps 4 - 6.

3. Finish the neck edge, using the instructions in section V. Neck Finishes, C. Bias Neck Binding on page 103, with the following addition:

   a. After step 1, measure the neck edge with the facings folded to the inside. Cut a 2^1/$_2$" wide strip of bias, twice the length of the neck edge plus 1". This strip will be the neck ruffle.

   b. Fold the ruffle strip in half along the length, with wrong sides together, and stitch two gathering rows across the long cut edges, through both layers, at ^{1}/$_8$" and ^{1}/$_4$" from the edge. About 1^1/$_2$" from each end, taper the stitching rows so that the stitching goes off on the folded edge (**fig. 1**).

   c. Place the ruffle to the right side of the neck edge with the raw edges meeting. Where the stitches taper off of the folded edge, let the ruffle curve off of the neck edge so that the folded edge of the ruffle meets the center back of each dress yoke (not the fold line) (**fig. 2**).

   d. Pull up the gathers of the ruffle to fit the neck edge and pin the ruffle in place. Baste the ruffle to the neck and treat as one layer for the next steps.

   e. Continue with section V.C. Bias Neck Binding, step 2 on page 103.

4. Refer to section IV. Finishing the Dress.

Navy Dress with Neck Ruffle

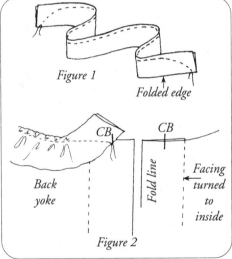

Figure 1

Folded edge

CB

CB

Back yoke

Fold line

Facing turned to inside

Figure 2

White Embroidered Dress

Supplies

✿ Refer to the supply chart on page 100. In addition, the following supplies are needed:

✿ 2¹/₂ yds. of edging lace, ³/₄" wide

✿ 3¹/₄ yds. of insertion lace, ³/₄" wide

✿ 1¹/₄ yds. of insertion lace, ³/₈" wide

✿ 1³/₄ yds. of entredeux

✿ Silver machine embroidery thread, or other color of choice

✿ Stabilizer for machine embroidery

✿ Hand embroidery supplies (optional)

✿ **Pattern Pieces Needed:** Front Yoke, Back Yoke, Armhole Guide and Sleeve found on the pattern pull-out

✿ **Template Needed:** White Dress Embroidery Template found 106

White Embroidered Dress

I. Cutting and Preparation

Refer to section I. Cutting on page 100, steps 1-4. No additions or alterations are needed.

II. Construction

A. Follow the steps in section II. Construction of the Yokes and Skirts on page 100, steps 1 - 12.

B. Refer to section III. Constructing the Sleeves on page 102. Make the following additions:

   1. For step 1, embroider a design centered on each sleeve. Use a large embroidery design from a machine, or use the template provided to work hand embroidery.

   2. Create a wide band of lace to be used as the sleeve ruffle, using the lace to lace technique for the following steps:

      a. Cut the following pieces, each twice the length of the sleeve band measurement given in the sleeve band chart on page 100; two strips of ³/₄" wide lace edging, four strips of ³/₄" wide lace insertion; two strips of ³/₈" wide lace insertion.

      b. Attach the strips in the following order to make two ruffles: edging, ³/₄" insertion, ³/₈" insertion, ³/₄" insertion. These ruffle pieces will be used as the edging for the sleeve bands.

   3. For step 3, see page 103, section VI. Sleeve Bands and Ruffles, A. Entredeux, Insertion and Gathered Lace. Use ³/₄" lace insertion, and use the ruffle created above as the edging.

   4. Continue the sleeve construction with steps 4 - 6.

C. Finish the neck edge, using the instructions in section V. Neck Finishes, A. Entredeux to Gathered Edging on page 102. Use ³/₄" wide edging.

D. Refer to section IV. Finishing the Dress. ▨

Template for White Embroidered Dress And Holiday Pinafore

Stitch Key

o *French Knot, 6 strands DMC*

∩∩ *Tiny Chain Stitch, 1 strand DMC*

\|\|\|\|\| *Satin Stitch, 2 or 3 strands DMC*

Square Collar Blouse

Fabric and Trim Requirements

Size	Fabric	Tatted Edging, 1/2"
4	1 1/4 yds.	1 1/4 yds.
6	1 3/8 yds.	1 3/8 yds.
8, 10, 12	1 1/2 yds.	1 3/4 yds.

✪ **Notions:** sizes 4 & 6, four 1/2" buttons; sizes 8 - 12, five 1/2" buttons; lightweight sewing thread; pattern tracing paper; see-thru gridded ruler; machine embroidery thread and stabilizer for machine embroidery; or hand embroidery supplies; Optional: gimp for cording collar edges

✪ **Pattern Pieces Required:** Dress Front Yoke, Dress Back Yoke, Armhole Guide, Sleeve, Square Collar found on pull-out section

✪ **Embroidery Template** (Optional) found on page 108

A. Modifying the Pattern

1. Trace the front yoke pattern onto tracing paper. Mark the lower yoke and armhole seam lines (**see fig. 1**).

2. Place the armhole guide over the yoke pattern, matching the seam lines and the side edges (**fig. 1**).

3. Trace around the armhole curve and side edge of the armhole guide.

4. Draw a line parallel to the center front line that will extend the side seam of the new pattern piece to the length given in the chart below (**see fig. 2**):

Size	Length
4	8"
6	9"
8	10 1/2"
10	10 3/4"
12	11"

5. Draw a line perpendicular to the side seam, extending toward the center front. This will be the blouse bottom edge (**see fig. 2**).

6. Lengthen the center front line to meet the new bottom edge line (**fig. 2**).

7. Repeat steps 1 - 6 for the back yoke.

8. Transfer pattern markings and seam allowances to the new pattern pieces.

B. Constructing the Blouse

All seam allowances are marked on the pattern pieces unless otherwise noted.

1. Cut one blouse front from the fold, two blouse backs from the selvage and two sleeves.

2. Make a complete collar pattern by tracing the pattern onto a piece of folded paper, then cut out the new pattern piece. Trace one collar onto a square of fabric, but do not cut the collar out.

3. Follow the instructions with the embroidery machine and work the embroidery design onto one collar piece, centered at the front. Option: a hand-embroidered design may be worked on the collar if preferred.

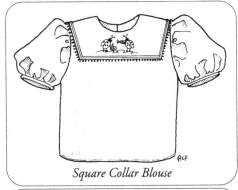

Square Collar Blouse

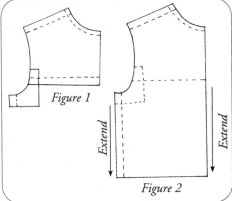

Figure 1

Extend *Extend*

Figure 2

4. Place the embroidered collar piece over a second square of fabric, with wrong sides together. Baste the two pieces together around the collar outline. Do not cut out.

5. Refer to Double Needle Edge Trim in the new technique section, page 253 and finish the collar outer edge. For a more pronounced piping look, place gimp under the zigzag rows and use a pintuck foot for the stitching. Use the tatted edging to finish the collar edge as described in the instructions.

6. Place the shoulders of the blouse front to the blouse back and stitch, then finish the seam edges with a serger or zigzag.

7. Cut out the collar neck edge and place the collar over the blouse, with the wrong side of the collar to the right side of the blouse. The back edges of the collar should meet the center back line of the blouse. Pin or baste in place.

8. Finish the neck edge with a bias facing, using the general dress instructions, section V. B. Bias Neck Facing. Stitch through all layers.

9. Make and attach the sleeves using the dress general instructions section III. Finish the sleeve ends according to section VI.B. Bias Sleeve Bindings.

10. Finish the bottom edge of the blouse with a serger or zigzag, then turn up a ¹/₂" hem and press in place. Hem the blouse by hand or machine.

11. Work buttonholes in the blouse back right, and attach buttons to the blouse back left. ▨

Template for Square Collar Blouse

White Embroidered Dress

Square Collar Blouse

Pink and Blue Silk Dresses with Bias Bindings

Navy Dress with Neck Ruffle

Girl's Pinafore - General Instructions

General Information

* Yardage given in this section is for the basic pinafore. Any additional requirements will be found in the specific directions for each pinafore (lace, entredeux, trims, notions, etc.).

* Pattern pieces and templates required are listed in the specific instructions for each pinafore, along with their location.

* All seam allowances are $1/4$" and seams are sewn with right sides together unless otherwise noted.

Fabric Requirements

* Amounts given are for 45" fabric.

Fabric

Size 4	$1^3/8$ yds.
Size 6	$1^1/2$ yds.
Size 8	$1^7/8$ yds.
Size 10	2 yds.
Size 12	$2^1/8$ yds.

Notions: Lightweight sewing thread, two $1/2$" flat buttons

* Skirt Chart

Size	Skirt Length
4	$19^1/4$"
6	$22^3/4$"
8	$28^3/4$"
10	$30^1/2$"
12	$33^1/4$"

* Cut two $36^1/2$" widths to the following measurements unless the specific directions say otherwise.

** Yoke and Yoke Trim Lengths

| Outer Edge - All Sizes | $1^1/2$ yds. |
| Neck Edge - All Sizes | $1^1/4$ yds. |

** Use these measurements as cutting lengths for bias strips or entredeux strips; these lengths are also used for making the decorative yoke strips unless indicated otherwise in the specific instructions. $1/4$" seam allowances are included in the measurements.

I. Cutting And Preparation

1. Decorate fabric for the yoke as directed in the specific instructions for each pinafore.

2. Cut the yoke pieces from plain or decorated fabric, as directed in the specific instructions.

3. Refer to the specific instructions for each pinafore to find cutting instructions for the skirt pieces. Cutting measurements are given in the chart on this page. Specific directions for any skirt alterations are given in the instructions for each specific pinafore.

4. Trace the armhole guide onto stiff paper and cut the armholes from the sides of the skirt front and back pieces.

II. Yoke Construction

A. Mitered Yoke - Entredeux Around Yoke Outer Edge And Neck

1. Decorate fabric for the yoke pieces as directed in the specific instructions.

2. Cut one front yoke on the fold, two shoulder straps on the fold, and two back yokes on the selvage if available. If selvage fabric is not available, serge or overcast the cut edges. Remember to keep the bottom edges of the yoke pieces and the outer edges of the shoulder straps lined up on the same edge of the fabric strip when cutting the pieces, so that if there is a design all the way around the yoke, the design will be continuous and matched. Mark the back yoke fold lines, center front and strap centers (**fig. 1**).

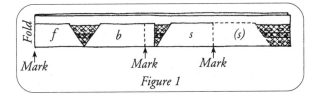

Figure 1

3. If the yoke will be lined, cut the same pieces from the lining fabric or self-fabric. Place the lining pieces to the yoke pieces and baste around the edges, then treat the two layers as one for the remaining steps.

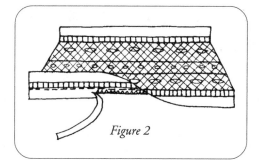

Figure 2

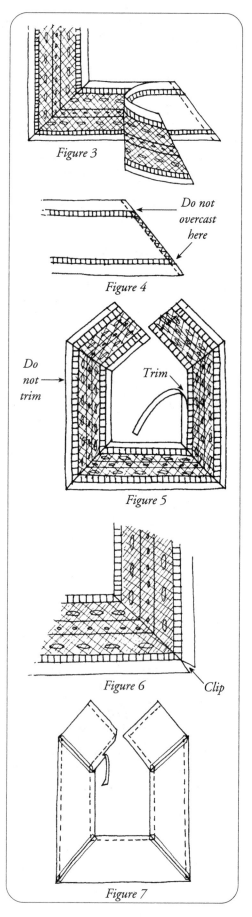

Figure 3

Do not overcast here

Figure 4

Do not trim

Trim

Figure 5

Figure 6

Clip

Figure 7

4. Attach a strip of entredeux across each long edge of the yoke pieces (top and bottom, inner and outer), using the entredeux to fabric technique. Do not trim away the remaining tape edge of the entredeux (**fig. 2**).

5. Place the shoulder pieces to the yoke pieces, right sides together. If there is a continuous design around the yoke, make sure that the design meets correctly at each seam. Sew with a straight stitch and a $^1/_4$" seam allowance (**fig. 3**).

6. Trim the seam allowance to $^1/_8$", then overcast with a zigzag only from the top edge of the top entredeux to the bottom edge of the bottom entredeux. In other words, do not overcast the entredeux tape edges at the top or bottom (**fig. 4**).

7. Trim the tape away from the entredeux at the neck edge. Do not trim the entredeux tape edge from the bottom and outer edges of the yoke (**fig. 5**).

8. Clip the remaining entredeux tape edges along the seam line, trimming off the seam allowance (**fig. 6**).

9. Set the yoke aside while constructing the skirt (refer to the specific instructions at this point).

B. Mitered Yoke - Lined, No Edge Trim

1. Refer to the specific directions if the yoke fabric is to be decorated.

2. From the yoke fabric and the lining fabric, cut one front yoke on the fold, two yoke backs, and two shoulder straps on the fold. Make sure to follow the specific instructions for grainline and design direction. Remember to keep the bottom edges of the yoke pieces and the outer edges of the shoulder straps lined up on the same edge of the fabric strip when cutting the pieces, so that if there is a design all the way around the yoke, the design will be continuous and matched. Mark the back yoke fold lines, center front and strap centers (**refer to fig. 1**).

3. Sew the yoke front and backs to the shoulder straps. If there is a continuous design around the yoke, make sure that the design meets correctly at each seam. Sew with a straight stitch and a $^1/_4$" seam allowance (**refer to fig. 3**). Press the seams open.

4. Sew the lining front and backs to the shoulder straps with a $^1/_4$" seam, using a straight stitch.

5. Place the yoke to the yoke lining, right sides together. Stitch around the neck edge and center back edges with a $^1/_4$" seam; clip the corners and trim the seam allowance to $^1/_8$" (**fig. 7**).

6. Stitch the outer edge of the shoulders with a $^1/_4$" seam, stopping the stitching at the corner seams. Trim the seam allowances to $^1/_8$" (**see fig. 7**).

7. Turn the yoke to the right side and press the seams well.

8. Set the yoke aside while constructing the skirt. Refer to the specific directions at this point.

C. Square Yoke - Bias Trimmed Edges

1. Decorate the yoke fabric according to the specific instructions.

2. Cut out one yoke front on the fold, two yoke backs on the selvage if available, and two shoulder straps on the fold. If selvage fabric is not available, serge or overcast the center back yoke edges. Mark the back yoke fold lines, center front and strap centers.

3. Use ¹/₄" finished double-fold bias tape to finish the inner edge of each strap piece:

   a. Open out the folds in the tape and pin the right side of the bias tape to the wrong side of the shoulder strap with the raw edges meeting (**see fig. 8**).

   b. Attach the bias to the strap, stitching in the crease with a ¹/₄" seam (**fig. 8**).

   c. Refold the bias, folding it to the outside over the strap edge (**see fig. 9**).

   d. "Baste" the bias in place with a liquid pins product.

   e. Topstitch the bias in place with a slightly shortened straight stitch along both long edges (**fig. 9**).

   f. Zigzag or serge across the short ends of the straps. Set the straps aside.

4. Create and attach the front and back skirt pieces, but do not sew the side seams. Refer to section III. steps 1 - 4, and section IV.C. steps 1 - 7.

5. Follow steps 3a - 3d in this section to finish the top edges of the yoke front and backs. Treat the yoke backs in the following manner (**refer to fig. 10**):

   a. Fold the back facings to the inside along the fold lines.

   b. When placing the bias to the top edge in step 3a, cut the bias ¹/₄" longer than the yoke edge.

   c. Fold the extra ¹/₄" to the inside and meet the folded edge to the fold line of the back facings.

   d. Continue with steps 3b - 3d.

6. Slide the strap ends under the top edges of the yoke front and backs. The right side of the strap will be against the wrong side of the yokes. The bias-finished edge of the straps will be toward the neck edge and the unfinished long edge will be even with the unfinished sides of the yokes. The short ends of the straps should barely overlap the bound top edge of the yoke (**see fig. 11**).

7. Pin the straps in place, then topstitch along both long edges of the bias tape at the yoke top edges, using a slightly shortened straight stitch. Both rows of stitching should catch the strap ends. At the back edges, topstitch across the short end of the bias also (**fig. 11**).

8. Refer to the specific instructions at this point for instructions on finishing the skirt.

III. Skirt Construction

1. Refer to the specific instructions for each pinafore for cutting and decorating instructions.

2. Cut a 4¹/₂" slit down the center of the skirt back (**fig. 12**) and insert a back placket:

   a. Cut a strip of fabric from the selvage ³/₄" wide by 10".

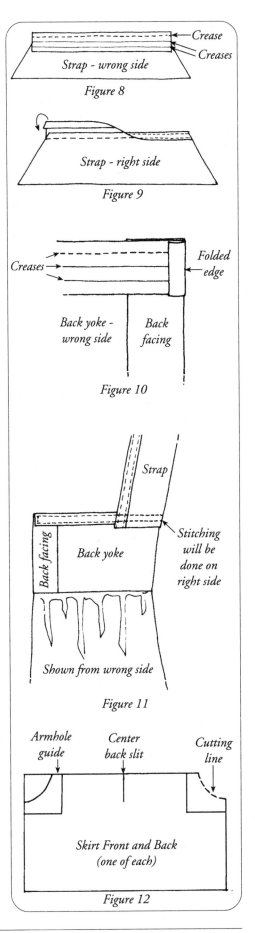

Crease
Creases
Strap - wrong side

Figure 8

Strap - right side

Figure 9

Creases →
Folded edge

Back yoke - wrong side

Back facing

Figure 10

Strap

Back facing

Back yoke

Stitching will be done on right side

Shown from wrong side

Figure 11

Armhole guide

Center back slit

Cutting line

Skirt Front and Back (one of each)

Figure 12

b. Pull the slit in the skirt apart to form a "V". Place the right side of the strip to the right side of the skirt slit. The stitching will be made from the wrong side with the skirt on top and the placket strip on the bottom. The placket strip will be straight and the skirt will form a "V" with the point of the "V" ¹/₄" from the edge of the placket. Stitch, using a ¹/₄" seam. As you stitch, you will just catch the tip (a few fibers) at the point of the "V" (**fig. 13**).

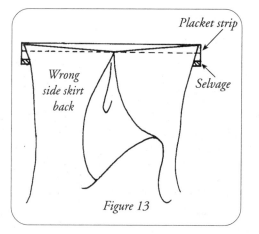

Figure 13

c. Press the seam toward the selvage edge of the placket strip. Turn the selvage edge to the inside of the dress, enclosing the seam allowance. Whip by hand or stitch in place by machine (**fig. 14**).

d. From the wrong side, fold the placket in half so that the top edges of the skirt are even. Stitch a small dart across the bottom fold of the placket, being careful not to catch the skirt in the stitching (**fig. 15**).

3. The back of the pinafore will lap right over left. Fold the right side of the skirt placket to the inside of the skirt and pin. Leave the left skirt placket open (**see fig. 16**).

4. Run two rows of gathering in the top edges of each skirt piece at ¹/₄" and ¹/₈" (**fig. 16**).

5. Refer to the specific instructions at this point and sew one or both side seams. Complete the skirt decoration if needed.

6. After both side seams are sewn, finish the armhole edges with a bias facing. To determine the amount of bias needed, measure one armhole edge and add 1", then double this amount so there will be enough bias for both armholes. See page 248 for instructions to make a ¹/₂" finished bias tape strip, then attach the facing in the following way:

a. Open out the bias strip and pin one raw edge to the raw edge of the armhole, right sides together (**see fig. 17**).

b. Straight stitch along the crease of the bias strip at the ¹/₄" seam line. Trim or clip the seam allowance (**fig. 17**).

c. Fold the bias strip to the inside of the pinafore and press in place (**see fig. 18**).

d. Topstitch the bias facing on the right side ³/₈" from the armhole edge (**see fig. 18**).

e. Trim the excess bias strip away at the top edge of the skirt back and front (**fig. 18**).

IV. Attaching The Skirt To The Yoke

(refer to the specific instructions for any necessary changes before attaching the skirt)

A. Yoke With Entredeux

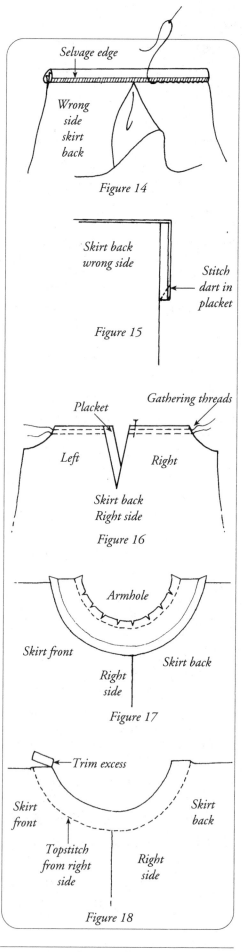

Figure 14

Figure 15

Figure 16

Figure 17

Figure 18

1. Pull up the gathering threads in the skirt front and skirt backs to fit the yoke bottom edges. Match the finished edge of the armholes to the side edges of the yokes. Do not let the skirt extend past the entredeux at the yoke edges. In other words, the entredeux tape at the armhole edges should not be caught in this seam (**fig. 19**).

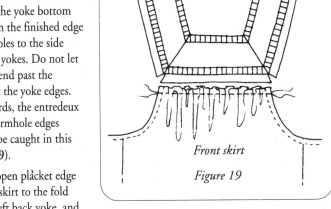

Front skirt

Figure 19

2. Match the open placket edge of the back skirt to the fold line of the left back yoke, and match the folded placket edge to the fold line of the right back yoke. The yoke facings will extend past the plackets (**fig. 20**).

3. Pin the skirt to the yoke, right sides together and attach the two pieces using the entredeux to gathered fabric technique.

4. Reinforce the seam well at the armhole edges and press the seam toward the skirt, away from the entredeux. There will still be entredeux tape along the armhole edges of the yoke; these should be left in place.

5. Refer to the specific instructions for each pinafore at this point. If no other lace or ruffles will be added to the yoke edge, topstitch with a tiny zigzag to hold the seam away from the entredeux.

B. Lined Yoke With No Edge Trim

1. Pull up the gathering threads in the skirt front and skirt backs to fit the yoke bottom edges. Match the finished edge of the armholes to the side edges of the yokes.

2. Pin the skirt to the yoke, right sides together and attach the two pieces using a ¼" seam. Do not catch the yoke lining in this seam (**fig. 21**).

3. Trim the seam to ⅛" and press the seam toward the yoke.

4. Press ¼" to the inside along the lining bottom edges. Pull the pressed edge of the lining pieces over the yoke/skirt seam and stitch in place by hand, or topstitch "in-the-ditch" from the right side (**fig. 22**).

5. Edge-stitch around the yoke on all edges, including the neck.

C. Unlined Yoke With Bias Trim

1. Cut the skirt pieces according to the specific instructions.

2. Insert a placket, using the instructions in section III. steps 1 - 4.

3. Pull up the gathering threads in the skirt front and skirt backs to fit the yoke bottom edges. Match the edges of the armholes to the side edges of the yokes.

4. Match the open placket edge of the back skirt to the fold line of the left back yoke, and match the folded placket edge to the fold line of the right back yoke. The yoke facings will extend past the plackets (**refer to fig. 20**).

5. Pin the skirt to the yoke, right sides together and attach the two pieces using a ¼" seam. Press the seams toward the yokes.

6. Place a strip of ¼" finished double-fold bias tape over the skirt/yoke seams and "baste" in place with a liquid pins product (**see fig. 23**).

7. Topstitch along both long edges of each bias strip with a slightly shortened straight stitch. The seam will be caught in the topstitching so that it will stay in place (**fig. 23**).

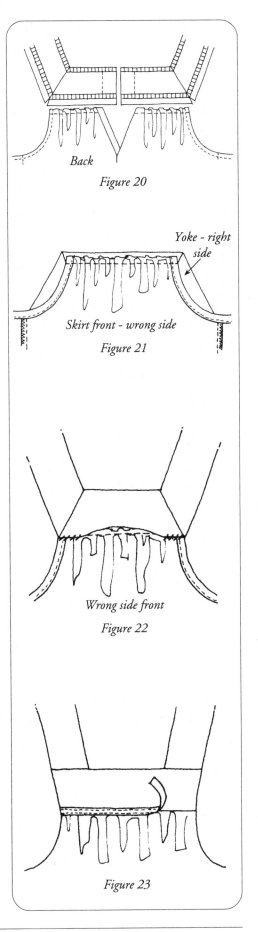

Back

Figure 20

Yoke - right side

Skirt front - wrong side

Figure 21

Wrong side front

Figure 22

Figure 23

8. Fold the back yoke facings to the inside along the fold lines and press in place. Tack the bottom facing edges to the yoke/skirt seams.

V. Yoke Finishes

A. Gathered Lace To Entredeux Around Yoke

1. Cut a piece of edging lace that is twice the length given in the Yoke and Trim chart on page 109. Mark the ruffle into quarters.

2. Pull the heading thread to gather the lace until it is the same as the measurement in the chart, plus $\frac{1}{2}$".

3. Trim the remaining tape edge from the entredeux at the yoke armhole edges (see fig. 24).

4. Butt the gathered edge of the lace to the entredeux edge of the yoke bottom and outer edges. Match the ruffle marks to the center front, strap centers and center backs. Turn $\frac{1}{4}$" to the inside at the back edges of the lace and then attach the edging to the entredeux, using the technique entredeux to gathered lace. The stitching will go through all layers at the skirt/yoke seams in the front and back (fig. 24).

B. Sleeve Ruffle
1. Fabric Or Lace Ruffle With Finished Ends

1. Construct the sleeve ruffle as directed in the specific instructions. Mark the ruffle center.

2. Run gathering rows across the unfinished edge of the ruffles at $\frac{1}{4}$" and $\frac{1}{8}$" from the raw edge, or pull the heading thread if the ruffle edge to be attached is lace.

3. Pull up the gathers to fit the shoulder edge, stopping the finished edge of the ruffle at the point given in the specific instructions (fig. 25).

4. If the ruffle edge is lace, and if there is entredeux tape along the armhole edge, trim away the tape edge. Butt the gathered edge of the lace to the trimmed edge of the entredeux or to the plain finished edge of the lined yoke. Match the ruffle center to the strap center. Attach the lace ruffle using the technique gathered lace to entredeux or lace to lace, using the finished edge of the fabric like a lace edge.

5. If the ruffle edge is gathered fabric, attach the ruffle to the entredeux tape edge using the gathered fabric to entredeux technique.

2. Lace Ruffle With Unfinished Ends

1. Construct the ruffle as directed in the specific instructions. Mark the ruffle center.

2. If there is entredeux tape along the armhole edge, trim it away.

3. Pull the heading thread if the ruffle edge to be attached is lace.

4. Pull up the gathers to fit the shoulder edge, stopping the gathered edge of the ruffle at the point given in the specific instructions. Let the unfinished ends of the ruffle taper off at the armhole edge until the outer edge of the ruffle meets the armhole edge (fig. 26).

5. Butt the gathered edge of the lace to the trimmed edge of the entredeux or to the plain finished edge of the lined yoke. Match the ruffle center to the strap center. Attach the lace ruffle using the technique gathered lace to entredeux or lace to lace, using the finished edge of the fabric like a lace edge.

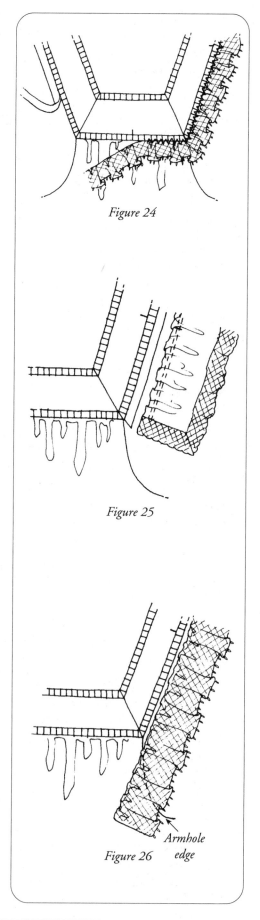

Figure 24

Figure 25

Figure 26   Armhole edge

6. At the point where the gathered edge of the lace stops, let the cut lace edge extend behind the finished armhole edge and taper until the outer edge of the lace meets the armhole edge.

7. From the right side, topstitch along the armhole edge at the edge and again ¼" away (see **fig. 27**).

8. Trim the excess lace away from the inside of the pinafore (**fig. 27**).

C. Fabric Ruffle To Entredeux Around Yoke

1. Create the fabric ruffle according to the specific instructions for the pinafore. Mark the ruffle into quarters.

2. Run gathering rows across the unfinished edge of the ruffles at ¼" and ⅛" from the raw edge.

3. After the yoke is created, pin the ruffle to the yoke, right sides together and raw edges meeting. Match the quarter marks to the center front, shoulder strap centers and center back edges.

4. Attach the ruffle to the entredeux, using a straight stitch "in-the-ditch". Sew in one continuous seam, pivoting at the yoke corners.

5. Refer to the specific instructions to create the skirt.

6. Attach the yoke to the skirt, using the instructions in section IV.A., steps 1 - 3. Continue the roll and whip around the entire yoke edge, finishing the armhole edges at the same time that the yoke seam is finished. Sew in one continuous seam, pivoting at the yoke corners.

D. Bias Trim

1. After the side seams are both sewn, finish the armhole edges with ¼" finished double-fold bias tape, following section II.C., steps 3a - 3e in this section. Begin and end the bias tape at the underarm seams, turning under the beginning end to make a neat overlap at the seam (**refer to figs. 8 and 9**).

VI. Neck Edge With Entredeux And Gathered Lace

1. If there is still an entredeux tape edge at the neck edge, trim away the entredeux tape.

2. Cut a piece of lace edging that is twice as long as the neck length given in the chart for Yoke and Trim Lengths on page 109. Mark the lace into quarters.

3. Pull the heading thread to gather the lace to fit the neck edge.

4. Butt the lace heading to the trimmed entredeux, matching the quarter marks of the lace to the center front, strap centers and center backs.

5. Attach the lace to the neck edge, using the technique lace to entredeux.

6. After the lace is attached, fold the back facings into place and press. Tack the entredeux edges of the facing to the yoke/skirt seam and the entredeux seam at the neck edge (**fig. 28**).

VII. Finishing

1. If the back yoke facings have not been folded to the inside, fold them in and tack the facing edges to the neck and yoke seams. If the facing edges were not cut on the selvage, serge or zigzag across the ends to finish the raw edges.

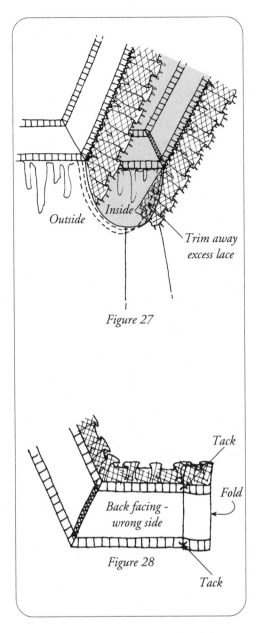

Outside   *Inside*

Trim away excess lace

Figure 27

Tack

Fold

Back facing - wrong side

Figure 28

Tack

2. Lap the back yokes right over left and close with snaps, or buttons and buttonholes.

3. If the skirt has not been hemmed or decorated, finish the bottom edge with a serger or zigzag. Turn the hem allowance to the inside and hem by hand or machine. ▨

Double Lace Scallops Pinafore

Made of pink Swiss Nelona batiste, this is a delightful little summer pinafore. The yoke has been constructed using a strip of pintucked fabric with entredeux attached to each edge. Narrow white French edging has been attached flat and mitered around the neck edge. A wide lace ruffle runs around the entire outer edge of the yoke; this ruffle is composed of strips of beading, insertion and edging. The full skirt falls to a wide bottom band which features vertical pintucks edged on the top and the bottom with lace-shaped beading scallops. Of course, all of the pintucks can easily be made by using a double needle and a pintuck foot. The bottom edge is finished with a wide ruffle made like the one which edges the yoke. The pinafore closes in the back with two buttons and button-holes.

Double Lace Scallops Pinafore

Supplies

In addition to the supplies listed in the general instructions on page 109, the following materials will also be needed:

- 2 yds. of ³/₈" lace insertion
- 20¹/₄ yds. of ⁵/₈" lace insertion
- 2¹/₂ yds. of ³/₈" lace edging
- 7³/₄ yds. of ³/₄" lace edging
- 2³/₄ yds. of entredeux
- **Pattern Pieces Needed:** Mitered Yoke Front, Mitered Yoke Back, Mitered Shoulder Strap, Armhole Guide found on pull-out section
- **Template Needed:** Lace Template for Double Lace Scallops found on page 117

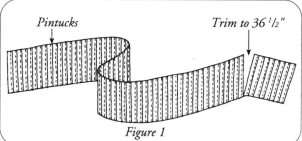

Figure 1

I. Cutting and Preparation

1. Cut or tear two 5" x 45" strips across the fabric. Place the 5" edges along the grain of the fabric. These strips will form the pintucked insert for the hem (see fig. 1).

2. With or without a pintuck foot, make ¹/₈" pintucks ¹/₄" apart and stitch along the 5" direction, covering each strip. When all of the tucks are made, cut the strips to 36¹/₂" long (fig. 1).

3. To decorate fabric for the yoke and shoulder pieces, cut or tear one strip of fabric that is 3" x 45", and one strip that is 3" x 15". Place the 3¹/₂" edges along the grain of the fabric.

4. Make ¹/₈" pintucks that run along the length of the strips. Place six tucks ¹/₄" apart. Make the first tuck ¹/₂" from one long edge of the strip, which will become the top edge (fig. 2).

5. Press all of the tucks toward the bottom of the strips.

6. Place the strips side by side with the tucks matched and tape the two strips together.

7. Before cutting the fabric pieces, a whole strap piece can be made by placing the strap on folded paper and cutting a whole strap.

8. Place the pattern pieces on the fabric strips with the top edges of the pattern pieces lined up on the top edge of the pintucked strips. Cut one front yoke on the fold, two back yokes on the selvage and two shoulder straps (fig. 3).

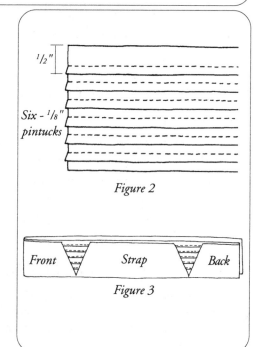

Figure 2

Figure 3

9. Refer to the skirt chart on page 109 and cut two pieces 36$^{1}/_{2}$" wide and 7" shorter than the lengths given in the chart.

II. Construction

1. Refer to the general instructions, section II.A - Mitered Yoke - Entredeux Around Yoke Outer Edge And Neck. Follow steps 2 - 9 to construct an unlined yoke.

2. Finish the Neck Edge as described in the general instructions, section VI. Neck Edge With Entredeux And Gathered Lace.

3. Insert a placket at the skirt center back. See the general instructions, section III. Skirt Construction, steps 2 - 5.

4. Sew the two 36$^{1}/_{2}$" pintucked skirt strips together at one end, right sides together. Trim and overcast the seam. Also sew one side seam of the upper skirt sections, right sides together.

5. Open out the skirt strip and trace the scallop template across the tucked strip at the top edge and the bottom edge. Place the edge of the template $^{1}/_{4}$" from the edge of the fabric, with the tops of the scallops at the top edge of the strip and the bottom curve of the scallops at the bottom edge of the strip.

6. Refer to the new technique section, page 249, and shape the double lace scallops across the pintucked skirt strip.

7. After the skirt decoration is finished, create a bottom ruffle:

    a. Cut two strips of $^{5}/_{8}$" lace insertion and one strip of $^{3}/_{4}$" lace edging, each twice as long as the width of the skirt edge.

    b. Attach the two strips of insertion, using the technique lace to lace.

    c. Attach the edging to one long edge of the insertions, using the technique lace to lace.

    d. Pull the heading thread in the free insertion edge and gather the ruffle to fit the bottom edge of the scalloped skirt.

    e. Attach the ruffle to the skirt bottom edge, using the technique lace to lace.

8. Sew the remaining side seam, from the bottom edge of the ruffle to the top edge of the skirt, with right sides together. Trim and overcast the seam.

9. Return to the general instructions, section III. Skirt Construction, step 6 and complete the skirt.

10. Attach the skirt to the yoke, general instructions section IV.A., Yoke With Entredeux.

11. Create a yoke ruffle by following steps 7a - 7e, replacing references to the skirt with yoke.

12. Refer to the general instructions, section V.A. Gathered Lace To Entredeux Around Yoke. Use the technique gathered lace to entredeux to attach the ruffle to the yoke.

13. Refer to the general instructions, VII. Finishing. ▨

Double Lace Scallops Pinafore with Dress

Double Lace Scallops Pinafore

Lace Template

Show 3

Ribbons and Lace Pinafore

Using purchased ribbon pieces with ribbon puffing built-in between the wonderful embroidered edges, the yoke of the pinafore was made by mitering this ribbon. Beautiful ribbons are hard to find, but you occasionally come upon a piece like this one. The mitered trim on the skirt is matching ribbon in a little more narrow version, with machine feather stitch following the mitered shapes. The machine feather stitching is done in shades of ecru, pink and lavender. The bottom row of ecru feather stitching also attaches the hem of the dress. White medium-weight linen is the pinafore fabric and beautiful wide ecru French lace forms the ruffles over the shoulders. The back closes with snaps.

Ribbon and Lace Pinafore

Supplies

In addition to the supplies listed in the general instructions on page 109, the following materials will also be needed:

- ✪ An additional ¹/₃ yd. of the pinafore fabric
- ✪ 3 yds. of 1" wide decorative ribbon
- ✪ 2 yds. of 1⁵/₈" wide decorative ribbon
- ✪ 2 yds. of 3¹/₂" wide lace edging
- ✪ Machine embroidery thread, one or more colors to coordinate with the decorative ribbon
- ✪ Notions: two snaps (no buttons)
- ✪ **Pattern Pieces Needed:** Mitered Yoke Front, Mitered Yoke Back, Mitered Shoulder Strap, Armhole Guide found on pull-out section
- ✪ **Template Needed:** Zigzagged Ribbon Template for Ribbons and Lace Pinafore found on pull-out section

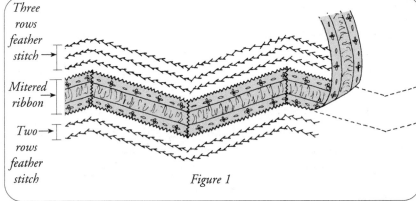

Figure 1

(labels in figure: Three rows feather stitch; Mitered ribbon; Two rows feather stitch)

I. Cutting and Preparation

1. Before cutting the fabric pieces, a whole strap piece can be made by placing the strap on folded paper and cutting a whole strap.

2. From plain fabric, cut two front yokes on the fold, four back yokes on the selvages and four shoulder straps.

3. Refer to the skirt chart on page 109 and cut two pieces 36¹/₂" wide and 6" longer than the lengths given in the chart.

II. Construction

1. Refer to the general instructions, section II.B. Mitered Yoke - Lined, No Edge Trim, steps 2 - 8.

2. Insert a placket at the skirt center back. See the general instructions, section III. steps 2 - 5.

3. Sew one side seam of the skirt; trim and overcast the seam allowance.

4. Trace the skirt zigzag template (including miter lines) onto the skirt piece, with the bottom edge of the template 5³/₄" above the bottom edge of the skirt. Place a "down" point at center front and back. "Down" points will also meet at the side seams.

5. Miter the 1" wide decorative ribbon over the template lines and zigzag in place along both edges. Also zigzag the miters in place. Refer to Making Lace Diamonds in the technique section for mitering instructions (**see fig. 1**).

6. Use the machine embroidery thread to stitch three rows of feather stitching above the ribbon, following the template lines and pivoting at the miter lines. A good stitching guide is the edge of the machine foot (**see fig. 1**).

7. Stitch two rows of feather stitching below the ribbon the same as the rows above. Do not stitch the third row until after the hem is in place (**fig. 1**).

8. Sew the second side seam of the skirt; trim and overcast the seam allowance.

9. Press under a 6" hem allowance and pin or baste in place.

10. Stitch the third row of feather stitching below the ribbon, catching the edge of the hem in the stitching. Trim the excess hem edge away from behind the stitching (**fig. 2**).

11. Continue with the pinafore general instructions, section III, step 6, a - c, on page 112. The facings will be topstitched in place after the lace armhole ruffles are attached.

12. Attach the yoke to the skirt, referring to the pinafore general instructions, section IV.B, steps 1 - 4. The facings will be in place on the inside of the pinafore, but are not yet stitched. Baste the lining in place with a liquid pins product, it will be stitched in a later step.

13. Cut the 3 1/2" wide lace edging into two pieces. Pull the heading thread to gather the lace to fit the armhole edges, stopping the headings of the lace at the yoke/skirt seam.

14. Adjust the gathers evenly, butt the headings to the armhole edges and zigzag, using the same technique as lace to lace.

15. Let the cut edges of the lace extend into the inside of the pinafore at the armhole edges so that the outer edge of the lace meets the finished armhole edge and extends 1/2" into the pinafore.

16. Topstitch through all layers at the armhole edges and again 1/4" away, catching the facings and the lace in the stitching. Trim away the excess lace ends.

17. Miter the 1 5/8" ribbon over the yoke, beginning and ending at the back edges. Leave 1" extended at each back edge to be turned in. Miter the ribbon at each corner. Topstitch the ribbon in place along both edges, and stitch the miters in place (**fig. 3**).

18. Zigzag the raw ends of the ribbon, then turn the ribbon ends to the inside and whip to the lining.

19. Refer to section VII of the general instructions to finish the pinafore, lapping the back edges right over left and using snaps as closures. Buttons may be sewn over the snaps if desired, but it will be best not to try to work buttonholes through the ribbon and yoke layers. ▨

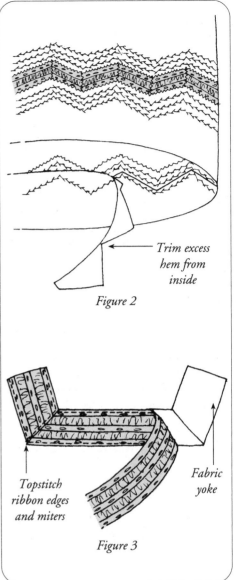

Trim excess hem from inside

Figure 2

Topstitch ribbon edges and miters

Fabric yoke

Figure 3

Ribbon and Lace Pinafore with Dress

Show 5
Smocked Pinafore and Square Collar Blouse

Red baby-wale corduroy is the perfect fabric for this school pinafore with smocking done in black and a plain turned up hem. It could just as easily be made into an elegant holiday outfit by using a silk fabric smocked in a complementary shade of floss or silk ribbon. The blouse is made as a variation of the dress pattern from this book using white Swiss batiste Nelona. The short puffed sleeves are finished with a narrow binding at the bottom. The blouse collar is perfectly fabulous with the machine-embroidered beetles playing a trombone and a drum. There is a wonderful border of double needle edge trim done in red and black thread around the outer edge of the collar; white tatting is shaped around this beautiful edge embellishment. The pinafore and the blouse close with buttons and buttonholes.

Square Collar Blouse found on page 107

Smocked Pinafore

Supplies

❁ Featherweight corduroy was used for the garment shown, and it is worn as a jumper over the Square Collar Blouse (instructions are included in the section for specific dress instructions). Do not use a fabric heavier than featherweight corduroy because of the smocking.

Additional Supplies

❁ An additional $^1/_3$ yd. of fabric is needed
❁ Black floss for smocking
❁ Replace $^1/_2$" buttons with $^5/_8$" - $^3/_4$" if corduroy is used
❁ **Pattern Pieces Required:** Mitered Front and Back Yokes, Mitered Shoulder Strap, Armhole Guide found on pull-out section
❁ **Smocking Graph:** Smocked Pinafore Graph found 121

I. Cutting and Preparation

1. From the fabric, cut two yoke fronts on the fold and four yoke backs on the selvage.

2. Cut or tear the skirt pieces, each 5" longer than the measurement given in the chart found on page 109.

3. Trace the armholes onto the skirt pieces, but do not cut them out.

4. Pleat eight whole-space rows across the top edge of the skirt front piece. Place the first pleating row $^1/_8$" from the top cut edge of the skirt. The top and bottom rows are holding rows and will not be smocked. Remove the pleating threads from the sides to a line $^3/_8$" inside the armhole seam line at the top edge of the skirt (**fig. 1**).

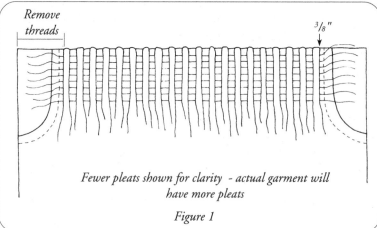

Fewer pleats shown for clarity - actual garment will have more pleats

Figure 1

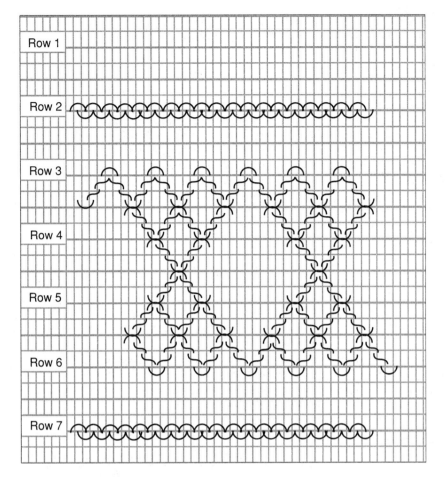

II. Construction

1. Construct the yoke according to the pinafore general directions, section II.B. Mitered Yoke - Lined, No Edge Trim.

2. Cut the armholes in the skirt pieces and construct the skirt, using the general pinafore instructions, section III, steps 2 - 6. Sew both side seams in step 5.

3. Follow the pinafore general instructions, section IV.B. Lined Yoke With No Edge Trim, to attach the skirt to the yoke.

4. Refer to the general pinafore instructions, section VII. Finishing. The hem allowance is 5". 🔲

Smocked Pinafore

5. Use three strands of floss to smock six rows as follows:

   a. Cable across row 2.

   b. Between rows 3 and $3^{1}/_{2}$, smock 2-step waves: * down cable on row $3^{1}/_{2}$, two steps up to row 3, up cable, two steps down to row $3^{1}/_{2}$, repeat from * across the row.

   c. Between rows $3^{1}/_{2}$ and 4, work two 2-step waves to form two diamonds under the previous row, beginning with an up cable under a down cable of the previous row. Skip one wave and work two more 2-step waves; repeat across the row. Refer to the graph.

   d. Begin with an up cable under the first down cable of the previous row and work one 2-step wave between rows 4 and $4^{1}/_{2}$, forming a diamond.

   e. Between rows $4^{1}/_{2}$ and 6, work a mirror image of rows 3 to $4^{1}/_{2}$.

   f. Work cables across row 7.

6. Steam and block the smocking. Do not remove the holding threads until the garment construction is completed.

Square Collar Blouse
Instructions found on page 107

Show 6

Antique Peek-a-Boo Pinafore

If you will look in the antique clothing section of this book, you will see the original antique garment from which we took this technique. The name of the antique dress is "Triangular Ruffle Christening Dress." We called the technique used on the center bodice and the skirt of this antique dress "peek-a-boo" lace. This pinafore is made of white Nelona Swiss batiste and the bodice uses round thread lace with bias strips crossed in the peek-a-boo fashion. Gathered white French edging goes around the bodice of this pinafore in both the front and the back. The underdress is blue silk dupioni. The peek-a-boo technique is used on the skirt also. The hem of the pinafore is double and the pinafore closes with two buttons and buttonholes.

Antique Peek-a-Boo Pinafore

Supplies

❁ In addition to the supplies listed in the general instructions, the following will also be needed:

❁ An additional ⁵/₈ yd. of pinafore fabric

❁ 3¹/₂ yds. of ⁵/₈" wide lace insertion

❁ 3 yds. of ⁷/₈" wide lace edging

❁ **Notions:** liquid pins product, ¹/₂" bias tape maker, water-soluble stabilizer

❁ **Pattern Pieces Required:** Square Yoke Front and Back, Square Yoke Shoulder, Armhole Guide found on pull-out section

I. Cutting and Preparation

1. Cut two back yokes on the selvage and two shoulder straps.

2. Cut or tear two skirt pieces, each 6" longer than the measurements given in the chart on page 109.

3. Cut enough 1" wide bias strips to make nine yards of bias tape.

4. Refer to the instructions on page 248 to make ¹/₄" finished double-fold bias tape for the Antique Peek-a-Boo technique.

II. Constructing the Yoke

1. Refer to the instructions for Antique Peek-a-Boo on page 251 and create a rectangle large enough to cut the front yoke from (**fig. 1**).

2. Refer to the general instructions, section II.C. Square Yoke - Bias Trimmed Edges, steps 3 - 7.

III. Constructing the Skirt

1. Refer to the general pinafore instructions, section III. Skirt Construction, steps 2 - 5. Sew both side seams.

2. Press the 6" hem allowance to the wrong side. Pin or baste in place.

3. Refer to the Antique Peek-a-Boo Lace Skirt Band instructions on page 251, steps 2 - 9. Since both side seams are already sewn, overlap the ends of the lace and the bias tape strips at one side seam and topstitch in place to finish the raw ends (**fig. 2**).

4. Follow the instructions in the pinafore general instructions, section III. Skirt Construction, step 6, finishing the armhole edges.

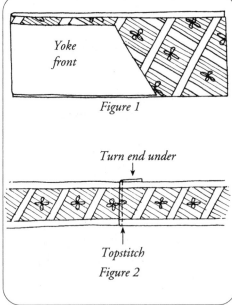

Yoke front

Figure 1

Turn end under

Topstitch

Figure 2

5. Attach the skirt to the yoke, following the instructions in the general pinafore instructions, section IV.C. Unlined Yoke With Bias Trim.

IV. Finishing the Pinafore

1. See section VII of the general pinafore instructions. ▨

Embroidered Panels Pinafore

I adore the new embroidery stitches on today's sewing and embroidery machines. What fun we in the heirloom industry are having since embroidery is our middle name. This paneled pinafore is made of baby blue Nelona Swiss batiste and it features ecru French laces around the neckline and around the angel sleeves. The panels in the dress have beautiful ecru heirloom machine embroidery running vertically. On the two front panels which do not have embroidery, there are three one-quarter-inch tucks in the middle. The vertical strips of ecru lace insertion are stitched to the dress using wing needle/machine entredeux. Even the bottom fancy band is gorgeous with three tucks of the baby blue batiste and a flat piece of ecru French lace insertion stitched to the bottom of the tucked strip. The perfect finish for the bottom of the dress is a piece of ecru French edging stitched on flat. The pinafore closes in the back with two buttonholes and pearl buttons. What a beautiful pinafore to be worn by itself for a sweet summer outfit or to be worn over a dress for almost anytime of year.

Embroidered Panels Pinafore

Supplies

❂ In addition to the supplies listed in the pinafore general instructions, the following supplies and notions will be needed:

❂ ⁵/₈" wide insertion lace: size 4, 8³/₄ yds.; size 6, 9¹/₄ yds.; size 8, 10 yds.; size 10, 10³/₄ yds.; size 12, 11¹/₄ yds.

❂ 1" wide edging lace - 5 yds., all sizes

❂ ¹/₂" wide edging lace - 1¹/₄ yds., all sizes

❂ entredeux - 2³/₄ yds., all sizes

❂ Notions: machine embroidery thread and stabilizer, or hand embroidery supplies

❂ **Pattern Pieces Required:** Mitered Yoke Front and Back, Mitered Yoke Shoulder Strap, Armhole Guide found on pull-out section

❂ **Template Required (optional):** Panel and Yoke Embroidery Templates for Embroidered Panel Pinafore found on page 124

I. Cutting and Preparation

1. Trace the front yoke onto a rectangle of fabric, but do not cut it out.

2. Cut two back yokes on the selvage, and cut two shoulder straps.

3. Cut two pieces for the armhole ruffles, each 3" wide and twice as long as the outer edge of the shoulder strap.

4. Cut or tear two skirt pieces 36¹/₂" wide and 3¹/₂" shorter than the measurements given in the chart on page 109. Use the armhole guide to cut the armholes in the skirt backs and front.

5. Cut two strips across the fabric, each 3³/₄" by 36¹/₂", with the long edge going across the fabric.

6. Make a line from the top edge to the bottom edge of the skirt front piece, 8" from one side edge. Repeat for the other side.

7. Between the two end lines, make four more lines 4" apart. This creates five 4" wide panels across the skirt front.

8. Refer to the new technique directions for Built-In Machine Embroidery on Heirloom Clothing, found on page 255. In the center panel and the two outer 4" panels of the skirt front, work a machine embroidery design from top to bottom, or work several

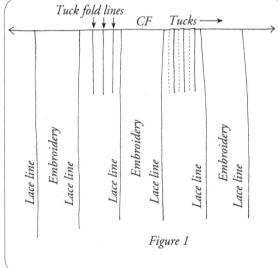

Figure 1

designs to fill in the panel. If no machine embroidery unit is available, use the template provided on page 124 and work the embroidery by hand or machine. Designs may be flipped from left to right to give a balanced look. Be sure that the designs are centered from side to side, because lace will be added along the lines separating the panels and if the designs are not centered, it will show.

9. Work a coordinating design centered on the front yoke by hand or machine, using a machine design or the template provided on this page. After the embroidery is complete, cut out the front yoke.

II. Construction

1. Refer to the pinafore general instructions, section II.A. Mitered Yoke - Entredeux Around Yoke Outer Edge And Neck, steps 2 - 9.

2. Place lace insertion along the panel lines on the skirt front , with the center of the lace over the lines. Make sure that the embroidery designs are centered between the lace strips.

3. Attach the insertion lace to the skirt piece with a machine pinstitch along each edge. Use a removable stabilizer if necessary. Carefully trim the fabric away from behind the insertion strips.

4. In the two un-embroidered panels, make three tucks (**refer to fig. 1**):

   a. Draw a line parallel to the lace that is closest to the center. The line should be 1" from the lace and 6" from the top edge of the skirt to the bottom of the line.

   b. Make two more lines, each 1" from the previous line and 6" long.

   c. Fold along the fold lines and press the tucks in place.

   d. Stitch the tucks in place, $^1/_4$" from the fold lines, through both layers.

   e. Press the tucks toward the outside edge of the skirt, away from the center.

5. Refer to the pinafore general instructions, section III, steps 2 - 5.

6. Work three tucks lengthwise in each $3^3/_4$" strip of fabric, placed as follows (refer to the finished drawing):

   a. Draw the first fold line $^3/_4$" from the top edge of the strip.

   b. Draw two more fold lines, each 1" below the previous line. The bottom line should be 1" above the bottom edge of the fabric strip.

   c. Fold along the fold lines and press the tucks in place.

   d. Stitch the tucks in place, $^1/_4$" from the fold lines, through both layers.

   e. Press the tucks toward the bottom edge of the fabric strip.

7. After both strips have been tucked, lace a strip of the lace insertion along the bottom edge and the top edge of each strip, letting the lace overlap the edge of the skirt by $^1/_4$". Attach the lace with a pinstitch and trim as before.

8. Attach the top edges of the strips to the bottom edges of the skirt pieces (remember that the tucks are pressed toward the bottom edge). Overlap the fabric with the lace by $^1/_4$" and pinstitch and trim as before.

9. Sew one side seam of the skirt, then attach 1" wide edging lace to the bottom insertion edge of the skirt, using the technique lace to lace.

10. Sew the remaining side seam of the skirt.

11. Refer to the general instructions, section III, step 6 to finish the armhole edges.

12. Attach the skirt, following the general instructions, section IV.A, steps 1 - 4.

13. Attach 1" wide edging to one long edge and both short ends of each ruffle piece. Overlap the lace headings onto the fabric by $^1/_4$" and attach with a pinstitch, then trim as before. Finish the yoke edge (general instructions section V.B1 Fabric Or Lace Ruffle With Finished Ends), stopping the edge of the lace at the yoke seam.

14. Finish the neck edge (general instructions section VI. Neck Edge With Entredeux And Gathered Lace), with the lace attached flat, not gathered (omit step 3).

15. Follow the instructions in the general instructions, section VII. Finishing. ◾

Hand embroidery template for yoke of Embroidered Panels Pinafore

Hand embroidery template for panels down skirt of Embroidered Panels Pinafore

♢ *Template repeats*

Show 9
Tone on Tone Corded Appliqué Pinafore

This has to be one of the most elegant garments ever made in heirloom sewing. Beautiful simplicity is the order of the day with the navy blue wool and cotton challis short sleeved dress. The neck ruffle is especially pretty since it is navy blue challis also. The white pinafore is made of white organdy with white batiste corded shadow appliqué scallops on both the front and the back. The mitered bodice of the pinafore is organdy lined with the white Swiss batiste. Entredeux is found around the neck opening and Swiss entredeux is stitched around the outer edge of the bodice also. French edging is gathered to the Swiss entredeux for a simple but elegant treatment. The scallops on this pinafore hem number three on the front and three on the back. The pinafore appears to tie under the arm; however, there is just a little bow stitched there because the pinafore front and back are actually joined under the arm. This is a very beautiful technique and I think a magnificent garment. The pinafore closes in the back with two buttonholes and two pearl buttons.

Tone on Tone Corded Appliqué Pinafore

Supplies

Purchase the amount of organdy called for in the general supplies; this is the pinafore fabric. In addition to the supplies listed in the general instructions, the following supplies and notions will also be needed:

- ✪ Swiss batiste for shadows - two skirt lengths plus 6"
- ✪ 6 yds. of ³/₄" wide edging
- ✪ 3 yds. of entredeux
- ✪ 3 yds. of 1¹/₂" wide decorative ribbon
- ✪ Cotton or rayon machine embroidery thread
- ✪ **Template Required:** Corded Appliqué Pinafore template found on center pull-out section
- ✪ **Pattern Pieces Required:** Panel and Yoke Templates for Shoulder Strap and Armhole Guide found on pull-out section

I. Cutting and Preparing the Skirt

1. Cut or tear two skirt pieces from the batiste and two from the organdy, each 42" wide and the length given in the chart on page 109. Starch and press the pieces.

2. Trace the skirt template lines onto the organdy skirt pieces, using a washable marker or pencil on the right side of the fabric. Place the bottom edge of the template ¹/₄" above the bottom edge of the skirt pieces.

3. Place one organdy skirt piece over one batiste piece, with the right sides up.

4. Baste the two layers together along the inner template lines with a straight stitch.

5. Refer to Corded Shadow Appliqué on page 244 and work the inner template lines, #1, #2, #3 and # 4, trimming away the areas shown on the template. Save the outer edge of the fabric that is trimmed away and the inner piece that is trimmed away (**fig. 1**).

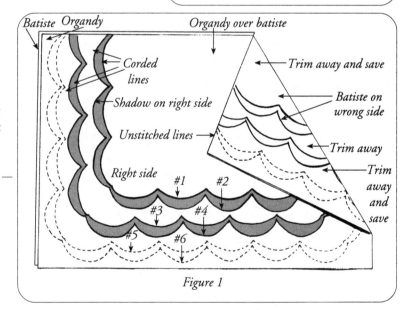

Figure 1

6. Place the outer trimmed piece of the batiste on the right side of the organdy skirt, matching the edges. Stitch along the outer template line #6, using a slightly shortened straight stitch (**see fig. 2**).

7. Use a short, close zigzag (L - 1.0, W - 1.0) to stitch just outside the straight stitches.

8. Trim away the seam allowance close to the zigzags, being very careful not to cut into the stitches (**see fig. 2**).

9. Turn the batiste edge to the inside underneath the organdy, enclosing the seam between the two layers. Carefully press the seam so that the seam is on the edge of the crease (**see fig. 2**).

10. Baste the layers together along the remaining template line, #5, then work the corded appliqué as before (**fig. 2**).

11. Repeat steps 3 - 10 for the remaining organdy and batiste skirt pieces.

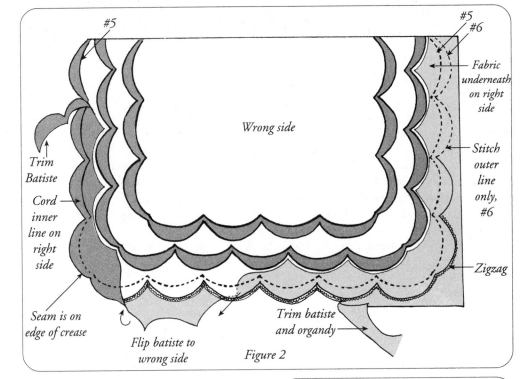

Figure 2

12. Use the armhole guide to trace and cut the armholes from the skirt pieces. Refer to the pinafore general instructions, section III. Skirt Construction, steps 2 - 5.

13. Place the two skirt pieces side by side, right sides up. Butt the two side edges together and zigzag the two edges together along the top 2" of the side seams, using a L - 1.5 and W - 1.5. Repeat for the remaining side seam.

14. Return to the pinafore general instructions section III, step 6. Use batiste scraps to make the bias facings from.

II. Yokes and Final Construction

1. Refer to the pinafore general instructions section II.A. Mitered Yoke - Entredeux Around Outer Edge And Neck, steps 2 - 9 to make a lined yoke. Use organdy as the outer layer and use the batiste scraps for the lining.

2. Refer to the pinafore general instructions, section IV. A. Yoke With Entredeux, steps 1 - 4.

3. Finish the yoke edges, using the pinafore general instructions section V.A. Gathered Lace To Entredeux Around Yoke.

4. See the pinafore general instructions section VI to finish the neck edge and section VII to finish the pinafore.

5. Cut the decorative ribbon in half and fold two bows with long streamers and bow knots (**fig. 3**). Stitch a bow at each side seam, below the armhole. ▨

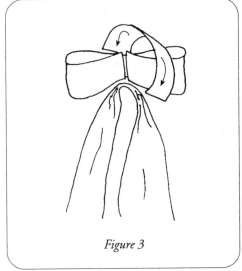

Figure 3

Lace and Tucks Pinafore

I love tucks. Many of you already know that since you have been reading my publications for years. Tucks are easy to make and don't cost any money, this tucked pinafore is a real beauty. A band made of French lace edged by Swiss insertion on each side is mitered to form the yoke. Wide white French lace makes the ruffles on the sleeves and narrow gathered French edging finishes the neck edge of the bodice. The skirt features five tucks with a feather stitch at the top and the bottom. The hem of the dress was folded up and the feather stitch not only embellishes this area but hems the garment. A beautiful wide white French lace edging is zigzagged to the bottom of the dress to make this a pinafore which could be worn for any occasion.

Lace and Tucks Pinafore

Supplies

In addition to the supplies listed in the general instructions, the following materials will also be needed:

❂ $3^1/2$ yds. of $1/2$" wide Swiss insertion

❂ $1^3/4$ yds. of $5/8$" wide lace insertion

❂ $3^1/2$ yds. of $2^1/4$" wide lace edging

❂ $2^1/4$ yds. of $3/8$" wide lace edging

❂ Notions: use two small snaps to close the back of the pinafore instead of buttons and buttonholes

❂ **Pattern Pieces Required:** Mitered Yoke Front and Back, Armhole Guide, Mitered Yoke Shoulder found on pull-out section

I. Cutting and Preparation

1. Cut or tear two skirt pieces, each $36^1/2$" wide and 4" longer than the measurements given in the chart on page 109.

2. Cut the $1/2$" Swiss insertion into two pieces, each $1^3/4$ yards long. Make a lace band in the following order: $1/2$" Swiss insertion, $5/8$" lace insertion, and $1/2$" Swiss insertion, using the entredeux to lace technique (**fig. 1**).

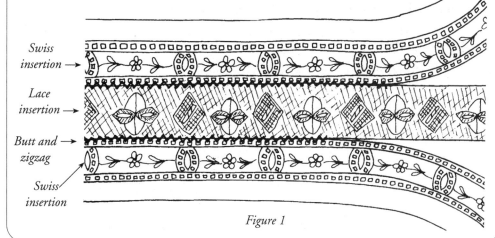

Swiss insertion →

Lace insertion →

Butt and zigzag →

Swiss insertion →

Figure 1

3. Place the outer seam line of the yoke and shoulder pattern pieces along the bottom entredeux edge of the lace band created in step 2 above. Make sure that the pattern edges line up all the way across, so that the design will be continuous around the yoke. Cut one front yoke on the fold, two yoke backs and two shoulder pieces on the fold, or create a full shoulder pattern and cut two shoulder pieces. Mark the back yoke fold lines, center front and shoulder centers (see general instructions fig. 1 on page 109).

II. Construction

Refer to the finished drawing during construction.

1. Place the shoulder pieces to the yoke pieces, right sides together and sew the seams. Finish the seams with a serger or zigzag.

2. Refer to the general pinafore instructions, section III, steps 2 - 5 to begin the skirt construction. Sew one side seam, and finish the seam edges.

3. Draw a line across the skirt pieces, 7" above the bottom cut edge. Working toward the bottom edge, draw four more lines, each $^1/_2$" below the previous line.

4. Fold the skirt along each line, wrong sides together, and press a crease on each line to mark five tucks.

5. Stitch $^1/_8$" from each folded line to create the tucks. Press the tucks toward the bottom edge of the skirt.

6. Press under $^1/_4$" along the bottom of the skirt edge, then press a $2^1/_2$" hem to the wrong side. Topstitch the hem in place from the right side, using a tiny feather stitch, by hand or machine.

7. Measure the distance from the bottom tuck to the feather-stitched hem edge. Make another row of feather stitches that same distance above the top tuck, so that the tucks are centered between the feather-stitched rows.

8. Butt the $2^1/_4$" wide lace edging to the folded bottom edge of the hem and zigzag the two together, using a zigzag set for L - 1.5, W - 1.5.

9. Sew the remaining side seam, being careful to match the tucks, feather stitching and lace-to-hem seams as they meet at the side seam.

10. Continue with section III, step 6 of the pinafore general instructions.

11. Attach the skirt to the yoke using the general instructions, section IV.A, steps 1 -5. Zigzag the skirts over the yoke seam to hold the seam away from the entredeux.

12. Make and attach sleeve ruffles using the remaining $2^1/_4$" wide lace edging, referring to section V.B.2.

13. Refer to the pinafore general instructions, section VI to finish the neck edge.

14. Refer to the pinafore general instructions, section VII, steps 1 and 2 to finish the pinafore. ▨

Lace and Tucks Pinafore with Dress

Antique Bonnet

Antique Pinafore Doll Dress

Antique Peek–A–Boo Pinafore

Machine Embroidery
Tatting Pillow

Shadow
Sandwich
Pinafore

Triangular Pillow

Scalloped
Lace
Pinafore

Pintucks and
Lace Pinafore

Heirloom Puffing Dress

French Knot Lamb
Pinafore

Oval Lace Picture
Transfer Pinafore

Shoe Bag, Ribbon Thread Pillow, Pintucked Doll Dress with Embellished Pinafore

Ribbons and Lace Pinafore, Dainty Photo Pillow and Corded Shadow Applique Pillow

Metallic Gimp Pillow

Lace Fan Pillow

Victorian Watch Brooch

Sweet Gloves

Lacy Bear

Victorian Picture Frame

Looking Glass

Shoe Ornament

Boot Ornament

Angel Stocking

Pillow/Lap Quilt

Crazy Patch Vest

Satin Party Dress

*Couched Ribbon
Pinafore*

*Holiday
Pinafore*

Embroidered
Panels
Pinafore

Antique Peek–A–Boo
Pinafore

Tone On Tone
Corded
Appliqué
Pinafore

Santa's Sack

Smocked
Pinafore

Pillow/Lap
Quilt

Lace and
Tucks
Pinafore

Ribbon Diamonds
Picture Transfer
Pinafore

Double Lace
Scallops Pinafore

Ribbons and Lace
Pinafore

Lace
Scallops On
Lace

Organdy
Pinafore
with
Serger
Ruffles

Corded
Appliqué
Pinafore

Above: Ribbon Message Board

Left: Fancy Napkin and Decorative Lunch Tray

Below: Mannequin, Armchair Hussif and Decoupage
*   Suitcases*

*Linen Bag, Metallic Trim Neck Roll Pillow,
Rose Pillow and Basketweave Scissors Case*

Ribbon Embellished Lamp Shades, Hearts and Vines Box Lid

*Decoupage Tissue Boxes, Baby Powder Cover
and Heart Door Hangers*

*Close–up of Bassinet Skirt and
Covered Hood with Paneled Canopy*

Above: Baby Blanket and Pillow Case

Left: Bassinet Skirt and Covered Hood, Paneled Canopy

Diaper Stacker

Detail of Bassinet Covered Hood

Close–up of Diaper Stacker

Above: Heirloom Angel Quilt

*Above: One of the lovely wreaths on the
Heirloom Angel Quilt*

*Above: Silk ribbon between the
squares on the Heirloom Angel Quilt*

Angel Square

Angel Square

Wreath Square

Corner Angel

Center Square

Angel Square

Left: Tone On Tone Corded
Appliqué Pinafore and Oval
Lace Picture Transfer Pinafore

Middle: Embroidered Panels
Pinafore and Lace Scallops
On Lace

Right: Holiday Pinafore
and French Knot Lamb
Pinafore

Martha's SEWING ROOM

P.B.S. T.V. Program Video Series 600

Filmed and produced by The University of Alabama Center For Public Television

600 Series Videos

A set of three videos is available for
the 100, 200, 300, 400, 500 series, also.

$29.95

For Each Video-American VHS Format*
(postage paid)
Video 600-A contains 5 (26 min.) shows: Video 600-B
and Video 600-C each contain 4 (26 min.) shows

Video 600-A

601 Double Lace Scallops: Host Martha Pullen shows how to make double lace scallops and pintucks on a girl's pinafore. Also shown are a ruffled rose pillow, silk ribbon fuchsias, an heirloom angel quilt square and a lace scalloped doll dress; vintage clothing.

602 Ribbon Thread Technique: The easy technique of using specialty threads in your bobbin is demonstrated on a ribbon thread pillow. Host Martha Pullen also shows a decoupage suitcase, heirloom angel quilt square, pintucks and scalloped lace doll dress, and vintage clothing.

603 Ribbon Manipulation: Ribbon manipulation techniques are shown on ribbon embellished lamp shades, ribbons and bows doll dress, and a ribbon message board. A silk ribbon iris is shown on an armchair hussif; vintage clothing.

604 Nursery Ensemble: Martha Pullen shows how easy it is to make an elegant ensemble to fit a purchased bassinet. Also shown are a beautiful linen set, lacy bear, baby powder cover and heart door pillow for the baby's room, a French knot lamb pinafore to dress your doll; vintage clothing.

605 Girl's Jumpers: Martha Pullen shows how easy it is to make a little girl's lined jumper. Also: a lace fan pillow, heirloom angel quilt square, silk ribbon side stitch, a shadow sandwich pinafore doll dress, and vintage clothing.

Video 600-B

606 Antique Peek-A-Boo: This elegant technique is one that Martha Pullen has updated to reproduce the antique look on a girl's pinafore and a doll pinafore. Also shown are a shoe bag, Victorian picture frame, and vintage clothing.

607 Sewing Machine Tatting: Sewing machine tatting is a great technique used on a cutwork/tatting pillow. Martha Pullen also shows a scalloped lace doll pinafore, embroidered panels pinafore for little girls, and an heirloom angel quilt square. A no-fail French knot is also shown; vintage clothing. Guest: Sue Hausmann.

608 Teddy Bear Dressing: Martha Pullen shows some cute ideas for dressing up your teddy bears in crazy patch vests, an elegant satin dress, and a fancy dress with puffing. You'll also see an embellished looking glass, heirloom angel quilt square, dress form mannequins, a pintucked dress and pinafore set for your doll, and vintage clothing.

609 Corded Shadow Appliqué: Making beautiful corded shadow appliqué is easy when Martha Pullen shows you how. Also shown are a metallic gimp pillow, silk ribbon weaving stitch, a girl's tone-on-tone corded appliqué pinafore as well as a corded appliqué pinafore doll dress; vintage clothing.

Video 600–C

610 Decorative Serging: Serging with decorative threads is fun and fast. See a beautiful metallic trim neckroll pillow and a doll dress with serger ruffles. Also included on the show are a decorative lunch tray, an heirloom angel quilt square, and vintage clothing. Guest: Ann Riegel

611 Picture Transfer: This fun new technique is shown in detail by host Martha Pullen. Projects include an oval lace picture transfer pinafore for a doll and a ribbon diamonds picture transfer pinafore for a little girl. Also shown are silk ribbon long and short stitch, a dainty photo pillow, a Victorian watch brooch, sweet gloves; vintage clothing.

612 Happy Holidays: Martha Pullen shows you how easy it is to make beautiful angel decorations, a Santa's sack, angel stocking, and boot and shoe ornaments for your tree. Also included on the show are a couched ribbon pinafore doll dress and a holiday pinafore for a little girl's dress and vintage clothing.

613 Hand Embroidery And Quilt Construction: Details on how to construct the heirloom angel quilt from the squares which have been described in earlier shows. Also, a segment on favorite heirloom embroidery stitches for babies. Other projects are an antique pinafore doll dress and a triangular pillow; vintage clothing.

VIDEO ORDER FORM

Check		Quantity	Price
☐	Video 600-A	____	29.95
☐	Video 600-B	____	29.95
☐	Video 600-C	____	29.95
☐	Video 500-A	____	29.95
☐	Video 500-B	____	29.95
☐	Video 500-C	____	29.95
☐	Video 400-A	____	29.95
☐	Video 400-B	____	29.95
☐	Video 400-C	____	29.95
☐	Video 300-A	____	29.95
☐	Video 300-B	____	29.95
☐	Video 300-C	____	29.95
☐	Video 200-D	____	29.95
☐	Video 200-E	____	29.95
☐	Video 200-F	____	29.95
☐	Video 100-A	____	29.95
☐	Video 100-B	____	29.95
☐	Video 100-C	____	29.95

TOTAL AMOUNT $_____

(Alabama Residents add 8% tax.)

please call for Canadian or Foreign Shipping charges

Name _____

Address _____

City/State/Zip _____

Daytime Phone # _____

Credit Card # _____ Exp. Date _____

☐ MasterCard ☐ Visa ☐ American Express ☐ Discover

Mail order to: *Martha Pullen Co.*
518 Madison Street • Huntsville, AL 35801
Phone: 1-800-547-4176 or 1-205-533-9586 or Fax: 205-533-9630

*American VHS Format does not work on all foreign video systems.

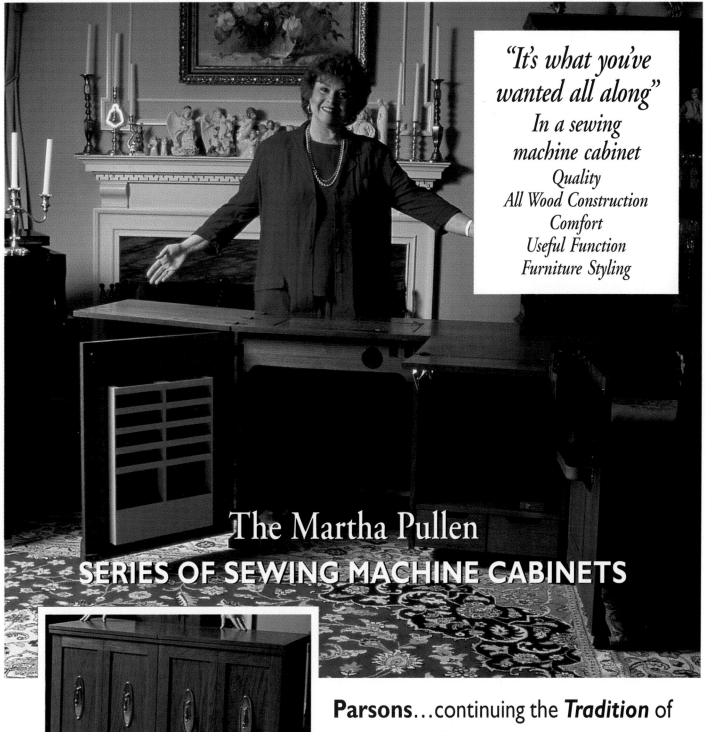

Linda's Silver Needle

1-800-SMOCK-IT!®

Let us bring our charming specialty sewing shop right to your mailbox! Call 1-800-766-2548 for a complimentary copy of our latest newsletter filled with wonderful fabric swatches and all the latest in specialty sewing supplies!

Visiting the Chicagoland area? We'd *love* to meet you in person! Stop in to see us at our lovely retail store in Naperville's historic Fifth Avenue Station Mall!

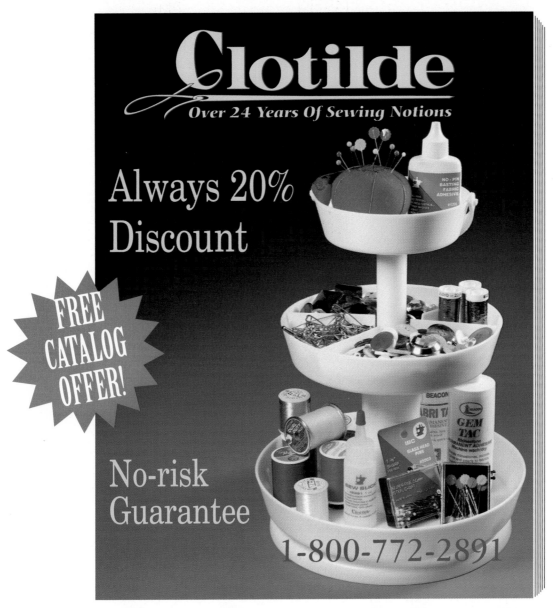

The Comfortable Edge!

Reach over the edge and grasp the comfort of Softouch! Fiskars proudly introduces the Softouch family– Softouch Craft Snip, Blunt-Tip, Micro-Tip and Multi-Purpose Scissors. These tools go hand-in-hand meeting your everyday cutting needs. Complemented by oversized cushion-grip handles, an easy-action spring gently re-opens blades after each cut and reduces fatigue. Ideal for left or right hand, the superior comfort and ease of use will take you over the edge.

FISKARS

Innovative Products For Creative People
Fiskars Inc. P.O. Box 8027, Wausau, WI 54402

SC4856

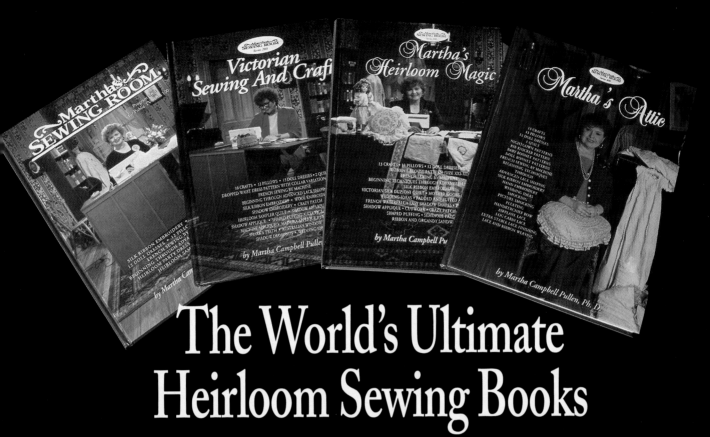

The World's Ultimate Heirloom Sewing Books

Each book is an encyclopedia of heirloom sewing! These books are a must for any lover of vintage sewing. Learn to create beautiful garments and gifts to pass down through generations as a symbol of your love of sewing.

MARTHA'S SEWING ROOM
Heirloom Party Dress Pattern
Beginning French Sewing by Machine • Plackets • Gathering French Lace • Machine Entredeux • Puffing • Basic Pintucking • Lace Shaping • Shaping a Lace Scalloped Skirt • Shaping Lace Diamonds • Shaping Flip-Flopping Lace Bows • Round Lace Portrait Portrait Collar • Hearts-Fold Back Miter Method • Curves & Angles with Pintucks • Silk Ribbon Embroidery Stitches • Crazy Patch • Doll Dresses • Pillows • Crafts • Heirloom Quilt • 308 pages

VICTORIAN SEWING AND CRAFTS
Child's Dropped Waist Dress Pattern with Variations
Beginning French Sewing Techniques • Shaped Puffing • Celtic Lace Designs • Appliqué • Appliqué Stitch Maneuvers • Shadow Appliqué • Madeira Appliqué • Shark's Teeth • Australian Windowpane • Shadow Diamonds • Shadowwork Embroidery • More Silk Ribbon Embroidery Stitches • Crazy Patch • Doll Dresses • Pillows • Crafts • Heirloom Quilt • Shadow Appliqué Quilt • 388 pages

MARTHA'S HEIRLOOM MAGIC
Woman's Blouse Pattern with Collar Variations
Complete French Sewing Techniques • Appliqué Stitch Maneuvers • Shadow Appliqué • Puffy or Padded Appliqué • Basic Crazy Patch • Cutwork • Easy Shadow Shapes • Normandy Lace • French Waterfall • Patchwork Lace • Ribbon & Organdy Sandwiches • Shaped Puffing • More Silk Ribbon Embroidery Stitches • Doll Dresses • Crafts • Quilts • 312 pages

MARTHA'S ATTIC
Bib Knickers, Baby Bonnet, and Woman's Nightgown
Complete French Sewing Techniques • Appliqué • Appliqué Stitch Maneuvers • Shadow Appliqué • Crazy Patch • Ribbon & Netting Diamonds • Smocking • Picture Smocking • Pleating • Constructing a Smocked Yoke Dress • Handkerchief Bow • Airplane Lace • Extra Stable Lace Finishing • Lace & Ribbon Weaving • Shaped Puffing • Hand Embroider Stitches • More Silk Ribbon Embroidery Stitches • Doll Dresses • Crafts • Quilt • 300 + pages

Each book contains ...
- Professional Step-by-Step Sewing Instructions
- Complete Heirloom Sewing By Machine Instructions
- Silk Ribbon Embroidery Instructions
- Color Photographs of Projects
- Professional Artist's Illustrations
- 12 - 13 Doll Dress Patterns (each in 13 sizes)
- Free Garment Pattern in each book
- 13 Crafts, 13 Pillows, and Quilt Projects with Instructions
- Hard cover book

HAVE YOU DRIVEN
A FORD LATELY?

Show 11
Ribbon Diamonds Picture Transfer Pinafore

This is a really fun and fancy dress using one of my favorite techniques, picture transfer. Not only do I love antique clothing, but I also love antique greeting cards and Valentines. From my personal collection we transferred beautiful Valentine pictures to the skirt and stitched down very fancy ribbons to make diamonds on the skirt. The ribbon is in shades of pink, dusty pink, green and gold on a pink background. The pinafore is of ecru Swiss batiste and the bodice is batiste with mitered pink ribbon trim. The ruffle around the dress is a shiny organza which is edged with an ecru French edging stitched on flat. The bottom of the pinafore is finished with a row of the fancy ribbon and ecru French insertion stitched first, then a narrow row of the shiny organza and finally a row of French edging on the bottom . The pinafore is divided at the sides and trimmed with ecru French edging stitched flat. The back of the pinafore closes with two buttons and buttonholes. What a fantasy dress. By the way, these valentines from my personal collection are available, ready to iron on, from Martha Pullen Company.

Ribbon Diamonds Picture Transfer Pinafore

Supplies

In addition to the supplies listed in the general supply list found on page 109, the following materials and notions will be needed:

- ❂ ³/₄" wide edging lace: size 4, 6 yds.; size 6, 8 yds.; size 8, 8¹/₂ yds.; size 10, 9 yds.; size 12, 9¹/₄ yds.
- ❂ 2 yds. of ⁵/₈" wide lace insertion
- ❂ 1¹/₄ yds. of ³/₈" wide edging lace
- ❂ 2³/₄ yds. of entredeux
- ❂ 15 yds. of ⁵/₈" wide tapestry ribbon
- ❂ 2 yds. of ¹/₂" wide sparkle chiffon ribbon
- ❂ 3 yds. of 2" wide sparkle chiffon ribbon
- ❂ Other supplies: nine picture transfers (on transfer paper), aluminum foil, hot dry iron, press cloth
- ❂ **Pattern Pieces Required:** Mitered Yoke Front and Back, Mitered Yoke Shoulder, Armhole Guide found on pull-out section
- ❂ **Template Required:** Picture Transfer Skirt Grid Template, Picture Transfer Side Seam Template found on pull-out section

I. Cutting and Preparation

1. Refer to the pinafore general instructions, section II.A. Mitered Yoke - Entredeux Around Yoke Outer Edge and Neck, steps 2 - 7.

2. After step 7 above, draw a line around the yoke, centered between the entredeux on all sides of the yoke. Place the ⁵/₈" wide tapestry ribbon over the drawn line, centered.

3. Beginning at one back edge, follow the line around the yoke, mitering the ribbon at the corners. Try to make the ribbon miters exactly over the yoke miters (**see fig. 1**).

4. Topstitch the ribbon in place along both edges and over the miter lines (**fig. 1**).

5. Cut two skirt pieces, each 36¹/₂" wide and 2" shorter than the measurements given in the chart found on page 109. Use the armhole guide to cut armholes from the skirt front and back.

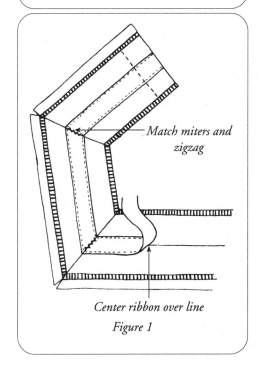

Match miters and zigzag

Center ribbon over line

Figure 1

6. Fold the skirt front in half to create a vertical crease running from the top edge to the bottom edge (see fig. 2).

7. Make a dot on the center front line, 12" above the bottom edge. Place the skirt template over the skirt, matching the dots and the center front line. Draw the first two lines of the grid, extending the lines beyond the template all the way to the edge of the fabric (see fig. 2).

8. To draw the remaining grid lines, draw parallel lines in each direction all the way across the fabric. Make the lines 9" apart, creating diamonds (fig. 2).

9. In the first row along the bottom, there will be four diamond "tips" and five large diamonds missing the lower points. In the five large diamond sections, place five picture transfers and fuse. Refer to the directions found on page 247 in addition to the instructions that come with the transfers (see fig. 2 for picture placement).

10. Also place and fuse picture transfers in the row of four complete diamonds above the five that were placed in step 9 above.

11. After the transfers are all placed and fused, place ⁵⁄₈" wide tapestry ribbon over all of the grid lines going in one direction. Topstitch the ribbon in place along both edge (see fig. 3).

12. Place ribbon over all of the lines going in the opposite direction and stitch them in place along both edges as before.

13. Serge or zigzag the bottom skirt edge before continuing with the pinafore construction.

II. Construction

1. Refer to the general pinafore instructions, section III, Skirt Construction, steps 2 - 5.

2. Cut two 37" long strips of the following: ⁵⁄₈" wide tapestry ribbon, ⁵⁄₈" wide insertion lace, ¹⁄₂" wide chiffon ribbon.

3. Use the cut pieces to make two bottom bands for the skirt, joining the pieces in the following order, top to bottom: tapestry ribbon, insertion lace, chiffon ribbon. Use the lace to lace technique, treating the finished edges of the ribbon like the heading of lace. Butt the two edges together and zigzag. Place the ribbon edge of the band so that it overlaps the skirt bottom edge by ¹⁄₄"; stitch in place with a straight stitch.

4. Using the ³⁄₄" wide lace edging, begin at one side seam and place ³⁄₄" wide lace edging along the edges of the skirt with the lace overlapping the skirt edge. Miter the lace along the side seam as shown on the side seam template. Continue down the side seam, miter at the bottom corner and continue around the skirt, finishing at the other side. Repeat for the other skirt piece. Trim the fabric away from behind the lace (fig. 3).

5. Sew the side seams of the skirt pieces together with a short seam that begins at the top edge and extends through the lace at the side seam. Finish the seam with a serger or zigzag.

6. Continue with the skirt construction, section III, step 6.

7. Attach the skirt to the yoke, referring to the pinafore general instructions, section IV.A. Yoke With Entredeux, steps 1 - 4.

8. Mark the 2" wide chiffon ribbon into quarters. Attach ³⁄₄" wide edging lace to one long side of the ribbon with the lace to lace technique, using the ribbon edge as if it were a lace heading. Hem the two short ends of the ribbon with a ¹⁄₄" double hem, stitched in place with a small zigzag or straight stitch. Run a gathering row very close to the edge of the ribbon that has no lace attached.

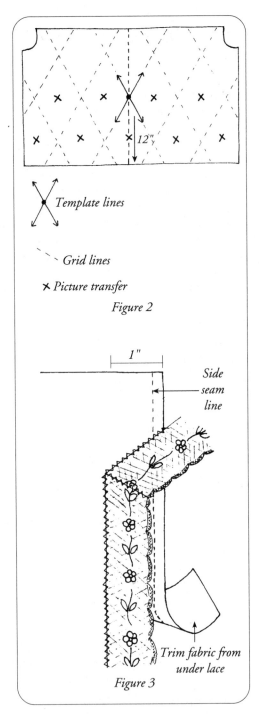

X Template lines

˙ ˙ Grid lines

✕ Picture transfer

Figure 2

1"

Side seam line

Trim fabric from under lace

Figure 3

9. Refer to the general pinafore instructions, section V.A. Gathered Lace To Entredeux Around Yoke, using the gathered edge of the ribbon the same as the heading edge of lace. At the back edges, stop the hemmed edge of the ribbon at the fold line.

10. Attach the ³⁄₈" wide lace edging to the neck edge, referring to the pinafore general instructions, section VI, then refer to section VII to finish the pinafore. ▨

Holiday Pinafore

I am sure that this pinafore winked at me when I opened the box and took it out. What excitement, what glamour, what fun! It reminded me of a Christmas dress that I had made for Joanna one year which incorporated gold and silver lamé fabric with batiste and ecru round thread lace. Joanna had announced, "I want glitz for my Christmas dance this year." Doesn't that sound like a 13-year old getting ready for the middle school dance? I guess nearly all little girls love glitz and this is one elegant glitz dress. The dress fabric is of white silk dupioni and the pinafore is made of silk organza; all of the laces are white. The machine embroidery on the sleeves of the dress and on the skirt of the pinafore is done in silver metallic thread. Beautiful intertwined lace loops travel vertically on the front of the pinafore and they are stitched down with the same metallic thread. Joanna used to call this lace shape, "footballs." The bodice of the pinafore is composed of three pieces of white French lace zigzagged together with metallic thread. The triple ruffle sections in the arms of the pinafore have organza, French insertion and slightly gathered French edging on the outside. The pinafore yoke has Swiss entredeux around both the top and bottom edges as well as gathered French edging at the neck edge. The back of the pinafore closes with two buttonholes and pearl buttons. The dress closes with buttons and buttonholes also. The neckline of the dress has white Swiss entredeux plus gathered French edging. The bottom of the puffed sleeves have a band made up of entredeux, insertion, entredeux, and a wide ruffle made up of three rows of French insertion with a row of French edging finishes the lower edges of the sleeve bands.

Holiday Pinafore

Supplies

- In addition to the supplies listed in the general instructions, the following materials will also be needed:
- An additional ¹/₃ yd. of the pinafore fabric
- 18¹/₂ yds. of ³/₄" wide lace insertion
- 1¹/₂ yds. of ³/₈" wide lace insertion
- 9 yds. of 1" wide lace edging
- 1¹/₂ yds. of ³/₈" wide lace edging
- 2 yds. of entredeux
- Notions: silver metallic thread, two buttons
- **Pattern Pieces Required:** Mitered Yoke Front and Back, Armhole Guide, Mitered Yoke Shoulder found on pull-out section
- **Templates Required:** "Football" lace template, zigzag lace template found on pull-out section, embroidery template found on page 106

I. Cutting and Preparation

1. Cut or tear two skirt pieces, to the length given on the chart (page 109) by 36¹/₂" wide.

2. Cut two pieces of ³/₄" lace insertion, one piece of ³/₈" lace insertion and two pieces of entredeux 1¹/₂ yds. long. Make a lace band in the following order: ³/₄" lace insertion, ³/₈" lace insertion and ³/₄" lace insertion. Butt the laces together and zigzag using a small narrow zigzag.

3. The lace strip will need to be backed with fabric. Cut two strips of fabric ¹/₂" wider than the lace band by 27" long. Cut one of the bands in half so that each piece measures 13¹/₂" in length. Place the fabric strips behind the lace strip with the 27" fabric piece in the center and the 13¹/₂" fabric pieces on each side. The fabric strips do not need to be stitched together. Center the fabric strips so that ¹/₄" of fabric extends above and below the lace strip. Stitch the lace strip to the fabric strip along the upper and lower edge of the lace using a straight stitch (**fig. 1**).

4. Attach entredeux to each side of the lace band using a ¹/₄" seam and the technique entredeux to fabric.

5. Place the outer seam line of the yoke and shoulder pattern pieces along the bottom entredeux edge of the lace band created in step 2 above. Make sure that the pattern edges line up all the way across, so that the design will be continuous around the yoke. Cut one front

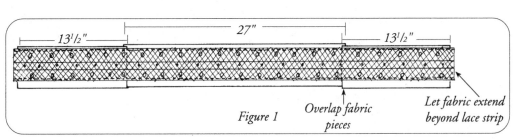

13¹/₂" — 27" — 13¹/₂"

Figure 1 Overlap fabric pieces Let fabric extend beyond lace strip

yoke on the fold and two yoke backs from the lace strip with the 27" piece of fabric behind the lace. Cut two shoulder pieces on the fold, or create a full shoulder pattern and cut two shoulder pieces from the 13^1/$_2$" fabric sections of the lace strip. Mark the back yoke fold lines, center front and shoulder centers (refer to general instructions fig. 1).

6. Using metallic thread, top stitch with a zigzag or featherstitch along the zigzag lines of the lace pieces. Also zigzag or featherstitch along the lace edge at the entredeux.

II. Construction

Refer to the finished drawing during construction.

1. Place the shoulder pieces to the yoke pieces, right sides together and sew the seams. Finish the seams with a serger or zigzag. Set aside.

2. Place the following lines along the skirt front: find the center front of the skirt by folding and placing a crease along the fold. Draw lines 4^1/$_2$" on each side of the center front crease, draw a second set of lines 9" from the 4^1/$_2$" lines (see fig. 2).

3. Trace the "football" lace template 1" from the bottom edge of the skirt front. The lace "footballs" should be centered along the drawn lines. The lower points of the zigzag template should end at the seam lines of the sides. Make any necessary adjustments to the template (fig. 2).

4. Shape lace along the template lines, following the directions for lace shaping. Stitch the lace in place using metallic thread and a zigzag or featherstitch. Do not stitch the bottom edge of the lace. Gathered edging lace will later be added to the lower edge of the insertion. It will not be necessary to cut the fabric from behind the lace "footballs". Trim the fabric from behind the lace along the bottom of the skirt.

5. Trace the zigzag lace template 1" from the bottom of the skirt back. The lower points of the zigzag should end at the seam lines of the sides. Make any necessary adjustments to the template. Shape lace along the template lines. Stitch the lace in place along the top edge only using metallic thread and a zigzag or featherstitch. Trim the fabric from behind the lace along the bottom of the skirt (fig. 3).

6. Refer to the pinafore general instructions, section III, steps 2 - 5 to begin the skirt construction. Sew one side seam matching the lace points, and finish the seam edges.

7. Gather 5 yards of edging lace to fit the bottom lace edge of the skirt. Attach the gathered edging to the lace insertion using the technique lace to lace.

8. Sew the other side matching the lace, and finish the seam edges.

9. Continue with section III, step 6 of the pinafore general instructions.

10. Attach the skirt to the yoke using the pinafore general instructions, section IV.A, steps 1 -5. Zigzag the skirts over the yoke seam to hold the seam away from the entredeux.

III. Making the Sleeve Ruffles

1. Cut six sleeve ruffle scallops from the organza.

2. Shape insertion lace along the template line of each scallop. Stitch the inside edge of the lace in place with a featherstitch or zigzag using metallic thread. Trim the fabric from behind the lace. Cut six pieces of edging lace to 24". Gather each piece of edging lace to fit the outer lace edge of the scallop. Attach the gathered lace to the insertion lace using a zigzag and white thread. Three scallops will be used on each shoulder ruffle (fig. 4).

3. Place two scallops side by side, right side up. Place the third scallop, right side up between the other two. Baste all three scallops together along the straight side to form one ruffle piece. Repeat for the other ruffle (fig. 5).

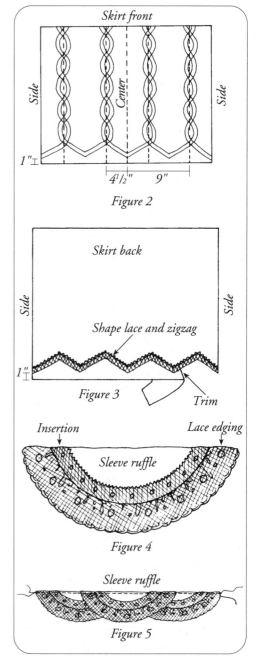

Figure 2

Skirt front

Side Center Side

4^1/$_2$" 9"

1"

Figure 3

Skirt back

Side Side

Shape lace and zigzag

1"

Trim

Figure 4

Insertion Lace edging

Sleeve ruffle

Figure 5

Sleeve ruffle

4. Attach the sleeve ruffles using the pinafore general instructions, section V.B.1.

5. Refer to the pinafore general instructions, section VI to finish the neck edge.

6. Refer to the pinafore general instructions, section VII, steps 1 and 2 to finish the pinafore.

7. Work the embroidery in the fabric sections between the lace "footballs". See "football" template for placement.

Introduction to Crafts

Entering into one of the supermarket sized craft stores is quite an experience. How I would have loved having one of these stores for shopping and ideas back when I was a Cub Scout or Brownie Scout leader. No matter what the project, they seem to have endless supplies. That holds true for ideas also; they are there for me to choose. Loving to make beautiful things holds fascination for many people. I remember that my second grade boyfriend made me a comb holder and a coin purse in his Cub scout troop. I did love the crafts as a scout myself. It would be a toss up as to whether I enjoyed earning badges or making crafts the most. Both activities are still with me as a permanent part of my life. I think I still like to complete the project and win badges. For me as an adult, completing the project is finishing a book or pattern and sending it to the printer. Making crafts completes a creative urge for me to "make it myself" and then enjoy it.

This section has some of the most creative crafts for you to enjoy. When I was a young bride, decoupage was brand new and I couldn't wait to save enough money to buy some of the "Mod-Podge." Since money was so scarce, I went to the local lumber yard and purchased scraps of old boards to be used for my "picture frames." I purchased brown stain to darken my "boards" and to serve as the base for some family photos. I practically decoupaged everything in the house and these pictures were wonderful for pictures to decorate my home since we had no money in the decorating budget. Our decoupage of an old suitcase purchased at the thrift store, plastic tissue boxes and a wooden paint box might inspire you to use some real "throwaways" that you thought had no use.

Speaking of recycling, you might enjoy refurbishing a mirror to use in your bedroom. An old picture frame becomes a Victorian beauty to hold a picture or an antique card of some kind. A teddy bear dressed in scraps of lace from your stash might be just the thing you need for a gift or to add a whimsical touch to your guest bedroom. Making jewelry is a cinch with our craft store brooch/watch embellished with tiny gold charms and other trims. An old pair of gloves become a potpourri-laden dresser knickknack.

Whatever your love in the craft area, I hope you enjoy these which we have made for you. All of them are easy and fun to make. Enjoy the lighter side of life by making fun crafts. Glue and little pieces of scraps make me feel young and like I am once again in my Girl Scout Troop with Mrs. Campbell and Mrs. Edge as my leaders. Maybe I will dream back a little further to my wonderful scouting days and remember Miss Will Maples and her camp-outs at the Girl Scout Cabin and those wonderful things we cooked on an open fire. Especially prominent in my memories are "some mores," "dough boy" biscuits, and stew in aluminum foil. Have fun with your crafts and make some memories for little ones in your family!

So many of you have written saying how much you enjoy the variety of projects on *Martha's Sewing Room*. We are indeed delighted that we have tickled your fancy. Our projects make us happy and we even like having a hot glue gun project every now and then. With our lives being just too busy, EASY is sometimes really appreciated. Thanks for your letters; always know that your suggestions for future projects are welcomed! ▨

Decoupage Suitcase

I have loved decoupage since the craft became popular in the mid-60's. Probably you have guessed that I love decoupage when done the easy way. This old suitcase was purchased in a thrift store and carries the name Amelia Earheart. Two old luggage identification pieces show that a Mrs. Pope traveled on Continental Trailways Busses from both Dallas and Alexandria, LA. I don't have the date; however, we had a suitcase just like this in the 1950s.

This suitcase has as its new identity being used as a silk ribbon embroidery case. The interior features a hand crocheted doily covering the back of the suitcase. This storage section would be great for placing one's books and pamphlets. Pieces of stiff cardboard are sectioned and painted gold; they serve as dividers in the bottom of the suitcase. Old crocheted doilies are used around the three bottom walls of the suitcase for holding goodies.

There is also an old oil paint carrying case which we have embellished, via decoupage, with old valentines, old cutouts and other cards, French lace and Swiss lace. The interior walls also have old laces glued in to serve as pockets for storing things.

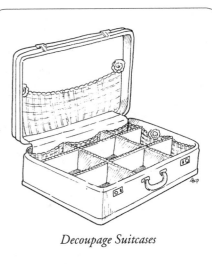

Decoupage Suitcases

Materials

* Old luggage
* Fabric to line interior of luggage. Yardage varies—measure old lining when it is removed
* Craft glue
* Decoupage paste
* Crochet doilies, antique valentines, paper or fabric cutouts, or anything you would like attached to your luggage
* Posterboard

A. Preparation

1. When choosing the luggage be sure to check the latches, handles, and check for inside damage. If latches are broken, ribbon can be used to tie it shut. Often latches and handles can be repaired at a luggage shop or shoe repair.

2. Remove the lining one layer at a time. Be sure to number the layers as you remove them. When new ones are cut, they will need to be replaced in the reverse order. After the linings are removed, you can measure to find out how much material is needed. If there is padding under the lining, replace this also. Padding is often the source of much of the musty smell in the luggage. Many old pieces of luggage are made of wood. If your piece happens to be wooden, lightly sand the interior of the luggage to prepare the surface for new padding and lining.

3. Old luggage usually smells musty. It may just need airing out. After old linings are removed, set the luggage outside on a sunny day. If there is still some odor, a few drops of perfume or refresher oil for potpourri seems to do the trick.

4. Wash the luggage well using a damp cloth and soap if necessary. Dry thoroughly.

B. Procedure

1. After the linings have been removed and numbered, cut new linings using the old ones as patterns (**fig. 1**).

2. If posterboard is to be used under the linings, cut it to the correct size. Remember to remove seam allowances before cutting the posterboard so that the piece will fit into the luggage smoothly.

3. If the old lining was glued to cardboard, glue the new lining to posterboard (**fig. 2**).

4. Pockets may be added to the interior of the luggage using crochet pieces or lace; fold the raw edges to the back of the lining piece. These may be stitched in place through the poster board using a long machine stitch and heavy-duty thread. The pockets may also be stitched to the lining by hand or machine before gluing the lining to the posterboard. Secure the stitching at the top edge of the pocket by pulling threads to the back side and securing (**fig. 3**).

5. Glue the linings in place with craft glue. Remember to replace the linings in the reverse order that they were removed. The linings may need to be secured in place with weights or clamps until they dry. Canned food makes good weights.

6. Decide how the decoupage design should appear. Will the luggage be carried? Will it be standing up as decoration, or laying down? The design pieces will need to be placed accordingly (see the finished drawing).

7. Place the decoupage pieces onto the luggage and rearrange them until the design looks right.

8. Remove the pieces and brush decoupage paste onto the luggage with a foam brush. Spread the paste evenly so that the decoupage pieces will lie flat against the surface.

9. Place a decoupage piece onto the luggage. Repeat with the other items to be decoupaged onto the luggage (see the finished drawing).

10. Spread an additional coat of paste on top of the pieces and allow the luggage to dry. ▣

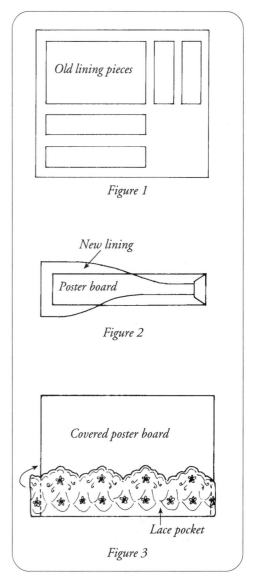

Old lining pieces

Figure 1

New lining

Poster board

Figure 2

Covered poster board

Lace pocket

Figure 3

Decoupage Tissue Box Covers

These tissue boxes, which have been covered with decoupage, are plastic. They feature old valentines and wrapping paper glued on first with an old bread cover of linen glued on over the pictures. Crochet or Battenburg doilies are also nice additions. Little bits of gold braid trim the top of the box. Decoupage paste is painted over all of this and it makes a wonderful Victorian decorative tissue box cover for any room of your house.

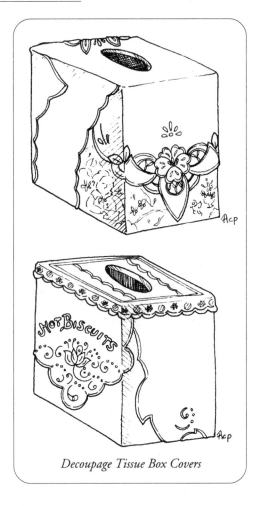

Materials

* Tissue box cover
* Assorted handkerchiefs or doilies
* Antique valentines, postcards, fabric or paper to cover box
* Decoupage paste

Procedure

1. Lightly sand the box and wipe it clean.

2. Place valentines or postcards to cover the box, cut out motifs from the paper to be overlapped to cover the entire box, or place large uncut pieces of the paper in the areas to be covered. Fabric may also be used to cover the box.

3. Starting near a lower corner, brush decoupage paste onto the box.

4. Place the paper or fabric over the box and smooth out any wrinkles. Let the edges of the paper or fabric extend below the lower edge of the and beyond the edges of the top opening (**fig. 1**). Apply another coat of paste on top of the paper or fabric.

5. Continue layering handkerchiefs and trims onto the box using the procedure in steps 3 and 4, covering the entire box.

6. Turn the edges of the fabric and paper to the inside of the box lower edge and the top opening. The edges will need to be clipped before turning to the inside of the box. Do not worry about fabric fraying because the decoupage paste will prevent fraying (**fig. 2**).

7. When all pieces have been applied and have dried, paint the finished box with a final coat of decoupage paste and allow it to dry completely before using. ▣

Decoupage Tissue Box Covers

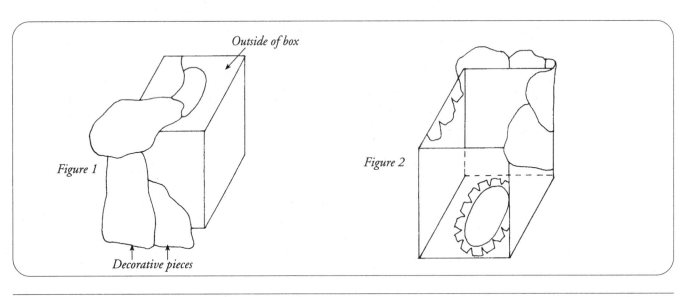

Figure 1 — Outside of box — Decorative pieces

Figure 2

Ribbon Message Board

An elegant message board can be a great addition to any room in a house. For teens, this could be the perfect message board as well as a "treasure" board to keep things like invitations, prom programs or pages torn from a favorite magazine. This board can be made to match any decor. Choosing gold and green upholstery fabric, we used gold silk ribbon to make the crisscrosses to hold the messages. Burnished gold upholstery tacks (look like thumb tacks) were placed where the ribbon crosses to hold it in place. There is an upholstery cord on the top to use for hanging. The base of the board is foam core which is very lightweight for hanging. A board like this would be a great idea for a teacher gift!

Ribbon Messsage Board

Materials

* ❋ 1 piece of foam core, cut to the desired size
* ❋ 1 piece of poster board, the same size as the foam core
* ❋ 1 piece of batting, the same size as the board
* ❋ 2 pieces of fabric, each larger than the foam core by at least 2" on each side
* ❋ $^3/_8$" wide ribbon, satin or silk (yardage will be determined based on the size of the board — see step 5)
* ❋ Upholstery tacks
* ❋ 1 piece of heavy cording, as long as the width of the board
* ❋ 1 piece of $^3/_8$" wide upholstery braid, long enough to go around the outer edge of the cut board
* ❋ Craft glue or hot glue

Assembly

1. Use a craft knife to cut the foam core and the poster board to the desired size.

2. Cut one batting piece that is the same size as the foam core; glue the batting to the foam core and let it dry.

3. Cut two pieces of fabric, each larger than the foam core by 2" on all sides.

4. Place one piece of the fabric over the batting on the foam core; wrap the edges to the back of the foam core and glue in place (**fig. 1**).

5. To determine how much ribbon is needed: measure the board diagonally from corner to corner, then measure diagonally every 3" - 4" apart in one direction, allowing room to turn the ribbon ends to the back. Double that amount and buy that much ribbon (**see fig. 2**).

6. Place the first piece of ribbon diagonally from corner to corner, wrap the ends to the back and glue in place. Repeat with other pieces of ribbon, placing the strips 3" - 4" apart all the way across the board (**see fig. 2**).

7. Repeat the ribbon placement in the other direction, starting diagonally from corner to corner as before. The second set of ribbons may be woven over and under the first set (**see fig. 2**).

8. Place an upholstery tack at each ribbon intersection. A drop of glue may be added to the tip of the tack to help hold it in place (**fig. 2**).

9. Unravel a short section of the cording at each end and flatten the cording, then glue the ends to the back of the board at the top edges (**see fig. 3**).

10. Cover the poster board with the remaining fabric piece and glue it to the back of the covered foam core to create a backing, with the cording sandwiched between the two layers (**see fig. 3**).

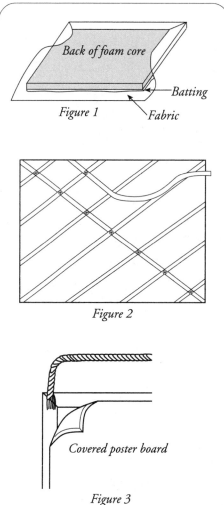

Back of foam core

Figure 1

Batting

Fabric

Figure 2

Covered poster board

Figure 3

11. Glue the upholstery braid around the outer edge of the finished board (refer to the finished drawing). ▨

Lacy Bear

Craft stores hold treasures for those of us who love Victorian crafts. This bear was purchased with furry arms, head and legs; her body is plain muslin. We decorated her body with scraps of lace, beading, buttons, and her skirt is a piece of an antique ecru handkerchief. Her "sleeves" consist of two pieces of scrap lace which don't match and her hairbow is of pink and ecru ribbon. Beads are found around her neck and she holds a little straw basket filled with white flowers and tied with a pink ribbon. Her shoes are pieces of crochet tied on with ribbon, and a little bow button is used for her shoe trim in the front. This little bear looks like a flapper bear with the dropped-waist look for her clothing. Have fun decorating a little bear like this!

Materials

* ✳ One craft bear or other animal to dress (one with a muslin torso is easier to work with)
* ✳ Handkerchiefs, lace scraps, small crochet doilies, strands of beads or pearls, ribbon roses, small wicker basket for bear to carry, assorted ribbons, tiny silk or dried flowers and greenery
* ✳ Glue gun
* ✳ Craft glue

Procedure

1. Arrange lace scraps on the bear, covering the torso to resemble a bodice of a dress. Lace edging can be gathered for the sleeve caps and buttons and ribbon roses can be added as desired (**fig. 1**).

2. Glue the bodice pieces into place. Buttons and roses may be either sewn on or glued on.

3. Two small doilies folded to cover the feet make cute shoes. Ribbon and buttons may be added here also. Run ribbon through the spaces in the doily and tie the "shoes" in place. The top edge may be folded over at the front with a bow or flower glued on (**fig. 2**).

4. A skirt can be made by cutting a circle from the center of a handkerchief large enough for the bear to fit through (**see fig. 3**).

5. Run a gathering stitch around the circle. Slide the skirt onto the bear, pull up the gathering stitches and secure. Decorative trim or a ribbon sash may be added to cover the stitching (**fig. 3**).

6. Add a beaded necklace and a bow atop one ear (see the finished drawing).

7. If you would like, the bear can carry a basket filled with flowers and greenery. Just glue the basket in place on the bear's wrist (see the finished drawing). ▨

Lacy Bear

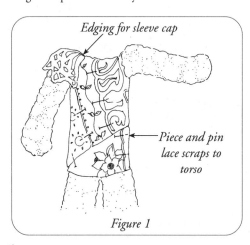
Edging for sleeve cap
Piece and pin lace scraps to torso
Figure 1

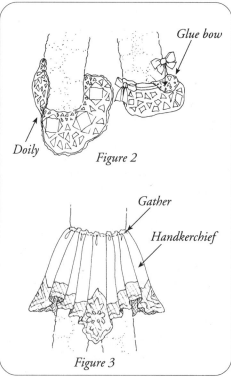
Glue bow
Doily
Figure 2
Gather
Handkerchief
Figure 3

Victorian Picture Frame

Victorian Picture Frame

Joanna always loved to collect picture frames. Taking pictures of her friends and family and framing them was one her favorite home decorating ideas. We began with a purchased wooden frame and other scraps of lace and ribbons. Our antique birthday card was used instead of a picture. Ecru lace trim is glued around the outside of the glass to frame the birthday card. Peach and green ombre wired ribbon is gathered in a most unusual way and glued all the way around the frame. Braid in pink, green, and gold is glued around the square frame on top of the ribbon and three antique buttons are glued on at one corner. By finding out the colors of a bedroom, one could make gifts for almost anyone on the Christmas list. This is a great way to use old picture frames which you don't particularly like or which are the wrong color for your house. By using correctly tinted ribbon, you can make it work for your house.

Materials

✳ Antique postcard or pretty postcard of your choice
✳ Frame larger than postcard by 1" to 1¹/₂" on all sides of card
✳ Heavy poster board
✳ 1¹/₂" wide wire-edged ribbon long enough to go around frame plus ¹/₂ yd.
✳ Braided trim to complement ribbon, long enough to go around the picture frame
✳ Novelty buttons or charms
✳ Tatted or crochet trim, ¹/₂" to ³/₄" wide
✳ Fabric to cover poster board backing beneath post card (fabric will show through crochet mat)
✳ Hot glue gun

Procedure

1. Cut a piece of poster board to fit inside the picture frame. Cut a piece of fabric large enough to cover the board and lap to the back of the board approximately 1" on all edges. Cover the board with fabric; wrap and glue the excess fabric edges on the back (**fig. 1**).

2. Center the postcard on the fabric-covered board and glue it into place (**see fig. 2**).

3. Place the mat and postcard in the frame under the glass and secure the backing to the back of the picture frame (**fig. 2**).

4. Tatting or crochet trim can be glued in place along the inside edge of the picture frame on top of the glass (the fabric-covered mat around the card will show through the trim) (**fig. 3**).

5. Gather the ribbon into a ruffled shape, following the directions for ruching on page 210.

6. Glue the ruched ribbon in place on the front of the picture frame. Glue braid along the center of the ribbon to cover the gathers, having the ends of the braid begin and end in the top left corner of the frame (**fig. 4**).

7. Glue buttons or charms or a combination of both in the top left corner where the braid meets (see the finished drawing). ▨

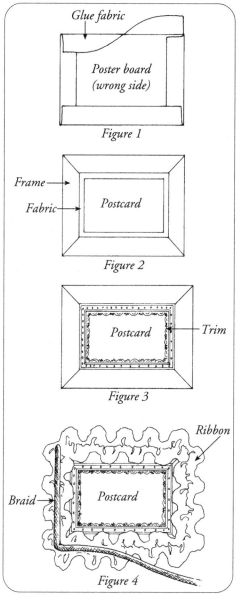

Glue fabric

Poster board (wrong side)

Figure 1

Frame
Fabric
Postcard

Figure 2

Postcard
Trim

Figure 3

Ribbon
Braid
Postcard

Figure 4

Looking Glass

Old dresser mirrors are relatively easy to find at flea markets or garage sales. Ours is a pretty brass-looking one which had a broken mirror on one side and a perfectly good one on the other. This is the perfect kind to recycle by making it very lovely and Victorian. Using a bit of black lace, an old handkerchief with pink bullion roses and black thread trim, peach silk roses, and a couple of gold charms, we glued them all on and tied the flowers with an unusual black ribbon. It is amazing what one can do to recycle old articles such as this broken mirror.

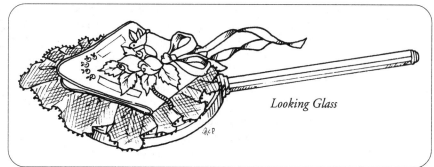

Looking Glass

Materials

* Old vanity mirror
* ³/₄ yd. of wide vintage lace (this measurement is approximate)
* 1 yd. of ribbon
* 1 pretty handkerchief
* 1 lace motif or large charm
* 2 small brass charms
* ¹/₂ yd. of entredeux or narrow braid
* Three small dried-look silk flowers with leaves
* Hot glue gun

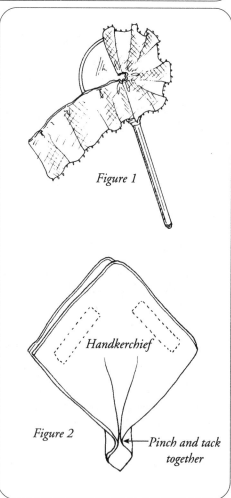

Figure 1

Assembly

1. Pull the flowers and leaves from the stem. Set aside.

2. Pinch up the lace by hand and glue it to back of the mirror. The lace should extend past the edge of the mirror. Pinch up the lace as you glue (**fig. 1**).

3. Fold the handkerchief and pinch it together at the bottom edge in a fan shape.

4. Glue or tack the bottom edge of the handkerchief together (**fig. 2**).

5. Glue the handkerchief in place on top of the lace.

6. Add the leaves and flowers on top of the handkerchief.

7. Tie the ribbon into a bow and arrange the remaining items as you desire.

8. The entredeux may be trimmed on both sides and used as a trim.

9. Glue everything in place. ▨

Handkerchief

Figure 2

→ *Pinch and tack together*

Decorative Lunch Tray

Whether you are serving cool drinks on a summer afternoon or delivering a meal-in-bed to a special someone, this decorative tray will add an elegant touch to the occasion. Take an inexpensive rattan tray, a piece of decorative fabric and some decoupage glue, add a little braid trim and in no time, you have a beautiful serving tray. This project is so easy, your children could help make one to use for serving breakfast-in-bed to Mom on Mother's Day!

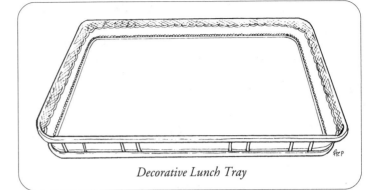

Decorative Lunch Tray

Materials

✳ One rattan serving tray
✳ Decorator fabric large enough to cover inside of tray
✳ One piece of iron-on vinyl, same measurement as fabric
✳ 1" wide crochet edging long enough to go around top edge of tray (if you choose to cover sides of tray)
✳ ¹/₄" wide crochet edging or trim long enough to fit around inside edge of tray where the sides meet the tray base
✳ Decoupage paste
✳ Craft glue
✳ Spray paint (optional)
✳ Clear spray acrylic (optional)

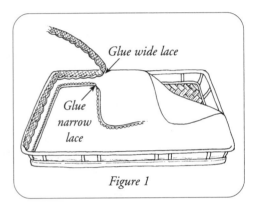

Glue wide lace

Glue narrow lace

Figure 1

Procedure

1. Paint the tray to complement the fabric, or leave the tray natural. If the tray is painted, allow it to dry overnight. In order to be able to wipe the tray off with a damp cloth, spray the outside of the tray with a clear acrylic and allow to dry overnight.

2. The fabric may cover only the inside base of the tray or extend up the inside sides to the top edge, which is how our tray was covered.

3. Place the fabric inside the tray and cut it out to fit the tray as desired (or make a paper pattern to cut the fabric from).

4. Remove the fabric from the tray and cut a piece of iron-on vinyl the same size as the fabric.

5. Following the manufacturer's instructions, apply the vinyl to the fabric.

6. Glue the vinyl-covered fabric to the inside of the tray (**see fig. 1**).

7. If the fabric extends up the sides of the tray, glue the wider crochet lace to cover the top edge of the fabric (**see fig. 1**).

8. Glue the narrow edging or trim on the inside of the tray where the fabric meets the joint of the base and sides (if only the base is covered, the narrow trim will cover the cut edge of the fabric) (**fig. 1**).

9. After gluing the trim in place, apply a coat of decoupage paste over the trims to protect them. 🖾

Victorian Watch Brooch

By purchasing an inexpensive watch at the craft store, you can make a masterpiece with trims and a hot glue gun. Tiny charms were glued on around the face of the watch. Since my name is Pullen, we chose a "P," as well as charms of flower baskets, bows, cherubs and a ballet dancer. Little gold outline pieces were glued on around the outside of the watch to make a frame. After having fun being creative with your things to glue on the watch, glue on a little jewelry catch on the back and you have a lovely watch brooch.

Materials

* One watch or clock insert (1¹/₂" diameter makes a nice brooch)
* 10 to 15 small charms (hearts, cupids, bows, flowers)
* Tiny buttons or other small jewelry findings
* 1 pin back
* Hot glue or epoxy

Procedure

(Refer to the finished drawing during assembly.)

1. Draw a circle the size of the watch face on a piece of paper. Arrange the charms around the circle until the placement looks right.

2. If any of the charms have rings at the top, these can usually be removed with wire snips. It may be necessary to lightly file or sand the cut edge, but be careful not to make that area more shiny than the rest of the charm.

3. Glue the charms in place around the watch face.

4. Glue the pin back to the back of the watch (**fig. 1**).

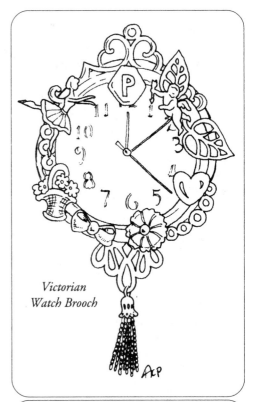

*Victorian
Watch Brooch*

Glue → pin   Back of brooch

Figure 1

Sweet Gloves

Old gloves aren't too difficult to find at an antique store or in an old attic. Some of you might remember the days when we wouldn't go anywhere "dress up" without a hat and gloves. I remember my mother always teaching me to wear only white, beige or black gloves even when colors were in style. Gloves seemed so civilized for dress wear that I wonder if they will ever come back. Using an old nylon (see through) glove as the base for this craft, we filled the glove, fingers and all, with a beautiful deep rose and cranberry potpourri. The top of the glove was tied with a pink to purple ombre wired ribbon and tied in a bow at the top. A dried cranberry rose was stuck in under the tied ribbon and the ruffle on the top of the glove peeks out. This little glove could be used for embellishment in many rooms of the house. It smells as lovely as it looks.

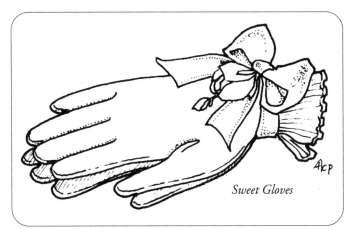

Sweet Gloves

Materials

* One pair of Victorian-style sheer gloves (bridal stores usually have them)
* Rose potpourri
* Thread to match gloves
* Two or three dried roses
* Wide ribbon to complement roses
* Hot glue gun

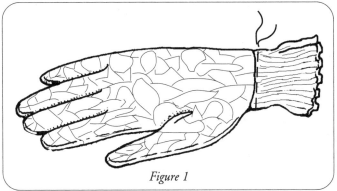

Figure 1

Assembly

1. Stuff rose potpourri inside one glove using a new, unsharpened pencil to push the potpourri into the fingers of the gloves. Fill the palm part of the glove, leaving room to stitch the glove closed at the wrist. Stitch across the glove (**fig. 1**).

2. Lay the filled glove, palm sides together, on top of the other glove.

3. Tie the ribbon around the gloves at the wrists.

4. Arrange the roses in the center of the bow and glue them down (see the finished drawing).

NOTE: These sweet gloves look nice lying on an entry table. However, do not lay the gloves directly on a wooden surface. The oils and colors from the potpourri may discolor the wood. 🖬

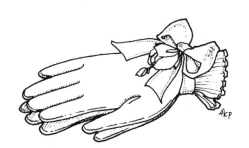

Happy Holidays

Santa's Sack

Magnificent Christmas Angels

Boot and Shoe Ornaments

Angel Christmas Stocking

Santa's Sack

Children of all ages will be fascinated with this great bag of goodies. It is packed so full of surprises that you may not see everything the first time. This is a great no-sew project - even the hem is done with a heat-fusible web. Using a circle of gorgeous Christmas plaid taffeta, add some batting and tie the top, then fill the top with some new or treasured ornaments and greenery. All that's left to do is to tie an elegant twisted cord around the top and then find just the right place to display your newest creation!

Santa's Sack

Materials

❋ ³/₄ yd. of fabric for sack

❋ ³/₄ yd. of batting, plus scraps of batting and polyfil

❋ 2¹/₄ yds. of ⁵/₈" wide fusible web

❋ 1 yd. of heavy braid or cord

❋ Miniature toy ornaments—teddy bears, plastic candy canes, small Christmas floral picks, and gift boxes

❋ Hot glue

❋ Heavy duty thread

Assembly

1. Cut a 26" diameter circle from the fabric.

2. Fold about 1" to the inside around the edge of the circle to form a hem (the fabric will pucker some) . This does not have to be precise. Fuse the hem down, placing the fusible web between the two fabric layers (**fig. 1**).

3. Thread a needle with a doubled heavy duty thread and sew a long gathering stitch approximately ³/₄" from the edge of the circle (**fig. 2**). This can be gathered by machine also.

4. Cut a circle from the batting, about 22" in diameter. Center the batting on the wrong side of the hemmed circle (**see fig. 3**).

5. Using scraps of batting and fiber fill, make a large ball that will fit inside the open circle of batting (**fig. 3**).

6. Pull up the gathers on the circle until you have an opening left at the top of the sack, about 5" in diameter. Tie off the gathering threads (**see fig. 4**).

7. Tie the heavy cording around the top of the sack over the gathering stitches. A little glue will hold the cord in place. Tie the cording in a knot, and tie knots in each end of the cording (**fig. 4**).

8. Add more stuffing if necessary to make a full sack.

9. Arrange the ornaments and toys in the top of the bag and glue them in place. Fill in any bare spots with greenery from the Christmas floral picks. The picks can be cut apart if necessary to fit in as needed (see the finished drawing). ▨

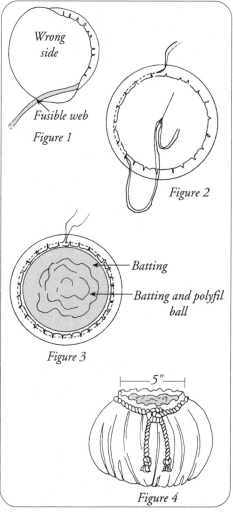

Wrong side

Fusible web

Figure 1

Figure 2

Batting

Batting and polyfil ball

Figure 3

5"

Figure 4

Magnificent Christmas Angels

These wonderful angels can be placed on top of your tree, nestled in among the branches or placed on a stand to sit on a shelf or table. The graceful, flowing skirts and peaceful faces are a beautiful expression of the joy we feel when celebrating the holidays with family and friends. Wherever you decide to use them, they will add an air of classic elegance to your home during the holiday season or all year long.

Many thanks to Roberta Przybylski for allowing us to use a variation of her angel designs. Her angel "Annalise" was shown in *Sew Beautiful* magazine, Holiday, 1996. For information about her other angel patterns and designs, you may write to Sewing Traditions, Roberta Przybylski, 575 Sand Piper Way, Boca Raton, FL 33431, (407) 362-4115.

Magnificent Christmas Angels

Materials

(The instructions and supplies given will duplicate the ivory angel. The other angels may be duplicated by changing the fabrics used. Fabric amounts and other supplies will remain the same.)

※ 1 porcelain angel head and attached breastplate, $3^1/2$" to $4^1/2$", with hands (craft stores)
※ $^1/4$ yd. of 1" wide satin ribbon
※ 9" x 3" piece of fabric for body
※ 1 doily or handkerchief, 12" in diameter
※ $3^1/2$ yds. of 3" to 4" wide wire-edged ribbon
※ $^3/4$ yd. of cotton netting or tulle
※ $^1/2$ yd. of $^1/4$" wide picot braid trim
※ $^1/2$ yd. of 1" wide lace edging
※ 8 yds. of $^5/8$" wide lace edging
※ two packages of bridal trims (ovals, leaves, etc.) for wings
※ two packages of beaded loops for wings
※ two sprays of beaded bridal trim for wings
※ Other Requirements: hot glue gun, craft glue, 18" of white florist's wire, 12" of white florist's wire, white floral tape, small amount of polyfil; Optional: doll stand or styrofoam cone
※ Pattern Pieces Required (found on pull-out section): Front Underskirt, Inner Skirt Back, Outer Skirt Back

I. Making the Body
A. Arms

1. Fold the 18" piece of florist's wire in half, making a double strand that is 9" long.

2. Fill the hands with glue and insert the ends of the wire into the hands. Let the glue dry before going to the next step (**see fig. 1**).

3. Cover the wire with glue and wrap a small bit of polyfil around the wire to build up an arm shape. Add some extra glue in the area where the wire goes into the hands and let all of the glue dry completely. After the glue is dry, wrap the top of the hands and the wire with white florist's tape to shape the arms and secure the polyfil to the wire (**fig. 1**).

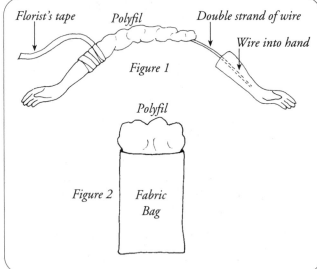

Florist's tape *Polyfil* *Double strand of wire*

Wire into hand

Figure 1

Polyfil

Figure 2 *Fabric Bag*

B. The Body Form

1. Use the 9" x 3" piece of fabric to make the body. Fold the fabric in half, right sides together, with the short ends meeting. Stitch the $4^1/2$" sides with a $^1/4$" seam, making a bag that is open at the top. Turn the bag to the right side (**see fig. 2**).

2. Fill the bag with polyfil, stuffing it firmly. Turn the ¹/₄" seam allowance to the inside and close the opening by hand or machine (**fig. 2**).

C. Assembling the Body

1. Turn the head piece upside down and fill the shoulder area with glue.

2. Press the arm assembly into the shoulder cavity, making sure that the hands face forward. Hold in place or set the head upside down in an egg carton to dry (**see fig. 3**).

3. Add more glue to the shoulder cavity and press one short end of the body form into the cavity. Let dry upside down, adding more glue if necessary to assure that the body is firmly attached (**fig. 3**).

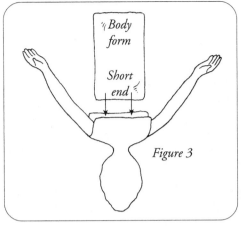

Figure 3

II. Skirts
A. Cutting

1. Cut one skirt piece from each pattern piece, with all pieces on a fold (it will be necessary to fold both selvage edges to the middle to create two folds).

2. Cut pieces of ⁵/₈" edging lace that are 1¹/₂ to 2 times as long as the outer edge of each skirt piece, depending on how full you want the gathers.

3. Gather the lace edging and attach it to the skirt outer edges (the lace will not go across the top edge) using the following technique (**see fig. 4**):

   a. Place the gathered lace over the skirt edge with the wrong side of the gathered lace to the right side of the skirt piece, and the scalloped edge of the gathered lace to the outer edge. The ruffle will overlap the edge of the skirt by ¹/₄".

   b. Stitch the gathered lace in place with a short, narrow zigzag (1.0 L, 1.0 W).

   c. Trim the excess skirt fabric from below the ruffle on the wrong side.

   d. Zigzag over the seam again, using a short stitch that is slightly wider than before (1.0 L, 1.5 W).

4. Beginning at the outer edge (in the middle of one side for a handkerchief), cut a 3" slit toward the center of the handkerchief or doily. Open out the slit to form a straight line (**fig. 5**).

5. Place the handkerchief or doily on top of the front underskirt, both with right sides up. The top cut edge of the skirt piece and the slit edge of the handkerchief or doily should be even at the top edge. Run two gathering rows through both layers, ¹/₄" and ¹/₈" from the cut edges (**fig. 6**).

6. Place the back inner skirt over the back outer skirt, both with right sides up. The top edges should be even. Run two gathering rows across the top edge, through both layers, ¹/₄" and ¹/₈" from the edge (**refer to fig. 6**).

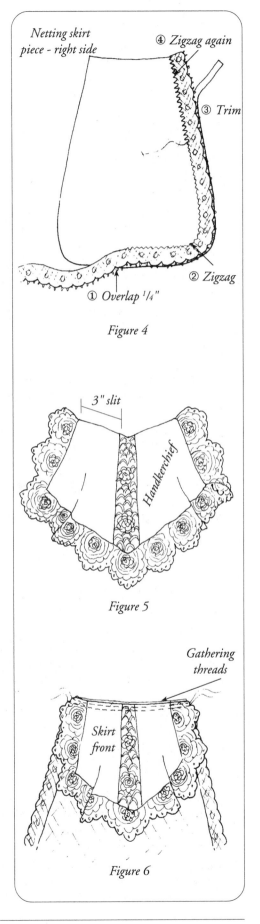

Netting skirt piece - right side
④ *Zigzag again*
③ *Trim*
② *Zigzag*
① *Overlap* ¹/₄"

Figure 4

3" slit
Handkerchief

Figure 5

Gathering threads
Skirt front

Figure 6

— III. Final Assembly —

1. Pull up the gathers in the skirt front to fit across the front of the angel, stopping just under the arms at the sides. Glue the front skirt in place (see **fig. 7**).

2. Pull up the gathers in the skirt back to fit across the back, letting the edges of the back skirt overlap the front skirt by ¹/₂". Glue the back skirt in place (**fig. 7**).

3. Cut the remaining ⁵/₈" lace edging in half and wrap one piece around each arm, covering the florist's tape. Let the scalloped edge of the lace point toward the hand to form a pretty "sleeve" edge (**fig. 8**).

4. Wrap the 1" wide satin ribbon around the top of the skirt at the "waist" and tie into a knot at the back, letting the ends hang down to form short streamers.

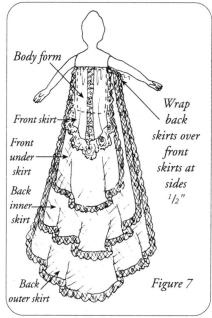

Body form
Front skirt
Front under skirt
Back inner skirt
Back outer skirt
Wrap back skirts over front skirts at sides ¹/₂"
Figure 7

5. Pull the top thread in the 1" wide lace edging and gather it to fit around the bottom edge of the porcelain breastplate; glue the lace in place to form the bodice ruffle (**see fig. 9**).

6. Beginning in the back, glue the ¹/₄" picot braid around the top edge of the gathered lace bodice ruffle. Also glue a small piece of the braid trim around the neck like a choker necklace (**fig. 9**).

7. Remove two stems from each beaded spray and set aside to form the halo in a later step.

8. Attach the wings in the following order, using half of each trim on each side:

   a. Wrap the stems of the beaded loops together with florist's tape; glue the two sections to the angel between the shoulder blades and fan the loops into a wing shape (**fig. 10**).

   b. Repeat step a with the oval or leaf shapes.

   c. Repeat step a with the beaded sprays.

9. Using the four beaded stems that were set aside earlier, bend the ends together to make circle for the halo, adjusting the circle so that it is large enough to reach from the bottom of the neck to the top of the head. Wrap the ends of the stems with a short piece of wire and glue the end of the wire into the area where the wings join the body, trimming away any excess wire (**fig. 11**).

10. Cut a one-yard long piece of the wide wire-edged ribbon and drape it loosely around the back of the angel, below the wings, and over the arms in the front, letting the ends fall below the hands to the bottom of the upper skirt. Glue the ribbon to the arms to hold it in place. Trim the ends of the ribbon at an angle (see the color photograph and finished drawing). Bend the ribbon into a pretty shape.

11. Fold the remaining wide wire-edged ribbon into a large-looped bow shape and fasten the center with a short piece of wire. Glue the bow to the back of the angel, over the area where the wings join the body. The bow tails will cover the knot in the satin ribbon. Trim the tails to a pretty length and bend the ribbon into a pretty shape.

12. The angel may be placed in the limbs of a Christmas tree, or displayed on a doll stand or attached to a styrofoam cone. The angel could also be attached to a hollow florist's cone to be placed on top of the Christmas tree. ▨

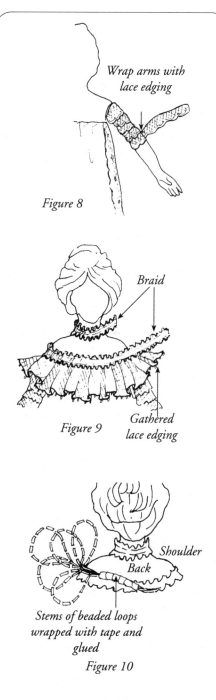

Wrap arms with lace edging
Figure 8

Braid
Gathered lace edging
Figure 9

Shoulder
Back
Stems of beaded loops wrapped with tape and glued
Figure 10

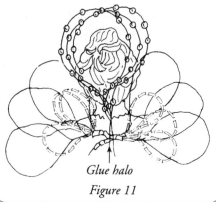

Glue halo
Figure 11

Boot and Shoe Ornaments

These cute little ornaments look like the real thing! The high-top boot has buttons up the front and a shaped heel at the back. The dainty shoe also has a shaped heel and elegant braid trim, ready for a special party. You might want to make one of these ornaments using scraps of fabric and trim from a special holiday dress, or some other special occasion during the year. This could be a nice gift for a bride, using fabrics from the wedding.

Materials

❋ Heavy poster board
❋ ¼ yd. of fabric (will make several ornaments)
❋ Braids, trims, and lace scraps
❋ 3 small buttons or beads for boots
❋ Ribbons
❋ Glue stick
❋ Craft glue
❋ Hot glue gun

❋ **Pattern Pieces Needed:** Boot Pattern and Shoe Pattern, found on page 257

Procedure

1. Cut two poster board pieces of each pattern, following the inner cutting line. Cut fabric to cover the board cutouts, following the outer cutting line.

2. Cover the board cutouts with the fabric with a glue stick, gluing the extra ½" to the back of the board. Clip the fabric where necessary to make it lie flat. Be sure to cover opposite sides of the ornaments (one left and one right) so that when they are glued wrong sides together, both front and back will be covered (**fig. 1**). It is only necessary to decorate one piece, but they are also very pretty with both sides decorated.

3. Make a loop with a piece of braid or cord and glue it in place at the top back edge of one shoe or boot piece. The ends may be placed between the two layers, or left on the outside to be covered by trim or a bow (**fig. 2**).

4. Glue a decorative trim around the top of the shoe and down the center front of the boot. Glue gathered lace where a shoe clip would be placed. Add a metallic or ribbon bow on top of the lace (**see fig. 3**).

5. Buttons are added to the boot down the center front (**fig. 3**).

6. Glue the decorated piece to the plain fabric-covered piece with craft glue, wrong sides together.

7. Press with something heavy and let dry overnight.

8. Attach corded trim around the edges of the shoe and boot where the two pieces are glued together (see the finished drawing). ▨

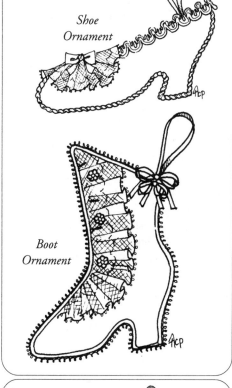

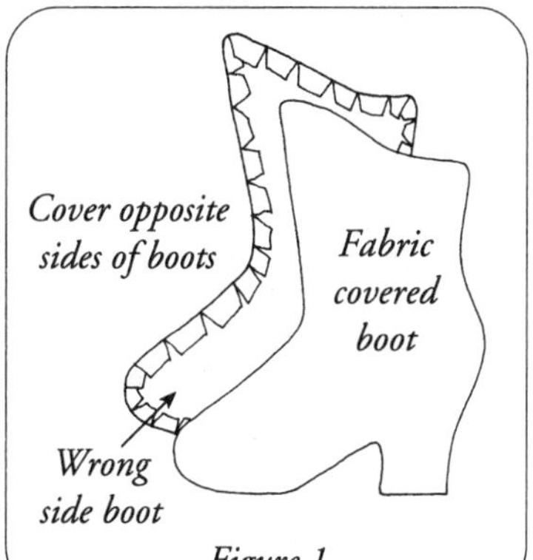

Shoe Ornament

Boot Ornament

Figure 1

Cover opposite sides of boots

Fabric covered boot

Wrong side boot

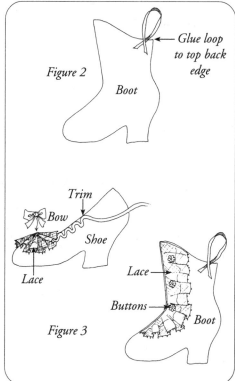

Figure 2

Boot

Glue loop to top back edge

Trim

Bow

Shoe

Lace

Lace

Buttons

Boot

Figure 3

Angel Christmas Stocking

What an elegant and beautiful stocking this is! The sweet little angel face is framed by loops of ribbon and a lace ruffle to create a skirt effect, while picot-edged pleated chiffon and beaded loops form wings. Her lace bodice is set off by a single folded rose and a tiny little satin bow. The top edge of the elegant brocade fabric stocking is edged with a gorgeous tapestry ribbon and an elegant velvet cord forms a hanging loop.

Materials

❋ ³/₄ yd. of Victorian or antique-style fabric
❋ ¹/₂ yd. of 1¹/₂" wide ribbon trim
❋ 8" of decorative cording for loop hanger on stocking
❋ 2" tall porcelain angel bust
❋ Scrap of lace or ribbon for bodice on angel
❋ 2 yds. of 1¹/₂" wide wire-edged ribbon for skirt of angel
❋ 2 yds. of 1" wide wire-edged ribbon for skirt of angel
❋ 10" of 2" wide scalloped lace edging
❋ 2 yds. of ¹/₈" wide satin ribbon
❋ One small ribbon rose
❋ ²/₃ yd. of picot edged pleated sheer trim
❋ One pearl bridal spray
❋ Hot glue gun
❋ **Pattern Piece Needed:** Stocking Pattern found on pull-out section

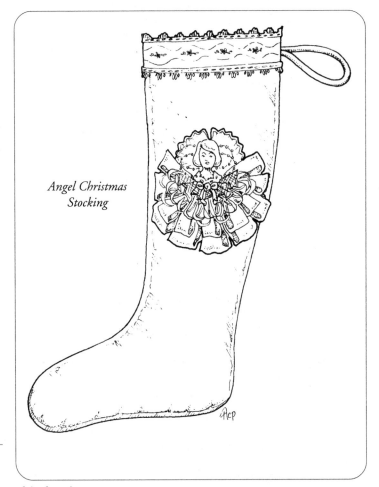

Angel Christmas Stocking

A. Stocking Construction

1. Cut two stocking pieces from the stocking pattern.

2. With right sides together, begin stitching the stocking at the top of the front leg seam. Stitch for 3 to 4" and stop.

3. Open the stocking pieces out flat and finish the top edge of the stocking front and back by serging or zigzagging across the edge.

4. Place the ribbon trim flush with the top of the stocking and stitch in place. The ends of the ribbon trim will be caught in the center back seam.

5. Fold the cording for the loop in half and pin it in place on top of the ribbon trim, having the ends flush with the raw fabric edge at the back of the stocking.

6. Place the pieces with right sides together again and continue stitching down the front of the leg, around the foot, and up the back to the top of the stocking. Stitch the seam across the loop several times to make it very secure. Finish the seam with a serger or zigzag and turn the stocking to the right side.

B. Making the Angel

1. Cut the pleated picot-edged trim in half, making two 12" pieces. Trim the ends of the trim as shown in figure 1 (**fig. 1**). Run a gathering stitch down the longest side of the trim. Pull up the gathers and tie off to form one side of the wings (**fig. 2**). Repeat with the other piece of trim for the other half of the wings.

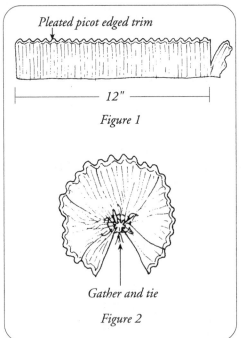

Pleated picot edged trim

|← 12" →|

Figure 1

Gather and tie

Figure 2

2. Glue the wings together at the center. Cut apart the pearl bridal spray and glue the ends at the center of the wings (**fig. 3**).

3. Glue a piece of lace or ribbon around the lower edge of the angel bust to make the bodice (see **fig. 4**).

4. Glue the angel bust in place on top of the wings (**fig. 4**).

5. Make the skirt by looping wide wire-edged ribbon and folding it every 4¹/₂". Make five loops. After the fifth loop, make five more loops towards the other side (as if you were making a bow). Stitch in the center at the folds to secure (**fig. 5**).

6. Repeat step 4 with the narrower wire-edged ribbon. Secure the narrow looped ribbon to the center of the wider loops.

7. Tie a small bow with a piece of the ¹/₈" wide satin ribbon. Set the bow aside.

8. With the remaining ¹/₈" ribbon, create a multi-looped bow approximately 5" wide. Secure the bow at the center. Glue this bow to the bottom of the angel bust with loops extending out both sides (**fig. 6**).

9. Glue the skirt in place against the bottom of the angel bust behind the narrow ribbon loops attached in step 8. Arrange the loops to create the skirt.

10. Trim the ends and gather the 10" piece of scalloped lace edging the same as the wing pieces in step 1.

11. Glue the lace in place at the back of the angel just under the bodice on top of the skirt (see the finished drawing).

12. Glue the bow made in step 7 to the lower edge of the bodice. Glue the ribbon rose in the center of the bow.

13. The angel may be either glued or stitched to the stocking. ▦

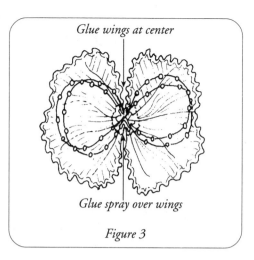

Glue wings at center

Glue spray over wings

Figure 3

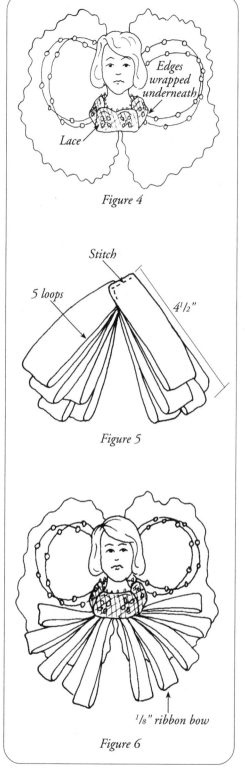

Edges wrapped underneath

Lace

Figure 4

Stitch

5 loops

4¹/₂"

Figure 5

¹/₈" ribbon bow

Figure 6

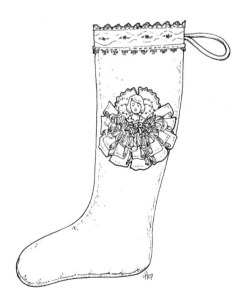

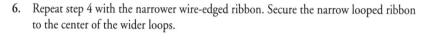

Introduction to Teddy Bear Dressing

Even my little dog, Jacob, loves to play with teddy bears. Never shall I forget my surprise years ago when I went to my first doll show to sell smocking machines, batiste and lace. Shortly after my arrival, I realized that there were as many teddy bears exhibited as dolls. Speaking with some of the "doll people," I realized that the teddy bear industry was included with the doll industry and that it was about as big as the doll craze. At the end of the show, after I had browsed every booth and sold 110 smocking machines, I figured out that if the teddy bear industry were as large as the doll, there surely weren't many books on dressing teddy bears. My first smocking book was called *Bearly Beginning Smocking* and featured teddy bear patterns and instructions as well as smocking instructions.

I featured Steiff bears in that book and we also used those beautiful Steiff bears on our television show. There are many wonderful bears on the market but my very favorite has always been Steiff. I appreciate their allowing us to use their bears once again.

Bear dressing is so much fun because you can do as much or as little as you wish. Since they are already completely dressed in their warm fur coats, you can just put a little hat and a collar on them and they look divine. We love to make dresses, suits and vests for our bears because we love to sew! Enjoy these patterns to make bear clothing. With the to-the-waist dress and the boy's shorts and vest, you can make many variations for your special bear. If your little ones love bears, you might enjoy making a bear outfit similar to and out of the same material as your little people's clothing. What a memory to have a bear dressed in the same type of suit or dress that mom or grandmother made for the child when he/she was little.

I am very happy to tell you that most people who are dressing dolls and bears aren't children at all, but real grown up people like you and me. How relieved I felt when I found out that it was all right to play with dolls again! I was a real doll and teddy bear person when I was little; I am more of a doll and teddy bear person at age 53. When I am 75, I expect to be even more of a doll and bear lover since I will probably have a little more time to sew and play. On second thought, my mother was busier at age 75 than she was at age 60 before she retired. Maybe I had better take the time to sew and play with dolls and bears right now. I have just given myself permission to do something I really like to do, and I give you permission also. Have fun dressing your bears! I would love for you to send me a picture of you and your bears that you dressed!

Crazy Patch Vest

I love crazy patch! This bear vest is made of tiny pieces of shiny fabrics. After the crazy patch piecing was completed, we stitched a beautiful machine feather stitch in gold lamé thread. We love combining solid colors and prints in the same outfit and we think your teddy bear will love this vest. It closes in the front with three buttonholes and buttons. Of course, we used pearl buttons to close this traditional garment for a wonderful bear.

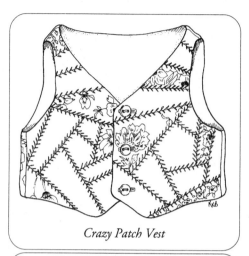

Crazy Patch Vest

Materials

- Scraps of fabrics for constructing crazy patch
- $^1/_4$ yd. of lining fabric to complement crazy patch colors
- Metallic thread
- Thread to match lining fabric for construction
- 3 buttons ($^3/_8$")
- $^1/_4$ yd. of muslin for crazy patch base fabric

Sizing

- Small—will fit 10$^1/_2$" bear
- Medium—will fit 12$^1/_2$" bear
- Large—will fit 16$^1/_2$" bear

- **Bear Pattern Pieces Needed:** vest front and vest back; pattern pieces can be found on pages 270-271

Directions

1. Trace a whole vest back pattern and two vest front patterns onto the muslin. Remember to trace a right side and left side of the vest front. Refer to the Crazy Patch instructions (pg. 240) and cover each of the three outlined pattern pieces with crazy patch. Be sure to keep the pieces of the crazy patch small. Embellish the seams of the crazy patch using metallic thread.

2. Cut one vest back and two vest fronts from the crazy patch fabric. From the lining fabric, cut one vest back from the fold and two vest fronts.

3. With right sides together, stitch the side seams of the crazy patch back and front pieces using a $^1/_4$" seam allowance. Press the seams open (**fig. 1**).

4. With right sides together, stitch the side seams of the vest lining front and back pieces using a $^1/_4$" seam. Press the seams open (**refer to fig. 1**).

5. Place the vest and lining with right sides together and pin in place. Stitch the lining and vest together using a $^1/_4$" seam allowance along all edges except the shoulder seams and 2" at the center back neck edge (**fig. 2**).

6. Clip the curves and points. Turn the vest through the opening at the center back and press.

7. Place the vest with right sides together and stitch the shoulder seams using a $^1/_4$" seam. Zigzag or serge the seam allowance. Fold the seam allowance toward the vest back and hand stitch to the lining (**fig. 3**).

8. Whip stitch the opening at the center back neck edge to close it.

9. Work 3 buttonholes on the left side of the vest and attach buttons to the right side. ▨

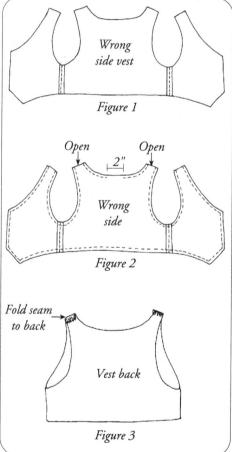

Wrong side vest

Figure 1

Open |—2"—| *Open*

Wrong side

Figure 2

Fold seam to back →

Vest back

Figure 3

Pull-On Shorts

After completing the sophisticated and very fancy crazy patch vest for your bear, you most certainly will want to make a pair of pants to complete his outfit. These little short pants are made of a bright green satin and have elastic around the waist. The green satin is also found in his crazy patch vest. The legs of the shorts are machine hemmed and I believe you will find this garment easy to make.

Materials

- ☙ ¹/₄ yd. of fabric (satin)
- ☙ ¹/₃ yd. of ¹/₂" wide elastic
- ☙ Thread to match fabric

Sizing

- ☙ Small—will fit 10¹/₂" bear
- ☙ Medium—will fit 12¹/₂" bear
- ☙ Large—will fit 16¹/₂" bear

- ☙ **Bear Pattern Piece Needed:** pants, found on pages 267-268

Directions

NOTE: All seam allowances are ¹/₄" unless otherwise noted. All seams are finished with a serger or zigzag.

1. Cut two pieces from the pattern piece for the pants. Mark the fold line and mark the center fronts.

2. Place the pieces right sides together and stitch the center front seam and the center back seam (**fig. 1**).

3. Place the lower crotch edges with right sides together and stitch, using a ¹/₄" seam (**fig. 2**).

4. Finish the raw edge at the leg openings using a zigzag or serger. Fold the hem up ¹/₈" and topstitch in place (**fig. 3**).

5. Finish the raw edge at the waistline of the pants using a zigzag or serger. Create a casing for the elastic by folding ³/₄" of the top edge to the inside of the pants and topstitch close to the edge, leaving a small opening to insert the elastic (**see fig. 4**).

6. Topstitch ¹/₈" away from the top folded edge of the casing (**see fig. 4**).

7. Measure around the waist of the bear. Cut the elastic 1" shorter than this measurement.

8. Insert the elastic into the casing and stitch the ends of the elastic together (**fig. 4**).

9. Whip stitch the opening closed (**fig. 5**). ▨

Pull-On Shorts

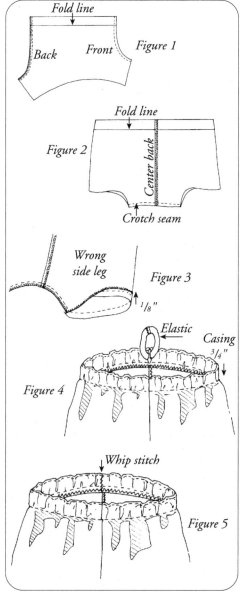

Fold line

Back   Front   Figure 1

Fold line

Figure 2   Center back   Crotch seam

Wrong side leg   Figure 3   ¹/₈"

Elastic   Casing ³/₄"

Figure 4

Whip stitch

Figure 5

Heirloom Puffing Dress

Our little girl bears love fancy and fluff just as much as Joanna did when she was little. The girl bears are always asking me, "Martha, when are we going to get a really fancy dress?" It seemed time to present them with one and we chose robin's egg blue Swiss Nelona batiste with white French laces and a delicate scalloped collar. The collar is finished with gathered white French lace edging. The puffing in the fancy band has a row of white French lace at the top and at the bottom. Around the bottom of the pretty ruffle is white French edging stitched on flat. The puffed sleeves have elastic and the bottom is finished with white French lace edging. A wing needle/entredeux stitch by machine has been used to stitch the gathered lace to the outside edge of the pretty white batiste collar and more wing needle work was used to attach the lace insertion to the top and bottom of the puffing. A beautiful machine embroidery design was stitched on the collar using some of the precious designs which are available. The bow is white, the leaves are green and the flowers are in two shades of pink. Buttons and buttonholes are used to close this dress.

Heirloom Puffing Dress

Materials

- ❧ ⁷/₈ yd. of robin's egg blue Swiss batiste (Nelona) for dress
- ❧ ¹/₄ yd. of white Swiss batiste (Nelona) for collar
- ❧ 2¹/₂ yds. of ¹/₂" wide lace insertion
- ❧ 4¹/₂ yds. of ¹/₂" wide lace edging
- ❧ 3 buttons (³/₈") - (only 2 buttons for small bear)
- ❧ Thread to match lace
- ❧ ¹/₄ yd. of ¹/₈" elastic
- ❧ *100 wing needle - optional
- ❧ *¹/₂ yd. of stabilizer - optional

Sizing

- ❧ Small—will fit 10¹/₂" bear
- ❧ Medium—will fit 12¹/₂" bear
- ❧ Large—will fit 16¹/₂" bear
- ❧ **Bear Pattern Pieces Needed:** front bodice, back bodice, sleeve, collar; pattern pieces can be found on pages 269-271
- ❧ **Template Needed:** Bear Collar Embroidery Template found on page 158

I. Cutting

1. Cut two front bodices on the fold. Cut two back bodices on the fold, and mark the fold on each back piece with a fabric marker or pencil. Cut two sleeves and transfer all markings, also mark the center of each sleeve (**fig. 1 - cutting guide**).

2. Upper skirt - Tear a strip of fabric to the following measurements according to the dress size: Small—4¹/₂" by 45"; Medium—5" by 45"; Large—5¹/₂" by 45". This strip should be torn across the fabric from selvage to selvage. If some of the length has to be removed to achieve a 45" width, overcast or serge the short cut edge with a zigzag or serger (**fig. 2**).

3. Tear two strips of fabric 2" by 45" for the puffing.

4. Tear two strips of fabric 2¹/₂" by 45" for the ruffle.

5. Cut a square of white fabric 9" by 9" for the collar.

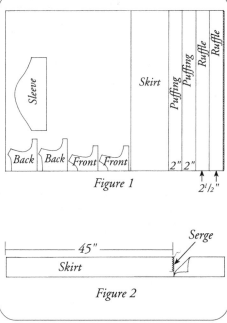

Figure 1

Figure 2

II. General Information

1. All seams are ¹/₄" unless otherwise indicated.

2. Several methods of lace to fabric have been used in constructing this dress. When the instructions state "using the technique lace to fabric", method I, II or III will also be given.

The three lace to fabric methods are given below:

- Method I- Refer to the Lace to Fabric technique found in the Beginning Techniques (pg. 213).

- Method II - Zigzagging the lace on top of the fabric. Place the lace on top of the fabric, overlapping the fabric by ³/₈". Stitch along the lace heading using a small, tight zigzag (length =1; width = 2 to 1¹/₂). Trim the excess fabric from behind the lace.

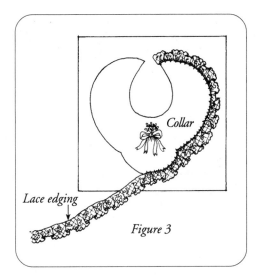

Figure 3

- Method III - Hemstitching the lace to the fabric. A wing needle and stabilizer will be needed for this method. Place the lace on top of the fabric overlapping the fabric by ³/₈". Place stabilizer behind the fabric to give the hemstitches stability. Stitch along the lace heading using a hemstitch (Refer to Machine Entredeux - pg. 216). Trim the excess fabric from behind the lace.

III. Constructing the Bodices, Collar and Sleeves

1. Trace the collar onto the white fabric with a washout marker or pencil. Embroider by hand or machine the design given or a design of your choice along the center front. Do not cut out the collar.

2. Measure around the outer edge of the collar. Do not include the neck opening. Cut a piece of lace edging twice this measurement. Gather the lace edging by pulling the top thread in the lace heading. Place the gathered lace on the drawn line. Attach the lace to the line using the technique lace to fabric - Method II or III (fig. 3). Trim the fabric from behind the lace and cut out the neck opening.

3. Place the shoulders of the front bodices to the shoulders of the back bodices, right sides together, and stitch (fig. 4). Finish the seams using a zigzag or serger and press.

4. Place the wrong side of the collar to the right side of the bodices, matching the neck edges and matching the center of the collar with the center of one front bodice (fig. 5). Fold the remaining front and back bodices on top of the collar along the back fold lines. The collar will be sandwiched between the two layers of the bodice.

5. Stitch along the neckline through both layers of the bodice and the collar. Clip the seam and flip the upper bodice layer to the wrong side. Press. This finishes the neck.

6. Match the edges of the bodices and treat both bodice layers as one for the remaining construction steps (fig. 6).

7. Sleeves - Run two rows of gathering stitches ¹/₈" and ¹/₄" from the raw edge between the marks on each sleeve cap.

8. Attach flat edging lace along the bottom edge of each sleeve using the technique, lace to fabric (Method I).

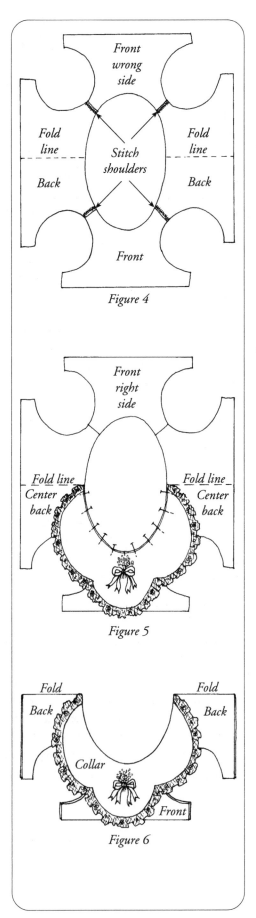

Figure 4

Figure 5

Figure 6

9. Draw a line across the wrong side of each sleeve ¹/₂" from the lace seam. Cut a piece of elastic 4¹/₄" long for each sleeve. Place the end of the elastic even with the edge of the fabric on the wrong side of the sleeve. Straight stitch a few tiny stitches through the elastic. With the presser foot down and the needle up, adjust the width of the stitch so that the zigzag will encase the elastic. You do not want the needle to pierce the elastic while zigzagging (**fig. 7**). Stretch the elastic as you stitch, ending with a few tiny straight stitches through the elastic to secure.

10. Place the sleeves to the arm opening, right sides together. Gather the sleeves to fit the arm opening. Stitch the sleeves into the dress (**fig. 8**). Be sure that the collar does not get caught in the sleeve seam.

11. Work buttonholes on the left side of the dress back, placing the top buttonhole ¹/₂" from the top finished neck edge. Place the bottom buttonhole ³/₄" from the bottom raw edge of the back bodice. For the medium and large dresses position another buttonhole between these two.

12. Place the sleeves/sides of the bodice right sides together. Stitch and overcast the seam allowance with a zigzag or serger (**fig. 9**).

IV. Decorating the Skirt

(refer to figure 10 for steps 1 - 9)

1. Stitch the 2" puffing strips together with a tiny seam. You now have a strip 2" by 90".

2. Run gathering rows at ¹/₂" on each side of the strip. Refer to the directions for making puffing found on page 219. This strip should be gathered with a 2-to-1 fullness, which means 90" should be gathered to 45".

3. Cut two pieces of lace insertion 45" long. Place one piece of lace insertion on top of the puffing with the heading of the lace even with the gathering row. Attach the lace to the fabric using Method II or III. Remember, if using a hemstitch, stabilizer will be needed under the puffing. Repeat, attaching lace on the other side of the puffing.

4. Tear away the stabilizer (if used) and trim away the excess fabric from behind the lace. Press.

5. Stitch the 2¹/₂" ruffle strips together with a tiny seam. You now have a ruffle strip 2¹/₂" by 90".

6. Attach flat lace edging to one long side of the ruffle using the technique lace to fabric (Method I).

7. Gather the ruffle using a machine gathering foot (stitch at a ¹/₂" seam) or run two rows of gathering stitches along the top of the ruffle at ¹/₄" and ¹/₂". The ruffle strip should measure 45" when gathered.

8. Place the lace/puffing/lace band on the ruffle with the heading of the lace over the gathering line of the ruffle. Stitch the band to the ruffle using the technique lace to fabric (Method II or III). Trim the excess fabric from behind the lace.

9. Attach the band/ruffle to the upper skirt piece using the technique lace to fabric (Method II or III) (**fig. 10**).

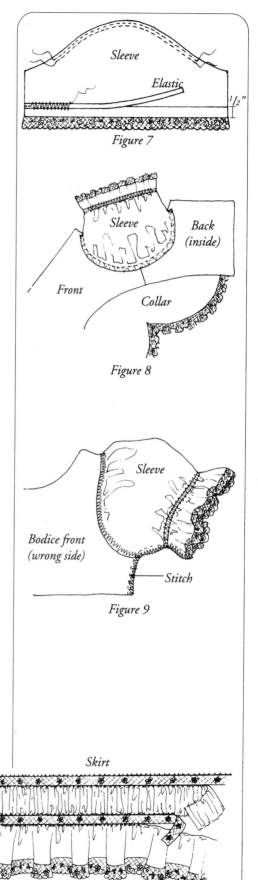

Figure 7

Figure 8

Figure 9

Figure 10

1. Fold the skirt piece in half, right sides together, matching the edges. Be sure to match the laces. Stitch a $^1/_2$" seam, starting at the bottom edge of the ruffle and stopping $^1/_2$" above the fancy band seam (**fig. 11**). From the wrong side, press the seam towards your right, also pressing the unstitched part. This creates an opening or placket in the skirt.

2. Run two rows of gathering stitches along the top of the skirt $^1/_8$" and $^1/_4$" from the top edge.

3. Adjust the gathers to fit the bottom of the bodice. The $^1/_2$" lap that is folded under at the center skirt back should be beneath the buttonholes and will lap over the other side. Stitch the skirt to the bodice and overcast the seam allowance with a zigzag or serger.

4. Attach the buttons along the back bodice opposite the buttonholes. ▧

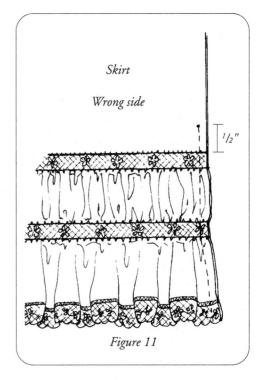

Skirt

Wrong side

$^1/_2$"

Figure 11

Collar Embroidery Template

Satin Party Dress

This green satin party dress features long sleeves, antique laces and a very festive look. The satin matches the little boy bear pants; perhaps this is a brother/sister outfit. A sweet piece of antique edging is slightly gathered around the collar and a piece of ecru silk ribbon has been run through the top of this lace, then tied in the back. A little piece of French ecru trim is stitched at the bottom of each sleeve and elastic is used to gather in the fullness at the bottom of each sleeve. The back is closed with three buttons and button-holes. Antique colored pearl buttons finish the look.

Satin Party Dress

Materials

- ⅔ yd. of satin fabric
- 3 buttons - size ⅜" (only 2 buttons for size small)
- ⅓ yd. of ⅛" wide elastic
- ½ yd. of 2" wide gallooning (scalloped edges on both sides of the lace) for the collar. The collar lace used in this dress was a piece of gallooning with a small "ladder" along the top edge. ⅔ yd. of ⅛" silk ribbon was woven through the "ladder".
- ⅔ yd. of ½" lace edging for sleeves
- 1 small silk ribbon rose
- Thread to match lace and fabric

Sizing

- Small—will fit 10½" bear
- Medium—will fit 12½" bear
- Large—will fit 16½" bear

- **Bear Pattern Pieces Needed:** front bodice, back bodice, and sleeve; pattern pieces can be found on pages 269-270.

I. Cutting

1. Cut two front bodices on the fold. Cut two back bodices on the fold, and mark the fold on each piece with a fabric marker or pencil. Add 1" to the lower edge of the sleeve pattern piece, then cut two sleeves and transfer all markings; also mark the center of each sleeve.

2. Tear or cut a skirt piece across the width of fabric by the following measurements according to the size you are making: Small—8½" by 45"; Medium—9½" by 45"; Large—10½" by 45". This strip should be torn across the fabric from selvage to selvage. If some of the length has to be removed to achieve a 45" width, overcast or serge the short cut edge with a zigzag or serger. Also, serge or zigzag along one long side of the skirt to finish the edge. The finished long side of the skirt will be the lower edge of the skirt (**fig. 1**).

II. Construction

1. All seams are ¼" unless otherwise noted, and finished with a serger or zigzag.

2. Place the shoulders of the front bodices to the shoulders of the back bodices, right sides together, and stitch (**fig. 2**). Finish the seams using a zigzag or serger and press.

3. Place the front and back bodices on top of each other, right sides together, folding along the back fold lines.

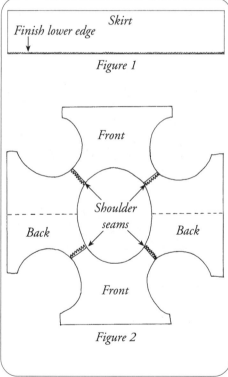

Skirt

Finish lower edge

Figure 1

Front

Back — Shoulder seams — Back

Front

Figure 2

4. Stitch along the neckline through both layers of the bodice. Clip the seam and flip one layer of the bodice to the wrong side. Press.

5. Turn the back, cut edges of the collar lace to the wrong side ¼" and ¼" again. Stitch in place.

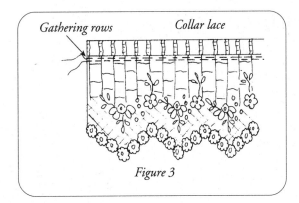

Gathering rows   Collar lace

Figure 3

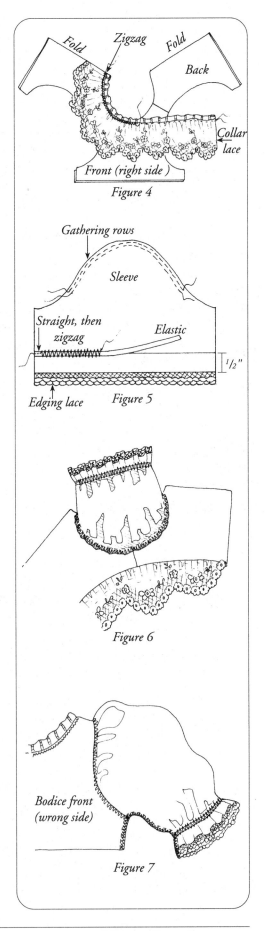

Fold   Zigzag   Fold

Back

Front (right side)

Collar lace

Figure 4

Gathering rows

Sleeve

Straight, then zigzag

Elastic

1/2"

Edging lace   Figure 5

Figure 6

Bodice front (wrong side)

Figure 7

6. Run two rows of gathering stitches ³/₈" and ¹/₂" from the top scalloped edge of the lace (**fig. 3**). Gather the lace to fit the neck edge. Place the wrong side of the lace along the right side of the bodice with the gathering rows at the top edge of the neck. Pin in place. Zigzag the collar to the dress between the two gathering rows (**fig. 4**).

7. Match the edges of the bodices and treat both bodice layers as one for the remaining construction steps (**refer to fig. 4**).

8. Sleeves - Run two rows of gathering stitches ¹/₈" and ¹/₄" from the raw edge between the marks along each sleeve cap.

9. Attach flat edging lace along the bottom edge of each sleeve, using the technique lace to fabric.

10. Draw a line across the wrong side of each sleeve ¹/₂" from the lace seam. Cut a piece of elastic 4¹/₄" long for each sleeve. Place the end of the elastic even with the edge of the fabric on the wrong side of the sleeve. Straight stitch a few tiny stitches through the elastic. With the presser foot down and the needle up, adjust the width of the stitch so that the zigzag will encase the elastic. You do not want the needle to pierce the elastic while zigzagging (**fig. 5**). Stretch the elastic as you stitch, ending with a few tiny straight stitches through the elastic to secure.

11. Place the sleeves to the arm opening, right sides together. Gather the sleeves to fit the arm opening. Stitch the sleeves into the dress (**fig. 6**).

12. Work buttonholes on the left side of the dress back, placing the top buttonhole ¹/₂" from the top finished neck edge. Place the bottom buttonhole ³/₄" from the bottom raw edge of the back bodice. For the medium and large dresses position another buttonhole between these two.

13. Place the sleeves/sides of the bodice right sides together. Stitch and overcast the seam allowance with a zigzag or serger (**fig. 7**).

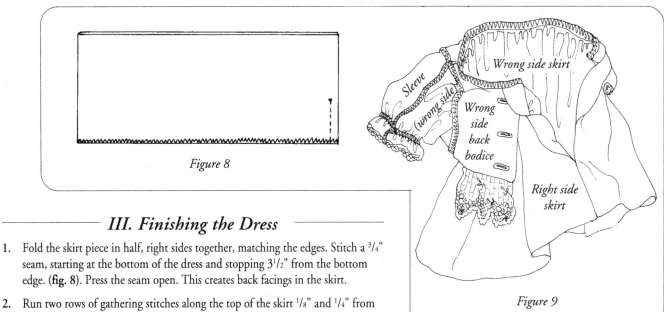

Figure 8

Figure 9

Wrong side skirt

Sleeve (wrong side)

Wrong side back bodice

Right side skirt

III. Finishing the Dress

1. Fold the skirt piece in half, right sides together, matching the edges. Stitch a $^3/_4$" seam, starting at the bottom of the dress and stopping $3^1/_2$" from the bottom edge. (**fig. 8**). Press the seam open. This creates back facings in the skirt.

2. Run two rows of gathering stitches along the top of the skirt $^1/_8$" and $^1/_4$" from the top edge.

3. Adjust the gathers to fit the bottom of the bodice so that the crease at the skirt center back will meet the center back fold of the bodice. Wrap the skirt facings to the outside, over the back bodice edge. Stitch the skirt to the bodice and overcast the seam allowance with a zigzag or serger (**fig. 9**).

4. Attach the buttons along the back bodice opposite the buttonholes.

5. Hem the skirt to the desired length.

6. If desired, run ribbon through the gallooning above the zigzag at the lace collar. Tie the excess ribbon into a bow at the back of the dress. Attach the silk rose at the center front neckline. ▨

Introduction To Nursery Ensemble

How exciting it is to prepare for the birth of a new baby! I have known several grandmothers who made absolutely gorgeous bassinet ensembles. Years ago when Joe and I were in London, I went into Harrod's and saw the most breathtaking bassinet that I have ever seen. It had a crown above the bassinet with netting falling around the crown to the floor. There were about 6 rows of smocking in pink, green, blue and yellow holding in the fullness of the batiste skirt. That is about all I remember about the bassinet except for the price. This was several years ago and the price was over $5,000 U.S. dollars. I gulped and quickly passed by this gorgeous thing but I couldn't get it out of my mind. Much to his disgust, I suggested to Joe that we go look at it one more time before we left London. Being the sweetheart that he his, Joe said, "O.K. we'll go to that baby department one more time." When we arrived, the bassinet was gone. I asked the sales person, "Where is that beautiful bassinet?" She replied, "We sold it yesterday." I then asked her, "Do you sell many of those?" She replied, "We sell all that we can get. Since it is handmade we can't get very many." I gulped and Joe was even more horrified. "Who in the world would pay $5,000 for a baby basket?" he inquired. I acted shocked also; however, in the back of my mind, I knew that it was worth $5000 and that if we had been rich, I might have bought it myself.

The vision of that baby bassinet has never left me. On the next two trips to Harrod's there was never another bassinet like that one. The sales personnel at Harrod's referred me to another VERY EXPENSIVE small store in London which did have pretty bassinets. Joe and I, once again, traipsed across London. This time we found a bassinet, also costing over $6,000 US dollars; however, it had no hand work, no smocking and it was made of a nylon organza. Don't misunderstand me, it was gorgeous, nylon and all. Joe was shocked even more and I just kept my mouth shut this time.

What did we decide that we had to do for this television series? You guessed it, a beautiful baby bassinet and I promise that it is even more beautiful than the one at Harrod's years ago. If you have a new baby coming in your family, you might consider making this bassinet for him/her. Even if you don't want to make the bassinet, I thought you would love the directions in case you ever decide to tackle a project like this. We have also included a diaper stacker, a bassinet blanket, a bassinet pillow, and a paneled canopy to hang from the ceiling. If you think you would love one of these for a future child or grandchild, my suggestion is to get started now, since this isn't a speedy project at all. But what a magnificent bassinet it is!

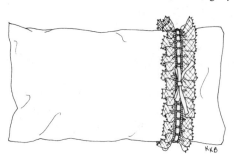

Bassinet

Our bassinet is made of a pale aqua silk dupioni and has cotton French netting over the silk dupioni. The lining on both the hood and in the bassinet is white. The smocking is white and the green roses and yellow flowers in the bottom border of the smocking are of silk ribbon embroidery. The skirt has two tiers and they are finished by stitching white polyester satin ribbon on the bottom. The hood of the bassinet is absolutely gorgeous also. It is covered with green silk dupioni and has several layers of white netting ruffles around the front of the hood. Buttons pull the fabric in on the underside of the hood. There is some beautiful silk ribbon embroidery on the center back of the hood. The colors are pale aqua, two shades of pink, yellow and pale blue. A beautiful white satin ribbon bow is stitched below the silk ribbon embroidery and four long streamers hang down. What an incredible way to welcome the new baby. What a lovely home decorating piece to leave in a bedroom forever. Just coordinate the room around the same colors you used for the bassinet. I would love to see a collection of dolls stored in this lovely piece long after the little baby has grown up.

In order to reproduce the bassinet shown, buy the total yardage given here. If the colors will be combined differently (for example: the inside lining of the bassinet will be the same color as the smocked skirt), refer to the instructions for each individual part of the bassinet. Yardage will be given for each section. The bassinet shown measures 88" around the top edge and 27" from the floor to the top edge of the bassinet, excluding the hood. Changes in height will require no change in yardage. If the bassinet used is significantly more than 88" around the top edge, add one extra yard of the colored silk.

Bassinet

Supplies

- 1 purchased baby bassinet with hood
- 8 yds. of aqua silk dupioni
- 3 yds. of white silk dupioni
- 16 yds. of cotton netting
- 9 button forms for covering, $^5/_8$"
- 1 twin size quilt batting
- 1$^1/_2$ yds. of 2$^1/_2$" wide decorative ribbon
- 13 yds. of $^1/_4$" wide double-faced white satin ribbon
- 7 yds. of $^1/_8$" white satin ribbon
- 7 yds. of $^1/_8$" aqua satin ribbon
- 1 yd. of pink and yellow $^1/_4$" double-faced satin ribbon
- Floss and silk ribbon: refer to smocking graph and template
- 2$^1/_2$ yds. of white $^3/_4$" wide Velcro
- Ten 2$^1/_2$" washers
- Fabric glue
- Craft glue
- **Templates Required:** Nursery Ensemble Embroidery Template found on page 168, Netting Curve Template found on page 171
- **Bassinet Smocking Graph** found on page 168

I. Lining the Bassinet

Supplies

- 2$^1/_2$ yds. of white silk dupioni
- Ten 2$^1/_2$" washers
- Craft glue
- 2$^1/_2$ yds. of $^3/_4$" white Velcro

1. Remove the hood from the bassinet.

2. Place the silk into the bassinet and smooth it into the bottom.

3. Use the craft glue to attach the washers to the bottom of the mattress, giving it extra weight to keep it in place. Cover the mattress with a sheet, then place the mattress into the bassinet to hold the fabric in the bottom; smooth the fabric up the sides and over the edge. Keep it smooth along the flat sides, head and foot, letting the excess fabric collect at the corners.

4. Fold three deep pleats in the fabric at each corner, having the folds of the pleats toward the sides of the bassinet (**fig. 1**).

5. Glue the fabric in place along the outer edge of the bassinet about 2¹/₂" from the top edge. Trim the raw edge of the silk to neaten it and make it an even width all the way around the bassinet. Make sure that it is securely glued (**see fig. 2**).

6. Glue the loop side of the Velcro around the top of the bassinet, 2¹/₂" from the top edge (it will cover the fabric edges) (**fig. 2**). The hook side of the Velcro will be attached to the smocked skirt in a later step.

II. Smocked Bassinet Skirt

Supplies

- 7¹/₂ yds. of aqua silk dupioni, 45" wide
- 15 yds. of cotton netting, 45" or wider
- 13 yds. of ¹/₄" wide double-faced white satin ribbon
- 7 yds. of ¹/₈" white satin ribbon
- 7 yds. of ¹/₈" aqua satin ribbon
- 1 yd. of pink and yellow ¹/₄" double-faced satin ribbon
- Floss and silk ribbon: refer to smocking graph and template
- **Template Needed:** Bassinet Skirt Smocking Graph and Template found on page 168

A. Cutting and Preparation

1. For the skirt shown (27" finished length), trim one selvage edge of the 7¹/₂ yard piece of silk dupioni to create a strip 7¹/₂ yards long and 36" wide.

2. Finish the long cut edge with a serger, zigzag or narrow hem.

3. Along one long edge, turn up a 5" hem. Press in place and then stitch the hem by machine, using matching thread. A straight stitch will be fine, the hem will not show through the netting overlay if the thread is a good match (**see fig. 3**).

4. Along the un-hemmed edge of the strip, press under a 4" hem. Set the silk aside while preparing the netting (**fig. 3**).

5. Cut the netting into two pieces, each 7¹/₂ yards long. Trim one piece to be 32" wide and 7¹/₂ yards long. Trim the other piece to be 22" wide and 7¹/₂ yards long.

6. On one long edge of each netting piece (this will become the bottom edge), use the template to mark a curve on each corner of the netting, and trim the corners along the curve lines (**see fig. 4**).

7. Place a strip of the white ¹/₄" ribbon under the edge of the 22" wide netting with one edge of the ribbon on the netting and the other edge barely off the netting. Begin at one top corner, go down the side and around the bottom curve, across the bottom and around the other bottom curve, then up the side back to the other top corner. Stitch in place along the edge that is on the netting (**fig. 4**).

8. Press the ribbon away from the netting, then fold the ribbon edge to the other side of the netting, forming a hemmed edge. Stitch the loose edge of the ribbon in place (**fig. 5**).

9. Using ³/₈" wide white ribbon, repeat the ribbon finish along the side and bottom edges of the remaining netting.

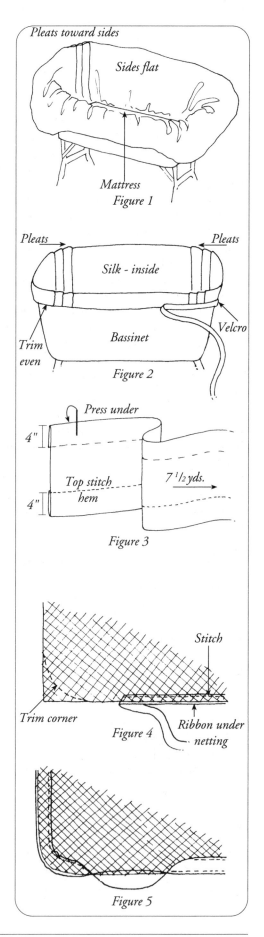

Pleats toward sides

Sides flat

Mattress
Figure 1

Pleats   Pleats

Silk - inside

Velcro

Trim even

Bassinet

Figure 2

Press under

4"

Top stitch hem

7 ¹/₂ yds.

4"

Figure 3

Stitch

Trim corner

Figure 4

Ribbon under netting

Figure 5

10. Attach a strip of ¼" ribbon along the same edges of the netting, 1" away from the ⅜" ribbon hem (**fig. 6**).

11. Place the shorter netting piece over the longer piece, having the top edges and side edges even. Fold a 4" hem to the inside along the top edge of the netting piece, folding both pieces as one; press the crease (**fig. 7**).

12. Lay the silk piece out as flat as possible and place the netting over the silk, matching the top folded edges. Let the side edges of the netting fall 1" from the side edges of the silk (**fig. 8**).

B. Pleating and Smocking

1. This step requires two people. It is practically impossible for one person to do this step alone, so please be sure that two people do this together.

2. Thread the pleater for 6 whole space rows. Use a white thread or a color to match the silk in the pleating rows, as these threads will be left in the skirt. Cut the threads 8 - 9 yards long or use a pleater which uses bobbins and be sure that the bobbins are full. Use a heavy quilting thread that will support the weight of the pleated fabric. Remember that the piece to be pleated is 7½ yards long!

3. Very carefully line up the top folded edges of the fabric and netting with the tenth whole-space groove of the pleater. Let one person guide the fabric to feed it through the pleater, while the other person turns the pleater. The fabric layers will have to be held fairly taut to prevent the layers from shifting a lot during pleating, but they should not be held so tightly that the fabric will not feed evenly through the pleater.

4. When the pleating is complete, remove the pleats at each end up to the point where the netting overlay begins. Tie off the pleating threads to the length around the top edge of the bassinet, in the sample it was 88".

5. Smock the bassinet skirt using the following instructions and the graph on page 168. Leave the top and bottom rows un-smocked, they are holding rows. Use three strands of DMC white floss to smock the geometric portion of the design.

   a. Work a row of outline stitches across row 1 (thread always above the needle).

   b. Work a row of stem stitches just below the first row (thread always below the needle).

   c. Between rows 1 and 2, work whole-space, 1-step waves across the row.

   d. Between rows 2 and 3, work a mirror image of the previous row so that the design forms diamonds.

   e. Begin on row 3, just below a down cable of the previous row. Between rows 3 and 4½, work 1½ space, 5-step waves; skip one space between each complete wave (follow the graph closely).

6. Work the silk ribbon embroidery in every other open space between the points (refer to the graph and stitch template for placement and colors).

7. When the smocking and embroidery are completed, remove the top holding row thread, but leave the bottom holding row thread in place to stabilize the smocking.

C. Finishing the Bassinet Skirt

1. Place the skirt around the bassinet and be sure that no adjustments are needed to make the edges of the netting and the smocking meet at the open edges of the skirt. Pin or baste the seam, then sew the seam below the smocking. Turn under a double hem on the silk edges, having the seam line as the fold line. Leave this section of the seam open (**fig. 9**).

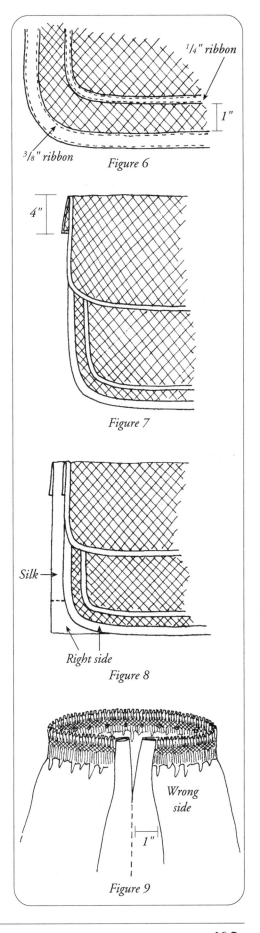

¼" ribbon

1"

⅜" ribbon

Figure 6

4"

Figure 7

Silk

Right side

Figure 8

Wrong side

1"

Figure 9

2. Use the fabric glue to attach the hook side of the Velcro to the back of the smocking, 2½" from the top edge of the ruffle.

3. Slip the skirt over the bassinet and press the Velcro in place. Pin the edges of the seam together, then whip the finished edges in place to complete the seam (**fig. 10**).

4. Make a very full ribbon rosette from the ¼" white satin ribbon, leaving tails at various lengths from 16" - 21" long (see page 239 for instructions). Tie knots about 6" apart along the length of the ribbon, then make loops so that the knots are at the tops of the loops. Optional: knots may be tied in the streamers, 2" - 3" apart.

5. Leave long tails of the aqua and white ⅛" ribbon, then make full loopy bows of those ribbons. Tack the ⅛" ribbon bows behind the ¼" ribbon bow. this creates a very large, full bow.

6. Fold the remaining ribbons off-center and attach to the back of the bow to create streamers.

7. Tack the rosette over the seam of the smocking, or attach it with a large snap.

— III. Covering the Hood —

Supplies

⊕+ ½ yd. of aqua silk dupioni
⊕+ ½ yd. of white silk dupioni
⊕+ 1 yd. of cotton netting
⊕+ 9 button forms for covering, ⅝"
⊕+ 1½ yds. of 2½" wide ribbon
⊕+ Floss and silk ribbon: refer to Bassinet Hood Template
⊕+ Polyfil batting
⊕+ **Template Needed:** Bassinet Hood Stitch Template found on page 168

1. Spread craft glue on the inside surface of the hood.

2. Press batting over the glue and let it dry until tacky.

3. Run a line of glue around the outside edge of the hood and fold the batting edges to the outside, pressing it in place over the glue (**see fig. 11**).

4. After the glue is dry, trim the excess batting away.

5. Place the white silk dupioni on the inside surface of the hood, over the batting. Leave enough silk to fold 1½" to the outside on all edges, then trim enough from the edges to cover the 9 buttons (**fig. 11**).

6. Cover the buttons, using two layers of silk or one layer of silk and a layer of interfacing so that the form will not show through.

7. Use a washout fabric marker or pencil to mark the button placement on the white silk dupioni inside the hood (**fig. 12**).

8. Using several strands of sturdy white thread, run the threads through the back of the buttons. Take the thread tails through the hood from the inside to the outside, attaching the buttons at the marks. Tie the threads into tight knots on the outside of the hood, giving the inside a padded look. Put a drop of craft glue on the knots to help secure them (**fig. 13**).

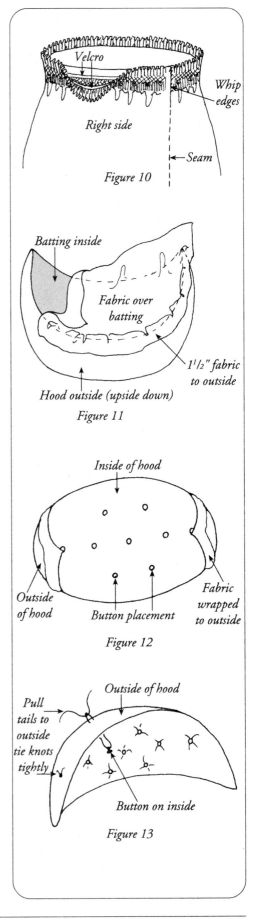

Velcro

Whip edges

Right side

Seam

Figure 10

Batting inside

Fabric over batting

1½" fabric to outside

Hood outside (upside down)

Figure 11

Inside of hood

Outside of hood

Button placement

Fabric wrapped to outside

Figure 12

Outside of hood

Pull tails to outside tie knots tightly

Button on inside

Figure 13

Bassinet Hood

9. Place a layer of batting over the outside of the hood and trim it to fit just inside the edge of the hood. Glue the batting in place.

10. For the next step, either make a paper pattern for the outside of the hood, or place the aqua silk over the hood and trace the shape onto the silk with a chalk pencil or crease the silk at the edges to show the shape. Transfer the embroidery design (pg. 168) to the fabric, centering the design on the back of the hood (see fig. 14).

11. Cut two pieces of the cotton netting that are larger than the hood shape on the aqua silk.

12. Place the two pieces of netting over the aqua silk. Baste the netting and silk layers together (fig. 14).

13. Working through all layers, stitch the embroidery design, using the template and stitch key found on page 168. Make and attach the ribbon bow, using the 2^1/$_2$" decorative ribbon. Add two extra tails to make the streamers.

14. Cut enough 3" wide strips of the cotton netting to make a two-layer ruffle that is four times as long as the front edge of the hood. Place two of the netting strips together and run a gathering stitch down the middle of the two pieces. At the end of the strips, place two more layered strips to slightly overlap the end of the first set and continue the gathering stitch. Repeat these steps until all of the netting has been used. Gather the ruffle to fit the front edge of the hood (fig. 15).

15. Cut out the hood cover, leaving a 1^1/$_2$" seam allowance on all edges. Place the embroidered hood fabric over the hood and turn the seam allowances under so that the folded edge of the fabric meets the edge of the hood. Pin or baste in place to be sure of the positioning (fig. 16).

16. When the hood cover is in place, whip it to the white fabric by hand around all edges. Make sure that the embroidery is centered and pull the fabric smooth and taut across the hood.

17. Place the ruffle across the front edge of the hood and adjust the gathers to fit. Pin the ruffle in place. Lift the ruffle away from the fabric along the front edge and whip the ruffle to the hood from underneath the gathering line (fig. 17).

18. Attach the hood to the completed bassinet. ▩

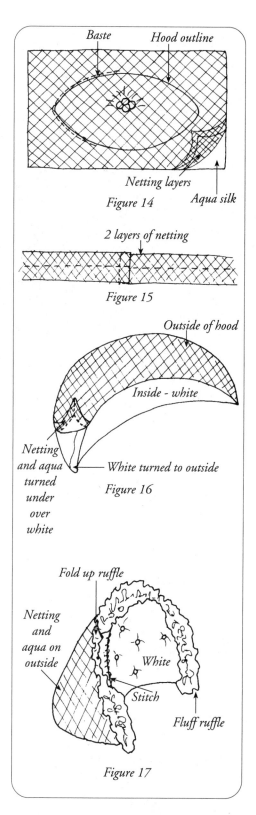

Baste   Hood outline

Netting layers   Aqua silk

Figure 14

2 layers of netting

Figure 15

Outside of hood

Inside - white

Netting and aqua turned under over white   White turned to outside

Figure 16

Fold up ruffle

Netting and aqua on outside   White

Stitch   Fluff ruffle

Figure 17

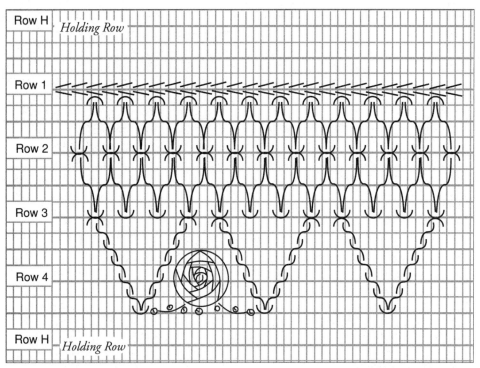

Row H — Holding Row
Row 1
Row 2
Row 3
Row 4
Row H — Holding Row

Smock with 3 strands of DMC white floss.

YLI Silk Ribbon 4mm #63

YLI silk ribbon 4mm #120

2 strands DMC 992

Bassinet smocking plate and template

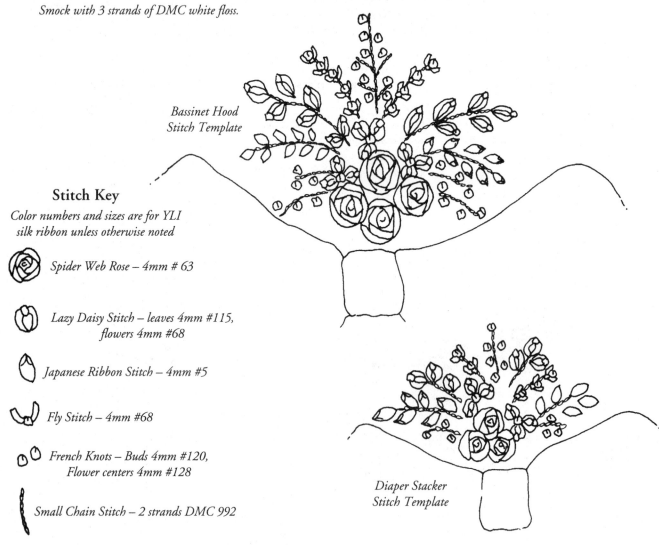

Bassinet Hood Stitch Template

Stitch Key

Color numbers and sizes are for YLI silk ribbon unless otherwise noted

Spider Web Rose – 4mm # 63

Lazy Daisy Stitch – leaves 4mm #115, flowers 4mm #68

Japanese Ribbon Stitch – 4mm #5

Fly Stitch – 4mm #68

French Knots – Buds 4mm #120, Flower centers 4mm #128

Small Chain Stitch – 2 strands DMC 992

Diaper Stacker Stitch Template

Paneled Canopy

From what I have been able to discover, canopies like these were originally used as mosquito nets to protect the baby. Thank goodness most of us don't have mosquitoes in our houses. I think this type of canopy is perfect for a beautiful room. Our canopy is made of the same white netting that is used around the bassinet. We attached ours to the ceiling and made it long enough to go to the bottom of the bassinet and puddle on the floor. White double-faced satin ribbon is stitched along the edges of the panels and beautiful pink, green, yellow and pink ribbons are used for the bows. We used brass rings for the two circles which form the crown of the canopy.

Supplies

- 18 yds. of cotton netting (45" wide)
- 2¹/₂ yds. of ³/₄" wide lace edging
- Optional: additional 83 yds. of ³/₄" wide lace edging
- 10 yds. of ⁵/₈" wide single-faced satin ribbon
- 10 yds. each of yellow and pink ¹/₄" double-faced satin ribbon
- 10 yds. each of white and green ¹/₈" double-faced satin ribbon
- 15 yds. of ⁵/₈" wide white double-faced satin ribbon
- 15 yds. of 2" wide white double-faced satin ribbon
- 5 yds. of 2" wide decorative ribbon
- Two brass rings: one 5" diameter, one 12" or 14" diameter (have each ring cut in one spot so that a casing can be threaded onto it)
- ¹/₂" wide cotton twill tape (white)
- Nylon filament, such as lightweight fishing line
- **Template Required:** Netting Curve Template found on page 171

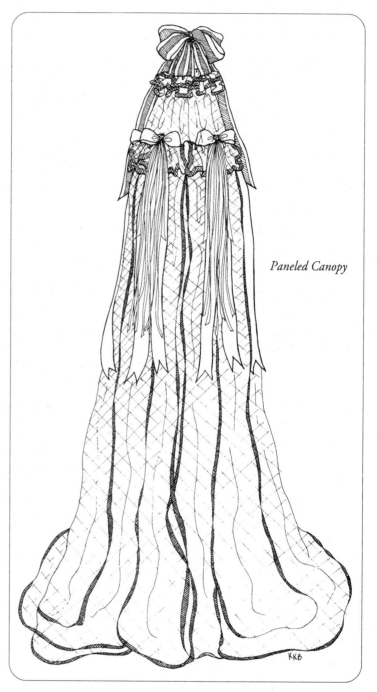

Paneled Canopy

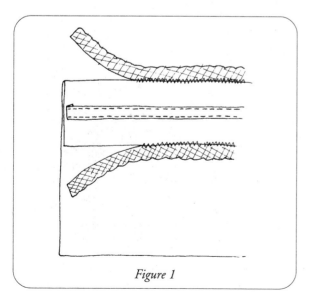

Figure 1

I. Making the Upper Tier

1. Cut a piece of netting 16" long and the full 45" width.

2. Along one 45" side, turn 6" to the outside and press a crease at the fold (**see fig. 1**).

3. Serge or machine roll and whip ³/₄" wide lace edging along the fold. Also attach ³/₄" lace edging to the cut edge of the lace that was folded over (**see fig. 1**).

4. Draw a line 3" from the fold of the netting. Center ⁵/₈" wide single-faced satin ribbon over the line and stitch both edges of the ribbon in place with a straight stitch; this forms a casing. Turn the raw ends of the ribbon under and catch them in the stitching (**fig. 1**).

5. Measure around the large brass ring and add ¹/₂" to the measurement. Cut a piece of cotton twill tape to that length.

6. Run a gathering stitch ¹/₄" from the 45" cut edge of the netting. Pull up the gathers to fit the twill tape (**see fig. 2**).

7. Fold the twill tape over the gathered edge of the netting to enclose the gathered seam allowance. Stitch the twill tape in place, making sure that both layers of the twill tape are caught in the stitching (**fig. 2**).

8. Thread the 5" diameter ring through the ribbon casing and set the upper tier aside while constructing the lower panels.

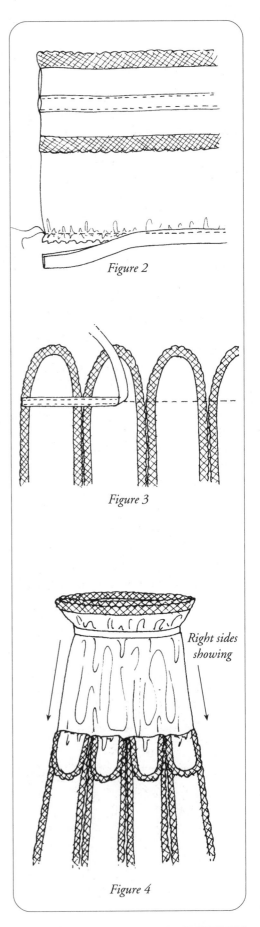

Figure 2

Figure 3

Right sides showing

Figure 4

II. Making the Lower Panels

1. Cut five pieces of the netting, each 45" wide and 120" long.

2. Split each of the five pieces in half lengthwise, giving ten pieces each 22¹/₂" wide and 120" long.

3. Round all four corners of each netting strip, using the template provided on page 171.

4. Optional: Attach ³/₄" wide lace edging all the way around each panel, using a serger or machine rolled hem. This lace may be omitted, leaving the edges of the netting plain. In this case, make a rolled edge along the edges of the netting, using a serger or sewing machine.

5. Draw a line 6" from one end of each panel. Place the ten panels right side up, side by side, having the top edges and the lines matched (**see fig. 3**).

6. Place ⁵/₈" wide single-faced satin ribbon over the line and stitch along both edges of the ribbon with a straight stitch, forming a casing. Turn the raw ends of the ribbon under and catch the edges in the stitching (**fig. 3**).

7. Thread the large ring through the ribbon casing. This will allow the top 6" of each panel to fold to the outside and create a scalloped ruffle. The wrong side of the panel will show at the top.

III. Assembly and Finishing

1. Place the twill edge of the upper tier inside the large ring and attach the upper tier by hand, stitching the twill edge to the ribbon edge through the netting. Stitch along both edges of the ribbon in order to keep the casing from rolling (**fig. 4**).

2. Cut the 2" wide double-faced satin ribbon into five 3-yard pieces. Tie each ribbon piece into a bow with long tails.

3. Attach a bow to the large ring through all layers where two of the netting panels meet. Skip every other meeting point and attach a bow, for a total of five evenly spaced around the ring.

4. Cut the ¹/₄" and ¹/₈" ribbons into 2 yard lengths. Place one strand of each color together to form a bundle and fold the bundle in two, with the ends a little uneven. Make five bundles.

5. Stitch the folded end of each bundle to one of the bows on the large ring. Make sure that every strand of ribbon is caught in the stitching.

6. Cut the ⅝" double-faced satin ribbon into five pieces. Make a cabbage rose in the center of each ribbon piece, leaving long tails on each end. Attach a rose over each ribbon bundle on the bows.

7. Cut the 2" wide decorative ribbon into four pieces.

8. Make four marks evenly spaced around the small ring at the top of the canopy. Attach one end of each ribbon piece at each of the four marks. Make sure to turn the raw ends under and stitch through all layers (**fig. 5**).

9. After all four ribbons are attached, tie two opposite ribbons together in a bow above the upper ring. Tie the other two ribbons into a bow also, at the same height above the ring (**fig. 6**).

10. Tie the two bows together with a piece of nylon filament and make a loop for hanging the canopy. ▨

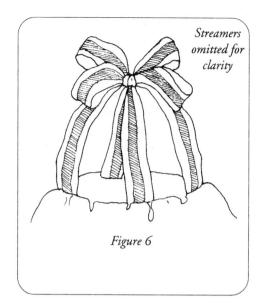

Streamers omitted for clarity

Figure 6

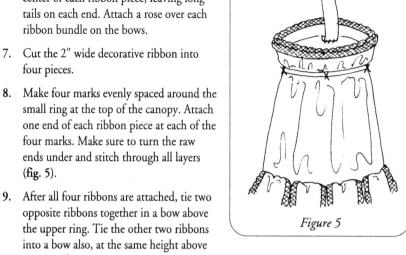

Figure 5

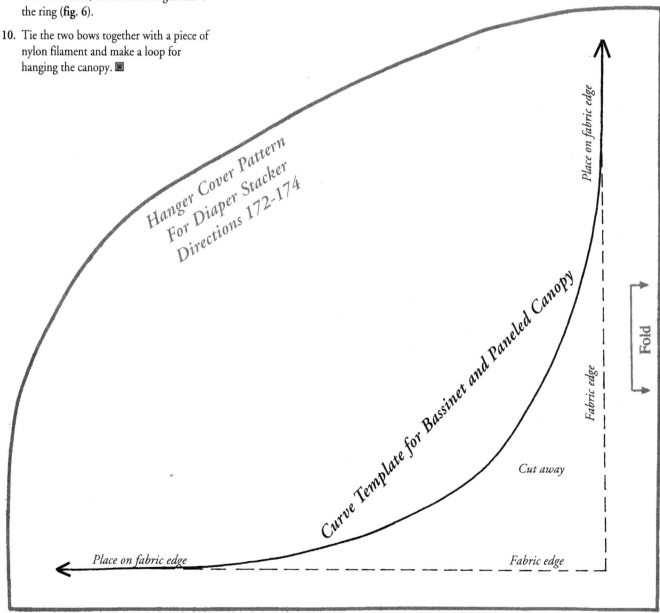

Hanger Cover Pattern
For Diaper Stacker
Directions 172-174

Curve Template for Bassinet and Paneled Canopy

Place on fabric edge

Fold

Fabric edge

Cut away

Place on fabric edge

Fabric edge

Diaper Stacker

This is a very convenient item to have with a new baby, especially with most disposable diapers coming folded the same way. Some of you are going to remember using cloth diapers and washing and folding every day. I don't even think disposable diapers were invented when my boys were little and unfortunately, they caused a rash on Joanna's tender skin. Just call me a diaper-washing mother!

This beautiful diaper stacker matches the other parts of the lovely bassinet ensemble. It is made of aqua silk dupioni covered with cotton netting at the top and the bottom section is made of white silk dupioni. A beautiful silk ribbon embroidery design, very similar to the one on the back of the hood, is found at the top. A pretty white ribbon is tied and stitched below the silk ribbon embroidery. This diaper stacker would make a beautiful baby gift even if you weren't going to make the bassinet.

Supplies

- ⊕ ¹/₂ yd. of aqua silk dupioni
- ⊕ ⁷/₈ yd. of white silk dupioni
- ⊕ 1 yd. of cotton netting
- ⊕ ³/₄ yd. of white broadcloth
- ⊕ Floss and silk ribbon: refer to the embroidery template
- ⊕ ¹/₄ yd. of woven interfacing
- ⊕ 1¹/₂ yds. of 2¹/₂" wide decorative ribbon
- ⊕ 1 child-size satin hanger
- ⊕ Lightweight cardboard or poster board, 14" square
- ⊕ **Pattern Piece Required:** Hanger Cover Pattern found on the page 171
- ⊕ **Template Required:** Diaper Stacker Stitch Template found on page 168

A. Making the Hanger Cover

1. Use the hanger cover pattern provided or one that has been drafted to fit a particular hanger. The measurements given in these instructions are for a padded hanger that is 10"-10¹/₂" across the bottom. For other sizes, the measurements must be adjusted.

2. Trace the pattern shape onto a piece of aqua silk dupioni for the front; also trace the embroidery design onto the fabric. Place two pieces of cotton netting over the silk, making sure that the netting is large enough to cover the traced pattern shape. Baste the netting layers to the fabric along the pattern outline and treat as one layer (**fig. 1**).

3. Work the embroidery design through all layers before cutting out the hanger cover. Do not add the bow at this point, it will be done in a later step. Cut the front piece out just outside the basting line.

4. Use the pattern piece to cut one back from the aqua silk, two backs from the netting, and two lining pieces from the broadcloth.

5. Place the two back netting pieces over the aqua silk back piece and baste the layers together, then treat as one layer.

6. Place the front and back lining pieces to the wrong side of the silk front and back pieces and baste in place, then treat as one layer (**see fig. 2**).

7. Serge or zigzag across the top of the hanger cover pieces to finish the fabric edge around the hanger opening (**fig. 2**).

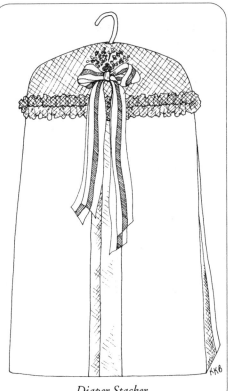

Diaper Stacker

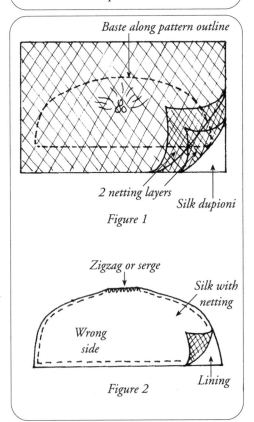

Baste along pattern outline

2 netting layers

Silk dupioni

Figure 1

Zigzag or serge

Silk with netting

Wrong side

Lining

Figure 2

8. Place the front and back with right sides together. Stitch from the bottom edges to the top, stopping at the top to leave an opening large enough to insert the hanger into (see fig. 3).

9. Fold the edges of the opening to the inside and stitch in place by hand (fig. 3). Turn the hanger cover to the right side.

10. Measure the bottom edge of the hanger cover across the front and back. Cut enough 2¹/₂" wide strips of cotton netting to go around the bottom edge four times.

11. Sew a gathering row down the middle of one netting strip. When the end of the strip is reached, place another strip at the end , slightly overlapping the first one. Continue the gathering row. Repeat these steps until all of the netting strips are used.

12. Pull up the gathering threads to fit the ruffle to the bottom edge of the hanger cover.

13. Place the ruffle on the right side of the hanger cover with the center of the ruffle (the gathering threads) resting ³/₈" above the bottom edge. Pin the ruffle in place and then stitch it to the hanger cover with a straight stitch down the middle, over the gathering threads (fig. 4).

— B. Making the Bag —

The measurements given in these instructions are for a hanger that is 14" across the bottom edge. For other sizes, the measurements must be adjusted.

1. Cut the following pieces:

   a. One piece of white silk dupioni that is 41" wide and 22" long.

   b. One piece of white silk dupioni that is 14¹/₂" x 6¹/₂".

   c. One piece of woven interfacing that is 14¹/₂" x 6¹/₂".

   d. Two pieces of cardboard for base, 13¹/₄" x 5¹/₄".

   e. Two pieces of white broadcloth, 14" x 6".

2. Make marks on the large rectangle in the following positions (see fig. 5):

   a. Place a dot 10¹/₂" from each short end at the top edge.

   b. Place a small clip 7¹/₂" from each short end on the bottom edge and the top edge.

   c. Place a small clip 13¹/₂" from each short end on the bottom edge and the top edge.

3. Serge or zigzag each front edge (the 22" edges). Stitch a strip of 2" wide white satin ribbon to the wrong side of each front edge with the edge of the ribbon meeting the fabric edge. Use a ¹/₄" seam. Press the ribbon to the outside, enclosing the seam allowance between the two layers (fig. 6).

4. Make an inverted pleat at each side of the bag:

   a. Make a line on the wrong side of the fabric at the dot that was placed 10¹/₂" from each front edge. The line should be 3" long and be perpendicular to the top edge (fig. 7).

   b. Fold the fabric with right sides together along the drawn line, matching the clips on each side of the line.

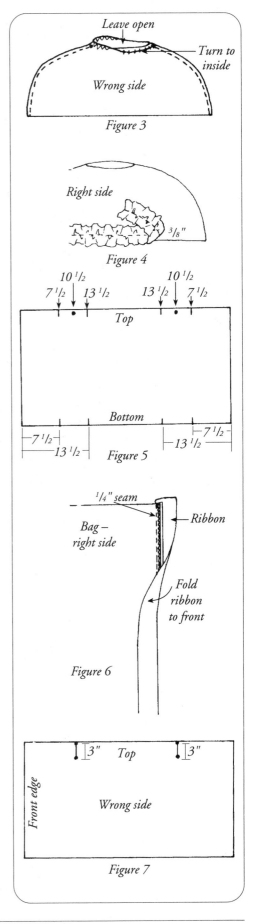

Figure 3

Figure 4

Figure 5

Figure 6

Figure 7

c. Draw a second line on the wrong side of the fabric where the clips are matched. This line will be parallel to the fold, 3" long and 3" from the folded edge (see fig. 8).

d. Stitch along the second line, backstitching at the beginning and end of the seam (fig. 8).

e. Place the stitching line against the fold where the first line was drawn. This will create a flat pleat. Press the pleat and baste across the top edge (fig. 9).

5. Overlap the top and bottom front edges by ¹/₂" and baste. Turn the bag wrong side out.

6. Press the ruffle away from the bottom edge of the hanger cover and pin it to keep it out of the seam allowance. The hanger cover should be right side out.

7. Slip the hanger cover upside down into the top of the bag. Place the top edge of the bag and the lower edge of the hanger cover with right sides together and stitch with a ¹/₄" seam. Make sure that the front of the bag is matched to the front of the hanger cover. Be sure to keep the ruffle edges out of the seam. Finish the seam with a serged edge or zigzag (fig. 10).

8. Turn the bag to the right side and unpin the ruffle, letting it fluff out over the seam.

9. Use the 2¹/₂" wide decorative ribbon to make a bow, adding two extra streamers. Attach the bow by hand to the front of the hanger cover underneath the embroidery.

10. Place the woven interfacing rectangle over the white silk that is the same size. Baste the two pieces together around the outer edges.

11. Use a ¹/₄" seam to sew the silk/interfacing base piece to the bottom of the bag with right sides together, matching the corners of the base to the clips in the bottom edge of the bag. Serge or zigzag the seam (fig. 11).

12. Place the broadcloth rectangles with right sides together and stitch around three sides with a ¹/₄" seam. Turn the piece right side out (see fig. 12).

13. Insert the cardboard into the pocket. Turn the open edges to the inside and slipstitch the opening (fig. 12).

14. Place the cardboard base into the bottom of the bag. ▨

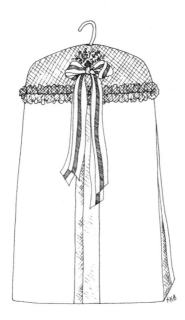

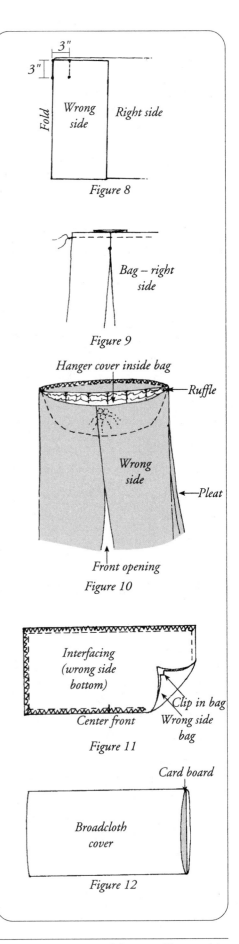

3"
3"

Fold

Wrong side   Right side

Figure 8

Bag – right side

Figure 9

Hanger cover inside bag

Ruffle

Wrong side

Pleat

Front opening

Figure 10

Interfacing (wrong side bottom)

Center front

Clip in bag

Wrong side bag

Figure 11

Card board

Broadcloth cover

Figure 12

Bassinet Blanket

Searching through antique stores, I have found many beautiful crib/bassinet blankets. What a wonderful idea to have a blanket just for baby's bassinet. To let you in on a little secret, this blanket can be used for the baby even if you don't have a bassinet. The top of the blanket is white Swiss Nelona batiste; it is lined in a lovely cotton flannel, also in white. Beautiful three-inch wide white French lace is attached around the edge and there is a magnificent shadow work embroidery bow in the center stitched in aqua. Surface embroidery worked in floss is used for the leaves, the pink flowers and the yellow French knots at the top of the flower spray.

Bassinet Blanket

Supplies

☙ 1 yd. of white batiste for top

☙ 1 yd. of fabric for lining

☙ 6 yds. of 3" wide lace edging

☙ Floss: refer to embroidery template found on page 176

☙ **Template Required:** Bassinet Blanket Embroidery Template found on page 176

Directions

1. Cut a 36" square of the batiste and the lining fabric.

2. Fold the batiste into fourths and mark the center at each side and also in the middle.

3. Spray starch and iron the batiste dry. Lightly trace the embroidery design (pg. 176) onto the batiste with a washout fabric marker or pencil.

4. Work the embroidery, using the template and stitch key on page 176. Wash out any markings that show after the embroidery is completed.

5. Place the batiste and the lining with right sides together and stitch around the edges with a ¹/₄" seam; leave a 4" opening on one side for turning the blanket through.

6. Turn the blanket right side out and press well. At the opening, press the seam allowances to the inside. The opening will be stitched as the lace is attached.

7. If the lace edging has a bold pattern, it should be matched on the sides and at the miters:

   a. Center one of the lace designs along one side edge of the blanket; leave the lace about 6" - 9" longer than the blanket at each end. The lace from each side should extend beyond the lace from the adjoining side. Repeat for the other sides (**fig. 1**).

   b. Pin the lace to the blanket. At the corners, let the lace extend and overlap the ends. Draw a line from the inside corner of the intersection to the outside corner; this will be the miter line (**fig. 2**).

   c. Set the machine for a small zigzag (L = 1.0, W = 1.0). Let the lace heading butt against or slightly overlap the blanket edge and zigzag it in place. Be sure to stitch through both layers of the opening (**fig. 3**).

   d. When the stitching is about 2" from a corner, fold the top layer of lace under on the miter line and pin in place (**fig. 4**).

   e. Continue stitching to the corner. When the corner is reached, pivot and stitch along the miter to the outside corner, then turn and stitch back down the miter to the blanket corner. Pivot and stitch along the next side of the blanket (**fig. 5**).

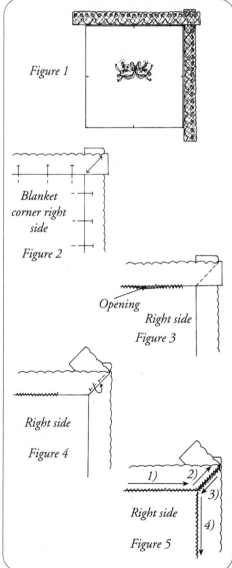

Figure 1

Blanket corner right side

Figure 2

Opening

Right side

Figure 3

Right side

Figure 4

1) 2) 3) 4)

Right side

Figure 5

f. After all of the lace is attached and the miters are stitched, cut away the lace from behind the miters, trimming close to but not into the stitches (**fig. 6**).

8. If the opening was not completely stitched, either re-stitch it or slipstitch by hand. ▓

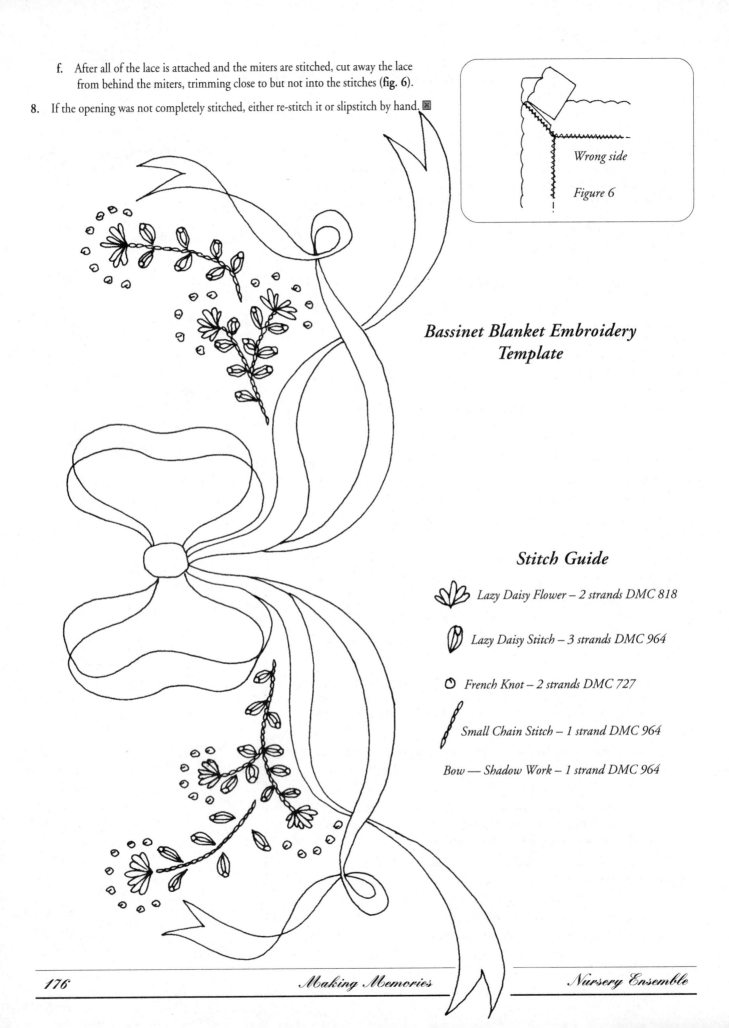

Wrong side

Figure 6

Bassinet Blanket Embroidery Template

Stitch Guide

Lazy Daisy Flower – 2 strands DMC 818

Lazy Daisy Stitch – 3 strands DMC 964

French Knot – 2 strands DMC 727

Small Chain Stitch – 1 strand DMC 964

Bow — Shadow Work – 1 strand DMC 964

Bassinet Pillow

This is the absolutely sweetest pillow case and pillow for a baby. The pillow case is made of white broadcloth and the pillow is white broadcloth also. The trim on the bottom of the pillow features entredeux beading with tightly gathered white French lace edging gathered on either side of this entredeux beading. It is stitched to the outside edge of the pillowcase and an aqua ribbon has been threaded through the entredeux beading. If you are so fortunate as to have a machine which does embroidery, the baby's name or monogram would be beautiful worked in the same color as the ribbon. This is a very easy baby gift to make. As a matter of fact, you might want to make several of these in one sitting and tuck them away for future baby showers.

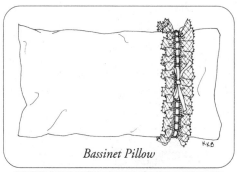

Bassinet Pillow

Supplies

- ⊕⊹ ¹/₂ yd. of white broadcloth
- ⊕⊹ ⁵/₈ yd. of Swiss beading for ¹/₄" ribbon
- ⊕⊹ ³/₄ yd. of ¹/₄" aqua double-faced satin ribbon
- ⊕⊹ 2¹/₂ yds. of ³/₄" wide lace edging
- ⊕⊹ Polyfil for stuffing pillow

I. Making the Pillowcase

1. Cut a piece of white broadcloth to measure 18¹/₂" x 16".

2. At one 18¹/₂" end, press ¹/₄" to the wrong side, then press a 2¹/₂" hem to the wrong side. Do not stitch the hem at this point.

3. Open the hem out flat and sew the two 16" sides of the pillowcase together with a ¹/₄" seam, right sides together. Finish the seam with a zigzag or serger (**see fig. 1**).

4. Stitch the seam at the end opposite the hem, taking a ¹/₄" seam allowance; finish the seam with a zigzag or serge (**fig. 1**).

5. Press the hem into place and stitch with a straight stitch.

6. Cut the lace edging into two 1¹/₄ yd. pieces and gather each piece to fit the beading.

7. Trim the batiste seam allowance away from one side of the beading and attach one piece of the lace to the edge of the beading, using the technique entredeux to lace (**fig. 2**). Repeat for the other side.

8. Place the beading/lace strip over the hem seam on the right side of the pillowcase and stitch it in place with a zigzag or straight stitch that goes into the holes of the entredeux edge along the beading. Turn the ends under to hide the raw edges (**fig. 3**).

9. Thread the ribbon through the beading, starting and ending on the front of the pillowcase. Tie the ends into a small bow.

II. Making the Pillow

1. Cut a piece of white broadcloth to measure 17¹/₂" x 13".

2. Fold the rectangle with right sides together and having the 13" sides meeting. Stitch the 13" sides together and stitch across one short end of the pillow, using a ¹/₄" seam (**fig. 4**).

3. Turn the pillow right side out and stuff with the polyfil.

4. Close the end of the pillow in one of the following ways:

   a. Serge the raw edges together (this seam will show).

   b. Turn the raw edges to the inside and stitch the seam by hand or machine.

5. Insert the pillow into the pillowcase. ▨

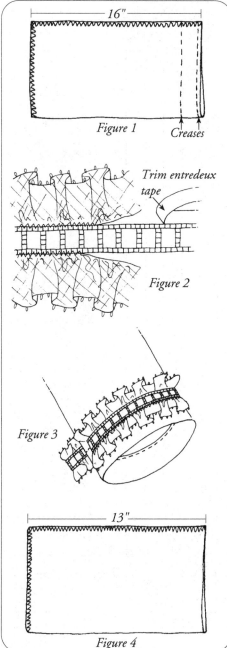

Figure 1

Creases

Trim entredeux tape

Figure 2

Figure 3

Figure 4

Heirloom Angel Quilt

This gorgeous quilt was designed by Angela Pullen and made by Margaret Taylor; what a great team they are! The angels look so delicate in their lace-shaped dresses with lacy wings against the burgundy silk dupioni background, and each plays a musical instrument. Their messages of love, peace, hope and joy are written inside wreaths of gorgeous silk ribbon flowers with filmy ribbon organza bows. A central message states that "My Angels Watch Over Me" and is surrounded by a ribbon wreath anchored with silk ribbon flowers. The corner angels are magnificent with their lace-shaped wings and full gathered lace skirts made of cotton English netting lace. Golden haloes are the crowning touch for all of the angels. This quilt is sure to be one that you will want to make for someone special. ▣

Heirloom Angel Quilt

General Directions

1. The templates for each square of the quilt are found on pages 257-264.

2. Directions for the different techniques used are in the technique section of this book.

3. All seam allowances are ¼" unless otherwise noted.

4. Individual squares are initially cut 15" by 15" but will be trimmed down to 12½" by 12½" after appliqués, embroideries and laces are finished.

Materials and Supplies

⚬ Silk dupioni and cotton netting:
  ⚬ 6 yards of maroon silk dupioni for quilt squares, sashings and backing
  ⚬ 12" by 12" square of sunset gold silk dupioni for hair, horn and book
  ⚬ 12" by 12" square of off-white silk dupioni for face, hands and feet
  ⚬ Scrap of brown silk dupioni for harp and lyre
  ⚬ ½ yard cotton netting
⚬ Laces:
  ⚬ 8 yards of ³⁄₈" wide lace insertion
  ⚬ 13 yards of 8 mm 100% cotton Battenburg picot-edged lace tape
  ⚬ 3 yards of ³⁄₈" wide lace beading
  ⚬ 2 yards of 6" wide embroidered lace edging for angel skirts
⚬ Threads:
  Maroon, sunset gold, brown, off-white, metallic gold Sulky thread #7004, monofilament thread, 14 yards of #16 metallic gold Balger braid
⚬ DMC Floss: #3326 pink, #801 brown
⚬ 4 mm silk ribbon in the following colors for silk ribbon embroidery:
  #179 Mauve, #163 Rose, #125 blue, #147 gold, #001 white, #170 green, #20 green, #86 navy
⚬ Ribbon:
  ⚬ 3 yards of ⅛" wide ribbon for angels' dresses
  ⚬ 5 yards of 1½" wide organza ribbon
⚬ Miscellaneous:
  ⚬ 6 squares of water soluble stabilizer (WSS), each 12" by 12"
  ⚬ 12" by 12" piece of tear-away paper stabilizer
  ⚬ 12" by 12" piece of fusible web
  ⚬ #3 tapestry needle
  ⚬ Black glass beads
  ⚬ Iridescent glass beads
⚬ Batting: 3 yards, 45" wide

I. Cutting

1. Cut out the following pieces and lay aside until needed:

   a. From the silk dupioni:
      18 squares of maroon silk dupioni, each 15" by 15"
      12 sashing strips of maroon silk dupioni, each 2½" by 12½"
      4 sashing strips of maroon silk dupioni, each 2½" by 45"
      2 sashing strips of maroon silk dupioni, each 2½" by 6 yards long (may be pieced)

      8 pieces of maroon for quilt border, each 8" by 60"

   b. From the batting:
      18 squares, each 15" by 15"
      12 strips, each 2½" by 12½"
      4 strips, each 2½" by 45"
      2 strips, each 2½" by 6 yards long (may be pieced)
      8 strips, each 8" by 60"

Refer to Finished Quilt Design Chart for Block Placement on page 178.

II. Angel Blocks

Block 2—Use Template B,
Block 4—Use Template C,
Block 6—Use Template E,
Block 8—Use Template F

The following instructions are general and can be followed for all four angel blocks listed above (**see fig. 1**). If instructions for appliqué are needed, please refer to *Martha's Attic,* Program Guide 400, or any other appliqué book of your choice. Refer to the embroidery sections of this book for specific embroidery stitch instructions.

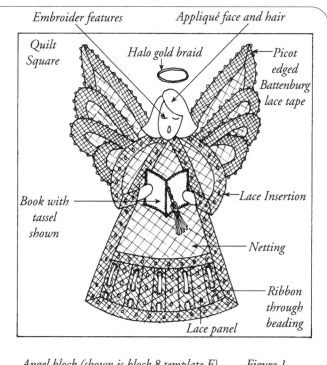

Embroider features   Appliqué face and hair

Quilt Square   Halo gold braid   Picot edged Battenburg lace tape

Book with tassel shown   Lace Insertion

Netting

Ribbon through beading

Lace panel

Angel block (shown is block 8 template F)   Figure 1

A. Shaping the Angels

1. Using the technique Lace to Lace, construct a panel of lace wide enough to fit across the bottom of the angel's skirt. The panel needs to be at least as wide as the template diagram and extend at the top and bottom by approximately ¹/₂". Alternate lace and beading as shown on the angel template. When panel is completed, press and run ribbon through beading with a tapestry needle. Place the lace panel on top of the template and draw a line across the lace panel at the top and bottom along template line. Use a fine point wash out marker to draw this line. Stay stitch along the two lines to keep the lace panel from distorting. Trim the lace panel ¹/₈" from the stitching.

2. Using an extra fine permanent marker, trace the angel design onto a square of WSS. Cut a piece of lace netting just larger than the angel. Baste the lace netting in place on top of the WSS.

3. Place the lace panel from Step 1 on top of the lace netting along the skirt bottom and pin in place. Place a piece of lace insertion across the top of the lace panel referring to the angel template. Stitch the piece of lace insertion in place at the top and bottom using a tiny zigzag.

4. Shape the picot-edged Battenburg lace tape on the angel wings, having the picots toward the outside edge. Begin shaping with the lace piece numbered 1, then 2, 3 and so on. Refer to the numbering on the template. Be sure to allow the ends of the lace tape to extend about ¹/₄" so that they will be caught underneath the pieces that will lay over them. The ends of lace pieces marked with a * need to be tucked under the previous pieces (refer to the template). Refer to Lace Shaping Techniques for shaping lace and mitering the top points of the wings. Stitch the lace tape in place on each edge using a tiny zigzag.

5. Shape the lace insertion on the remaining portion of the angel's dress. Shape the sleeves last. Stitch the insertion in place with a tiny zigzag. Refer to Lace Shaping Techniques.

6. Carefully trim the excess lace netting from around the angel's dress. Center the angel on the quilt square and stitch in place along the outer edge of the lace using a tiny zigzag.

7. Place the angel's face and hair on the quilt square and appliqué in place. Be sure the hair overlaps the face. The part in the angel's hair is created by using a triple straight stitch (reinforced straight stitch) on the machine.

8. The eyes and mouth are embroidered with a stem stitch using a single strand of DMC floss. Use brown or blue floss for the eyes and light rose floss for the mouth.

9. The halo is created by stitching a piece of #16 metallic gold Balger braid in place. The raw ends of the braid are taken to the back by threading the braid through a tapestry needle. Use a small zigzag and monofilament thread to secure the braid. Be sure to secure the point where the braid ends were taken to the back.

B. Appliqué the Appropriate Instrument or Book

1. Horn—The horn is appliquéd in place using Sulky metallic thread. The openings in the horn are embroidered French knots or black glass beads stitched in place.

2. Harp—The harp is appliquéd in place with thread to match the harp fabric. The strings on the harp are pieces of #16 metallic gold Balger braid zigzagged in place. The ends of the braid can be taken to the back with a tapestry needle.

3. Lyre—The lyre is appliquéd in place using thread to match the lyre. The strings are the metallic braid zigzagged in place. Secure the ends as before. The tuning knobs are glass beads stitched in place.

4. Book—On a small block of gold fabric, trace the outline of the book from the template. Place a square of stabilizer to the wrong side of the fabric. Place another block of gold fabric underneath the stabilizer with the wrong side of the fabric facing the stabilizer. You now have two blocks of gold fabric, wrong sides together, with a piece of stabilizer sandwiched between them. Stitch around the outline of the book with a tiny zigzag, then stitch a tiny zigzag down the center of book to form the spine. Trim away the excess fabric very close to the zigzag along the outside edge of the book. Increase the width of the zigzag slightly and satin stitch around the book, finishing the raw edge of the fabric. Make a tassel by cutting six strands of metallic braid, each 3" long. Fold the strands in half and wrap a length of braid around the folded loops about ¹/₂" from the fold. Secure the wrap. Attach a length of braid to the top of the tassel and attach the tassel to the center top of the book. Position the book on the appropriate angel so that the book will be held in place when the hands are stitched.

5. Appliqué the hands in place. Refer to the template for placement of hands on each square.

6. Feet, if shown on template, are appliquéd in place using white or metallic thread.

Template I

A. Blocks 1, 3, 7, and 9 — Using Template A (see fig. 2)

1. Trace the wreath design onto the square. Embroider the design using the wreath template as a guide. Refer to the embroidery sections of this book for specific embroidery stitch instructions.

2. The words are worked with one strand of Sulky metallic gold thread using the stem stitch. Refer to the finished drawing for word placement.

3. The bow is made by threading a #3 tapestry needle with the organza ribbon. Knot the end of the ribbon. Bring the ribbon to the front at the center of the bow, make a loop and take the ribbon to the back at the center. Pin the loop to the quilt square at the halfway point of the loop, opposite the center of the bow; repeat for the other side of the bow. For the tie ends of the bow, bring the ribbon up from the back at the bow center. Tie an overhand knot loosely near the end of the tie end. Take the needle to the back of the square where you want the tie end to stop and tie the ribbon off on the back. Secure the bow loops by stitching glass beads in place where the loops are pinned, and stitch behind the knots in the tie ends. For the center "knot" of the bow, bring the ribbon to the front just above the center (there is no need to knot the ribbon at the back). Take the ribbon to the back just below the bow center, then tie the two ends together on the back to secure. Make sure the knot on the front is not pulled too tightly.

B. Block 5—Template D (see fig. 3)

1. Trace the design from the template by placing an X at the "knot" of the bow. Place an X at each embroidery design around the oval. Trace the words in the center of the oval.

2. The words are worked with one strand of sulky metallic thread using a stem stitch. Refer to the finished drawing for word placement.

3. Thread a #3 tapestry needle with the organza ribbon. Bring the ribbon to the front at the center top of the design, leaving a tail at the back for securing later. Take the ribbon to the back at the first X and bring ribbon back to the front 1/4" away on the other side of the X; leave the loop puffy. Continue around the oval, going in and out at the X's. Do not pull the loops too tightly. At the top of the oval, take the ribbon to the back. Bring the ribbon to the front close to the previous hole and make the loop for the bow. Take the ribbon to the back at the center, pinning the loop to the square opposite the center of the bow. Do not pull too tightly, the bow needs to be puffy. Repeat for the other side of the bow. Secure the bow at each side by stitching glass beads in place at the pins. Bring the ribbon to the front just above the center point. Take the ribbon to the back, creating the "knot" of the bow. Tie off with the tail which was left at the beginning.

4. Embroider the flower design at each X around the oval. Refer to the template for placement

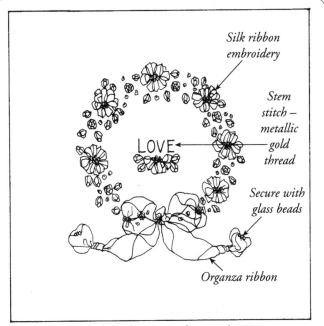

Wreath blocks 1,3,7 and 9, template A

Figure 2

Embroidered oval with bow, block 5, template D

Figure 3

IV. Quilt Construction

A. Block Preparation

1. Press each of the 9 blocks for the quilt and set them aside.

2. Place a square of batting on the wrong side of each block. Place a lining block behind the batting. Pin the layered square well to keep the fabric from shifting. This creates a sandwich of fabric, batting and fabric.

3. Find the center of the first block. Measure 6¼" from the center of the block to all four sides of the block and mark with a washout marker. This will need to be done in several places to ensure that the block is square. Be sure that the design on the block is still centered.

4. Draw a line along the markings. The block will now measure 12½" by 12½". Cut away the excess fabric outside the markings. This will need to be done for all nine blocks. Leave block 1 pinned together but remove the pins from the other eight blocks.

B. Embroidering and Attaching the Sashing Strips

1. On four of the 2½" by 12½" sashing strips, embroider three colonial knots on one end of each strip (**fig. 4**).

2. On two of the 2½" by 12½" sashing strips, embroider three colonial knots on both ends of each strip (**fig. 5**).

3. Place one short piece of sashing with the colonial knots at bottom right sides together along the right side of block 1. Place a lining piece of sashing right sides together on the back of block 1. Place a short piece of batting on the back of the sashing lining (**fig. 6**). Pin all layers in place; stitch through all the layers with a ¼" seam.

4. Flip the sashing and batting strips away from the square, then press both pieces of sashing together and pin the sashing sandwich layers together along the edge (**fig. 7**).

NOTE: Quilting on individual blocks may be done as each panel is completed. This will allow most of the quilting to be done before the quilt becomes bulky. Blocks 1, 3, 5, 7 and 9 are quilted with a decorative machine stitch approximately ½" from the outside edge of the silk ribbon embroidery. Begin as close to the bow as possible

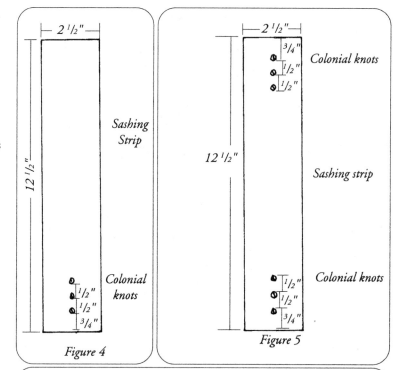

Figure 4

Figure 5

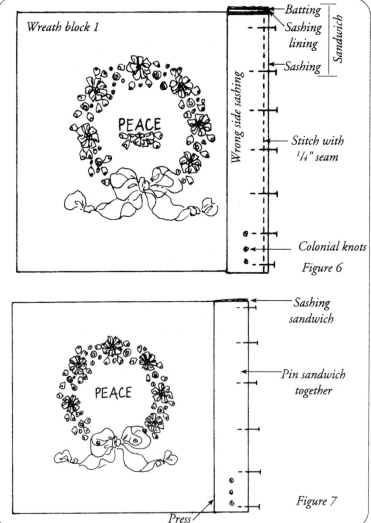

Figure 6

Figure 7

and continue around to the other side close to the bow (**fig. 8**). Blocks 2, 4, 6 and 8 are quilted with a straight stitch around the perimeter of the angel, approximately $^1/_2$" away from the angel (**fig. 9**).

5. Place block 2 on top of the sashing sandwich, right sides together. Place the lining of block 2 on the lining side of the sashing sandwich, followed by the square of batting. Remove the pins from the sashing sandwich and re-pin through all layers. Stitch in place with a $^1/_4$" seam. Press top, lining and batting of block 2 together creating a sandwich. Pin at right edge.

6. Repeat steps 3, 4 and 5, adding another sashing strip and block 3.

7. Repeat steps 3 through 6 to attach blocks 4, 5 and 6 to make a panel and blocks 7, 8 and 9 to make a panel. There are now three panels composed of three blocks with strips of sashing between each block. NOTE: Be sure to use the sashing strips with the colonial knots on each end for blocks 4, 5 and 6. Use sashing strips with colonial knots at the top for blocks 7, 8 and 9.

The embroidery design from Template I (page 180) will be traced onto the two 2$^1/_2$" by 45" sashing strips after the panels of three blocks across are completed, just before the long sashing strip is attached at the bottom of each panel. Make sure that the embroidery design is centered above and below the colonial knots on the shorter sashing strips of the panels. Mark and embroider each long strip just before attaching it to the panel.

8. Refer to step 3 and add a long sashing sandwich to the bottom of the first panel. Mark and embroider the strip as directed above.

9. Continue by adding the second panel to the sashing strip, stitching the panel to the sashing with right sides together through the top sashing layer and batting only; the sashing lining will be left loose on the back.

10. Add the other long sashing sandwich to the bottom of the second panel. Be sure to embroider the long sashing strip as before. Add the third panel to the bottom, following step 9 above. This creates the center portion of the quilt, consisting of nine squares with sashings between the squares. Stitch the loose edges of the long sashing strips to the back of the quilt by hand, turning under a $^1/_4$" seam allowance.

11. The two long pieces of 2$^1/_2$" wide sashing and one long piece of batting are attached around the center portion of the quilt in the same manner as step 3, creating a sashing sandwich around the center portion of the quilt. At the corners, flip the sashings away from the center and use the fold back miter method found on page 233 to miter the corners. Once the miters are folded in, turn the sashings back over the quilt and continue pinning. Stitch the sashing to the quilt, then flip the sashing layers away from the quilt and press. Pin the sashing sandwich through all layers.

12. Place a length of #16 metallic gold Balger braid around block 1, in the "ditch" of the seams. The ends of the braid are taken to the middle of the sandwich in one corner of the block with a tapestry needle. Zigzag over the braid with monofilament thread, securing well where the braid ends were inserted through the fabric. Repeat for the remaining squares.

13. Attach the 8" wide panel around the outside of the sashing strip in the same way as step 11. Miter the corners in the same manner as in step 11. Press the panel, batting and lining together.

14. At this point, make and attach the four corner angels to the top layer of the panel (see **fig. 10**).

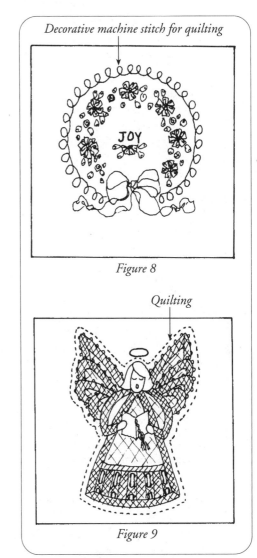

Decorative machine stitch for quilting

Figure 8

Quilting

Figure 9

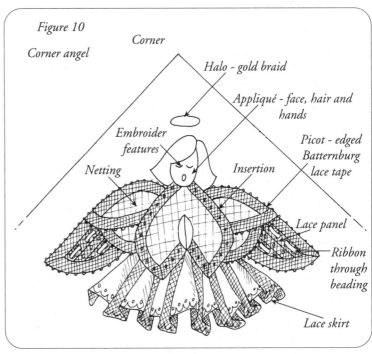

Figure 10

Corner
Corner angel

Halo - gold braid

Appliqué - face, hair and hands

Embroider features

Netting

Insertion

Picot - edged Batternburg lace tape

Lace panel

Ribbon through beading

Lace skirt

a. Cut a piece of WSS 12" by 6". With an extra fine point permanent marker, trace the corner angel design from Template G. There is no need to trace the skirt. Cut a piece of netting just larger than the drawn design. Baste the lace netting in place on top of the WSS.

b. For each angel, cut a piece of 6" wide embroidered lace edging 18" long. Finish both ends of the lace with a narrow hem. Gather or pleat the top raw edge of each lace piece. This may be done with the Perfect Pleater from Clotilde or a smocking pleater, or simply gathered on the machine. Pull up the gathers to the width of the arms at their widest point. Fan out the bottom of the skirt. Refer to the template. Set the skirt aside.

c. Using the technique Lace to Lace, construct a panel of lace insertion and beading wide enough to fit the end section of the wings. The panel needs to be slightly larger on all sides to be sure it is caught in the stitching.

d. Refer to the Angel Block instructions, step 4, to shape the wings.

e. Place the skirt on top of the netting and baste in place. Shape the sleeves on top of the skirt and stitch with a narrow zigzag on each side of the lace.

15. Fold the batting and outer panel lining out of the way and pin. NOTE: The top of the angel's head stitched in step 16 must be at least 4¹/₂" from the corner point of the quilt. This will allow room for the angel's halo and the 1" binding around the quilt. Place the angel's body on the top layer of fabric in the corner of the quilt (leaving room for the head) and stitch around the outside edges of the lace on the wings and sleeves. Do not stitch the sides or bottom of the skirt.

16. Appliqué the face, hair and hands in place with thread to match the fabrics.

17. Embroider the eyes and mouth using a stem stitch and a single strand of DMC floss. Use the same colors as for the other angels.

18. The halo is a piece of gold braid stitched in place with a narrow zigzag using monofilament thread. Treat the ends as before.

C. Finishing

1. After corner angels are stitched in place, unpin the batting and lining and smooth the layers beneath the panel top layer. Pin in several places around the outside edge of the panel sandwich.

2. Stitch around the top portion of the angel through all three layers, stitching approximately ¹/₂" away around the perimeter of angel's body. Do not stitch the angel's skirt, leave the skirt loose at this point.

3. The 8" panel around the quilt will be channel quilted. These rows of quilting are spaced 1¹/₂" apart. Stitch the channels as close to the corner angels as possible. Lift the angel skirts and stitch the channels underneath the skirts.

4. Since the corners of this quilt are shaped, the bias band around the outside is done separately from the corners.

5. Place the Corner Template H at the corners of the quilt and cut the corners in the shape of the template. Pin the layers together.

6. Straight stitch around the entire quilt 1¹/₄" from the raw edge, following the shape of the corners.

7. Cut the four corner pieces from the quilt material using the Template H. Place one corner piece on the lining side of one corner of the quilt, right sides together. Match the edges and stitch a ¹/₄" seam from the raw edge. Leave 1" unstitched on each end of the corner piece. This will allow you to attach the strip for the straight sides of the binding. Repeat for the other 3 corners.

8. Attach a long piece of binding 1¹/₂" wide to the end of a corner piece. Be sure to place the binding piece to the corner piece with right sides together so that the seam will be under the binding when it is flipped to the quilt top. Stitch the straight piece of the binding with a ¹/₄" seam along the side. Trim and attach the end of the binding to the next corner piece. Repeat for the other three sides.

9. Flip the binding over to the quilt top and press, having the seam along the edge of the quilt. Turn under ¹/₄" along the raw edge of the binding. Pin or baste the binding in place. Blanket stitch the binding in place from the right side.

10. Stay stitch the bottom edge of the angel skirts in three or four points.

11. Straight stitch the curve above the hands of the corner angels through all layers. ▨

Silk Ribbon Projects

Linen Bag

Fancy Napkins

Basket Weave Scissors Case

Armchair Hussif

Hearts and Vines Box Lid

Linen Bag

Why throw your nicest lingerie into just any old laundry bag? Put it in this elegant embroidered linen bag instead. With one flower stitch repeated over the bag, a large area can be decorated very quickly. Construction of the bag is also easy, so this is a great gift item that would be enjoyed by any lady on your gift list.

Supplies

- 1 yd. of 45" fabric
- ¹/₄ yd. of lightweight iron-on interfacing
- Silk ribbon (see stitch key for colors and sizes)
- Instructions for the silk ribbon fuchsias are found on page 201.

Directions

1. Cut the fabric; mark and label the fold lines as indicated on the layout (**fig. 1**).

2. Fuse iron-on interfacing to the wrong side of the pieces for the bow, the drawstring and the bow knot.

3. With right sides together, stitch the bow with a ¹/₄" seam allowance, leaving 2" open along the long side (**fig. 2**).

4. Trim the corners and turn the bow right side out. Stitch the opening to close.

5. Repeat steps 3 and 4 for the drawstring.

6. Using the bag pieces, stitch or serge both sides from the bottom up to point A (**fig. 3**).

7. Turn the bag to the right side. Press under ¹/₄" at the top edge, then fold the upper hem to the outside along the fold line, right sides together (**fig. 4**).

8. Stitch from point B to point D on each hem edge (**fig. 5**). Turn the hem to the inside.

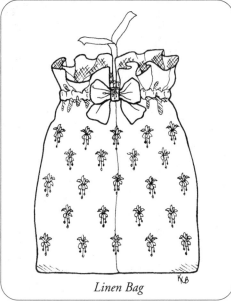

Linen Bag

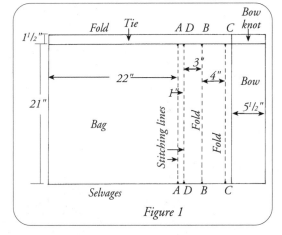

Figure 1

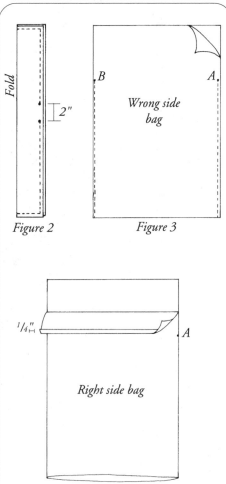

Figure 2

Figure 3

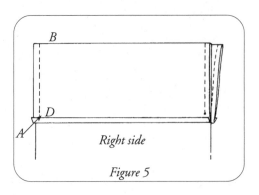

Right side

Figure 5

Figure 4

9. Stitch across the bag at points A and D to form a casing 1" wide (**fig. 6**).

10. Embroider the bag, working on a 4" grid with the design centered on the seam line (**fig. 7**). Instructions for the fuchsias are found on page 201.

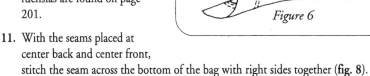

Right side

Figure 6

11. With the seams placed at center back and center front, stitch the seam across the bottom of the bag with right sides together (**fig. 8**).

12. Embroider the center of the bow knot, press the side edges to the back and slipstitch the edges together.

13. Fold the bow piece into a bow shape. Wrap a doubled thread around the center of the bow to hold the shape (**see fig. 9**).

14. Place the bow over the center of the drawstring and then fold the bow knot over both and secure it at the back, stitching through the back of the knot, the drawstring and the bow (**see fig. 9**).

15. Insert each end of the tie through the casing from front to back and tie the drawstring in a loose knot at the center back (**fig. 9**).

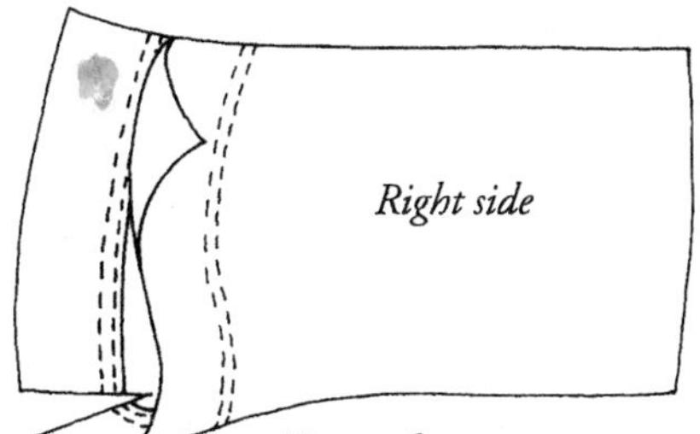

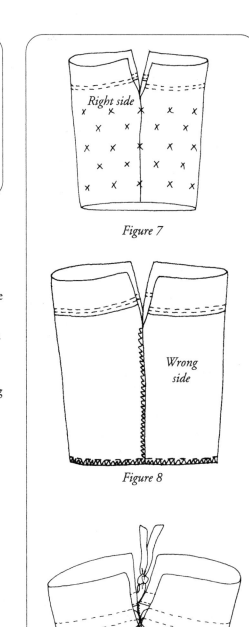

Right side

Figure 7

Wrong side

Figure 8

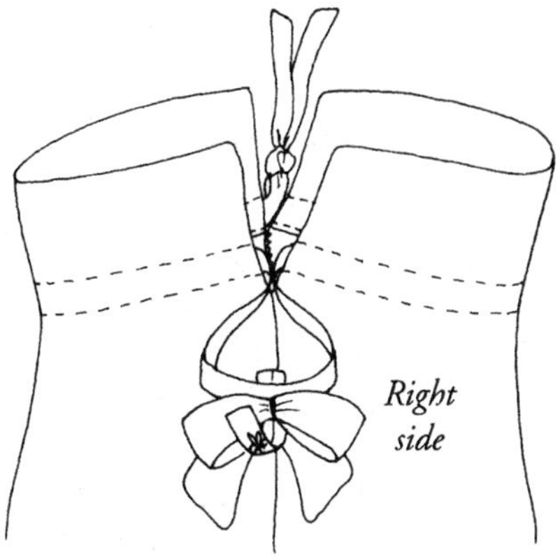

Right side

Figure 9

Stitch Key

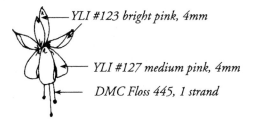

YLI #123 bright pink, 4mm

YLI #127 medium pink, 4mm

DMC Floss 445, 1 strand

Fancy Napkins

Everyone knows that a beautifully set table is the finishing touch that makes a good meal taste even better. With napkins like this, a gorgeous table is guaranteed. This is also a great way to dress up a breakfast tray. A meal served this elegantly would certainly brighten a day! Side ribbon stitch, Japanese ribbon stitch, a loop stitch flower, lazy daisies, chain stitch and pistil stitches are all fast and easy to work, so a lot of elegance is attained for very little effort.

Materials

* 1 set of ready-made hemstitched linen napkins
* Silk ribbon (see template for sizes and colors)
* **Template Required:** Fancy Napkins Template found on page 188
* Stitch instructions can be found on pages 196 to 212.

Directions

1. Trace the major template markings onto one corner of the napkin (**finish drawing**).

2. Embroider the design according to the template and stitch key (refer to the color photograph and finished drawing). Instructions for specific stitches can be found on pages 196 to 212.

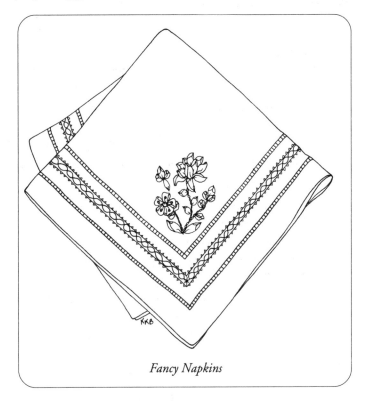

Fancy Napkins

Fancy Napkins Template

Stitch Key

Specific stitch instructions can be found on pages 196 to 212.

 Loop Stitch Flower — YLI #112 light rose, 7mm

 Japanese Ribbon Stitch — YLI #21 green, 7mm

 Lazy Daisy Stitch — YLI #21 green, 7mm

 Side Ribbon Stitch Rose — YLI #112 light rose , 7mm

 Chain Stitch — DMC 502 green, 2 strands

 Pistil Stitch — DMC ecru, 2 strands

Basket Weave Scissors Case

What better place to put basket weave stitch than on a basket! And the shape of this basket is just perfect for making a cute scissors holder. The design is not only pretty, but functional - it is made to pin on a garment or sewing bag, so that the small scissors will not be accidentally misplaced. Use all of those little scraps of silk ribbon that are not large enough to complete another full project, but are just to good to throw away. This will give a real country garden effect to the embroidery.

Materials

- 4 pieces of linen, each 4" x 5"
- 2 pieces of fusible lightweight fleece or batting, each 4" x 5"
- 1 shank button, $^1/_4$" in diameter
- Silk ribbon (refer to template for sizes and colors)
- **Pattern piece and template required:** Basket weave Scissors Case Pattern found on page 190
- Specific stitch instructions can be found on pages 196 to 212.

Directions

1. Trace the pattern onto each of the four linen pieces and the two batting pieces.

2. Trace the major template markings onto one of the four linen pieces (**fig. 1**).

3. Cut out and fuse the two batting shapes to the wrong side of two linen pieces inside the pattern lines, with one piece being the one with the embroidery markings on it.

4. Work the embroidery according to the template and stitch key. Specific stitch instructions can be found on pages 196 to 212. The handle and the ends of the basket weave will be finished after construction.

5. Cut out the four linen shapes.

6. Place one fused linen shape to one plain linen shape, right sides together. Stitch the two pieces together with a $^1/_4$" seam, leaving a 1" opening on one side of the basket for turning the piece to the right side (**see fig. 2**).

7. Repeat step 6 for the remaining two linen pieces, one being fused and the other being plain. Before stitching the two pieces together, add a small silk ribbon loop to the top edge. Tie a knot in each end of a $1^1/_4$" long piece of 4mm silk ribbon. Place the knotted ends in the seam allowance, with the loop extending toward the center of the basket (**fig. 2**).

8. Turn the pieces to the right side and press, making sure that the seam allowance of the opening is turned to the inside. These pieces form the front and back of the scissors case.

9. Place the front and back pieces with wrong sides together. Whip the pieces together from one top edge of the basket, down the side and across the bottom, then up the other side and stop at the top edge of the basket. Be sure that the openings are stitched closed with this whipped stitch and make sure that the bottom edge is especially secure (**fig. 3**).

10. Using the basket color in 4mm ribbon, work a chain stitch around the basket shape. Also work the basket handle with a chain stitch (see finished drawing).

11. Attach the button to the top edge of the scissors case on the piece without the loop (see the color photograph and the finished drawing). ▨

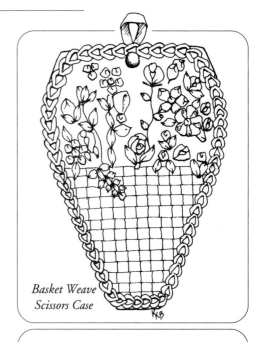

Basket Weave
Scissors Case

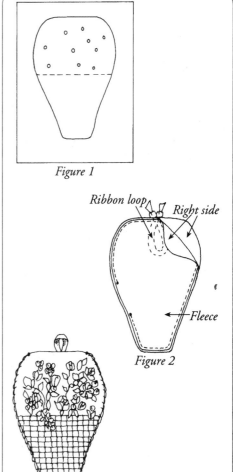

Figure 1

Ribbon loop   Right side

Fleece

Figure 2

Figure 3

Basket Weave Scissors Case

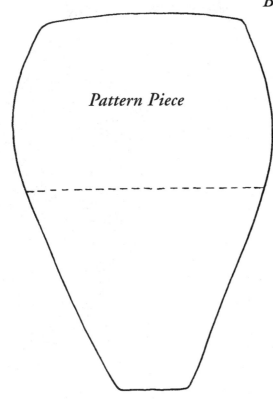

Pattern Piece

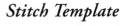

Stitch Template

Stitch Key

Specific stitch instructions can be found on pages 196 to 212.

This cheerful embroidery design looks best when worked in a variety of colors and sizes. The colors listed on the sample are given below. Feel free to sue odds and ends of ribbon in any color combination you lie. All Color numbers are for YLI; sizes are 4mm and 7mm. 120 Yellow, 126 Blue, 154 Lt. Green, 74 green, 114 Deep Rose, 112 Lt. Rose, 113 Med. Rose, 93 Red, 6 Lt. Pink and 123 Bright Pink.

 Spider Web Rose

 Loop Stitch Flower

 Chain Stitch

 Stem Stitch

 Lazy Daisy Stitch

 Japanese Ribbon Stitch

 French Knots

 Loop Stitch French Knot

Armchair Hussif

This gorgeous project is one of the most functional you will ever make, and also one of the prettiest. Using beautiful shades of silk ribbon to embroider easy irises, this little hussif consists of a pin cushion, scissors keeper and needle keeper. It is cleverly designed with small weights in the ends of the straps to hold it in place over the arm of your favorite sewing chair. The black silk dupioni is perfectly suited to the bright ribbon colors.

Materials

- ❀ ¹/₄ yd. of 45" fabric, or ¹/₃ yd. of 36" fabric
- ❀ 1 piece of wool flannel, 6" x ³/₄"
- ❀ 1 piece of synthetic suede, 6" x ³/₄"
- ❀ Iron-on fusible interfacing to fit the pieces listed above
- ❀ Silk ribbon (see template for colors and sizes)
- ❀ DMC floss, one color to match the fabric, the other to coordinate with the flower color
- ❀ One small button, ⁵/₈"
- ❀ One large snap
- ❀ Wool batting for stuffing
- ❀ **Pattern Piece Needed:** Hussif Pumpkin Pattern found 192
- ❀ **Template Needed:** Silk Ribbon Embroidery Templates for Hussif Pumpkin and Strap on page 193
- ❀ Silk Ribbon and Floss Stitch instructions can be found on pages 196 to 212.

Armchair Hussif

A. Making the Pumpkin

1. Cut two 5" x 5" squares of the fabric. Fuse iron-on interfacing to the wrong side of each square.

2. Using the template, draw a circle on the interfacing side of one piece of the fabric (do not cut out the circle).

3. Divide the circle into eight equal segments and mark with drawn lines. This can be done by folding the circle in half, half again, and once more for a total of three folds (**fig. 1**).

4. Using the divisions as your guide, embroider the flowers on the right side.

5. With a short machine stitch, stitch along the edge of the circle for approximately 1". This will be used later for the opening (**see fig. 2**).

6. Using a tack stitch, mark the center point on the front circle and the back fabric piece (**see fig. 2**).

7. Place the front over the back, right sides together, with the center points matched.

8. Using a short machine stitch, carefully stitch around the circle, leaving the seam open in the area of the previous stitching. Trim, leaving a ¹/₈" seam allowance. DO NOT CLIP (**fig. 2**).

9. Turn the pumpkin to the right side through the opening and stuff as tightly as possible with wool batting. Whip the opening together.

10. Blanket stitch around the pumpkin on each side of the seam line, using the floss that matches the fabric. Whip the blanket stitches together using the contrast color (**fig. 3**).

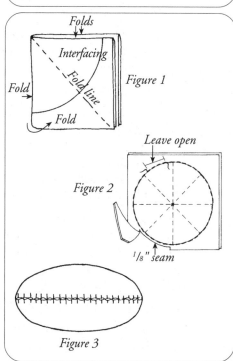

Figure 1

Figure 2

Figure 3

11. Using a double strand of the contrasting floss, put a knot approximately 6" from the end. When the thread is taken through the fabric, this will form a tail.

12. Using a long needle, come through the fabric from back to front at the marked center points. Take the needle over the edge, between the flowers and around to the back. Working alternately on opposite edges, divide the pumpkin into sections, first halves then quarters, then eighths, pulling the thread firmly to make the sections clearly divided (**fig. 4**).

13. When the divisions have all been made, bring the needle to the front and work a spider web over the center spokes; the needle will not go through the fabric, it will only go over and under the thread (see the finished drawing).

14. Take the thread to the back and secure, leaving a tail.

B. Making the Strap

1. Cut a piece of fabric 5$^{1}/_{2}$" wide x 27" long. Cut a piece of iron-on interfacing the same size and fuse it to the wrong side of the fabric strip.

2. Fold in half lengthwise and stitch with a $^{1}/_{4}$" seam, using a short stitch (**fig. 5**).

3. Clip the corners and turn the strap through to the right side.

4. Measure 4$^{1}/_{2}$" from each end and mark; these are fold lines. Also mark 6" from each end and stitch across the strap with a short stitch (**see fig. 6**).

5. Insert small weights into each end of the strap, then stitch across the strap at the fold lines. Whipstitch the opening at each end of the strap (**fig. 6**).

6. Blanket stitch around the strap on both sides along the edges, using the thread to match the fabric. Also blanket stitch along both sides of the stitching on the fold line (**fig. 7**).

7. Mark the placement for the strap embroidery at each end, just on the outside of the fold line. Work the embroidery at each end, through all layers (**fig. 8**).

8. Choose one end for the scissors end of the strap. Place the strip of synthetic suede 1" from the end of the strap on the wrong side (behind the embroidery) and buttonhole stitch it in place around all four sides (**fig. 9**).

9. At the opposite end of the strap, place the wool strip on the inside of the strap (behind the embroidery) and buttonhole stitch around all edges. This is the needle strip (**refer to fig. 9**).

10. Fold on the fold line of the scissors end *only* (the needle end will be left free) and pin the end to the strap. Using the contrast thread color, whip blanket stitches all the way around the strap in the following order (**fig. 10**):

    a. Begin at the scissors end of the strap, with the end folded in place. Begin the whipping 1" from the loose end of the folded strap (where the synthetic suede begins) and whip toward the loose end, across the short end and down the other side of the loose end to the 1" mark, where the synthetic suede begins.

    b. At this point, whip both layers of buttonhole stitches together, forming a pocket which is lined with the synthetic suede. Whip across the folded end and back up the other side to the point where the whipping is already worked in the loose end.

    c. At this point, whip the single-layer edge of the strap all the way around the remaining end, back to the point where the double-layer whipping was worked.

    d. Work a bullion stitch on each side of the scissors end of the strap at the top edge of the pocket to strengthen the stitching (**fig. 11**).

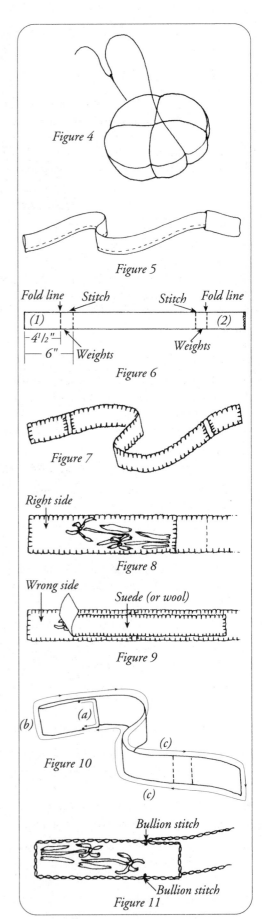

Figure 4

Figure 5

Fold line   Stitch   Stitch   Fold line

(1)   (2)

4$^{1}/_{2}$"   Weights
6"   Weights

Figure 6

Figure 7

Right side

Figure 8

Wrong side   Suede (or wool)

Figure 9

(b)   (a)   (c)

Figure 10   (c)

Bullion stitch

Bullion stitch

Figure 11

11. Fold up the needle end of the strap along the fold line and attach a large snap to hold it in place (**fig. 12**).

— C. Attaching the — Strap to the Pumpkin

1. Using the tails left at the back of the pumpkin, stitch the pumpkin to the center of the strap, putting a button at the back of the strap for greater strength (**fig. 13**). ▨

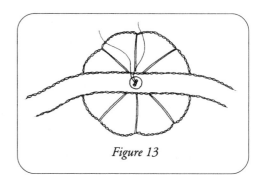

Figure 12

Figure 13

Stitch Key

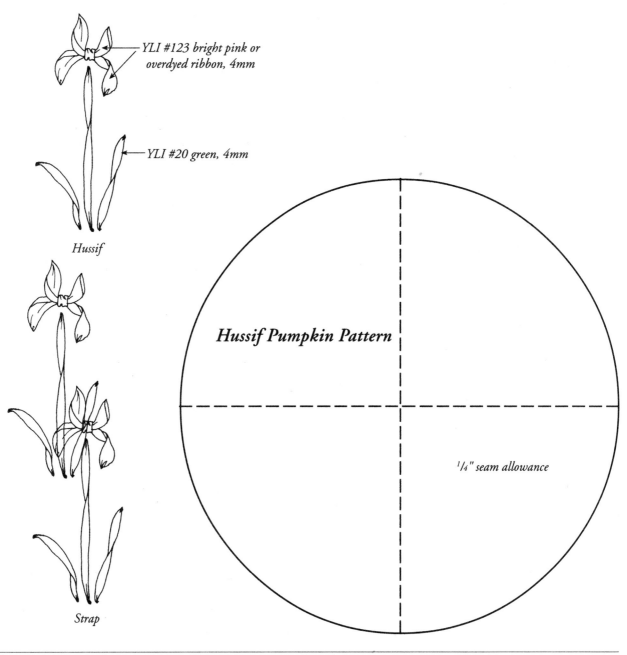

YLI #123 bright pink or overdyed ribbon, 4mm

YLI #20 green, 4mm

Hussif

Hussif Pumpkin Pattern

¹/₄" seam allowance

Strap

Hearts and Vines Box Lid

This little box is such a beautiful way to store those tiny treasures! Give it as a gift, or use it as "wrapping" for a very special gift. There will be many uses for something this elegant and pretty. The beautiful long and short stitched heart seems to be a reminder for Valentine's Day or Mother's Day, or any other special occasion. The best part is that it takes very little time to make, and it is very easy! Long and short stitch, spider web rose, French knots, stem stitch and cascaded ribbon are some of the easy stitches used.

Hearts and Vines Box Lid

Supplies

- One porcelain box with lid for embroidered insert
- One piece of linen, larger than the lid by at least 1" on all sides
- Silk ribbon for the design (refer to the template for sizes and colors)
- Posterboard for lid insert (if lid insert is not included with box)
- Lightweight batting for padding
- Optional: felt or paper for lid lining
- **Template Required:** Hearts and Vines Template found on page 195
- Stitch instructions can be found on pages 196 to 212

Directions

1. Use the lid liner or pattern provided with the box to trace the shape onto the linen piece, but do not cut it out. If a lid liner is not provided with the box, trace around the lid on a piece of posterboard. Trim the posterboard shape until it will fit snugly inside the lid. This will be the insert form.

2. Use a washout pencil or pen to mark the placement of the major design elements on the linen (**fig. 1**).

Figure 1

3. Refer to the template on page 195 and work the embroidery design. Refer to the color photograph and finished drawing. Instructions for specific stitches can be found on pages 196 to 212.

4. After the embroidery is complete, stitch just inside the lid outline to stabilize the shape (**see fig. 2**).

5. Mount the embroidery into the lid as directed in the instructions that come with the box, or use the following instructions.

6. Add a ³/₄" seam allowance all the way around the insert outline on the fabric and cut out along the new outline (**fig. 2**).

Figure 2

7. By hand or machine, run a gathering row around the edge of the shape, ¹/₄" from the cut edges (**fig. 3**).

8. Cut a piece of lightweight batting that is the size and shape of the lid insert form. Glue the batting to the top of the insert form.

Figure 3

9. Center the embroidered piece over the insert form and pull up the gathering thread to pull the cut edges to the back of the form. Smooth the fabric in place and glue the edges to the back of the insert form (**fig. 4**).

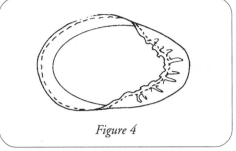

Figure 4

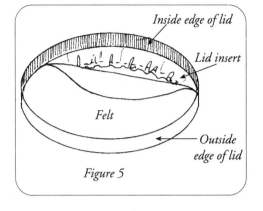

Figure 5

10. Once the embroidered piece is glued to the lid insert, place it into the lid. Add a bead of glue to the inside edge of the lid if necessary to hold the insert in place.

11. Cut a piece of paper or felt that is the same size as the insert form and glue it in place to line the lid (**fig. 5**). 🔲

Hearts and Vines Template

Stitch Key

Specific stitch instructions can be found on pages 196 to 212.

🌹 *Spider Web Rose, YLI #113 medium rose, 4mm*

🍃 *Japanese Ribbon Stitch, YLI #21 green, 4mm*

🍃 *Straight Stitch, YLI #21 green, 4mm*

● *French Knot, DMC floss 3752 blue, 1 strand*

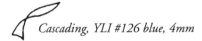 *Cascading, YLI #126 blue, 4mm*

 *Stem Stitch, DMC floss 502 green 1 strand*

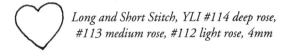 *Long and Short Stitch, YLI #114 deep rose, #113 medium rose, #112 light rose, 4mm*

Hand Stitches

Bullion Stitch

Loop Stitch French Knot

Buttonhole/Blanket Stitch

Cascading • Chain Stitch

Colonial Knot • Feather Stitch

Fly Stitch • No Fail French Knot

Fuchsia • Japanese Ribbon Stitch

Iris • Lazy Daisy Stitch

Satin Stitch

Long and Short Stitches

Loop Stitch • Maggie's Rose

Pistil Stitch • Side Ribbon Stitch

Side Stitch Rose • Silk Ribbon Weaving

Stem/Outline Stitch

Spider Web Rose

Straight Stitch Rose

Twisted Straight Stitch

Woven Spider Web

Bullion Stitch

Use a 24 or 26 chenille needle.

1. Bring the needle up from under the fabric at point "A" and take a stitch down in "B" about ³/₈" to ¹/₄" away and come back up through "A" beside (not through) the floss. <u>Do not pull the needle all the way through</u> (**fig. 1**). **Note:** The distance from "A" to "B" will determine the length of the bullion.

2. Now, hold the end of the needle down with your thumb. This will pop the point of the needle up away from the fabric. Wrap the floss or floss coming from point "A" around the needle 5 to 6 times (**fig. 2**).

3. With your finger, push the wraps of floss to the bottom of the needle next to the fabric so that they are all lined up tight (**fig. 3**). With your other hand, place your finger under the fabric and your thumb on top of the bullion and gently pull the needle and floss through the wraps (**fig. 4**).

4. You almost have a bullion, but first you most lay the coils over to the opposite side and take up the slack floss (**fig. 5**). To do this, lay the bullion over and place your finger under the fabric and your thumb on top of the bullion and gently pull the floss until the slack is out (**fig. 6**). Insert the needle into the fabric at the end of the bullion (**fig. 7**) and tie off. ▨

Loop Stitch French Knot

1. Come up at A and make a loop. Hold the loop in place with a pin.

2. Wrap the ribbon around the needle tow times. Insert the needle at B, close to the pin. Gently pull the two wraps down the needle until they rest on the fabric. Holding the ribbon tight, gently pull the needle through the fabric forming a French Knot (**fig. 1**). ▨

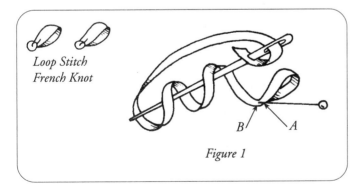

Loop Stitch
French Knot

B   A

Figure 1

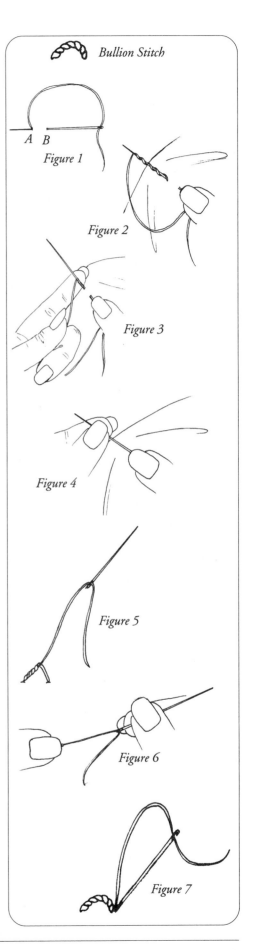

Bullion Stitch

Figure 1

Figure 2

Figure 3

Figure 4

Figure 5

Figure 6

Figure 7

Buttonhole/Blanket Stitch

I. On the Fabric

1. Bring the needle up through the fabric at A. Pull the ribbon above and to the right of A and hold it in place with your thumb (**fig. 1**).

2. Insert the needle in B and up through C in one stitch, keeping the ribbon under the needle (**fig. 2**). Pull through.

3. C now becomes A and the sequence repeats. You may see the sequence as A-B, A-B, and on and on (**fig. 3**). Notice that the stitch looks like a series of upside down "L's".

II. Over the Edge

1. Use the instructions given for On the Fabric with the following exceptions:

   a. Put a narrow hem in the edge of the fabric.

   b. Bury the beginning knot in the fold of the fabric at point A (**fig. 4**).

   c. Work stitch B through the fabric below the hem (**see fig. 5**).

   d. Bring the needle behind the edge of the fabric at point C, making the loop but not catching any fabric (**fig. 5**).

   e. Repeat across the edge (**fig. 6**).

III. Whipped Buttonhole/Blanket Stitch:

1. After the buttonhole stitches are complete, wrap each stitch with a matching or contrast floss or ribbon. The wrapping may be done over a single-layer edge (**fig. 7**), or it may be used to whip two layers together (**fig. 8**). ▨

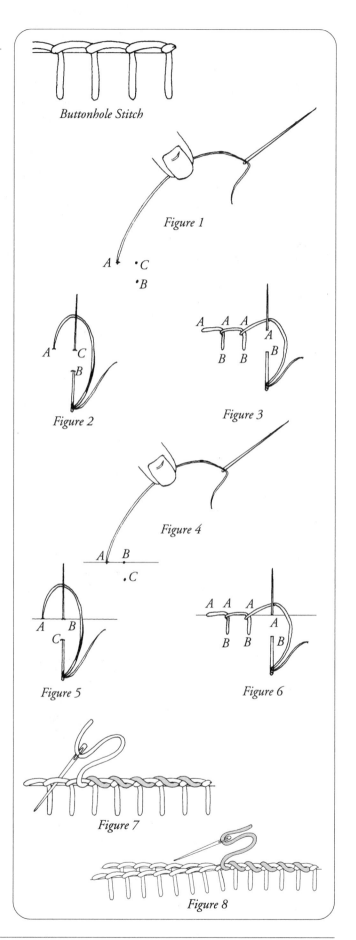

Buttonhole Stitch

Figure 1

Figure 2

Figure 3

Figure 4

Figure 5

Figure 6

Figure 7

Figure 8

Cascading

Bring the needle up through the fabric from underneath a bow or flower, or from wherever your streamers will be attached (**fig. 1**). Next, take a small stitch in the fabric about 1 inch or more away from where you came up and twist the ribbon so that it rolls and loops (**fig. 2**). Pull the ribbon very loosely and let it lie naturally. The loops may be tacked in place with French knots or seed beads. ◉

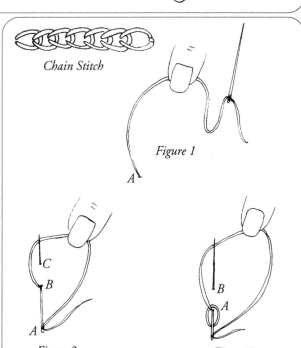

Cascading

Figure 1

Figure 2

Chain Stitch

This is a glorified lazy daisy stitch that works beautifully on smocking and adds dimension to silk ribbon embroidery. It is a great outline stitch for stems and vines when done with one or two stands of floss.

1. Bring the needle up through the fabric at A. Swing the floss or ribbon around in a loop and hold the loop with your thumb (**fig. 1**).

2. While holding the loop, insert the needle in at B and out through C in one stitch. Keep the needle and floss or ribbon going over the loop (**fig. 2**).

3. Instead of inserting the needle to the other side like a lazy daisy, you will make another loop and insert the needle down, right beside C were you last came up, this will become a new A. In the same stitch bring the needle through B and pull (**fig. 3**). Keep the needle over the loop.

4. Continue looping and stitching in an "A, B" – "A, B" sequence. ◉

Chain Stitch

Figure 1

Figure 2

Figure 3

Colonial Knot

These basic knot stitches are used in a variety of ways. They are the centers of daisies and the blossoms of hyacinths. They are grapes on a vine or tiny rosettes in a bouquet. It is good to know at least one; choose your favorite.

1. Come up from beneath the fabric and wrap the needle under the ribbon once (**fig. 1**).

2. Next, wrap the ribbon over the needle once (**fig. 2**) and back under once (**fig. 3**). This makes a figure eight.

3. Insert the needle just beside the original hole (**fig. 4**). While holding the needle vertically, pull the slack out of the ribbon so that the knot tightens around the needle (**fig. 5**). Continue holding the ribbon taut until the needle and ribbon have been pulled all the way through. ◉

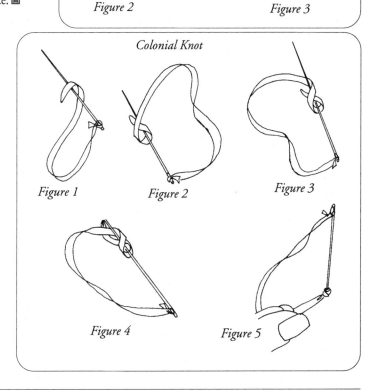

Colonial Knot

Figure 1

Figure 2

Figure 3

Figure 4

Figure 5

Feather Stitch

1. Bring the needle up through the fabric at A (**fig. 1**). Insert the needle down about ¼" to ⅜" across from A and into the fabric at B. In the same stitch bring the needle out of the fabric ¼" to ⅜" down and slightly to the right of center at C (**fig. 2**). With the ribbon behind the needle, pull the ribbon through (**fig. 3**). This stitch is much like the lazy daisy only the needle does not insert into the same hole in which it came up. Notice that the stitch is simply a triangle.

2. Now you will begin working your triangle from right to left, or left to right. C will now become A for your next stitch. Repeat the stitch as in step 1 (**fig. 4**).

3. Next time repeat the stitch on the other side (**fig. 5**). The trick is that A and B will always be straight across from each other and that A, B, and C will line up vertically (**fig. 6**). ▨

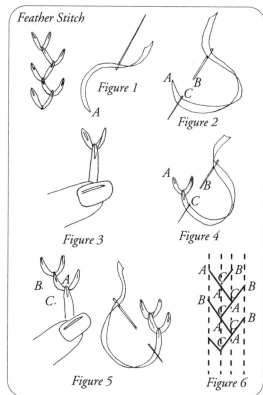

Feather Stitch

Figure 1

Figure 2

Figure 3

Figure 4

Figure 5

Figure 6

Fly Stitch

This stitch may be used for leaves at the base of flowers, it may be worked singly or in rows to give the appearance of ferns. This is an easy stitch to master and you will find many uses for it as fillers.

1. Come up at A. Insert the needle in the fabric at B, coming out of the fabric at C, making sure the loop of ribbon is below C (**fig. 1**). Keep the needle on top of the loop of ribbon.

2. The length of the anchor stitch is determined by the length of the stitch taken between C and D. The floss or ribbon comes out of the fabric at C and the needle is inserted into the fabric at D. The longer the distance between C and D, the longer the anchor stitch. Gently pull the ribbon to the wrong side (**figs. 2 and 3**). ◉

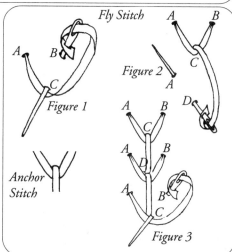

Fly Stitch

Figure 1

Figure 2

Figure 3

Anchor Stitch

No Fail French Knot

The most asked question about French knots is "How many wraps?". The number of wraps will depend on the size of the knot desired, the type of thread or floss being used, and personal preference. Generally, use one strand of floss or 2mm silk ribbon with one to two wraps per knot. If a larger knot is needed, use more strands of floss or larger silk ribbon. Often times, French knots will not lay flat on the fabric. To eliminate this problem, once the needle has been reinserted in the fabric (**fig. 3**), slip the wrapped floss or ribbon gently down the needle until it rests against the fabric. Hold the wraps against the fabric and slowly pull the floss or ribbon through the wraps to the wrong side. This will cause the knot to be formed on the surface of the fabric and not float above it.

1. Bring the needle up through the fabric (**fig. 1**).

2. Hold the needle horizontally with one hand and wrap the ribbon around the needle with the other hand (**fig. 2**). If you are using a single strand of floss, one or two wraps will create a small knot. If you are making French knots with 2mm silk ribbon, the knot will be larger. As stated above, the size of the knot varies with the number of strands of floss or the width of the silk ribbon being used.

3. While holding the tail of the ribbon to prevent it from unwinding off the needle, bring the needle up into a vertical position and insert it into the fabric just slightly beside where the needle came out of the fabric (**fig. 3**). Pull the ribbon or floss gently through the fabric while holding the tail with the other hand. ▨

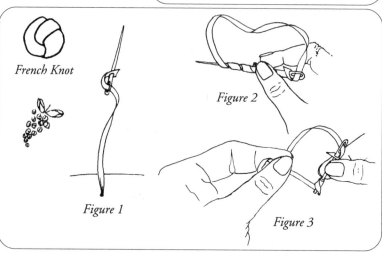

French Knot

Figure 1

Figure 2

Figure 3

Fuchsia

This flower uses two shades of the same color, one dark and one light, in addition to yellow floss or floche for the pistils.

1. Use the lighter ribbon for the bottom petals. Work the center petal first.

2. Bring the needle up at a point that is halfway between the center of the flower and the point where the bottom tip of the petal should end.

3. Fold the thread over one finger or a laying tool, forming a loop. The loop should be ¹/₂ the total length of the petal. Carry the ribbon to the wrong side just below the center of the flower (**fig. 1**).

4. Holding the loop firmly in place with your thumb, bring the ribbon up beside the center petal and form the second stitch following the directions given above. This stitch should be worked at a slight angle and shorter than the center stitch (**fig. 2**). Now put your thumb firmly on this loop.

5. Repeat this process on the other side of the center loop. Always remember to put your thumb firmly on the top of the loop before pulling the threads through because they are very unstable at this point.

6. Using the second (darker) color, bring the needle up just above the center petal leaving just a small gap between the lower stitches and the new stitches.

7. Work a straight stitch the same length as the middle loop petal, pulling the thread flat against the fabric (**see fig. 3**).

8. The second straight stitch is made beside the first straight stitch and it is approximately ³/₄ of the length of your first stitch (**fig. 3**).

9. The side stitches are made by working from the outside to the center of the flower. They are worked in reverse order because the loop stitches are still unstable and you do not want to pierce the ribbon and distort them. These stitches are worked at a sight 45 degree angle. Do not pull the ribbon tight and if the ribbon twists, leave the twists for a more natural appearance. Work one of these stitches on each side of the straight stitches (**see fig. 4**).

10. Tie off or simply move to the next flower.

11. Cut two 18" strands of DMC floss or one strand of DMC flower thread or floche. Bring the floss up underneath the first loop.

12. In order to secure the ribbon loops, make a small catch stitch through the bottom portion of each loop, making sure not to bring the catch stitch all the way through both pieces of the ribbon loop. The top piece of ribbon must remain loose.

13. When all of the loops are secure, work four pistil stitches (pg. 204) at different lengths underneath the center loop, with one center stitch being the longest (**fig. 4**).◼

Japanese Ribbon Stitch

Use any size ribbon. Bring the needle up from under the fabric, loop it around and insert the needle down into the center of the ribbon a short distance in front of where the needle came up. Pull the ribbon so that the end curls in on itself loosely so that it does not disappear. ◼

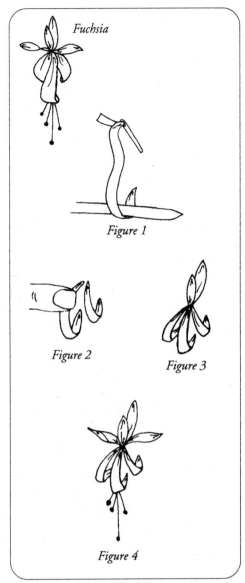

Fuchsia

Figure 1

Figure 2

Figure 3

Figure 4

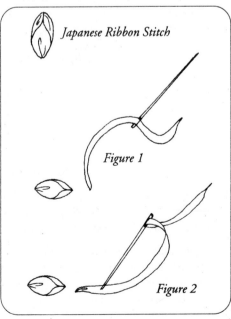

Japanese Ribbon Stitch

Figure 1

Figure 2

Iris

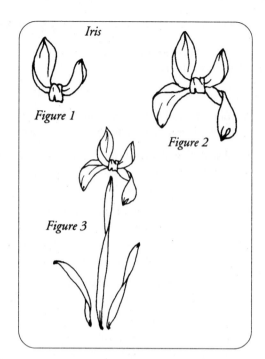

Iris

Figure 1

Figure 2

Figure 3

1. Begin with a fly stitch for the top petals (see pg. 200 for instructions). Make one arm of the stitch shorter than the other and bring the stitches closer together than usual. Leave the ribbon loose enough on the fabric to look fluffed up, not flat (**see fig. 1**).

2. Make the anchor stitch short, and leave it loose enough to puff up also (**fig. 1**).

3. Bring the needle back out at a point to the right of and below the right arm of the fly stitch. Use the eye of the needle to thread the ribbon through the anchor stitch of the fly stitch. Insert the needle to the left of and below the left arm of the fly stitch. Be sure that the lower stitches form an angle and do not stand out straight. It is all right for these stitches to be twisted a little. These bottom petals should be the same length as the top of the flower, but wider apart (**fig. 2**).

4. The stalk should be twice the length of the flower. Start at the bottom of the flower and lay the ribbon on the fabric. Insert the needle at the correct length below the flower and pull through. It is not a problem if the stem is twisted (**see fig. 3**).

5. Make two twisted straight stitch leaves at a slight angle to the stalk. Make one leaf half as tall as the stalk, and make the second leaf slightly shorter than the first one (**fig. 3**).

Lazy Daisy Stitch

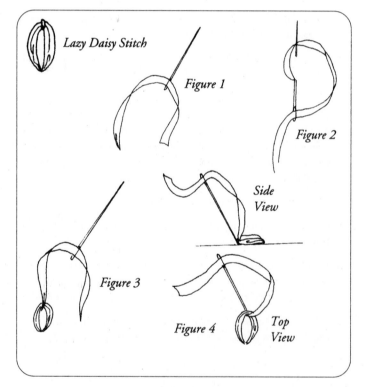

Lazy Daisy Stitch

Figure 1

Figure 2

Side View

Figure 3

Figure 4

Top View

1. Bring the needle up through the center point if you are stitching a flower, and up just next to a vine or flower for leaves (**fig. 1**).

2. Insert the needle down into the same hole in which you came up. In the same stitch come through about $^1/_8$ " to $^3/_8$ " above that point (**fig. 2**). Wrap the ribbon behind the needle and pull the ribbon through, keeping the ribbon from twisting (**fig. 3**).

3. Insert the needle straight down into the same hole or very close to the same hole at the top of the loop (**fig. 4**). Notice in the side view of figure 4 that the needle goes down underneath the ribbon loop. The top view of figure 4 shows that the stitch is straight and will anchor the ribbon loop in place.

Satin Stitch

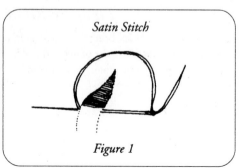

Satin Stitch

Figure 1

1. It generally helps if you have the area to be filled traced on the project so that you have two definite lines to guide and maintain the varying width of the stitch as it fills different shapes. Secure in embroidery hoop.

2. Begin at one end and work the needle from one side to the other, stacking the thread up just below and next to the previous stitch (**fig. 1**). Continue this wrapping process, keeping the fabric secured and taut while the stitches are pulled with light tension so that the fabric will not tunnel.

Long and Short Stitches

This stitch is used as a fill-in stitch or padding stitch.

1. Work the first row of stitching alternating long and short stitches (**fig. 1**).

2. Work the all middle rows with stitches of equal length that fit into the alternating stitches (**fig. 2**).

3. Continue stitching rows, filling in the middle of the design.

4. Work the last row with alternating long and short stitches to fit the shape of the design (**fig. 3**). ▣

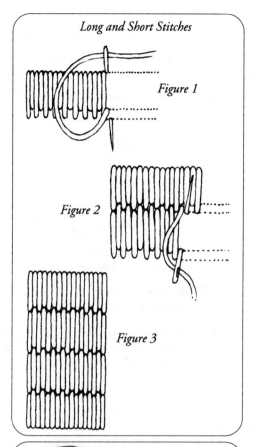

Long and Short Stitches

Figure 1

Figure 2

Figure 3

Loop Stitch

1. Insert the needle up through the fabric and loop around away from you, inserting the needle just slightly beside where you came up (**fig. 1**).

2. Pull the ribbon straight (without twists) and loosely adjust the loop to the desired size (**fig. 2**). ▣

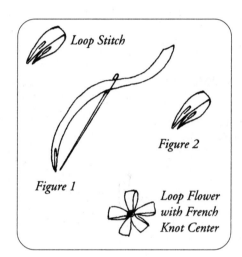

Loop Stitch

Figure 2

Figure 1

Loop Flower with French Knot Center

Maggie's Rose

Supplies

Crewel needle, 8 or 10
Two shades of floss, one light pink and one medium pink (use one strand)

Directions

1. Using the darker floss, bring the needle to the front and take three or four small stitches for the center of the rose, having all of the stitches go into and out of the same holes (**fig. 1**).

2. Change to the lighter floss and bring the needle up at one end of the stitches. Insert the needle at the other end of the stitches, then bring it halfway out at the end where the needle came up; do not pull the needle all the way through (**fig. 2**).

3. Using the end of the floss that is at the tip end of the needle, wrap the floss to the back and under the eye of the needle, then to the front and under the tip of the needle. The wrap should be formed smoothly and close to the needle, but not pulled tightly. That completes one wrap. Make two more wraps for a total of three (**fig. 3**).

4. After the third wrap, hold one thumb over the wraps and gently pull the needle through until the last loop of thread lies flat against the fabric. Take the needle over the wrapped threads and to the back, making a small stitch to secure the wraps at the front end of the rose (**fig. 4**).

5. Bring the needle out at the back end of the rose and take a small stitch over the wraps to hold them securely in place (**fig. 5**). ▣

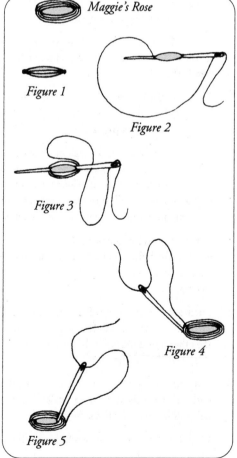

Maggie's Rose

Figure 1

Figure 2

Figure 3

Figure 4

Figure 5

Pistil Stitch

1. Come up at A. Allow a short length of the ribbon to extend above A. Keep the ribbon flat and taut (**fig. 1**).

2. Wrap the ribbon around the needle two times. Insert the needle at B, gently pull the wrapped ribbon down the needle until it rests against the fabric. Hold the ribbon taut as you pull the needle through the fabric forming a two wrap French knot (**fig. 2**). ■

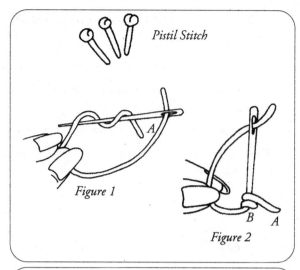

Pistil Stitch

Figure 1

Figure 2

Side Ribbon Stitch

1. Bring the needle up at the base of the stitch and lay the ribbon along the fabric in the direction of the stitch (**fig. 1**).

2. At the point where the stitch should end, insert the needle into the ribbon, close to one side edge (**fig. 2**).

3. Pull the ribbon through carefully, letting the ribbon roll to one side. Be sure to leave the ribbon loose and do not pull the curl to the back side of the fabric (**fig. 3**). ■

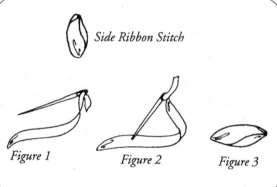

Side Ribbon Stitch

Figure 1   Figure 2   Figure 3

Side Stitch Rose

(Refer to the stitch diagram while forming the rose.)

1. Starting from the center of the flower, make a side ribbon stitch with the needle inserted on the right edge of the ribbon. Do not pull the stitch too tightly (**fig. 1**).

2. Make another side ribbon stitch to the right of the first stitch, this time inserting the needle on the left edge of the ribbon. Remember to leave the ribbon slightly loose (**fig. 2**).

3. Make the third stitch at an angle and slightly shorter than the two previous stitches. Make a fourth stitch on the opposite side of the flower. On each petal, insert the needle on the inside edge of the ribbon. The stitches should not all come from the same center hole, but should begin a slight distance from the center to leave a center space (**fig. 3**).

4. Stitches five and six are made the same as three and four, each at an angle and slightly shorter than three and four. Insert the needle in the inside edge of the stitches (see **fig. 4**).

5. Stitches seven and eight will extend below the flower center and each stitch should drop at a different angle, with one being a little longer than the other. Insert the needle in the right edge of stitch eight and in the left side of stitch nine (**fig. 4**).

6. More stitches may be worked in among the first layer, using a lighter or darker shade of the ribbon in a smaller size. Let the second layer of stitches fall at different angles to the first layer.

7. Optional: A center may be worked in the flower, using yellow ribbon French knots. ■

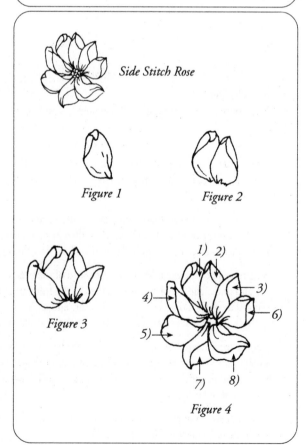

Side Stitch Rose

Figure 1   Figure 2

Figure 3

1) 2)
3)
4)
6)
5)
7) 8)

Figure 4

Silk Ribbon Weaving

1. Trace the shape of the weave on the fabric. Begin at the top or the bottom of the shape and work to the other end. Bring the needle up through the fabric on one side of the traced line and insert it down through the fabric on the other side into the traced line (**fig. 1**). Keep the ribbon completely flat and smooth. If fraying occurs switch to a bigger needle.

2. Make the next stitch come up through the fabric next to the last inserted stitch (**fig. 2**) so that the back side becomes simply an outline of the shape and not covered with ribbon (**fig. 3**). In other words you will not carry the ribbon across the back side of the fabric. When bringing the needle up for another stitch allow room for the ribbon width. You want the ribbon edges to touch but not to overlap.

3. Continue filling the shape with horizontal stitches following the shape of the traced lines.

4. Once the shape is filled with horizontal stitches, it is time to repeat the process vertically, only this time you will weave the ribbon through the horizontal ribbons before you insert the needle on the other side (**fig. 4**).

5. Tie off when complete and embellish the edges with flowers and leaves or with an outline stitch. 🔲

Silk Ribbon Weaving

←*Front of weave*

Figure 1

Figure 2

Leave space between stitches

Back of weave

Figure 3

Figure 4

Stem/Outline Stitch

Worked from left to right, this stitch makes a line of slanting stitches. The thread is kept to the left and below the needle. Make small, even stitches. The needle is inserted just below the line to be followed, comes out to the left of the insertion point, and above the line, slightly.

1. Come up from behind at A and go down into the fabric again at B (**see fig. 1**). This is a little below the line. Come back up at C (**fig. 1**). This is a little above the line. Keep the thread below the needle.

2. Go back down into the fabric at D and come up a little above the line at B (**fig. 2**).

3. Continue working, always keeping the thread below the needle (**fig. 3**). 🔲

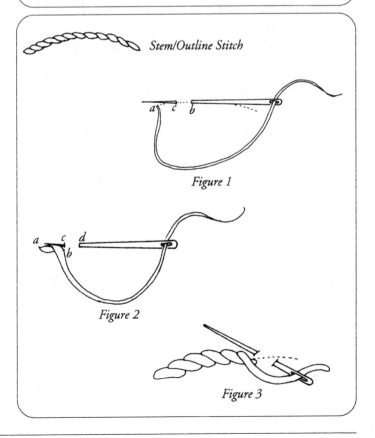

Stem/Outline Stitch

Figure 1

Figure 2

Figure 3

Spider Web Rose

Begin with a five legged "spider," or five spokes, stitched with either a single strand or a double stand of embroidery floss. For larger roses use a double strand. It may be helpful to mark a center with five evenly spaced dots around it using a washout pen or pencil as you are learning to make this rose.

1. To stitch the spider, come up from the bottom of the fabric with your needle through dot "a" then down in the center dot "b" (**fig. 1**). Come up through "c" then down in "b" (**fig. 2**). Continue around; up in "d" down in "b", up in "e" down in "b" etc… until the spider is complete and tie off underneath (**fig. 3**).

2. Now, with your silk ribbon, insert the needle up through the center "b" (**fig. 4**). Slide the needle under a spoke or "spider leg" and pull ribbon through loosely (**fig. 5**).

3. Skipping over the next spoke go under the third spoke (**fig. 6**) and begin weaving in a circle over and under every other spoke (**fig. 7**).

4. Continue weaving until the spokes are covered. Insert the needle underneath the last "petal" and pull through to the back.

You may stitch leaves first and then stitch the rose on top, or you may bring your needle up from underneath a "petal" and stitch leaves under the rose. ▣

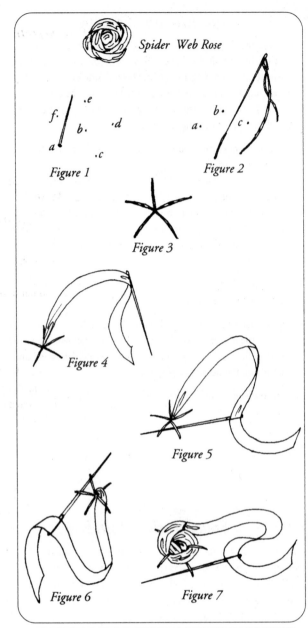

Spider Web Rose

Figure 1   *Figure 2*

Figure 3

Figure 4

Figure 5

Figure 6   *Figure 7*

Straight Stitch Rose

A straight stitch rose is simple and easy to make. Refer to the instructions given for a straight stitch in this section.

1. Work 3 French knots or Colonial knots in the center (**fig. 1**).

2. Work 3 straight stitches in a triangle around the center French knots. The straight stitches need to partially cover the stitch before (**fig. 2**).

3. Continue making rows of straight stitches being careful to overlap the stitches slightly as you work around the rose. The size of the rose is determined by the number of rows worked (**fig. 3**). ▣

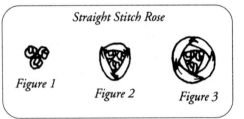

Straight Stitch Rose

Figure 1   *Figure 2*   *Figure 3*

Straight Stitch

Simply bring the needle up from under the fabric and insert it down into the fabric a short distance in front of where the needle came up. It is an in–and–out stitch. Remember to pull the ribbon loosely for nice full stitches. ▣

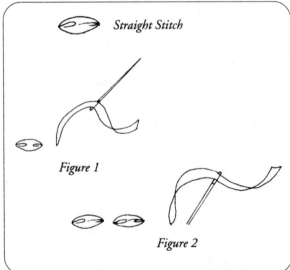

Straight Stitch

Figure 1

Figure 2

Twisted Straight Stitch

1. Following the instructions given for the straight stitch, bring the ribbon up at A and twist it one time, going back into the fabric at b (**fig. 1**).

2. Allow the twisted straight stitch to sit on top of the fabric. If pulled tightly against the fabric, you will loose the curl of the ribbon (**fig. 2**). 🔲

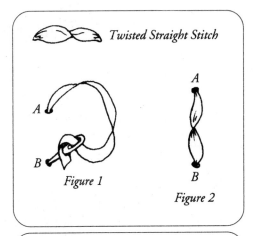

Twisted Straight Stitch

Figure 1

Figure 2

Woven Spider Web

1. Stitch six to eight "spokes" (straight stitches) to form a circle (**fig. 1**). Note: the number of spokes can vary. Take the needle to the back.

2. Bring the needle up to the left of the first spoke, close to the center of the circle. Take the thread under and over the first spoke (do not pick up any fabric) (**fig. 2**). All further stitching will be under and over the spokes and not into the fabric.

3. Place the needle under the first and second spoke creating a "wrap" stitch on the first spoke.

4. Take the needle over the second spoke and under the second and third spoke creating a "wrap" stitch on the second spoke. Take the needle over the third spoke and under the third and fourth spoke creating a "wrap" stitch on the third spoke (**fig. 3**). Continue stitching in this manner until all spokes are covered creating the spider web. Note: Gradually loosen the tension on the outer stitches of the circle to achieve better coverage. 🔲

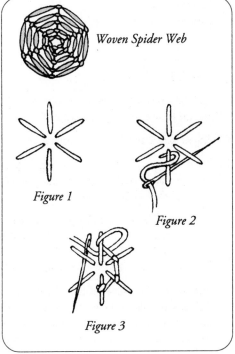

Woven Spider Web

Figure 1

Figure 2

Figure 3

Ribbon Flowers and Trims

Pansy

✂ 12" of ³/₄" wide medium blue ribbon, satin or French grosgrain

✂ 9" of ³/₄" wide light blue ribbon, satin or grosgrain

✂ 6" of yellow cording for center

✂ 2" square of buckram

✂ all-purpose thread

✂ large needle

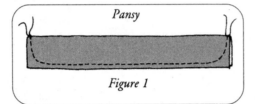

Pansy

Figure 1

1. Cut the 12" piece of ribbon into three 4" pieces; cut the 9" piece of ribbon into two 4¹/₂" pieces.

2. Run a gathering thread across one long side and both short ends of one ribbon piece, rounding off the corners (**fig. 1**).

3. Pull the gathers up tightly and tie off. The gathered edge is the inner edge of the petal and the loose edge is the outer edge of the petal (**fig. 2**).

4. Repeat steps 2 and 3 for the remaining ribbon pieces.

5. Tie several knots in the yellow cording as close together as possible. Cut a tiny hole in the center of the buckram piece and slip the ends of the cording through to the back side; tack the ends of the cording to the buckram and trim away the excess (**fig. 3**).

6. Place two of the medium blue petals on the buckram in the positions shown in fig. 4. If the buckram were a watch face and the yellow cording were at the center, the petals would be at 10 and 2, meeting in the center. Allow the inner edges of the petals to slip underneath the knots of the cording. Stitch the petals in place (**fig. 4**).

7. Place the two light blue petals on the buckram as shown in fig. 5. Using the watch face reference, the petals will be placed at 4 and 8. Let the outer edges of the two lower petals slightly overlap the upper petals and slip the inner edges of the lower petals underneath the knots. Stitch the petals in place (**fig. 5**).

8. The last petal (medium blue) will be centered over the bottom two petals, at 6 on the watch face. Stitch the petals in place (**fig. 6**).

9. Make sure that all petals are securely stitched in place. Trim away the excess buckram and glue or stitch the pansy in place. ▨

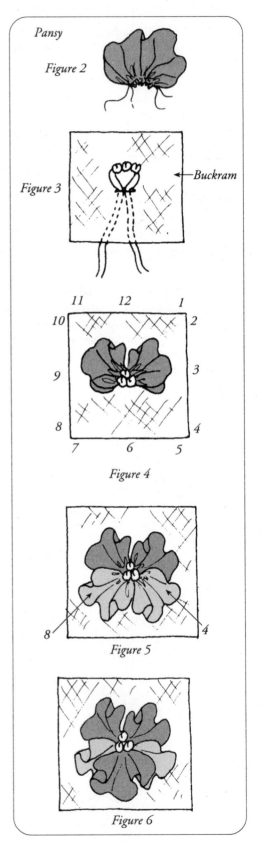

Pansy

Figure 2

Figure 3 ← Buckram

11 12 1
10   2
9   3
8   4
7   6   5

Figure 4

8   4

Figure 5

Figure 6

Cabachon Roses and Buds
Supplies

✂ 18" of wire-edged ribbon for each rose
✂ 9" of wire-edged ribbon for each bud
✂ Buckram, 2" square for each flower or bud
✂ All-purpose sewing thread to match ribbon
✂ Large needle
✂ Scissors to cut through wire edge

1. Cut each of the ribbons into 18" pieces for flowers, 9" for buds. Cut the buckram into 2" squares.

2. Fold down the right end of one piece of ribbon so that 2" hangs below, forming a "handle" to hold onto (**fig. 1**).

3. Gently and loosely roll the fold to the left to begin shaping the center of the flower or bud (**fig. 2**).

4. Treat the top and bottom selvages of the ribbon as if they were train tracks. Roll along the tracks until you have created a perfect circle.

5. To create the first petal, fold back the length of the ribbon to form a bias fold. Roll the bud along the tracks to completely enclose the fold in the bud (**fig. 3**). Make and roll another bias fold. Stop at this point for the buds and go to step 7 for finishing. Continue with these instructions for the remaining flowers.

6. Find the lower wire in the edge of the ribbon and gather the remaining ribbon to be about 4" to 5" long (**fig. 4**).

7. At this point, center the bud over a 2" square of buckram and sew the bud securely to the buckram, stitching through the rolled selvage edges at the base of the bud. Trim away the excess ribbon of the "handle" at this point.

8. Wrap the gathers counterclockwise around the bud, allowing ⅛" space on the buckram between the rows of gathers. Wrap the gathers around the bud until the flower is as large as desired, then trim away the excess length (**fig. 5**). Stitch the gathers to the buckram as the ribbon is wrapped and fold the raw end under before stitching.

9. Trim the excess buckram away from behind the rose. ▣

Serpentine Ribbon Manipulation

This gathered ribbon technique may be worked by hand or by machine. The instructions are the same for either method.

1. Make marks along each edge of the ribbon, with the distance between the marks being twice the width of the ribbon and the marks along the bottom edge should be directly under the marks along the top edge (**fig. 1**).

2. By hand or machine, run a sturdy gathering stitch between the first two dots on the upper edge, then stitch straight down to the second dot on the bottom edge (**fig. 2**).

3. Stitch along the bottom edge between the second and third dots, then stitch straight up to the third dot on the top edge (**fig. 3**).

4. Continue stitching in this pattern to the end of the ribbon.

5. Pull the gathering threads to gather the ribbon. The gathering threads will pull into a straight line and the ribbon will gather into a serpentine shape, with a loose ruffle first on one edge and then on the other edge (**fig. 4**). ▣

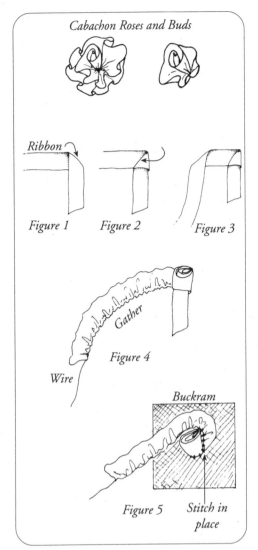

Cabachon Roses and Buds

Ribbon

Figure 1   *Figure 2*   *Figure 3*

Gather

Figure 4

Wire

Buckram

Figure 5   Stitch in place

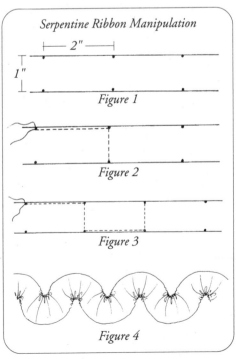

Serpentine Ribbon Manipulation

2"

1"

Figure 1

Figure 2

Figure 3

Figure 4

Ruched Ribbon

Ruching may be done by hand or by machine.

Method I - Hand

1. Place dots along one edge of the ribbon, with the spacing between the dots being twice the ribbon width.

2. Place dots along the opposite edge of the ribbon with the spacing being the same, but let the dots alternate with the first row (**fig.** 1).

3. Using a doubled thread, run gathering stitches from dot to dot in a zigzag pattern from one edge to the other (**fig.** 2).

4. When the gathering thread is pulled up, the gathering thread will become straight and the ribbon will be ruched (**fig.** 3).

Method II - Machine

1. The machine method works best with ³/₈" ribbon, due to the width of the machine stitch.

2. Use the three-step zigzag stitch and a loosened top tension, and just stitch down the length of the ribbon. The stitches will form a zigzag shape from side to side (**fig.** 4).

3. When the gathering thread is pulled up, the gathering thread will become straight and the ribbon will be ruched (**refer to fig.** 3). 🏵

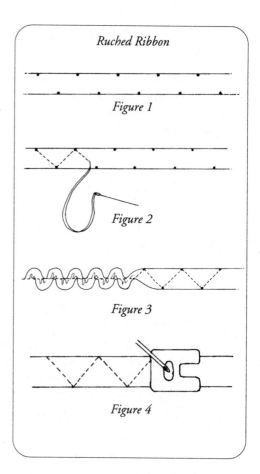

Ruched Ribbon

Figure 1

Figure 2

Figure 3

Figure 4

Ribbon Leaves

Supplies

✄ 6" to 9" of green wire-edged ribbon for each leaf, depending on the width of the ribbon and the finished size needed

✄ all-purpose sewing thread to match the ribbon

✄ scissors to cut through wired edges

1. Cut the green wire-edged ribbon into 6" - 9" pieces, depending on the size needed for the finished leaves.

2. Fold each piece of ribbon in half, end to end.

3. Fold the top edge of the fold down to meet the lower selvage edge (**see fig.** 1).

4. Beginning at the cut ends, sew a running stitch from the bottom edge diagonally up to the top edge, across the top, and diagonally down the fold to the bottom edge (**fig.** 1).

5. Pull up the gathers and open the ribbon to form the leaf. Adjust the gathers until the leaf is the desired shape and size, then tie-off the thread. 🏵

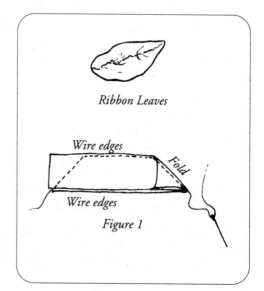

Ribbon Leaves

Wire edges

Fold

Wire edges

Figure 1

Cabbage Rose

Any project graced by this luxurious rose is instrantly touched with a Victorian appeal. It is a wonderful ornament for hats, boxes, pillows, and wedding dresses and veils. Technically, it is a variation of the hand wrapped rose. It is made exactly the same way only there is a twist at the end. It takes a little practice so don't be discouraged the first time.

1. Beginning with a flat piece of ribbon about 15 inches long, fold down about three inches at a right angle (**fig. 1**). Fold again, this time folding the ribbon back on itself. This will create a triangle in the corner (**fig. 2**).

2. Place a pointed object such as the sharp tip of a chalk pencil or light colored pencil up through the "triangle" (**fig. 3**) and begin twisting with about two twists (**fig. 4**).

3. Begin folding the ribbon back while twisting the pencil (**fig. 5**). Continue folding and twisting until you have about 5 to 7 ful twists for a ful rose and about 4 twists for a small rosette.

4. Remove the rose from the pencil and hold it between your thumb and finger. Tack the bottom securely with a needle and thread, leaving the tails dangling (**fig. 6**).

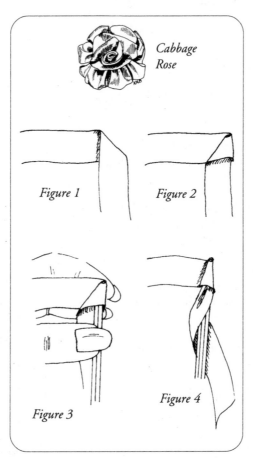

Cabbage Rose

Figure 1

Figure 2

Figure 3

Figure 4

5. Now, here's the tricky part. After you have tacked the rose to keep it from falling apart as you finish, take the tail of the ribbon and create loops as you would when making a Christmas bow (**fig. 7**). The point of the loop will be on bottom. Tack stitch each loop as it is formed to the bottom of the rose to secure it. Make four loops, one one each side of the rose. After the last loop, fold the raw edge under and stitch it securely (**fig. 8**).

6. Pinch together the ends of the loop and take a couple of tiny stitches to secure (**fig. 9**). gently pull the tacked ends to the bottom center and take loose stitches to hold it in place. Tie a knot, then go to the next petal and repeat until all of the loops are tacked to the bottom. As you will notice, the tacked loops create puffy petals on the bottom of the rose and give the wrapped rose more volume (**fig. 10**). ▨

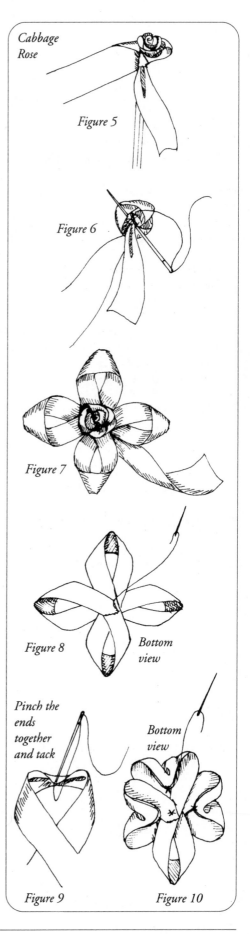

Cabbage Rose

Figure 5

Figure 6

Figure 7

Figure 8

Bottom view

Pinch the ends together and tack

Bottom view

Figure 9

Figure 10

Flower Bud

- ✂ $2\frac{1}{2}$" of $\frac{3}{4}$" wide ribbon for each bud, satin or French grosgrain
- ✂ 6 artificial flower stamens with wire stems
- ✂ all-purpose sewing thread to match ribbon
- ✂ large needle
- ✂ 2" square of buckram

1. Fold the ribbon with the short ends meeting. Stitch across the short ends and turn the ribbon so that the seam is on the inside (**fig. 1**).

2. Run two gathering rows around the ribbon cylinder, one at one edge (which will become the bottom) and one about $\frac{2}{3}$ of the way to the top, beginning and ending the gathering threads at the seam (**fig. 2**).

3. Cut the wire stems of the stamens so that the stamens are about $1\frac{1}{4}$" long. Place a bend in the wire about $\frac{1}{4}$" from the end to form a hook. Make a bundle of the stamens and insert the bundle into the cylinder with the bend of the wire at the bottom edge of the cylinder (**fig. 3**).

4. Thread the ends of the bottom gathering thread into the needle and gather the bottom edge tightly. Stitch into the hook of the stamens several times and then tie off (**fig. 4**).

5. Pull up the remaining gathering thread just enough to make a cupped ruffle around the top edge of the bud. Tie off the thread (**fig. 5**).

6. Place the bud on the buckram with the seam side down. Stitch the bud to the buckram.

7. Stitch or glue the bud in place. ▣

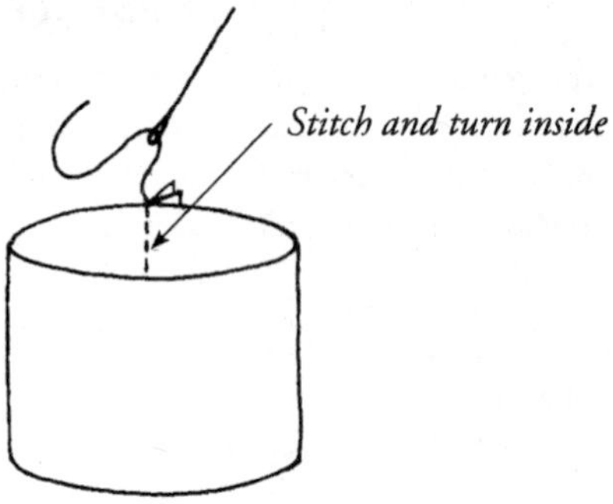

Figure 1

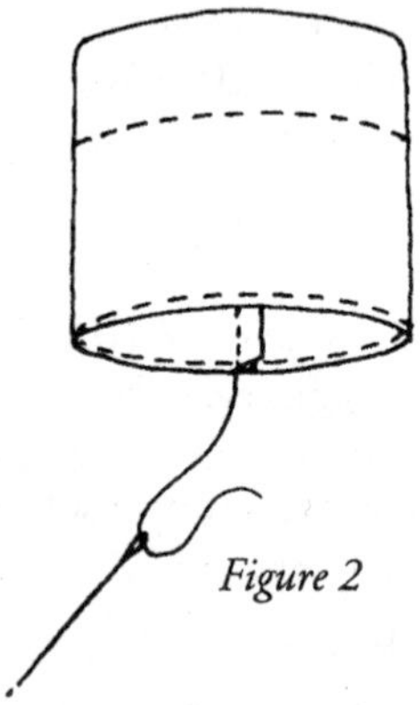
Figure 2

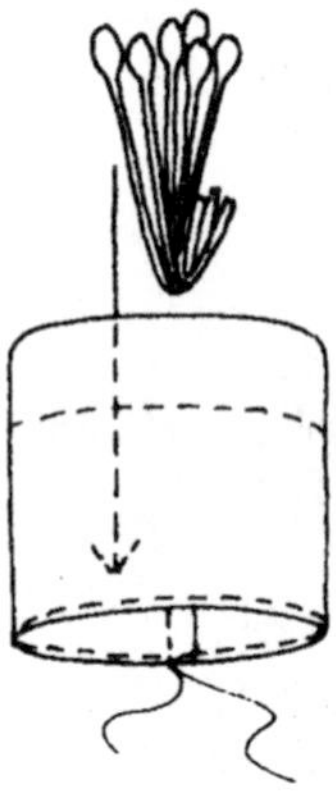
Figure 3

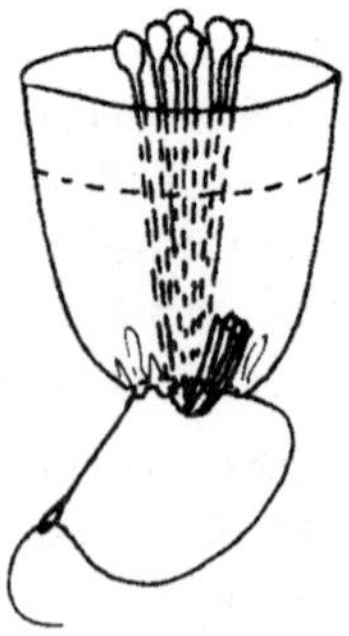
Figure 4

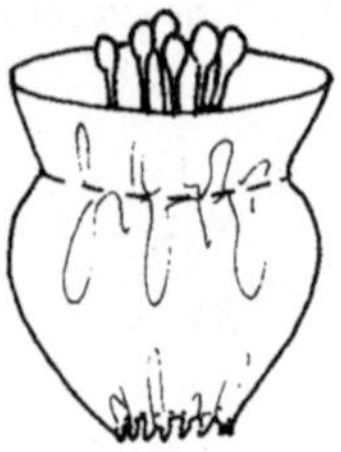
Figure 5

Beginning French Sewing Techniques

Lace to Lace

Butt together and zigzag.

Suggested Machine Settings: Width $2^1/_2$, Length 1.

Lace to Fabric

Place right sides together.

Fabric extends $^1/_8$" from lace.

Zigzag off the edge and over the heading of the lace.

Suggested Machine Settings: Width $3^1/_2$, Length $^1/_2$ to 1
(almost a satin stitch).

Lace to Entredeux

Trim batiste from one side of the entredeux.

Butt lace to entredeux and zigzag.

Suggested Machine Settings: Width $2^1/_2$, Length $1^1/_2$.

Gathered Lace to Entredeux

Trim one side of the entredeux.

Gather lace by pulling heading thread.

Butt together and zigzag.

Suggested Machine Settings: Width $2^1/_2$, Length $1^1/_2$.

Entredeux to Flat Fabric

Place fabric to entredeux, right sides together.

Stitch in the ditch with a regular straight stitch.

Trim seam allowance to $^1/_8$".

Zigzag over the seam allowance.

Suggested Machine Settings: Width $2^1/_2$, Length $1^1/_2$.

Entredeux to Gathered Fabric

Gather fabric using two gathering rows.

Place gathered fabric to entredeux, right sides together.

Stitch in the ditch with a regular straight stitch.

Stitch again $^1/_{16}$" away from the first stitching.

Trim seam allowance to $^1/_8$".

Zigzag over the seam allowance.

Suggested Machine Settings: Width $2^1/_2$, Length $1^1/_2$.

Top Stitch

Turn seam down, away from the lace, entredeux, etc.

Tack in place using a zigzag.

Suggested Machine Settings: Width $1^1/_2$, Length $1^1/_2$.

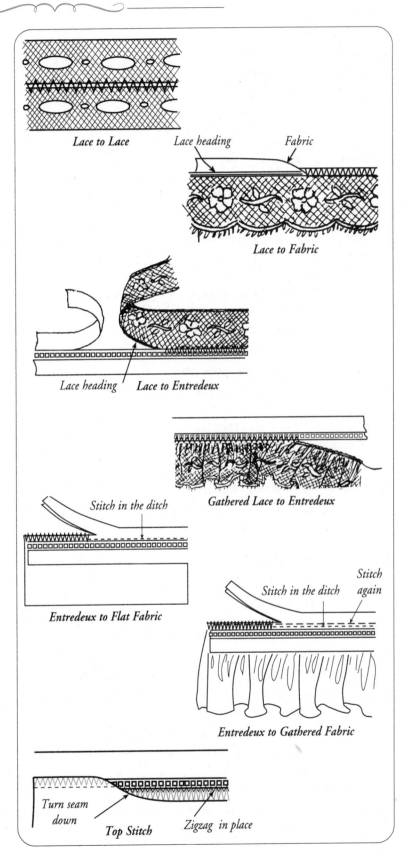

Lace to Lace

Lace heading   Fabric

Lace to Fabric

Lace heading   Lace to Entredeux

Gathered Lace to Entredeux

Stitch in the ditch

Entredeux to Flat Fabric

Stitch in the ditch   Stitch again

Entredeux to Gathered Fabric

Turn seam down   Zigzag in place   Top Stitch

Cutting Fabric From Behind Lace
That Has Been Shaped and Zigzagged

I absolutely love two pairs of Fiskars Scissors for the tricky job of cutting fabric from behind lace that has been shaped and stitched on. The first is Fiskars 9491, blunt tip 5" scissors. They look much like kindergarten scissors because of the blunt tips; however, they are very sharp. They cut fabric away from behind laces with ease. By the way, both of the scissors mentioned in this section are made for either right handed or left handed people.

The second pair that I really love for this task are the Fiskars 9808 curved blade craft scissors. The curved blades are very easy to use when working in tricky, small areas of lace shaping. Fiskars are crafted of permanent stainless steel and are precision ground and hardened for a sharp, long lasting edge.

Repairing Lace Holes Which
You Didn't Mean To Cut!

Trimming fabric away from behind stitched-down lace can be difficult. It is not uncommon to slip, thus cutting a hole in your lace work. How do you repair this lace with the least visible repair? It is really quite simple.

1. Look at the pattern in the lace where you have cut the hole. Is it in a flower, in a dot series, or in the netting part of the lace (**fig. 1**)?

2. After you identify the pattern where the hole was cut, cut another piece of lace $^1/_4$" longer than each side of the hole in the lace.

3. On the bottom side of the lace in the garment, place the lace patch (**fig. 2**).

4. Match the design of the patch with the design of the lace around the hole where it was cut.

5. Zigzag around the cut edges of the lace hole, trying to catch the edges of the hole in your zigzag (**fig 3**).

6 . Now, you have a patched and zigzagged pattern.

7. Trim away the leftover ends underneath the lace you have just patched (**fig. 3**).

8. And don't worry about a piece of patched lace. My grandmother used to say, "Don't worry about that. You'll never notice it on a galloping horse."

Piecing Lace Not Long Enough
For Your Needs

From my sewing experience, sometimes you will need a longer piece of lace than you have. Perhaps you cut the lace incorrectly or bought less than you needed and had to go back for more. Whatever the reason, if you need to make a lace strip longer, it is easy to do.

1. Match your pattern with two strips that will be joined later (**figs. 1 and 3**).

2. Is your pattern a definite flower? Is it a definite diamond or some other pattern that is relatively large?

3. If you have a definite design in the pattern, you can join pieces by zigzagging around that design and then down through the heading of the lace (**fig. 2**).

4. If your pattern is tiny, you can zigzag at an angle joining the two pieces (**fig. 2**). Trim away excess laces close to the zigzagged seam (**fig. 4**).

5. Forget that you have patched laces and complete the dress. If you discover that the lace is too short before you begin stitching, you can plan to place the pieced section in an inconspicuous place.

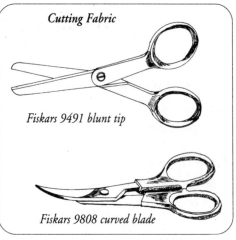

Cutting Fabric

Fiskars 9491 blunt tip

Fiskars 9808 curved blade

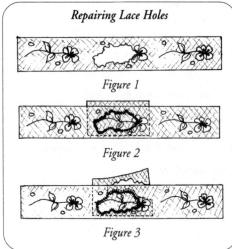

Repairing Lace Holes

Figure 1

Figure 2

Figure 3

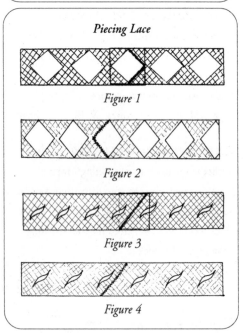

Piecing Lace

Figure 1

Figure 2

Figure 3

Figure 4

6. If you were already into making the garment when you discovered the short lace, simply join the laces and continue stitching as if nothing had happened.

If Your Fancy Band Is Too Short

Not to worry; cut down the width of your skirt. Always make your skirt adapt to your lace shapes, not the lace shapes to your skirt.

Making Diamonds, Hearts, Tear-Drops, Or Circles Fit Skirt Bottom

How do you make sure that you engineer your diamonds, hearts, teardrops, or circles to exactly fit the width skirt that you are planning? The good news is that you don't. Make your shapes any size that you want. Stitch them onto your skirt, front and back, and cut away the excess skirt width. Or, you can stitch up one side seam, and zigzag your shapes onto the skirt, and cut away the excess on the other side before you make your other side seam.

Ribbon To Lace Insertion

This is tricky! Lace has give and ribbon doesn't. After much practice, I have decided that for long bands of lace to ribbon, as in a skirt, it is better to place the lace on top of the ribbon and straight-stitch (Length 2 to $2^{1}/_{2}$). For short strips of lace to ribbon, it is perfectly OK to butt together and zigzag.

Directions for Straight-Stitch Attachment (fig. 1):

1. Press and starch your ribbon and lace.

2. Place the heading of the insertion just over the heading of the ribbon and straight-stitch (Length=2 to $2^{1}/_{2}$).

Directions for Zigzag-Stitch Attachment (fig. 2):

1. Press and starch your ribbon and lace.

2. Place the two side by side and zigzag (Width=$1^{1}/_{2}$ to $2^{1}/_{2}$, Length 1-2). ▨

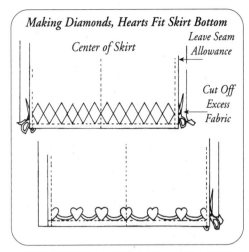

Making Diamonds, Hearts Fit Skirt Bottom

Center of Skirt — Leave Seam Allowance — Cut Off Excess Fabric

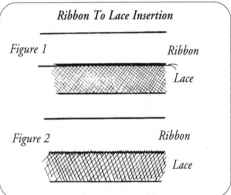

Ribbon To Lace Insertion

Figure 1 — Ribbon — Lace

Figure 2 — Ribbon — Lace

Machine Entredeux

Making Entredeux (Or Hemstitching) On Today's Computer Sewing Machines

About eight years ago I was conned into purchasing a 1905 hemstitching machine for $1500. I was told that it had a perfect stitch and that stitch (about 2 inches) was demonstrated to me by the traveling salesman. I was very happy to finally have one of those wonderful machines. Guess how long that wonderful machine lasted before it broke down? I stitched about 10 inches more which looked great; at that point, the stitching was awful. I called several repairmen. It never made a decent hemstitch again.

The good news to follow this sad story is that today's new computer machines do an excellent job of making hemstitching and they work! I am going to give our favorite settings for our favorite sewing machines. Before you buy a new sewing machine, if you love heirloom sewing, please go try out each of these machines and see if you love these stitches as much as we do.

Using A Stabilizer With Wing Needle Hemstitching Or Pinstitching

Before you do any hemstitching or any decorative work with a wing needle which involves lots of stitching on these wonderful machines, first let me tell you that **you must use a stabilizer**! You can use stitch-n-tear, computer paper, tissue paper (not quite strong enough but o.k. in certain situations), wax paper, physician's examining table paper, typing paper, adding machine paper or almost any other type of paper. When you are doing heavy stitching such as a feather stitch, I recommend that type of paper which physicians spread out over their examining tables. You can get a roll of it at any medical supply place. If you use stitch-n-tear or adding machine paper in feather stitch type stitches, it is difficult to pull away all of the little pieces which remain when you take the paper from the back of the garment. This physician's paper seems to tear away pretty easily.

I do not like the thin, plastic looking, wash away stabilizers for heavy stitching with a wing needle because it doesn't have enough body. There is another type of wash away stabilizer which is absolutely wonderful. It is the paint on, liquid kind. In this country it is called Perfect Sew. You simply paint it on with a paint brush; let it dry, and stitch. You don't have to use any other stabilizer underneath it. It washes out after you have finished your stitching. It is available in this country from Pati Palmer, Palmer/Pletsch Publishing, Perfect Sew, P.O. Box 12046, Portland, OR 97212. 1-800-728-3784.

Make your own wash away stabilizer by using some water in a container and by dropping this wash away plastic looking sheet of stabilizer into the container. Some of the brand names are Solvy™ and Aqua Solve™. Stir with a wooden spoon; keep adding the plastic looking wash away stabilizer sheets until it becomes the consistency of egg whites. Then, paint it on or brush it on with a sponge. Let it dry and then stitch. Both of the liquid, wash out stabilizers make batiste-type fabrics about as stiff as organdy which is wonderful for stitching. After stitching, simply wash the stabilizer away.

Preparing Fabric Before Beginning Hemstitching or Pinstitching

Stiffen fabric with spray starch before lace shaping or decorative stitching with the hemstitches and wing needles. Use a hair dryer to dry the lace before you iron it if you have spray starched it too much. Also, if you wet your fabrics and laces too much with spray starch, place a piece of tissue paper on top of your work, and dry iron it dry. Hemstitching works best on natural fibers such as linen, cotton, cotton batiste, silk or cotton organdy. I don't advise hemstitching a fabric with a high polyester content. Polyester has a memory. If you punch a hole in polyester, it remembers the original positioning of the fibers, and the hole wants to close up.

Threads To Use For Pinstitching Or Hemstitiching

Use all cotton thread, 50, 60, 70, 80 weight. If you have a thread breaking problem, you can also use a high quality polyester thread or a cotton covered polyester thread, like the Coats and Clark for machine lingerie and embroidery. Personally, I like to press needle down on all of the entredeux and pin stitch settings.

Pinstitching Or Point de Paris Stitch With A Sewing Machine

The pin stitch is another lovely "entredeux" look on my favorite machines. It is a little more delicate. Pin stitch looks similar to a ladder with **one of the long sides of the ladder missing**. Imagine the steps being fingers which reach over into the actual lace piece to grab the lace. The side of the ladder, the long side, will be stitched on the fabric right along side of the outside of the heading of the lace. The fingers reach into the lace to grab it. You need to look on all of the pinstitch settings given below and realize that you have to use reverse image on one of the sides of lace so that the fingers will grab into the lace while the straight side goes on the outside of the lace heading.

Settings For Entredeux (Hemstitch) And Pinstitch

Pfaff 7570

Pinstitch
  -100 wing needle, A - 2 Foot, Needle Down
  -Stitch 112, tension 3, twin needle button, 4.0 width, 3.0 length

Entredeux
  -100 wing needle, A - 2 Foot, Needle Down

	width	length
Stitch #132	3.5	5.0
Stitch #113	4.0	2.0
Stitch #114	3.5	2.5
Stitch #115	3.5	3.0

Bernina 1630

Pinstitch
  - 100 wing needle
  - 1630 menu G, Pattern #10, SW - 2.5, SL - 2

Entredeux
  - 100 wing needle
  - 1630 menu G, pattern #5, SW - 3.5, SL - 3

Viking#1+

Pinstitch
  - 100 wing needle
  -Stitch D6, width 2.5-3; length 2.5-3

Entredeux
  - 100 wing needle
  -Stitch D7 (width and length are already set in)

Elna 9000 and DIVA

Pinstitch
  - 100 wing needle
  -Stitch #120 (length and width are already set in)

Entredeux
  - 100 wing needle
  -Stitch #121 (length and width are already set)

Singer XL - 100

Pinstitch
  – 100 Wing Needle
  – Screen #3
  – Stitch #7
  – Width 4 (length changes with width)

Entredeux
  – 100 Wing needle
  – Screen #3
  – Stitch #8
  Width 5 (Medium) or 4 (small)

New Home 9000

Pinstitch
  – 100 Wing Needle
  – Stitch #26 (width 2.5; length 2.5)

Hemstitch
  - 100 wing needle
  - Stitch #39 (width 4.0; length 1.5)

Attaching Shaped Lace To The Garment With Machine Entredeux Or Pinstitching And A Wing Needle

Probably my favorite place to use the machine entredeux/wing needle hemstitching is to attach shaped laces to a garment. Simply shape your laces in the desired shapes such as hearts, diamonds, ovals, loops, circles, or bows, and stitch the stitch. In addition to stitching this gorgeous decorative stitch, it also attaches the shaped lace to the garment (**fig. 1**). Always use stabilizer when using this type of heavy hemstitching.

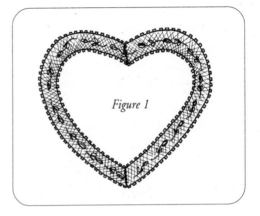

Figure 1

Attaching Two Pieces Of Lace With Machine Entredeux

There is nothing prettier than a garment which has entredeux in between each layer of fabric and lace. That would take a million years to stitch with purchased entredeux, not to mention the cost. Here is how you can use your hemstitch/machine entredeux stitch and wing needle and make your laces look as if they had been joined with entredeux.

1. Butt two pieces of lace insertion together. Since entredeux/hemstitching with a wing needle on your machine needs fabric underneath the stitching to hold the stitches perfectly, you need to put a narrow strip of batiste or other fabric underneath the place where these two laces will be joined.

2. Put a strip of stabilizer underneath the butted laces and the fabric strip.

3. Stitch using a wing needle and your hemstitching stitch. If your machine has an edge joining or edge stitching foot this is a great time to use it. It's little blade guides in between the two pieces of butted lace and makes it easy to stitch straight (**fig. 1**). You can see that the entredeux stitching not only stitches in one of the most beautiful stitches, it also attaches the laces.

4. When you have finished stitching, tear away the stabilizer and turn each side of the lace back to carefully trim away the excess fabric (**fig. 2**).

5. Now it looks as if you have two pieces of lace with purchased entredeux stitched in between them (**fig. 3**).

Making Machine Entredeux Embroidery Designs Or Initials

You can take almost any larger, plain embroidery design and stitch the entredeux stitch around it. You may find it necessary to put the design into an embroidery hoop for maximum effectiveness. I have some old handkerchiefs and some old tablecloths which actually look as if hemstitching has made the design. You can place several rows of entredeux stitching together to form a honeycomb effect which might be used to fill in embroidery designs.

Some of the prettiest monograms are those with hemstitching stitched around the letter. Once again, I think the liquid stabilizer and the embroidery hoop will be wonderful assets in doing this kind of wing needle work. Let your imagination be your guide when thinking of new and elegant things to do with these wonderful wing needle/entredeux stitches (**fig. 4**).

One of my favorite things to do with this entredeux stitch or pin stitch is simply to stitch it around cuffs, across yokes, around collars, down the center back or center front of a blouse. It is lovely stitched down both sides of the front placket of a very tailored woman's blouse. Some people love to machine entredeux in black thread on a black garment. The places you put this wing needling are endless. It is just as pretty stitched as a plain stitch as it is when it is used to stitch on laces. ▨

Attaching Two Pieces of Lace With Machine Entredeux

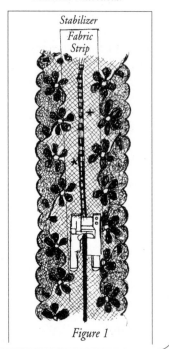

Stabilizer
Fabric Strip

Figure 1

Attaching Two Pieces of Lace With Machine Entredeux

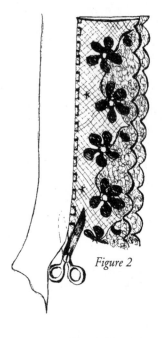

Figure 2

Figure 3

Making Machine Entredeux, Embroidery Designs Or Initials

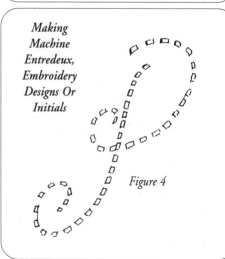

Figure 4

Puffing Method I

Gathering The Puffing Using The Gathering Foot On Your Machine

Two years ago, I wouldn't have told you that this was the easiest method of applying puffing into a round portrait collar. The reason being I didn't know how to make perfect puffing using the gathering foot for the sewing machine. I thought you used the edge of the gathering foot to guide the fabric underneath the gathering foot. This left about a $1/4$" seam allowance. It also made the gathers not perfect in some places with little "humps" and unevenness on some portions. Therefore, I wasn't happy with puffing made on the gathering foot. When I asked my friend, Sue Hausman, what might be wrong, she explained to me that to make perfect gathering, you had to move the fabric over so that you would have at least a $1/2$" seam allowance. She further explained that there are two sides to the feed dogs; when you use the side of the gathering foot, then the fabric only catches on one side of the feed dogs. It works like magic to move your fabric over and guide it along one of the guide lines on the sewing machine. If your machine doesn't have these lines, simply put a piece of tape down to make a proper guide line.

Making Gathering Foot Puffing

1. The speed of the sewing needs to be consistent. Sew either fast or slow but do not sew fast then slow then fast again. For the beginner, touch the "sew slow" button (if available on your machine). This will help to keep a constant speed.

2. The puffing strip should be gathered with a $1/2$ seam allowance, with an approximate straight stitch length of 4, right side up (**fig. 1**). Remember that you can adjust your stitch length to make your puffing looser or fuller. Do not let the strings of the fabric wrap around the foot of the machine. This will cause to fabric to back up behind the foot causing an uneven seam allowance, as well as uneven gathers. Leave the thread tails long in case adjustments are needed. One side of the gathering is now complete (**fig. 2**).

3. Begin gathering the second side of the strip, right side up. This row of gathering will be made from the bottom of the strip to the top of the strip. In other words, bi-directional sewing (first side sewn from the top to the bottom, second side sewn from the bottom to the top) is allowed. Gently unfold the ruffle with the left hand allowing flat fabric to feed under the foot. **Do not** apply any pressure to the fabric (**fig. 3**). The feeding must remain constant. Leave the thread tails long in case adjustments are needed. The puffing strip in now complete.

Placing Machine Gathered Puffing Into A Collar

1. Cut your strips of fabric.
2. Gather both sides of the puffing, running the fabric under the gathering foot. Be sure you have at least a $1/2$" seam allowance. When you use a gathering foot, the moveability of the puffing isn't as great as when you gather it the other way.
3. You, of course, have two raw edges when you gather puffing with the gathering foot (**fig. 1**).
4. Shape the puffing around the fabric board below the row of lace (or rows of lace) that you have already shaped into the rounded shape. Place the pins into the board through the outside edge of the puffing. Place the pins right into the place where the gathering row runs in the fabric (**fig. 2**).

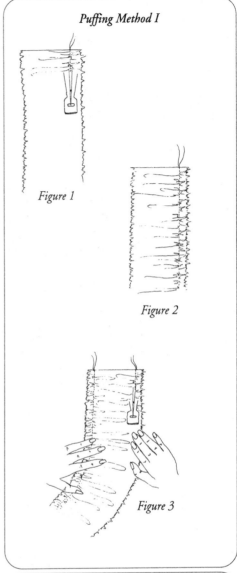

Puffing Method I

Figure 1

Figure 2

Figure 3

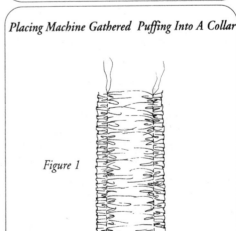

Placing Machine Gathered Puffing Into A Collar

Figure 1

5. Pull the raw edge of the machine puffed strip up **underneath the finished edge of the curved lace**, so that your zigzagging to attach the puffing will be on the machine gathering line. Put the rounded lace edge on top of the puffing. Pin the bottom edge of the puffing first so you can "arrange" the top fullness underneath the curved lace edge which is already in place (the top piece of lace) (**fig. 2**).

6. It will be necessary to "sort of" arrange the machine gathered puffing, especially on the top edge which will be gathered the fullest on your collar, and pin it where you want it since the machine gathering thread doesn't give too much. After you have pinned and poked the gathering into place where it looks pretty on the top and the bottom, flat pin it to the tissue paper and zigzag the puffing strip to the lace, stitching right on top of the lace.

NOTE: **You will have an unfinished fabric edge underneath the place where you stitched the lace to the puffing.** That is o.k. After you have zigzagged the puffing to the lace, then trim away the excess fabric underneath the lace edge. Be careful, of course, when you trim this excess fabric, not to accidentally cut the lace.

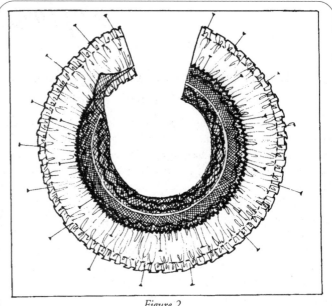

Figure 2

7. If you have a machine entredeux/wing needle option on your sewing machine, you can stitch this beautiful stitch in place of the zigzagging. Since the fabric is gathered underneath the lace, you will have to be very careful stitching to get a pretty stitch.

8. Shape another piece of lace around the bottom of this puffing, bringing the inside piece of curved lace exactly to fit on top of the gathering line in the puffing. Once again, you will have unfinished fabric underneath the place where you will zigzag the lace to the puffing collar. After zigzagging the lace to the puffing collar, trim the excess fabric away.

9. Continue curving the rest of the laces to make the collar as wide as you want it to be. ▨

Basic Pintucking

Double Needles

Double needles come in different sizes. The first number on the double needle is the distance between the needles. The second number on the needle is the actual size of the needle. The chart below shows some of the double needle sizes. The size needle that you choose will depend on the weight of the fabric that you are pintucking (**fig. 1**).

Let me relate a little more information for any of you who haven't used the double needles yet. Some people have said to me, "Martha, I only have a place for one needle in my sewing machine." That is correct and on most sewing machines, you probably still can use a double needle. The double needle has only one stem which goes into the needle slot; the double needles join on a little bar below the needle slot. You use two spools of thread when you thread the double needles. If you don't have two spools of thread of the fine thread which you use for pintucking, then run an extra bobbin and use it as another spool of thread. For most shaped pintucking on heirloom garments, I prefer either the 1.6/70, the 1.6/80 or the 2.0/80 size needle.

Figure 1

Fabric

a. 1.6/70 - Light Weight
b. 1.6/80 - Light Weight
c. 2.0/80 - Light Weight
d. 2.5/80 - Light Weight
e. 3.0/90 - Medium Weight
f. 4.0/100 - Heavy Weight

Pintuck Feet

Pintuck feet are easy to use and they shave hours off pintucking time when you are making straight pintucks. They enable you to space straight pintucks perfectly. I might add here that some people also prefer a pintuck foot when making curved and angled pintucks. I prefer a regular zigzag sewing foot for curved pintucks. Pintuck feet correspond to the needle used with that pintuck foot; the needle used corresponds to the weight of fabric. The bottom of these feet have a certain number of grooves 3, 5, 7, or 9. The width of the groove matches the width between the two needles. When making straight pintucks, use a pintuck foot of your choice. The grooves enable one to make those pintucks as close or as far away as the distance on the foot allows (**fig. 2**).

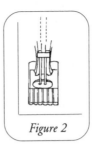

Figure 2

Preparing Fabric For Pintucking

Do I spray starch the fabric before I pintuck it? I usually do not spray starch fabric before pintucking it. Always press all-cotton fabric. A polyester/cotton blend won't need to be pressed unless it is very wrinkled. Tucks tend to lay flatter if you stiffen fabric with spray starch first; that is why I don't advise spray starching the fabric first in most cases. Pintuck a small piece of your chosen fabric with starch and one without starch, then make your own decision.

Straight Pintucking With A Pintuck Foot

Some of my favorite places for straight pintucks are on high yoke bodices of a dress and along the sleeves. On ladies blouses, straight pintucks are lovely running vertically on the front and back of the blouse, and so slenderizing! One of the prettiest treatments of straight pintucks on ladies blouses is stitching about three to five pintucks right down the center back of the blouse. Tuck a little shaped bow or heart on the center back of the blouse; stitch several tiny pintucks and top them off with a lace shape in the center back. Horizontally placed straight pintucks are lovely running across the back yoke of a tailored blouse. Tucks are always pretty running around the cuff of a blouse. I love pintucks just about anywhere.

1. Put in your double needle. Thread machine with two spools of thread. Thread one spool at a time (including the needle). This will help keep the threads from becoming twisted while stitching the tucks. This would be a good time to look in the guide book, which came with your sewing machine, for directions on using pintuck feet and double needles. Some sewing machines have a special way of threading for use with double needles.

2. The first tuck must be straight. To make this first tuck straight, do one of three things: (a.) Pull a thread all the way across the fabric and follow along that pulled line. (b.) Using a measuring stick, mark a straight line along the fabric. Stitch on that line. (c.) Fold the fabric in half and press that fold. Stitch along that folded line.

3. Place the fabric under the foot for the first tuck and straight stitch the desired length of pintuck. (Length=1 to $2^1/_2$; Needle position is center) (**fig. 1**).

4. Place your first tuck into one of the grooves in your pintuck foot. The space between each pintuck depends on the placement of the first pintuck (**fig. 2**).

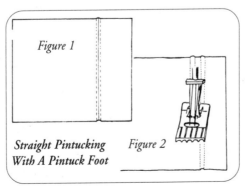

Figure 1

Straight Pintucking With A Pintuck Foot   Figure 2

5. Continue pintucking by placing the last pintuck made into a groove in the foot.

Straight Pintucking Without A Pintuck Foot

1. Use a double needle. Use your regular zigzag foot.

2. Thread your double needles.

3. Draw the first line of pintucking. Pintuck along that line. At this point you can use the edge of your presser foot as a guide (**fig. 3**).

NOTE: You might find a "generic" pintuck foot for your particular brand of machine.

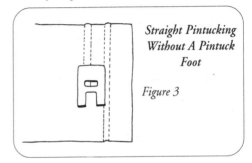

Straight Pintucking Without A Pintuck Foot

Figure 3

Properly Tying Off Released Pintucks

A released pintuck is usually used to give fullness to a skirt. It is a perfectly elegant way to add detail to a garment which is easy to do using today's double needles. If you have a pintuck foot, please do use it for this treatment.

Straight pintucks that are made on a piece of fabric, cut out and stitched into the seams garment, do not have to be tied off. Why? When you sew the seam of the garment, the pintucks will be secured within that seam. Released pintucks stop at a designated point in the fabric. They are not caught in a seam and, therefore, have to be tied off. To make the most beautiful released pintuck possible, you must properly tie it off. If you want to take a short cut, then either back stitch on your machine or use the tie off feature that some of the modern machines offer. Please do not use a clear glue sold for tying off seams in sewing. One of my friends had a disastrous experience when making a lovely Susan York pattern featured in *Sew Beautiful* several years ago with over a hundred gorgeous released pintucks. She dabbed a little of this glue product at the end of each pintuck; when she washed and pressed the dress, each place on the Swiss batiste garment where that product had been touched on, turned absolutely brown. The dress with all of the money in Swiss batiste and French laces, had to be thrown away.

Properly tying off released pintucks is a lot of trouble. Remember, you can back stitch and cut the threads close to the fabric. The result isn't as pretty but it surely saves time. The choice, as always, is yours. If you are going to properly tie off those released pintucks, here are the directions.

1. End your stitching at the designated stopping point (**fig. 1**).

2. Pull out a reasonable length of thread before you cut the threads for this pintuck to go to the next pintuck. Five inches should be ample. You can use more or less.

3. Pull the threads to the back of the fabric (**fig. 2**). Tie off each individual pintuck (**fig. 3**).

Bi-Directional Stitching Of Pintucks

The general consensus, when stitching pintucks, is to stitch down one side and back up the other side instead of stitching pintucks all in the same direction.

To prevent pintucks from being lopsided, stitch down the length of one pintuck, pull your sewing machine threads several inches, and stitch back up in the opposite direction (**fig. 4**). ▨

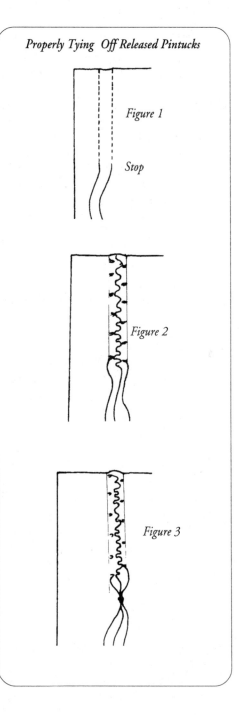

Properly Tying Off Released Pintucks

Figure 1

Stop

Figure 2

Figure 3

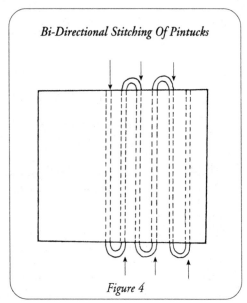

Bi-Directional Stitching Of Pintucks

Figure 4

Lace Shaping Techniques

General Lace Shaping Supplies

- ❧ Fabric to apply lace shape
- ❧ Lace (usually insertion lace)
- ❧ Glass head pins
- ❧ Spray starch
- ❧ Lightweight sewing thread
- ❧ Lace shaping board or covered cardboard
- ❧ Washout marker or washout pencil
- ❧ Wing needle (optional)
- ❧ Stabilizer (If a wing needle stitch is used)

Using Glass Head Pins

Purchasing GLASS HEAD PINS is one of the first and most critical steps to lace shaping. All types of lace shaping must be pinned in place, starched lightly and pressed. The iron is placed directly on top of the pins. Since plastic head pins melt onto your fabric and ruin your project, obviously they won't do. Metal pins such as the iris pins with the skinny little metal heads won't melt; however, when you pin hundreds of these little pins into the lace shaping board, your finger will have one heck of a hole poked into it. Please purchase glass head pins and throw away your plastic head pins. Glass head pins can be purchased by the box or by the card. For dress projects, as many 100 pins might be needed for each section of lace shaping. So, make sure to purchase enough.

Shape 'N Press (Lace Shaping Board)

I used fabric boards (covered cardboard) until the June Taylor's Shape 'N Press board became available. It is truly wonderful. This board measures 24" by 18" and has permanent lace shaping templates drawn right on the board. I never have to hunt for another lace shaping template again. Here is how I use it. I place my skirt, collar, pillow top or other project on top of the board with the desired template positioned correctly (I can see the template through the fabric), shape the lace along the template lines pinning into the board, spray starch lightly, re-pin the lace just to the fabric. Now I can move the fabric, correctly positioning the template, and start the process again. Did you notice, I never mentioned tracing the design on the fabric? With the Shape 'N Press, drawing on the fabric can be omitted so you never have to worry about removing fabric marker lines. I also use the flip side of the board. It has a blocking guide for bishops and round collars (sizes newborn to adult).

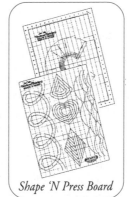

Shape 'N Press Board

Making A Lace Shaping Board or Fabric Board

If a lace shaping board is not available, a fabric board can be made from cardboard (cake boards, pizza boards or a cut up box) covered with fabric or paper. A child's bulletin board or a fabric covered ceiling tile will work. Just staple or pin fabric or white typing paper or butcher paper over the board before you begin lace shaping. Just remember you must be able to pin into the board, use a bit of stray starch and iron on it.

Tracing the Template

Trace the template on the fabric with a wash out marker. Margaret Boyles taught me years ago that it is simpler to draw your shapes on fabric by making dots about one half inch apart than it is to draw a solid line. This also means less pencil or marker to get out of the fabric when your lace shaping is finished. Mark all angles with miter lines (a line dividing the angle in half). Sometimes it is helpful to make the solid lines at the angles and miter lines (**fig. 1**). Hint: If you do not want to draw the template on the fabric, trace the template on stabilizer or paper with a permanent marker. Place the template under the fabric. Because the fabric is "see-through" the lines can be seen clearly. Shape the lace along the template lines. Complete the design as stated in the lace shaping directions. Remember to remove the template paper before stitching so that the permanent pen lines are not caught in the stitching.

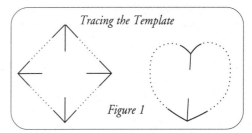

Tracing the Template

Figure 1

Shish Kabob Sticks

I first learned about using wooden shish kabob sticks from some of the technical school sewing teachers in Australia. By the way, where does one get these wooden shish kabob sticks? At the grocery store! If you can only find the long ones, just break them in half to measure 5″ or 6″ long and use the end with the point to push and to hold laces (or other items) as they go into the sewing machine. These sticks are used instead of the usual long pin or worse still, seam ripper that I have used so often. Using this stick is a safety technique as well as an efficient technique.

Liquid Pins

This is one of the most unique notions I have ever seen. It works like glue, but when dry it does not "gunk" up your needle. It washes out easily and does not stain. It is perfect for holding things like snaps, buttons, zippers, lace, Battenburg tape and shaped bias tape in place to make stitching easier. It is truly the greatest thing going for lace shaping. It is a solvent-based water dissolvable glue. Simply run a thin line of Liquid Pins over hems, lace shaping template lines, seams or appliqué areas. To speed up drying time, place a press cloth over the treated fabric and iron dry with a hot iron. Try it. I think you will like it. ▨

Scalloped Skirt

I have always loved scalloped skirts. The first one that I ever saw intimidated me so much that I didn't even try to make one for several years after that. The methods which I am presenting to you in this section are so easy that I think you won't be afraid to try making one of my favorite garments. Scalloping lace can be a very simple way to finish the bottom of a smocked dress or can be a very elaborate way to put row after row of lace scallops with curved pintucks in-between those scallops. Plain or very elaborate - this is one of my favorite things in French sewing by machine. Enjoy!

Preparing The Skirt For Lace Scallops

Before I give you the steps below, which is one great way to prepare scallops on a skirt, let me share with you that you can also follow the instructions found under the beginning lace techniques for scallops as well as diamonds, hearts, teardrops or circles. These instructions are that you can use any size scallop that you want to for any width skirt. How do you do that? Stitch or serge up one side seam of your whole skirt before placing the scallops.

1. Pull a thread and cut or tear your skirt. I usually put 88 inches in my skirt, two 44-inch widths - one for the front and one for the back. Make the skirt length the proper one for your garment. Sew one side seam.

2. Trace one scallop on each side of the side seam. Continue tracing until you are almost at the edge of the fabric. Leave a seam allowance beyond the last scallops and trim away the excess (**fig. 1**).

3. Now you are ready to shape the lace along the template lines.

Pinning The Lace Insertion To The Skirt Portion On The Fabric Board

1. Cut enough lace insertion to go around all of the scallops on the skirt. Allow at least 16 inches more than you measured. You can later use the excess lace insertion in another area of the dress. If you do not have a piece of insertion this long, remember to piece your laces so that the pieced section will go into the miter at the top of the scallop.

2. Pin the lace insertion to the skirt (one scallop at a time only) by poking pins all the way into the fabric board, through the bottom lace heading and the fabric of the skirt. Notice on (**figure 2**) that the bottom of the lace is straight with the pins poked into the board. The top of the lace is rather "curvy" because it hasn't been shaped to lie flat yet.

3. As you take the lace into the top of the first scallop, carefully place a pin into the lace and the board at **points C and D**. Pinning the D point is very important. That is why you drew the line bisecting the top of each scallop (**fig. 2**). Pin the B point at exactly the place where the flat lace crosses the line you drew to bisect the scallop.

4. Fold back the whole piece of lace onto the other side (**fig. 3**). Remove the pin at **C** and repin it to go through both layers of lace. Leave the pin at point **D** just as it is.

5. Then fold over the lace to place the next section of the lace to travel into the next part of the scallop (**fig.4**).

NOTE: If a little bit of that folded point is exposed after you place the lace into the next scallop, just push it underneath the miter until the miter looks perfect (**fig. 5**). I lovingly call this "mushing" the miter into place.

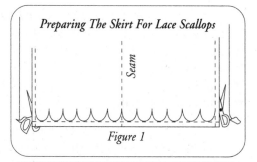

Preparing The Skirt For Lace Scallops

Seam

Figure 1

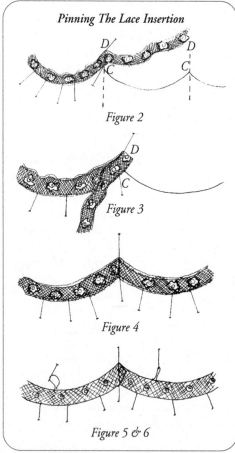

Pinning The Lace Insertion

Figure 2

Figure 3

Figure 4

Figure 5 & 6

6. To shape the excess fullness of the top of the scallop, simply pull a gathering thread at the center point of each scallop until the lace becomes flat and pretty (**fig. 6**).

7. Place a pin in the lace loop you just pulled until you spray starch and press the scallop flat. Remember, it is easier to pull the very top thread of the lace, the one which makes a prominent scallop on the top of the lace. If you break that thread, go in and pull another one. Many laces have as many as 4 or 5 total threads which you can pull. Don't worry

about that little pulled thread; when you zigzag the lace to the skirt or entredeux stitch it to the skirt, simply trim away that little pulled thread. The heaviness of the zigzag or the entredeux stitch will secure the lace to the skirt.

8. Spray starch and press each scallop and miter after you finish shaping them.

9. After finishing with the section of scallops you have room for on that one board, pin the laces flat to the skirt and begin another section of your skirt (**fig 7**). You have the choice here of either zigzagging each section of the skirt as you complete it, or waiting until you finish the whole skirt.

10. If you choose to use a decorative stitch on your sewing machine (entredeux stitch with a wing needle) you will need to stitch with some sort of stabilizer underneath the skirt. Stitch 'n Tear is an excellent one. Some use tissue paper, others prefer wax paper or adding machine paper. Actually, the paper you buy at a medical supply store that doctors use for covering their examining tables is great also. As long as you are stitching using a wing needle and heavy decorative stitching, you really need a stabilizer.

11. If you have an entredeux stitch on your sewing machine, you can stitch entredeux at both the top and bottom of this scalloped skirt (**fig. 8**). There are two methods of doing this:

Method Number One

1. After you finish your entredeux/wing needle stitching on both the top and the bottom of the scalloped skirt, trim away the fabric from behind the lace scallop.

2. Carefully trim the fabric from the bottom of the skirt also, leaving just a "hair" of seam allowance (**fig. 9**).

3. You are now ready to zigzag over the folded in miters (**fig. 10**). Use a regular needle for this zigzag.

4. Now zigzag the gathered laces to the bottom of this machine created entredeux.

Method Number Two

1. Machine entredeux the top only of the scallop (**fig. 11a**). Don't cut anything away.

2. Butt your gathered lace edging, a few inches at a time, to the shaped bottom of the lace scallop. Machine entredeux stitch in between the flat scalloped lace and the gathered edging lace, thus attaching both laces at the same time you are stitching in the machine entredeux (**fig. 11b**). Be sure you put more fullness at the points of the scallop.

3. After the gathered lace edging is completely stitched to the bottom of the skirt with your machine entredeux, cut away the bottom of the skirt fabric as closely to the stitching as possible (**fig. 12**).

4. Zigzag over your folded in miters (**fig. 12a**).

5. If you are going to attach the lace to the fabric with just a plain zigzag stitch, you might try (Width=1^1/$_2$ to 2, Length=1 to 1^1/$_2$). You want the zigzag to be wide enough to completely go over the heading of the laces and short enough to be strong. If you are zigzagging the laces to the skirt, zigzag the **top only** of the lace scallops (**see fig. 13**).

6. After you zigzag the top only of this skirt, carefully trim away the bottom portion of the fabric skirt, trimming all the way up to the stitches (**fig. 13**).

7. Now you have a scalloped skirt. Later you might want to add entredeux to the bottom of the scalloped skirt. It is perfectly alright just to add gathered laces to this lace scallop without either entredeux or machine stitched entredeux. Just treat the bottom of this lace scallop as a finished edge; gather your lace edging and zigzag to the bottom of the lace (**see fig. 14**).

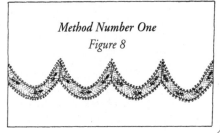

Pinning The Lace Insertion

Pin Flat

Figure 7

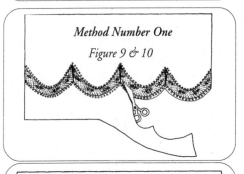

Method Number One
Figure 8

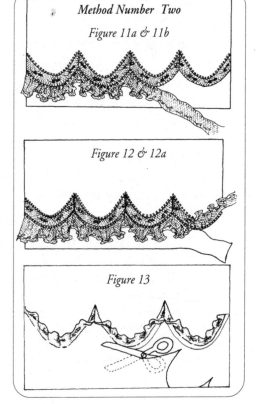

Method Number One
Figure 9 & 10

Method Number Two
Figure 11a & 11b

Figure 12 & 12a

Figure 13

Finishing The Center Of The Miter

After Attaching It To The Skirt and Trimming Away
The Fabric From Behind the Scallops

I always zigzag down the center of this folded miter. You can leave the folded lace portion in the miter to make the miter stronger or you can trim away the folded portion after you have zigzagged over the miter center (fig. 14).

Shaping And Stitching Purchased
Entredeux To Scallops

1. Trim off one side of the entredeux completely (see fig. 15).

2. Clip the other side of the entredeux (fig. 15).

3. **You must pin, starch, and press the entredeux before sewing it to the scallops.** It won't hang right, otherwise.

4. Here is a great trick. In order to pin the entredeux into the points of the scallops most effectively, trim entredeux about 1½" on either side of the point. This allows you to see exactly where you are placing the entredeux (fig. 16).

5. After pinning the entredeux into the points, starch, and press the entredeux into its shape.

6. Remove the pins from the skirt.

7. Zigzag the lace to the entredeux trying to go into one hole and off onto the lace (W=3, L=1½).

8. As you go into the points with the entredeux, simply "smush" the entredeux into the point, stitch over it, and turn the corner (fig. 17).

9. There is an optional method for sewing entredeux on to scallops. Some people prefer to put entredeux on the bottom of a lace shaped skirt by using short pieces of entredeux which go only from top of the curve to top of the next curve (fig. 18). Treat it exactly as you did in steps 1-6 in this section. Overlap the trimmed edges in each point. When you attach the gathered laces by zigzagging, these cut points will be zigzagged together.

Adding Gathered Lace To The Entredeux
At the Bottom of Scallops

1. Measure around the scalloped skirt to get your measurement for the gathered lace edging you are going to attach to finish the skirt bottom.

2. Double that measurement for a 2-1 fullness. Remember that you can piece your laces if your piece of edging isn't long enough.

3. Cut your lace edging.

4. Using the technique "Sewing Hand-Gathered French Lace To Entredeux Edge," zigzag the gathered lace to the bottom of the entredeux (fig. 19).

Gathering French Laces By Hand
Pull Thread In the Heading of Laces

On the straight sides of French or English cotton laces are several threads called the "heading." These threads serve as pull threads for lace shaping. Some laces have better pull threads than others. Before you begin dramatically-curved lace shaping, check to be sure your chosen lace has a good pull thread. The scallop on the top of most laces is the first pull thread that I pull. Most French and English laces have several good pull threads, so if you break the first one, pull another. If all the threads break, you could probably run a gathering thread in the top of the lace with your sewing machine.

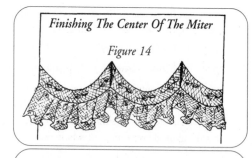
Finishing The Center Of The Miter
Figure 14

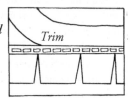
Shaping And Stitching Purchased Entredeux To Scallops
Trim
Figure 15

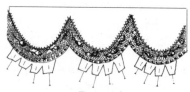
Figure 16

Figure 17

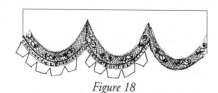
Figure 18

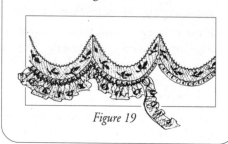
Adding Gathered Lace
Figure 19

1. Cut a length of lace 2-3 times the finished length to have enough fullness to make a pretty lace ruffle.

2. To gather the lace, pull one of the heavy threads that runs along the straight edge or heading of the lace (**fig. 20**).

3. Adjust gathers evenly before zigzagging.

Sewing Hand-Gathered French Lace To Entredeux Edge

1. Gather lace by hand by pulling the thread in the heading of the lace. I use the scalloped outside thread of the heading first since I think it gathers better than the inside threads. Distribute gathers evenly.

2. Trim the side of the entredeux to which the gathered lace is to be attached. Side by side, right sides up, zigzag the gathered lace to the trimmed entredeux (Width=1¹/₂; Length=2) (**fig. 21**).

3. Using a wooden shish kabob stick, push the gathers evenly into the sewing machine as you zigzag. You can also use a pick or long pin of some sort to push the gathers evenly into the sewing machine.

Hint: To help distribute the gathers evenly fold the entredeux in half and half again. Mark these points with a fabric marker. Before the lace is gathered, fold it in half and half again. Mark the folds with a fabric marker. Now gather the lace and match the marks on the entredeux and the marks on the lace (**fig. 22**).

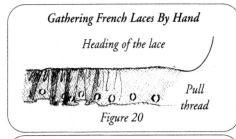

Gathering French Laces By Hand

Heading of the lace

Pull thread

Figure 20

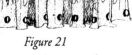

Sewing Hand-Gathered French Lace To Entredeux Edge

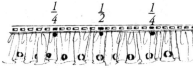

Figure 21

¼ ½ ¼

Figure 22

Shaping Lace Diamonds

Making Lace Diamonds

Lace diamonds can be used almost anywhere on heirloom garments. They are especially pretty at the point of a collar, on the skirt of a dress, at angles on the bodice of a garment, or all the way around a collar. The easiest way to make lace diamonds is to work on a fabric board with a diamond guide. You can make your diamonds as large or as small as you desire. I think you are really going to love this easy method of making diamonds with the fold back miter. Now, you don't have to remove those diamonds from the board to have perfect diamonds every time.

Making Lace Diamonds

Materials Needed

♦ Spray starch, iron, pins, fabric board

♦ Lace insertion

♦ Diamond guide

1. Draw the diamond guide or template (**fig. 1**).

2. Tear both skirt pieces. French seam or serge one side only of the skirt.

3. Working from the center seam you just made, draw diamonds all the way around the skirt. This way you can make any sized diamonds you want without worrying if they will fit the skirt perfectly. When you get all the way around both sides of the skirt you will have the same amount of skirt left over on both sides.

Figure 1

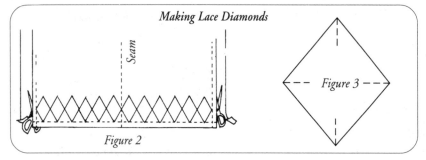

Figure 2

Making Lace Diamonds

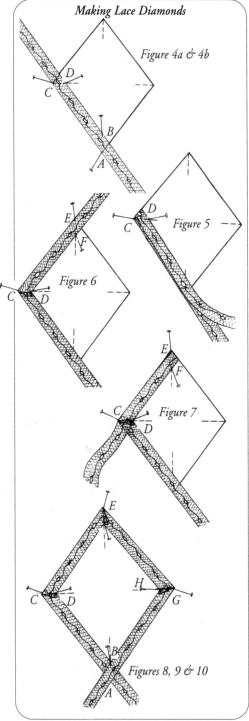

Figure 4a & 4b

Figure 5

Figure 6

Figure 7

Figures 8, 9 & 10

4. Simply trim the excess skirt away. Later you will French seam or serge the skirt on the other side to complete your skirt. This is the easy way to make any type of lace shaping on any skirt and it will always fit perfectly (**fig. 2**).

5. The guide or template, which you have just drawn, will be the outside of the diamond. Draw lines going into the diamond, bisecting each angle where the lace will be mitered. This is very important, since one of your critical pins will be placed exactly on this line. These bisecting lines need to be drawn about 2 inches long coming in from the angles of the diamonds (**fig. 3**). If you are making a diamond skirt, it is easier to draw your diamond larger and make your diamond shaping on the inside of the diamond. That way, the outside points of your diamond can touch when you are drawing all of your diamonds on the skirt.

6. As I said earlier, you can shape the laces for diamonds on either the outside or the inside of the template. I actually think it is easier to shape your laces on the inside of the template.

7. Place your skirt with the drawn diamonds on a fabric board.

8. Place the lace flat and guiding it along the inside of the drawn template, put a pin at **point A** and one at **Point B** where the bisecting line goes to the inside (**fig. 4a**). The pin goes through both the lace and the fabric into the fabric board.

9. Guiding the edge of the lace along the drawn template line, place another pin into the fabric board through the lace (and the fabric skirt) at **point C** and another one at **point D** on the bisecting line (**fig. 4b**).

10. Fold back the lace right on top of itself. Remove the pin from the fabric board at **point D**, replacing it this time to go through both layers of lace rather than just one. Of course, the pin will not only go through both layers of lace but also through the skirt and into fabric board (**fig. 5**).

11. Take the lace piece and bring it around to once again follow the outside line. You magically have a folded miter already in place (**see fig. 6**).

12. Guiding further, with the edge of the lace along the inside of the drawn template line, place another pin into the fabric board through the lace at **point E** and another at **point F** on the bisecting line (**fig. 6**).

13. Fold the lace right back on top of itself. Remove the pin at **point F**, replacing it this time to go through both layers of lace rather than just one (**fig. 7**).

14. Take the lace piece and bring it around to once again follow the outside line. You magically have a folded miter already in place (**fig. 8**).

15. Guiding further, with the edge of the lace along the inside of the drawn template line, place another pin into the lace at **point G** and another pin at **point H** on the bisecting line.

16. Fold the lace right back on top of itself. Remove the pin at **point H**, replace it this time to go through both layers of lace rather than just one.

17. Take the lace piece and bring it around to once again follow the outside line. You magically have a folded miter already in place (**fig. 9**).

18. At the bottom of the lace diamond, let the laces cross at the bottom. Remove the pin at **point B** and replace it into the fabric board through both pieces of lace. Remove the pin completely at **point A** (**fig. 10**).

19. Taking the top piece of lace, and leaving in the pin at **point B** only, fold the lace under and back so that it lies on top of the other piece of lace. You now have a folded in miter for the bottom of the lace.

20. Put a pin in, now, at **point B** (**fig. 11**). Of course you are going to have to cut away this long tail of lace. I think the best time to do that is before you begin your final stitching to attach the diamonds to the garment. It is perfectly alright to leave those tails of lace until your final stitching is done and then trim them.

21. You are now ready to spray starch and press the whole diamond shape. After spray starching and pressing the diamonds to the skirt, remove the pins from the fabric board and flat pin the lace shape to the skirt bottom. You are now ready to zigzag the diamond or machine entredeux stitch the diamond to the garments. Suggested zigzag settings are Width=2 to 3, Length=1 to $1^{1}/_{2}$.

Finishing The Bottom Of The Skirt

These techniques are for finishing the bottom of a Diamond Skirt, a Heart Skirt, a Bow Skirt, or any other lace shaped skirt where the figures travel all the way around the bottom touching each other.

Method One

Using Plain Zigzag To Attach Diamonds (Or Other Shapes) To The Skirt

1. First, zigzag across the top of the diamond pattern, stitching from **point A** to **point B**, again to **point A** and finish the entire skirt (**fig. 12**). Your lace is now attached to the skirt all the way across the skirt on the top. If your fabric and diamonds have been spray starched well, you don't have to use a stabilizer when zigzagging these lace shapes to the fabric. The stitch width will be wide enough to cover the heading of the lace and go off onto the fabric on the other side. The length will be from $^{1}/_{2}$ to 1, depending on the look that you prefer.

2. Zigzag all of the diamonds on the skirt, on the inside of the diamonds only (**fig. 13**).

3. You are now ready to trim away the fabric of the skirt from behind the diamonds. Trim the fabric carefully from behind the lace shapes. The rest of the skirt fabric will now fall away leaving a diamond shaped bottom of the skirt (**fig. 14**). The lace will also be see through at the top of the diamonds.

4. If you are going to just gather lace and attach it at this point, then gather the lace and zigzag it to the bottom of the lace shapes, being careful to put extra fullness in the points of the diamonds (**fig. 15**). If your lace isn't wide enough to be pretty, then zigzag a couple of pieces of insertion or edging to your edging to make it wider (**fig. 16**).

5. If you are going to put entredeux on the bottom of the shapes before attaching gathered lace to finish it, follow the instructions for attaching entredeux to the bottom of a scalloped skirt given earlier in this lace shaping section. Work with short pieces of entredeux stitching from the inside points of the diamonds to the lower points of the diamonds on the skirt.

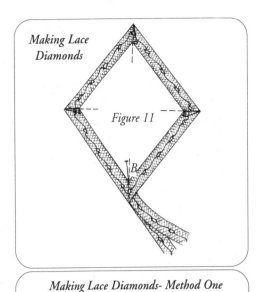

Making Lace Diamonds

Figure 11

Making Lace Diamonds- Method One

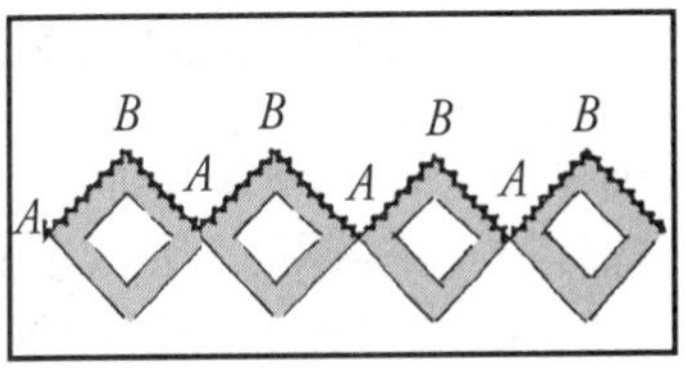

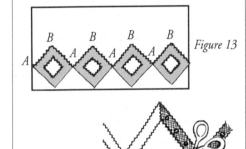

Figure 12

Figure 13

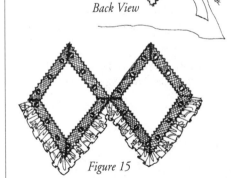

Figure 14

Back View

Figure 15

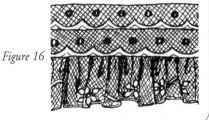

Figure 16

Finishing The Bottom Of The Skirt

Method Two

Using A Wing Needle Machine Entredeux Stitch To Attach Diamonds
(Or Other Lace Shapes) To The Skirt

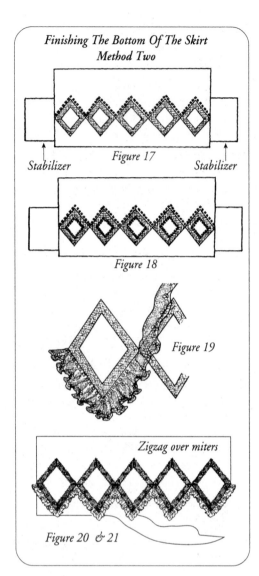

Finishing The Bottom Of The Skirt
Method Two

Stabilizer   *Figure 17*   Stabilizer

Figure 18

Figure 19

Zigzag over miters

Figure 20 & 21

1. If you are going to use the wing needle/entredeux stitch on your sewing machine to attach your diamonds or other lace shapes to the skirt, use the entredeux stitch for all attaching of the lace shapes to the skirt. Remember **you must use a stabilizer** when using the entredeux stitch/wing needle on any machine.

2. Place your stabilizer underneath the skirt, behind the shapes to be stitched. You can use small pieces of stabilizer which are placed underneath only a few shapes rather than having to have a long piece of stabilizer. Just be sure that you have stabilizer underneath these lace shapes before you begin your entredeux/wing needle stitching.

3. First, stitch the top side of the diamonds entredeux stitching from point A to point B all the way around the skirt. (**fig. 17**).

4. Secondly, stitch the inside of the diamonds using the entredeux stitch (**fig. 18**). Do not cut any fabric away at this point. Remember to continue using stabilizer for all entredeux/wing needle stitching.

5. You are now ready to gather your lace edging and machine entredeux it to the bottom of the skirt, joining the bottom portions of the diamonds at the same time you attach the gathered lace edging. If your machine has an edge joining or edge stitching foot with a center blade for guiding, this is a great place for using it.

6. Gather only a few inches of lace edging at a time. Butt the gathered lace edging to the flat bottom sides of the diamonds.

7. Machine entredeux right between the gathered lace edging and the flat side of the diamond. Remember, you are stitching through your laces (which are butted together, not overlapped), the fabric of the skirt and the stabilizer (**fig. 19**). Put a little extra lace gathered fullness at the upper and lower points of the diamonds.

8. After you have stitched your machine entredeux all the way around the bottom of the skirt, you have attached the gathered lace edging to the bottom of the skirt with your entredeux stitch.

9. Trim the fabric from behind the lace diamonds. Trim the fabric from underneath the gathered lace edging on the bottom of the skirt (**fig. 20**).

10. Either zigzag your folded miters in the angles of the diamonds or simply leave them folded in. I prefer to zigzag them (**fig. 21**). You also have the choice of cutting away the little folded back portions of the miters or leaving them for strength.

Shaping Flip-Flopped Lace Bows

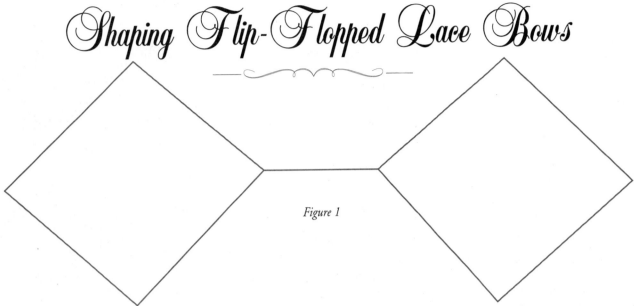

Figure 1

I make lace bows using a technique called "flip-flopping" lace — a relatively unsophisticated name for such a lovely trim. I first saw this technique on an antique teddy I bought at a local antique store. It had the most elegant flip-flopped lace bow. Upon careful examination, I noticed the lace was simply folded over at the corners, then continued down forming the outline of the bow. The corners were somewhat square. Certainly it was easier than mitering or pulling a thread and curving. I found it not only looked easier, it was easier.

Follow the instructions for making a flip-flopped bow, using a bow template. This technique works just as well for lace angles up and down on a skirt. You can flip-flop any angle that traditionally would be mitered. It can be used to go around a square collar, around diamonds, and around any shape with an angle rather than a curve.

Flip-Flopping Lace

1. Trace the template onto the fabric exactly where you want to place bows (**fig. 1**). Remember, the easy way to put bows around a skirt is to fold the fabric to make equal divisions of the skirt. If you want a bow skirt which has bows all the way around, follow the directions for starting at the side to make the bows in the directions given for a diamond skirt.

2. Draw your bows on your garment or on a skirt, where you want this lace shape.

3. Place your garment on your fabric board before you begin making your bow shapes. Beginning above the inside of one bow (**above E**), place the lace along the angle. The template is the inside guide line of the bow (**fig. 2**).

4. At the first angle (**B**), simply fold the lace so that it will follow along the next line (**B-C**) (**fig. 3**). This is called flip flopping the lace.

5. Place pins sticking through the lace, the fabric, and into the shaping board. I like to place pins on both the inside edges and the outside edges. Remember to place your pins so that they lie as flat as possible.

6. The lines go as follows: A-B, B-C, C-D, D-A, E-F, F-G, G-H, H-E. Tuck your lace end under E, which is also where the first raw edge will end (**fig. 4**).

7. Cut a short bow tab of lace that is long enough to go around the whole tie area of the bow (**fig. 4**). This will be the bow tie!

8. Tuck in this lace tab to make the center of the bow (**fig. 5**). Another way to attach this bow tie is to simply fold down a tab at the top and the bottom and place it right on top of the center of the bow. That is actually easier than tucking it under.

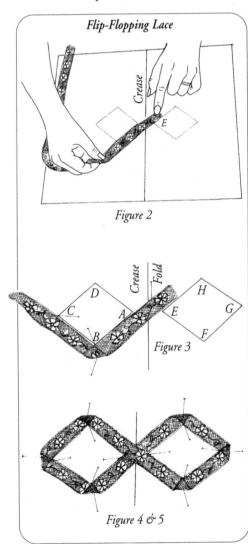

Flip-Flopping Lace

Figure 2

Figure 3

Figure 4 & 5

Since you are going to zigzag all the way around the bow "tie" it really won't matter whether it is tucked in or not.

9. Spray starch and press the bow, that is shaped with the pins still in the board, with its bow tie in place (**fig. 6**). Remove pins from the board and pin the bow flat to the skirt or other garment. You are now ready to attach the shaped bow to the garment.

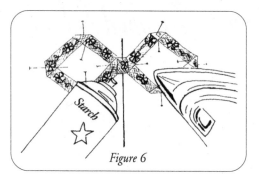

Figure 6

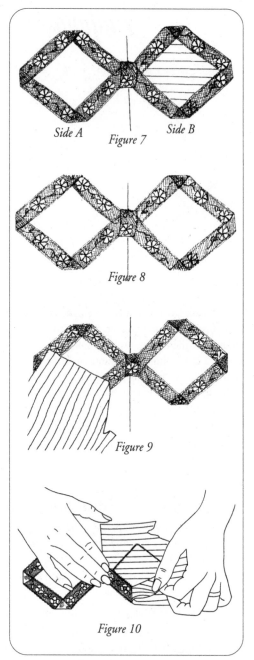

Side A   Figure 7   Side B

Figure 8

Figure 9

Figure 10

10. This illustration gives you ideas for making a bow two ways. First, the "A" side of the bow has just the garment fabric peeking through the center of the bow. Second, the "B" side of the bow illustrates what the bow will look like if you put a pintucked strip in the center. Both are beautiful (**fig. 7**).

11. If you prefer the bow to look like side (A), which has the fabric of the garment showing through the middle of the bow, follow these steps for completing the bow. Zigzag around the total outside of the bow. Then, zigzag around the inside portions of both sides of the bow. Finally, zigzag around the finished bow "tie" portion (**fig. 8**). The bows will be attached to the dress.

12. If you prefer the bow to look like side (B), which will have pintucks (or anything else you choose) inside, follow the directions in this section. (These directions are when you have bows on areas other than the bottom of a skirt or sleeve or collar. If you have bows at the bottom of anything, then you have to follow the skirt directions given in the diamond skirt section.)

13. Zigzag the outside only of the bows all the way around. Notice that your bow "tie" will be partially stitched since part of it is on the outside edges.

14. I suggest pintucking a larger piece of fabric and cutting small sections which are somewhat larger than the insides of the bows (**fig. 9**).

15. Cut away fabric from behind both center sections of the bow. I lovingly tell my students that now they can place their whole fists inside the holes in the centers of this bow.

16. Place the pintucked section behind the center of the lace bows. Zigzag around the inside of the bows, which will now attach the pintucked section. From the back, trim away the excess pintucked section. You now have pintucks in the center of each side of the bow (**fig. 10**).

17. Go back and stitch the sides of the bow "tie" down. After you have zigzagged all the way around your bow "tie," you can trim away excess laces which crossed underneath the tie. This gives the bow tie a little neater look. ▨

Tied Lace Bows

This method of bow shaping I saw for the first time years ago in Australia. It is beautiful and each bow will be a little different which makes it a very interesting variation of the flip flopped bow. Your options on shaping the bow part of this cute bow are as follows:

1. You can flip flop the bow, or
2. you can curve the bow and pull a string to make it round, or
3. you can flip flop one side and curve the other side. Bows can be made of lace insertion, lace edging, or lace beading. If you make your tied lace bow of lace edging, be sure to put the scalloped side of the lace edging for the outside of the bow and leave the string to pull on the inside.

Tied Lace Bow

Materials Needed

✧ 1 yd. to 1¹/₄ yds. lace insertion, edging or beading for one bow

Directions

1. Tie the lace into a bow, leaving equal streamers on either side of the bow.

2. Using a lace board, shape the bow onto the garment, using either the flip flopped method or the pulled thread curved method.

3. Shape the streamers of the bow using either the flip–flopped method or the pulled thread method.

4. Shape the ends of the streamer into an angle.

5. Zigzag or machine entredeux stitch the shaped bow and streamers to the garment. ▨

Hearts-Fold-Back Miter Method

Curving Lace

Since many heirloom sewers are also incurable romantics, it's no wonder hearts are a popular lace shape. Hearts are the ultimate design for a wedding dress, wedding attendants' clothing, or on a ring bearer's pillow. As with the other lace shaping discussed in this chapter, begin with a template when making hearts. When using our heart template, we like to shape our laces inside the heart design. Of course, shaping along the outside of the heart design is permitted also, so do whatever is easiest for you.

With the writing of the *Antique Clothing* book, I thought I had really figured out the easy way to make lace hearts. After four years of teaching heart making, I have totally changed my method of making hearts. This new method is so very easy that I just couldn't wait to tell you about it. After shaping your hearts, you don't even have to remove them from the skirt to finish the heart. What a relief and an improvement! Enjoy the new method of making hearts with the new fold-back miters. It is so easy and you are going to have so much fun making hearts.

1. Draw a template in the shape of a heart. Make this as large or as small as you want. If you want equal hearts around the bottom of a skirt, fold the skirt into equal sections, and design the heart template to fit into one section of the skirt when using your chosen width of lace insertion.

2. Draw on your hearts all the way around the skirt if you are using several hearts. As always, when shaping lace, draw the hearts onto the fabric where you will be stitching the laces.

3. Draw a 2" bisecting line at the top into the center and at the bottom of the heart into the center (**fig. 1**).

Figure 1

NOTE: I would like to refresh your memory on lace shaping along the bottom of a skirt at this time. You make your hearts (or whatever else you wish to make) above the skirt while the skirt still has a straight bottom. Later after stitching your hearts (or whatever else) to the skirt, you cut away to make the shaped skirt bottom.

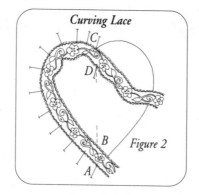

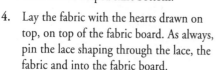
Curving Lace

Figure 2

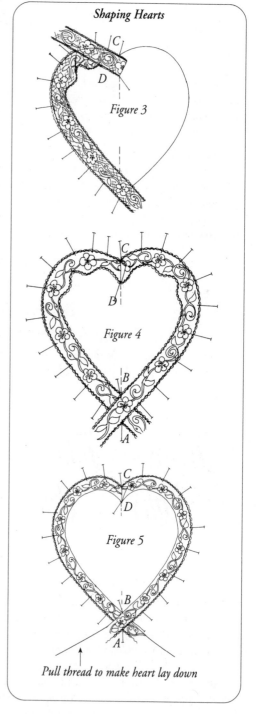
Shaping Hearts

Figure 3

Figure 4

Figure 5

Pull thread to make heart lay down

4. Lay the fabric with the hearts drawn on top, on top of the fabric board. As always, pin the lace shaping through the lace, the fabric and into the fabric board.

5. Cut one piece of lace which will be large enough to go all the way around one heart with about 4" extra. Before you begin shaping the lace, leave about 2" of lace on the outside of the bottom line.

6. Place a pin at **point A**. Beginning at the bottom of the heart, pin the lace on the inside of the heart template. The pins will actually be on the outside of the lace insertion; however, you are shaping your laces on the inside of your drawn heart template.

7. Work around the heart to **point C**, placing pins at ¹/₂" intervals. Notice that the outside will be pinned rather tightly and the inside will be curvy. **Note:** One of our math teacher students told me years ago, while I was teaching this lace shaping, a very important fact. She said, "Martha did you know that a curved line is just a bunch of straight lines placed in a funny way?" She said this as I was trying to explain that it was pretty easy to get the straight lace pinned into a curve. Since I remembered as little about my math classes as possible, I am sure that I didn't know this fact. It makes it a lot easier to explain taking that straight lace and making a curve out of it to know that fact.

8. After finishing pinning around to the center of the heart, place another pin at **point D (fig. 2)**.

9. Lay the lace back on itself, curving it into the curve that you just pinned (**fig. 3**). Remove the pin from **Point C** and repin it, this time pinning through both layers of lace.

10. Wrap the lace to the other side and begin pinning around the other side of the heart. Where you took the lace back on itself and repinned, there will be a miter which appears just like magic. This is the new fold-back miter which is just as wonderful on hearts as it is on diamonds and scalloped skirts.

11. Pin the second side of the lace just like you pinned the first one. At the bottom of the heart, lay the laces one over the other and put a pin at **point B (fig. 4)**.

12. It is now time to pull the threads to make the curvy insides of the heart lay flat and become heart shaped. You can pull threads either from the bottom of the heart or threads from the center of each side of the heart. I prefer to pull the threads from the bottom of the heart. Pull the threads and watch the heart lay down flat and pretty. (**fig. 5**). After teaching literally hundreds of students to make hearts, I think it is better to pull the thread from the bottom of the heart. You don't need to help the fullness lay down; simply pull the thread. On other lace shaped curves such as a scalloped skirt, loops, or ovals, you have to pull from the inside curve.

13. Spray starch and press the curves into place.

14. To make your magic miter at the bottom of the heart, remove the pin from **Point A**, fold back the lace so it lays on the other piece of lace, and repin **Point A**. You now have a folded–back miter which completes the easy mitering on the heart (**fig. 6**). You are now ready to pin the hearts flat onto the garment and remove the shaping from the fabric board.

15. You can trim these bottom "tails" of lace away before you attach the heart to the garment or after you attach the heart to the garment. It probably looks better to trim them before you stitch (**fig. 7**).

16. You can attach the hearts just to the fabric or you can choose to put something else such as pintucks inside the hearts. If you have hearts which touch going all the way around a skirt, then follow the directions for zigzagging which were found in the diamond section.

17. If you have one heart on a collar or bodice of a dress, then zigzag the outside first. If you choose to put something on the inside of each heart, cut away the fabric from behind the shape after zigzagging it to the garment. Then, put whatever you want to insert in the heart behind the heart shape and zigzag around the center or inside of the heart. Refer to the directions on inserting pintucks or something else in the center of a lace shape in the flip-flopped bow section.

18. You can certainly use the entredeux/wing needle stitching for a beautiful look for attaching the hearts. Follow the directions for machine entredeux on the lace shaped skirt found in the diamond section of this lace shaping chapter.

19. After you cut away the fabric from behind the hearts, go back and zigzag over each mitered point (**fig. 8**). You then have the choice of either leaving the folded over section or of cutting it away. Personally, I usually leave the section because of the strength it adds to the miters. The choice is yours. ▨

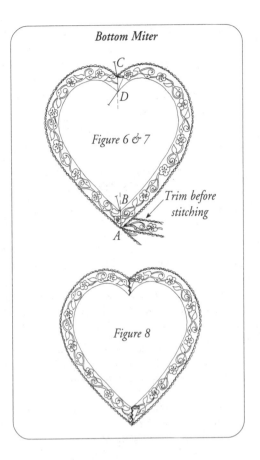

Bottom Miter

Figure 6 & 7

Trim before stitching

Figure 8

Shaping Curves And Angles With Pintucks

Pintucks are inexpensive to make. They add texture and dimension without adding cost to the dress. They're rarely found on store-bought clothing. One of my favorite things in the whole world to do is to follow lace shapes with pintucks or decorative stitches on your machine for an enchanting finish. Or you may simply use your template and pintuck the shape instead of using lace. For threads, use white-on-white, ecru-on-ecru, or any pastel color on white or ecru.

The effect of shaped pintucks is so fabulous and so interesting. Virtually everybody is afraid that she doesn't know how to make those fabulous pintucks thus making a garment into a pintuck fantasy. It is so easy that I just can't wait to share with you the tricks. I promise, nobody in my schools all over the world ever believes me when I tell them this easiest way. Then, everybody, virtually everybody, has done these curved and angled pintucks with absolute perfection. They usually say, "This is really magic!"

The big question here is, "What foot do I use for scalloped pintucks?" For straight pintucks, I use a pintuck foot with the grooves. That foot is fine for curved or scalloped pintucks also, but I prefer either the regular zigzag foot or the clear applique foot, which is plastic and allows easy "see through" of the turning points. Try your pintuck foot, your regular sewing foot, and your clear applique foot to see which one you like the best. Like all aspects of heirloom sewing, the "best" foot is really your personal preference. Listed below are my absolute recommendations for curved and angled pintucks.

— Martha's General Rules — Of Curving And Angling Pintucks

1. Use a regular zigzag foot, or a pintuck foot (**fig. 1**).

2. Either draw on your pintuck shape, or zigzag your lace insertion to the garment. You can either draw on pintuck shapes or follow your lace shaping. My favorite way to make lots of pintucks is to follow lace shaping which has already been stitched to the garment.

Martha's General Rules Of Curving And Angling Pintucks

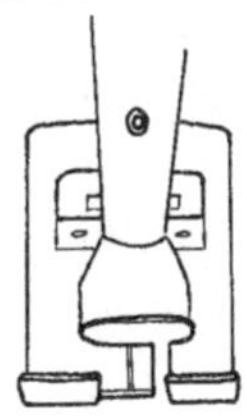

Figure 1

3. Using a ruler, draw straight lines with a fabric marker or washable pencil, bisecting each point where you will have to turn around with your pintuck. In other words, draw a line at all angles where you will have to turn your pintuck in order to keep stitching. This is the most important point to make with curved and angled pintucks. When you are going around curves, this bi-secting line is not necessary since you don't stop and pivot when you are turning curves. Everywhere you have to stop and pivot, these straight lines must be drawn (**fig. 2**).

4. Use a 1.6 or a 2.0 double needle. Any wider doesn't curve or turn well!

5. Set your machine for straight sewing, L=1.5. Notice this is a **very short stitch**. When you turn angles, this short stitch is necessary for pretty turns.

6. Press "Needle Down" on your sewing machine if your machine has this feature. This means that when you stop sewing at any time, your needle will remain in the fabric.

7. Stitch, using either the first line you drew or following around the lace shaping which you have already stitched to your garment. The edge of your presser foot will guide along the outside of the lace shape. When you go around curves, turn your fabric and keep stitching. Do not pick up your foot and pivot, this makes the curves jumpy, not smooth (**fig. 3**).

8. When you come to a pivot point, let your foot continue to travel until you can look into the hole of the foot, and see that your double needles have **straddled the line you drew on the fabric**. Remember your needles are **in the fabric** (**fig. 4**).

9. Sometimes, the needles won't exactly straddle the line exactly the way they straddled the line on the last turn around. Lift the presser foot. (Remember, you needles are still in the fabric.) Turn your fabric where the edge of the presser foot properly begins in a new direction following your lace insertion lace shaping or your drawn line, lower the presser foot, and begin sewing again (**fig. 5**).

10. Wait A Minute! Most of you are now thinking, "Martha, You Are Crazy. There are two major problems with what you just said. You said to leave the double needles in the fabric, lift the presser foot , turn the fabric, lower the presser foot and begin sewing again. If I do that I will probably break my double needles, and there will be a big wad or hump of fabric where I twisted the fabric to turn around to go in a new direction. That will never work!" I know you are thinking these two things because everybody does. Neither one of these things will happen! It is really just like MAGIC. TRY THIS TECHNIQUE AND SEE WHAT I AM SAYING. Ladies all over the world absolutely adore this method and nobody believes how easy it is.

11. After you get your first row of double needle pintucks, then you can use the edge of your regular zigzag sewing machine foot, guiding along the just stitched pintuck row as the guide point for more rows. The only thing you have to remember, is to have made long enough lines to bisect each angle that you are going to turn. You must have these turn around lines drawn so you can know where to stop sewing, leave the needles in the fabric, turn around, and begin stitching again. These lines are the real key. ▨

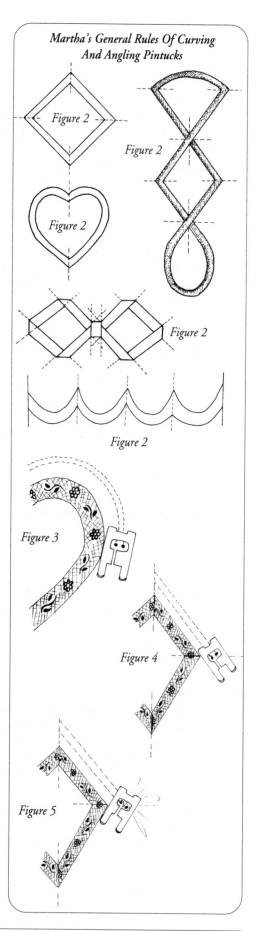

Martha's General Rules Of Curving And Angling Pintucks

Figure 2

Figure 2

Figure 2

Figure 2

Figure 2

Figure 2

Figure 3

Figure 4

Figure 5

Extra-Stable Lace Finishing

A. Extra-Stable Lace Finish for Fabric Edges

1. If the lace is being attached to a straight edge of fabric, pin the heading of the lace to the right side, ¹/₄" or more from the cut edge, with the right side of the lace facing up and the outside edge of the lace extending over the edge of the fabric. Using a short straight stitch, stitch the heading to the fabric (**fig. 1**).

2. If the lace is being attached to a curved edge, shape the lace around the curve as you would for lace shaping; refer to "Lace Shaping" found on page 223. Pull up the threads in the lace heading if necessary. Continue pinning and stitching the lace as directed in Step 1 above (**fig. 2**).

3. Press the seam allowance away from the lace, toward the wrong side of the fabric (**fig. 3**). If the edge is curved or pointed, you may need to clip the seam allowance in order to press flat (**fig. 4**).

4. On the right side, use a short, narrow zigzag to stitch over the lace heading, catching the fold of the pressed seam allowance (**fig. 5**).

5. On the wrong side, trim the seam allowance close to the zigzag (**fig. 6**).

B. Extra-Stable Lace Finish for Lace Shapes

1. Trace the lace design onto the fabric. Shape the lace according to the directions in "Lace Shaping" found on page 223 (**fig. 7**).

2. Using a short straight stitch, stitch the heading to the fabric on both edges of the lace (**fig. 8**).

3. After both sides of the lace have been stitched, carefully slit the fabric behind the lace, cutting in the middle between the two stitching lines. Be very careful not to cut through the lace (**fig. 9**).

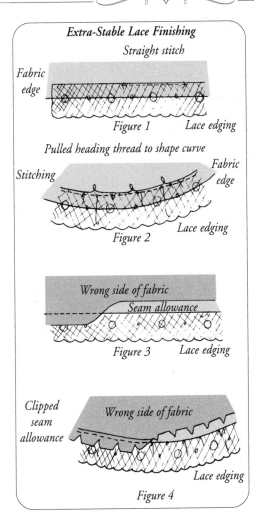

Extra-Stable Lace Finishing

Straight stitch

Fabric edge — Lace edging

Figure 1

Pulled heading thread to shape curve

Stitching — Fabric edge — Lace edging

Figure 2

Wrong side of fabric — Seam allowance — Lace edging

Figure 3

Clipped seam allowance — Wrong side of fabric — Lace edging

Figure 4

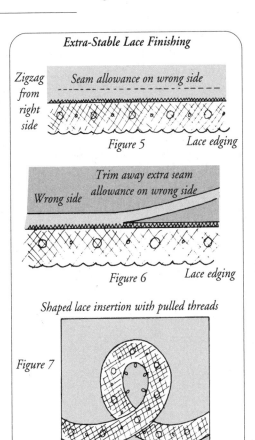

Extra-Stable Lace Finishing

Zigzag from right side — Seam allowance on wrong side — Lace edging

Figure 5

Wrong side — Trim away extra seam allowance on wrong side — Lace edging

Figure 6

Shaped lace insertion with pulled threads

Figure 7

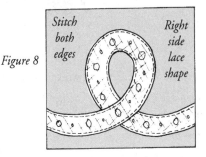

Stitch both edges — Right side lace shape

Figure 8

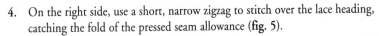

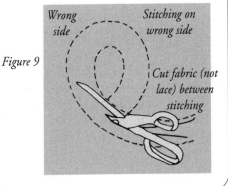

Wrong side — Stitching on wrong side — Cut fabric (not lace) between stitching

Figure 9

4. Press the seam allowance away from the lace, toward the wrong side of the fabric. If the edge is curved or has a corner, you may need to clip the seam allowance in order to press flat (**fig. 10**).

5. On the right side, use a short, narrow zigzag to stitch over the lace heading, catching the fold of the pressed seam allowance (**fig. 11**).

6. On the wrong side, trim the seam allowance close to the zigzag (**fig. 12**). ▨

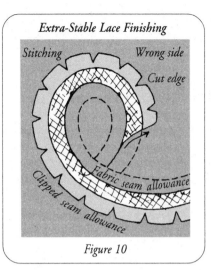

Extra-Stable Lace Finishing

Stitching   Wrong side

Cut edge

Fabric seam allowance

Clipped seam allowance

Figure 10

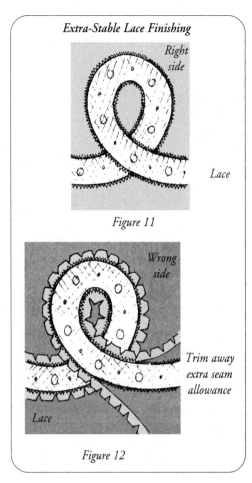

Extra-Stable Lace Finishing

Right side

Lace

Figure 11

Wrong side

Trim away extra seam allowance

Lace

Figure 12

𝒻rench 𝒮eam

1. Place the fabric pieces with wrong sides together.

2. Stitch a row of tiny zigzag stitches (L 1.0, W 1.0) $^3/_{16}$" outside the seam line (**see fig. 1**).

3. Press the seam flat and trim away the seam allowance outside the zigzags (**fig. 1**).

4. Open out the fabric and press the seam to one side.

5. Fold the fabric along the seam line with right sides together, encasing the zigzag stitching (**fig. 2**).

6. Stitch a $^3/_{16}$" seam, enclosing the zigzag stitching (**fig. 3**).

7. Press the seam to one side.

Note: A serged rolled edge may be used for the first seam, when the fabric pieces are wrong sides together. No trimming will be needed, as the serger cuts off the excess seam allowance. If a pintuck foot is available, use it to stitch the second seam for either the zigzag or serger method. Place the tiny folded seam into a groove of the foot so that the needle will stitch right along beside the little roll of fabric (**fig. 4**). ▨

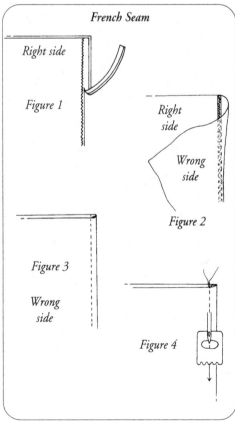

French Seam

Right side

Figure 1

Right side

Wrong side

Figure 2

Figure 3

Wrong side

Figure 4

Ribbon Rosettes

Ribbon Rosette

Ribbon rosettes are used to embellish children's dresses, doll dresses, craft projects, pillows and other home decorating projects. Ribbon rosettes are most commonly made from double-faced satin ribbon or silk ribbon. The width and length of the ribbon will vary according to the project. Commonly used ribbon widths are $1/16$", $1/8$" or $1/4$" while the lengths will vary from 18" to 5 yards.

1. Place dots on the ribbon evenly spaced apart, usually 1" to 2", leaving ribbon at each end un-dotted for the streamers. The directions for the project will give the length of the ribbon to be used and the dot spacing (**fig. 1**).

2. Thread a needle with a doubled thread and begin picking up the dots on the ribbon (**fig. 1**). Thread the dots onto the needle and pull them up tightly to form a rosette. Take a few stitches to secure the loops together (**fig. 2**).

3. Tack the rosette in place or pin in place using a small gold safety pin.

Knotted Ribbon Rosette

1. Make dots on the ribbon as described in step 1 of Ribbon Rosettes. At every other dot, tie a knot in the ribbon (**see fig. 3**).

2. Thread a needle with a doubled thread and begin picking up the dots on the ribbon. Thread the dots onto the needle (**fig. 3**) and pull them up tightly to form a rosette. Take a few stitches to secure the loops together.

3. Tie knots in the streamers, if desired (**fig. 4**).

4. Tack the rosette in place or pin in place using a small gold safety pin. ▨

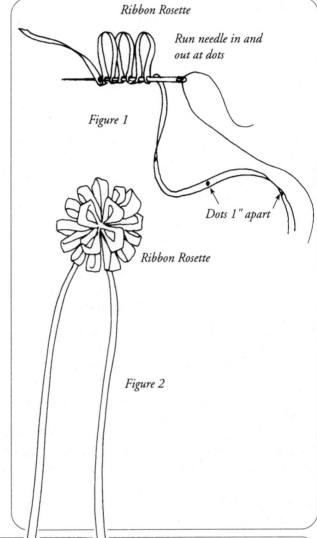

Ribbon Rosette

Run needle in and out at dots

Figure 1

Dots 1" apart

Ribbon Rosette

Figure 2

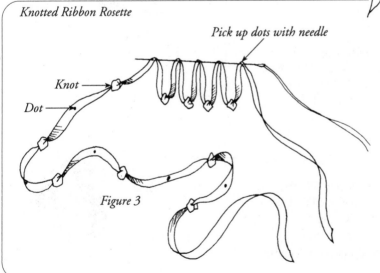

Knotted Ribbon Rosette

Pick up dots with needle

Knot

Dot

Figure 3

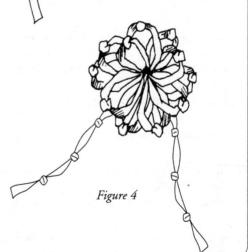

Figure 4

Basic Crazy Patch

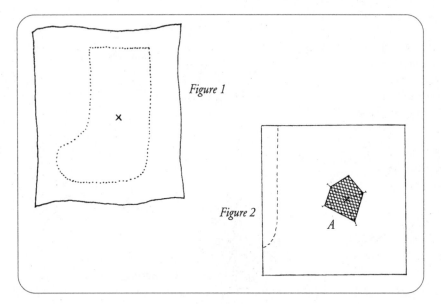

Figure 1

Figure 2

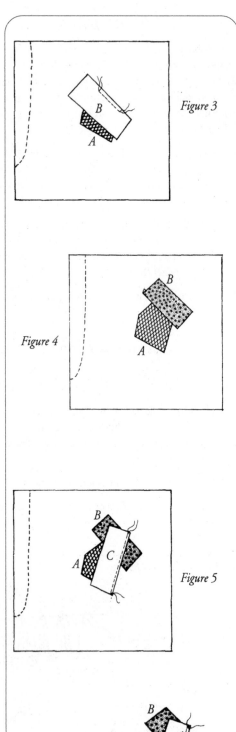

Figure 3

Figure 4

Figure 5

Figure 6

Directions

1. Cut a piece of base fabric larger than each pattern piece to be crazy patched. This base fabric can be any fabric since it will not show when the crazy patch is complete. We prefer to use unbleached muslin as the base fabric.

2. Outline the pattern piece on the base fabric. Find the center of the base fabric and mark with a fabric marker (**fig. 1**).

Optional: For a quilted look, batting may be placed under the base fabric. Pin the batting to the base fabric in several places to prevent the batting from slipping.

3. For the patchwork, start with a multi-sided fabric piece (patch "A") with at least five sides.

4. Pin patch "A" to the center of the base fabric (**fig 2**).

5. Place patch "B" to patch "A", right sides together. Line up one side of patch "B" with one side of patch "A". Patch "B" will overhang patch "A". Stitch using a $^1/_4$" seam the length of the edge of patch "A" (**fig. 3**). This stitching will be made through the two patch pieces and the base fabric. The stitch length should be about a 3, which is a little longer than a normal stitch. Use a straight stitch.

6. Flip patch "B" to the right side and press (**fig. 4**).

7. Place one of the straight sides of patch "C" overlapping patches "A" and "B". The edge of patch "C" may extend beyond the length of the patches underneath. The patches underneath may extend above the straight edge of patch "C" (**fig. 5**).

8. Stitch along the straight edge of patch "C" the length of the under pieces. Trim away any excess of the "A" and "B" patches (**fig. 6**).

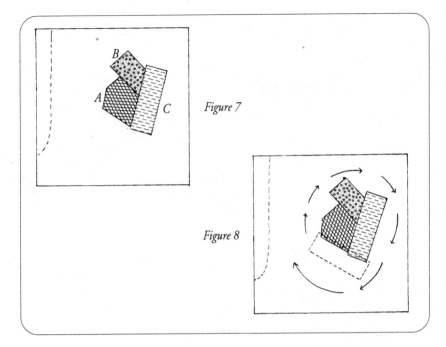

Figure 7

Figure 8

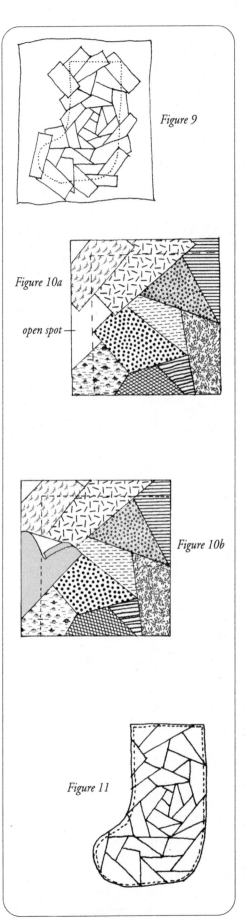

Figure 9

Figure 10a

open spot —

Figure 10b

Figure 11

9. Flip patch "C" to the right side and press (**fig. 7**).

10. Continue working in a clockwise direction adding patches until the needed base fabric is covered (**fig. 8**). The patches should extend beyond the traced pattern lines. This will insure that the crazy patch design will fit the pattern piece (**fig. 9**).

Note: Eventually, when stitching crazy patch, an unusual angle will develop or you will come to an unfinished space. A piece of ribbon, lace or any trim can be hand or machine stitched in that space or a piece of fabric can be used to cover the space by turning the edge or edges of the fabric under and top stitching in the desired area. In other words, use anything and any technique to cover these unusual or hard-to-stitch spaces (**fig. 10a and 10b**).

11. Place the pattern piece on top of the crazy patch fabric. Trace around the pattern and stitch just inside the traced line. Cut out the pattern piece (**fig. 11**).

New Techniques

Ribbon Thread Bobbin Technique

Corded Shadow Appliqué

Girl's Lined Jumper

Picture Transfer

Making Bias Tape

Double Lace Scallops

Hemstitching A Scalloped Hem

Antique Peek-a-Boo

Machine Tatting

Double Needle Edge Trim

Shadow Sandwich Technique

Built-In Machine Embroidery on Heirloom Clothing

Decorative Serged Seams

New Technique
Ribbon Thread Bobbin Technique

This is a fun technique which allows the use of heavier decorative threads for machine embroidery; this is accomplished by using the decorative thread in the bobbin, since it is too heavy to go through the needle. This allows the use of textured threads which could not be used otherwise, giving bolder designs which are particularly suited to pillows, pictures and other decorative items. Also try this technique on medium to heavy weight tailored clothing, such as jackets and blouses.

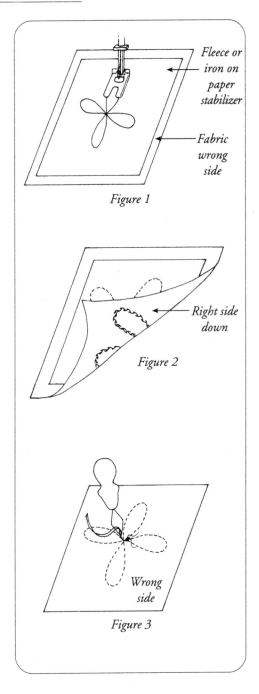

Fleece or iron on paper stabilizer

Fabric wrong side

Figure 1

Right side down

Figure 2

Wrong side

Figure 3

Supplies

* Iron-on fleece or iron-on paper stabilizer
* Decorative thread or ribbon
* Invisible (transparent) thread
* Washout fabric marker or pencil

Directions

1. Wind ribbon thread, silk ribbon or perle cotton onto a bobbin. The bobbin may be wound by machine, but wind slowly and guide by hand so that the thread winds evenly and does not pull too tightly.

2. Place the bobbin into the bobbin case of the machine and run the ribbon thread through the by-pass hole on the bobbin case, or purchase a spare bobbin case and lower the tension on the case to allow the thread to flow freely off of the bobbin.

3. Thread the needle with transparent (invisible) thread or with sewing thread to match the decorative bobbin thread (do not try to put the heavy decorative thread through the needle). Tighten the upper tension. Practice on a sample to determine the correct tension settings for each individual machine.

4. If the project will be backed with fleece, trace the design onto the fleece. If no fleece will be used, trace the design onto iron-on paper stabilizer.

5. Place the design (fleece or paper) on the wrong side of the fabric, with the design facing out so that it can be seen and iron in place (**see fig. 1**).

6. Place the fabric under the needle with the fabric to the feed dogs and the design facing up. Lower the presser foot and hold the thread ends while beginning to stitch (**fig. 1**).

7. Stitch over the design with a straight stitch or an open decorative stitch, such as a zigzag or feather stitch. Do not use satin stitches or very tiny stitches, they will knot up and not form a pretty design. Remember that the decorative design will be seen on the underside of the work, which is the right side of the fabric (**fig. 2**).

8. If the design does not look pretty, adjust the tensions if needed and sew a little more slowly than normal.

9. After the stitching is complete, use a small needle threader or large-eyed needle to pull the thread tails to the back of the fabric and tie in a knot. Place a drop of seam sealant over the knot and allow it to dry before clipping the thread tails. This will prevent the slippery threads from coming untied (**fig. 3**).

10. If paper stabilizer was used, carefully remove it. ▨

Corded Shadow Appliqué

This easy technique is one which uses a colored fabric to show a shape underneath a sheer top layer. The shape is clearly defined by a small corded outline, which also enhances the color of the fabric showing through. With a little practice, even very intricate designs can be successfully worked.

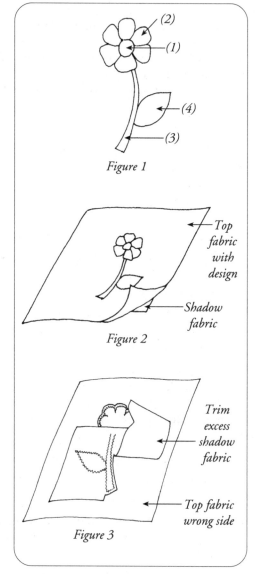

Figure 1

Figure 2

Top
fabric
with
design

Shadow
fabric

Figure 3

Trim
excess
shadow
fabric

Top fabric
wrong side

Supplies

✳ Lightweight white batiste, linen or organdy for top layer
✳ Colored fabric for shadow color
✳ Machine embroidery thread
✳ Gimp cording
✳ Tear-away paper stabilizer
✳ Washout lead pencil
✳ Spray starch
✳ Open-toe foot
✳ Appliqué scissors or other small scissors for close trimming

Directions

1. A lightweight or sheer fabric must be used for the top layer in order to let the color for the shadow show through.

2. The shadow fabric may be broadcloth, linen or other tightly woven fabric. The color should be bright and clear. For a deeper shadow, choose a brighter shade rather than a darker shade; the darker shades become muddy and lose their color. To test colors, place a piece of the colored fabric between two pieces of the top fabric and check the color.

3. While the shadow color is between the top fabric layers, choose the thread color to be used. Match the thread to the color of the shadow by placing a strand of the thread on the top layer beside the edge of the shadow. Use a slightly brighter shade of thread to enhance the color of the shadow and keep it from becoming dull.

4. Thread the needle with the decorative thread. The needle tension should be slightly loosened. The bobbin may be filled with lightweight white cotton machine embroidery thread. Use a #70 or #80 embroidery needle. Attach the appliqué foot.

5. Lightly spray starch and press dry the top piece of fabric. Lightly trace the design onto the top fabric. The pencil marks will rinse out with the starch if they are drawn lightly. Heavy, dark lines are ground into the fibers of the fabric and may not wash out.

6. Begin working the shadow design from the foreground to the background. In other words, the center of a flower would be worked before the petals. A section which overlaps another section would be worked before the area that is partly covered (**fig.** 1).

7. Place the top fabric over the shadow fabric, right side up. Make sure that the shadow fabric is under the traced design (**fig.** 2).

8. Set the machine for a narrow, close zigzag, not quite a satin stitch. Stitch around the design.

9. From the back side, trim away the excess fabric. Be very careful that the front fabric does not get cut (**fig.** 3).

10. Work the next section of the design, remembering to work from the foreground to the background.

11. After all of the shadow areas have been stitched and trimmed, it is time to add the gimp. This time, the sections will be worked from the background to the foreground. In other words, any line that goes under another line will be stitched first, so that the raw ends of the gimp will be stitched under the next stitching. The stitching order will just the reverse of when the shadow pieces were applied.

12. Set the machine for a medium-length zigzag, wide enough to encase the gimp cording, with the length at a satin stitch setting. Place a piece of stabilizer under the area to be worked first. Remember to work the design from foreground to background if there are overlapping areas.

13. Place one end of the gimp over the design line, with the beginning at a place where one line comes out from under another. If there are no overlapping areas, begin the gimp at a section which is not at a point or corner. Take a few stitches to anchor the gimp in place, then trim the thread tails.

14. Stitch around the design with the gimp on the lines. When stitching around curves, pivot with the needle on the outer edge of the curve so that gaps will not be formed in the stitches (**fig. 4**). When turning corners, pivot with the needle on the inside so that the gimp can be pulled around the needle to form the corner (**fig. 5**). Once the corner is anchored, stitch the same as for a curve.

15. If the line comes to a place where it goes under another line, tie off the stitching and cut the gimp. When the stitching returns to the beginning point of a design with no overlaps, trim the gimp so that the two ends butt together and zigzag over the ends (**fig. 6**).

16. Pull the threads to the back and tie a knot rather than reverse stitching. Reverse stitching will cause a lump in the satin stitching.

17. From the back side, carefully tear away the stabilizer (**fig. 7**). ▩

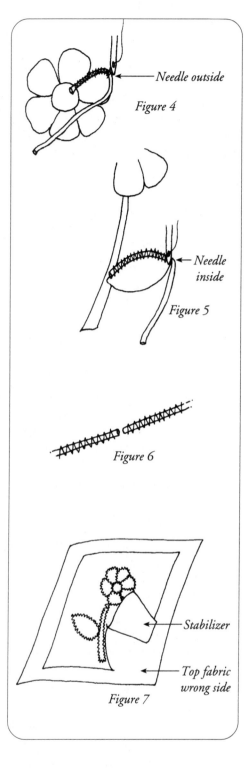

Needle outside

Figure 4

Needle inside

Figure 5

Figure 6

Stabilizer

Top fabric wrong side

Figure 7

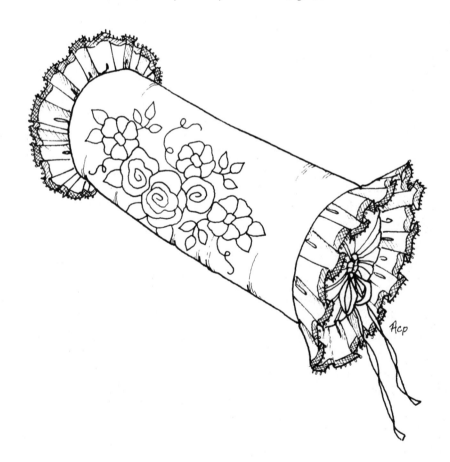

Girl's Lined Jumper

This jumper is reversible, if desired. The underside or second side of the jumper is referred to in these directions as the lining. This will be one of the easiest garments you have ever constructed. Use any button–on–the–shoulder jumper pattern.

Materials

Yardages are approximate, depending on what pattern is used (the pattern shown on *Martha's Sewing Room* is the Girl's Jumper from *Appliqué - Martha's Favorites* by Martha Pullen; these yardages are for that pattern).

✳ 45" fabric for jumper (buy the same amount for the lining)

sizes 1-2	$^2/_3$ yd.
sizes 3-4	$^3/_4$ yd.
sizes 5-6	1 yd.

✳ Other Requirements: thread, four $^1/_2$" buttons, paper for tracing pattern

I. Preparation and Cutting

1. Trace the correct size of the pattern onto paper and cut it out.

2. Pin the pieces together along the seam lines. Make any alterations necessary. If the length is shortened, fold up the desired amount and straighten the sides. If the pattern is lengthened, spread the pattern and straighten the sides.

3. Cut one jumper front and one jumper back, both on the fold. Cut one lining front and one lining back, both on the fold.

II. Construction

(All seams are $^1/_4$ inch.)

1. Place the jumper front and jumper back, right sides together, with the jumper front on top of the jumper back. Stitch the pieces together along the right side seam (**fig. 1**). Press the seam open. Appliqué or decorate the jumper at this time, if desired.

2. Place the lining front and lining back, right sides together, with the lining front on top of the lining back. Stitch the pieces together along the left side seam (**fig. 2**). Press the seam open. Applique or decorate the lining (if reversible) at this time, if desired.

3. Place the lining to the jumper with right sides together. Stitch along the top edge and along the hems; do not stitch the sides. Clip the curves (**fig. 3**).

4. Place one hand between the lining and the jumper at side #1. Reach through this opening and grab the jumper at side #2 (**fig. 4**).

5. Pull side #2 to side #1. Match the lining with the lining, the jumper with the jumper and match the seams. This will create a circular opening on the un-sewn sides. Pin in place (**see fig. 5**).

6. Stitch the sides (circular opening), leaving a 3-inch opening in the lining (**fig. 5**).

7. Turn the garment through the opening left in the side seam of the lining.

8. Stitch the opening closed (**fig. 6**).

9. Work buttonholes on the front tabs of the dress. Attach buttons on the back tabs of the dress. If the dress is reversible, attach buttons to both sides of the back tabs (**fig. 7**). ▣

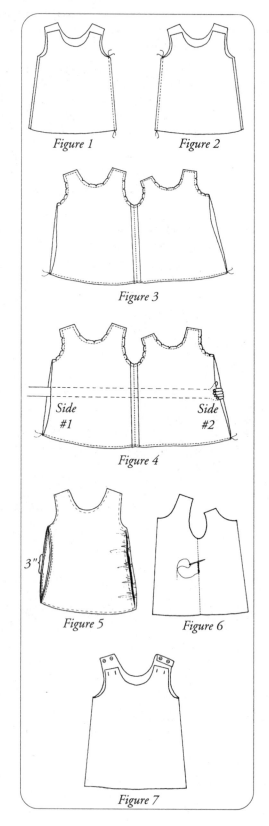

Figure 1   *Figure 2*

Figure 3

Side #1   Side #2

Figure 4

3"

Figure 5   *Figure 6*

Figure 7

New Technique

Picture Transfer

Borrowing the technique of transferring pictures to knit T-shirts and using the same technique to transfer antique valentines to heirloom projects seemed like a great new idea. Imagine my surprise at finding an antique pillow cover with a family portrait transferred onto it! Even though the idea was not as new as I had thought, the pillow cover certainly reinforced my idea that this technique was appropriate for heirloom projects!

Supplies

* One photo to be transferred, color or black and white
* Fabric for transfer
* Iron
* Aluminum foil

Directions

1. Take the photo to a copy service and have it copied onto transfer paper. Be sure to ask for transfer instructions, such as how long to heat the transfer. The photo will be reversed when it is copied onto the paper, but will reverse back to the original when it is transferred to the fabric.

2. Trim the excess paper from around the design. Any of the transfer film that is left around the design will be transferred to the fabric and will show on the finished project (**fig. 1**). It may help in positioning to mark the center top and bottom, left and right sides on the back of the transfer paper because you will not be able to see the front of the design while positioning it on the fabric.

3. When choosing the fabric, realize that some of the fabric color may show through the transfer and change the picture color. Stripes or prints may show through. If it is important that the picture retain the original color, use a light fabric such as white or pale ecru. Also choose a fabric without a lot of surface texture, because the transfer may crack a little over rough areas. This may be advantageous if an antique look is to be the end result.

4. It will help to work on a board or other hard, flat surface that can withstand the heat of the iron. Pressure is as important to a good transfer as heat. Place a piece of aluminum foil over the ironing surface. Place the fabric on the foil, right side up (**see fig. 2**).

5. Place the transfer design over the fabric, right side down. Cover the paper with a press cloth (**fig. 2**).

6. Using a hot iron with no steam, press the back of the design for the amount of time recommended by the copy service. Press hard, but do not rub the iron back and forth; this can cause the transfer to shift and blur.

7. Let the paper and fabric cool slightly, then carefully peel the paper away from the design (**fig. 3**).

8. If the paper seems to stick to the design, stop immediately and slightly rewarm the area, then carefully peel again.

9. To care for the finished project, hand wash and drip dry. Be careful that the transfer area is not scrubbed or wrung, so that the transfer does not peel off. If possible, do not iron over the transfer on the finished project. If it is necessary to iron over the transfer, a Teflon pressing sheet must be used to prevent the transfer from sticking to the iron and peeling off. ▨

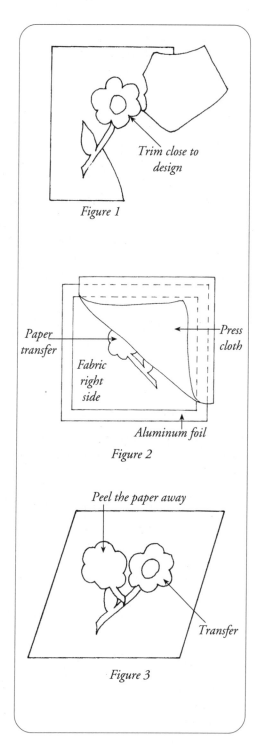

Trim close to design

Figure 1

Paper transfer

Press cloth

Fabric right side

Aluminum foil

Figure 2

Peel the paper away

Transfer

Figure 3

New Technique

Making Bias Tape

In order to have a beautifully finished garment, perfectly matched bias tape is a must. Custom-made bias tape also ensures that the tape is not too heavy or too wide and bulky for delicate projects. Techniques like Antique Peek-A-Boo require the use of tape which is self-made. Self-made bias tape is easy to make, especially with the use of a bias tape maker. Instructions are given for both methods, with or without the bias tape maker.

Supplies

* Fabric to be cut into bias strips
* Bias tape maker of correct finished size
* Optional: Rotary cutter, mat and ruler for cutting bias strips

A. Using a Bias Tape Maker

1. Choose the correct size bias tape maker for the desired finished width of the tape. Cut the bias strips twice the finished width of the finished tape. Bias strips are cut at a 45° angle to the straight grain.

2. Piece the bias strips into one long strip (**fig. 1**).

3. Cut the end of the bias strip at a slant so that it will slide into the bias tape maker more easily (**fig. 2**).

4. Insert the bias strip into the wide end of the bias tape maker, right side up. It may be necessary to use a pin or large needle to help push the end of the fabric into the tape maker.

5. The fabric will come out of the small end of the tape maker, with the edges folded to the wrong side. Press the fabric as it comes out, creasing the folded edges (**fig. 3**).

6. Slide the bias tape maker along the bias strip, pressing as it comes out the small end, until all of the tape is creased. It may be helpful to pin the finished end of the tape to the ironing board so that it is easier to slide the tape maker along the strip (**fig. 4**).

B. Without a Bias Tape Maker

1. Cut the bias strips twice the width of the finished tape.

2. Piece the bias strips into one long strip (**refer to fig. 1**).

3. Fold each long edge to the middle and press (**fig. 5**).

C. Double-Fold Bias Tape

1. After the bias tape is made with the long edges pressed to the middle, fold the tape in half along the length, meeting the long edges. Stop at this point if the tape will be used in the Antique Peek-a-Boo technique (**fig. 6**).

2. If the double-fold tape will be used to encase an edge, fold the tape slightly off-center so that one edge extends slightly beyond the other. Place the tape over the edge with the shorter edge on top, then topstitch through all layers. The wider layer underneath will be stitched at the same time (**fig. 7**). ▨

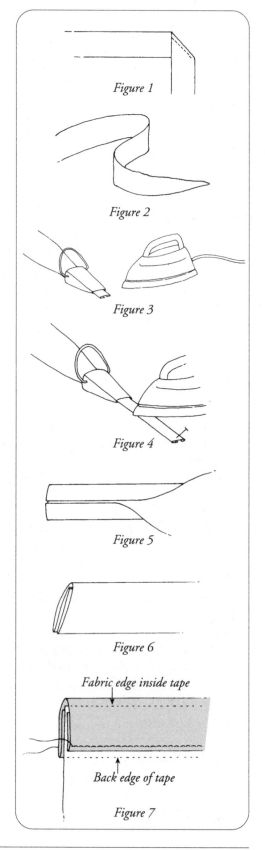

Figure 1

Figure 2

Figure 3

Figure 4

Figure 5

Figure 6

Fabric edge inside tape

Back edge of tape

Figure 7

Double Lace Scallops

Double lace scallops are formed by creating two rows of lace scallops with a space between them. The space may be filled with plain fabric, pintucked fabric, embroidered fabric, fabric of a different color or lace insertions stitched together, just to name a few options. The instructions below are to be used with any of these techniques. Two methods are given; the one to be used will be determined by personal preference unless a method is specified in the instructions for a particular project.

Supplies

* Fabric on which scallops will be placed
* Lace insertion for shaping scallops
* Scallop template
* Washout marking pen or pencil

A. Method I

1. Trace or cut out the pattern piece to be embellished, as directed in the specific instructions. Trace only the upper row of scallops onto the fabric. Center the design at center front and mark the template so that the lower row of scallops will match the upper row (**fig. 1**).

2. Place the fabric on a lace-shaping board and shape the scallops onto the right side of the fabric, using lace insertion and following the steps for shaping scallops on page 224.

3. Stitch across only the upper edge of the scallops, using a tiny zigzag (**see fig. 2**).

4. Trim the fabric from below the stitching, leaving the lace scallops on the edge of the fabric (**fig. 2**).

5. Create the fabric to be inserted between the scalloped rows, making the fabric as wide as the instructions call for.

6. Trace the same scallop design onto the bottom edge of the fabric strip, making sure that the scallops will match those on the upper piece (**see fig. 3**).

7. Place the fabric strip onto a lace-shaping board and shape the scallops onto the right side of the fabric strip as before.

8. Use a tiny zigzag and stitch across only the upper edge of the insertion as before. Trim the fabric away from below the scallops (**fig. 3**).

9. Place the top edge of the fabric strip underneath the upper row of scallops, overlapping the two edges so that the top edge of the fabric strip is just above the top point of the scallops on the wrong side, or placing the strip according to the project instructions. Pin in place (**see fig. 4**).

10. With the right sides of both pieces facing up, zigzag along the lower edge of the upper row of scallops. Trim away the excess of the fabric strip from behind the upper scallops (**fig. 4**).

11. Finish the bottom edge of the embellished pattern piece as directed in the project instructions.

B. Method II

1. Trace or cut out the pattern piece to be embellished, as directed in the specific instructions.

2. Create the fabric strip that will be placed between the two scalloped rows.

3. Trace both rows of the scallops onto the fabric strip, one row at the top and one row at the bottom. Make sure that the centers of the scalloped designs are lined up at the center of the fabric strip (**fig. 5**).

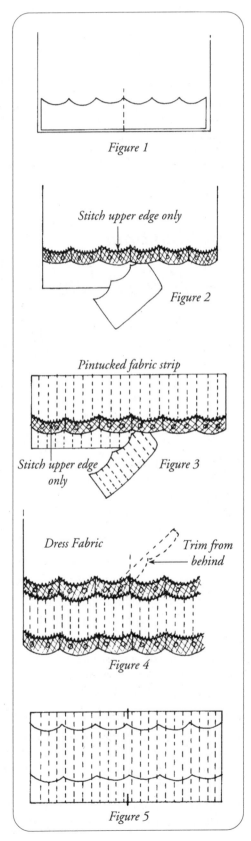

Figure 1

Stitch upper edge only

Figure 2

Pintucked fabric strip

Stitch upper edge only

Figure 3

Dress Fabric

Trim from behind

Figure 4

Figure 5

4. Place the fabric strip onto a lace-shaping board and shape the scallops, referring to the instructions on page 224.

5. Use a tiny zigzag to stitch across only the lower edge of the top row of scallops, and across only the top edge of the lower row of scallops (see **fig. 6**).

6. Trim the excess of the fabric strip away from behind the scallops (**fig. 6**).

7. Place the scalloped strip over the lower edge of the pattern piece to be embellished. Overlap the edges so that the fabric extends to just below the upper row of scallops, or place the strip as directed in the project instructions. Pin the strip in place (see **fig. 7**).

8. Use a tiny zigzag to stitch across the upper edge of the top row of scallops, attaching the scalloped strip to the fabric pattern piece. Trim away the excess skirt fabric from behind the scallops (**fig. 7**).

9. Finish the bottom edge of the embellished pattern piece as directed in the project instructions. ▣

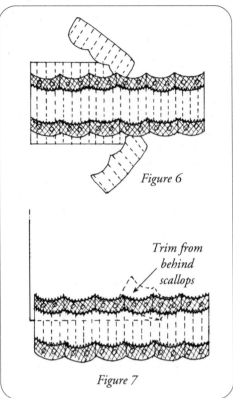

Figure 6

Trim from behind scallops

Figure 7

New Technique
Hemstitching A Scalloped Hem

This technique offers a beautiful method to make a scalloped/hemstitched effect while stitching in a hem at the same time. What an easy way to hem an elegant skirt!

Supplies

✴ Wing needle or large general purpose needle (the needle must be large enough to create a hole in the fabric)
✴ Washout fabric marker or pencil
✴ Tear-away or water-soluble stabilizer
✴ Spray starch

Directions

1. Sew one or both side seams of the skirt, according to the instructions.

2. Lightly spray starch the fabric and iron it dry.

3. Press the hem allowance to the wrong side.

4. Place the scallop template on the skirt right side with the points of the scallops ¹/₄" below the turned-up edge on the inside. Be sure that the template is centered as directed in the instructions (see **fig. 1**).

5. Trace the scallops onto the fabric with a washout fabric marker or pencil (**fig. 1**).

6. Place a suitable stabilizer underneath the fabric.

7. Insert a wing needle or large general purpose needle into the machine and thread with the same thread on top and in the bobbin. Do a practice piece to adjust the tension. Set the machine for a hemstitch (most stitches that go into the same hole more than once will work).

8. Stitch along the scallop lines with a steady speed, leaving the needle in the fabric at the points to pivot for a sharp point (**fig. 2**).

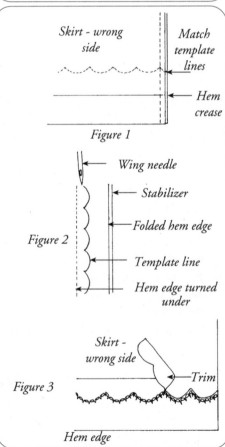

Skirt - wrong side   *Match template lines*

Hem crease

Figure 1

Wing needle

Stabilizer

Folded hem edge

Figure 2

Template line

Hem edge turned under

Skirt - wrong side

Trim

Figure 3

Hem edge

9. After the hem is stitched, remove the stabilizer and trim the excess fabric away from above the scallops on the wrong side (**fig. 3**). ▣

New Technique

Antique Peek-a-Boo

The antique peek-a-boo technique may be made in bands, or in blocks for use in making shapes such as hearts, diamonds, etc. In either case, the strips to be joined may be fabric, lace, or a combination. The lace should be insertion, at least ⁵/₈" wide, and have an isolated, repeated pattern (see fig. 1). The first instructions below are written for a skirt band using fabric for the skirt and the hem, with a lace strip between. The second set of instructions are for making a block using lace only, from which shapes can be cut, or the yoke for a jumper.

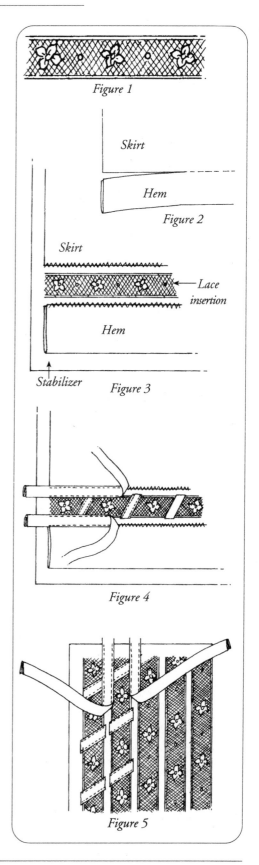

Figure 1

Figure 2

Figure 3

Figure 4

Figure 5

Supplies

* Fabric for garment
* Bias strips cut from the garment fabric
* Water-soluble stabilizer (WSS)
* Liquid pinning product for temporary gluing

A. Making a Peek-a-Boo Lace Skirt Band

1. Cut the skirt pieces to the required size as directed in the garment instructions. Sew the skirt pieces together at one side seam, right sides together, and finish the seam.

2. Press up the hem, then cut the skirt apart where the raw edge of the pressed hem meets the skirt (fig. 2).

3. Cut a strip of lace insertion long enough to go across the bottom edge of the skirt.

4. Place the lace strip on a piece of water-soluble stabilizer and press in place (use very little or no steam, otherwise the WSS will dissolve; however, a small amount of steam may be needed to make the lace adhere to the WSS. Do a practice piece first.) (see fig. 3).

5. Place the cut edges of the skirt and hem (with the hem folded) over the WSS along the edges of the lace insertion, leaving a small space between the lace and the fabric, about ¹/₈". Use a tiny zigzag and stitch the fabric edges to the WSS (fig. 3).

6. Decide whether the bias strips will cross the lace at an angle, or straight. Count how many bias pieces will be needed to go across the lace, then add twice the width of the skirt to determine how much bias tape to make.

7. Cut enough 1" wide bias strips to make the length needed. Follow the instructions on page 248 to make double-fold bias tape, using a ¹/₂" bias tape maker or following the instructions in section B if no bias tape maker is available.

8. Cut enough short bias tape strips to cross the lace between the patterns. Place the strips over the lace and "glue" in place with a liquid pins product. The strips may be stitched in place along both edges at this point, or they may be caught only at the ends when the long strips are stitched in place (see fig. 4).

9. After the short strips have been glued and/or stitched in place over the lace, place long strips of the bias tape over the spaces left between the long edges of the lace and fabric. Glue the long strips in place with the liquid pins product and stitch in place along both long edges of each bias tape strip. Be sure that the stitching connects the bias tape to the lace and fabric on each side (fig. 4).

B. Making an Antique Peek-a-Boo Block

1. Place parallel strips of lace over WSS, covering an area large enough to cut the shape or pattern piece from. Be careful to arrange the patterns in the lace strips so that a nice grid will be formed when the strips are placed across the lace (see fig. 5).

2. Leave a ¹/₈" space between the strips and press to adhere the lace to the WSS.

3. Continue with steps 6 - 9 above. Remember that there is no fabric in this method, the long strips of bias tape will connect two strips of lace (fig. 5). ▨

Machine Tatting

This great technique allows the addition of an openwork machine edging similar to tatting or crochet in a fraction of the time it would take to make the same edging by hand. Using lighter weight thread produces a tatted look, while the use of heavier thread gives a crocheted look.

Supplies

* Silk or cotton machine embroidery thread
* Heat-Away or other iron-off stabilizer

Directions

1. The edge that the tatting will be applied to must be a finished edge, either hemmed or folded.

2. Thread the machine with the embroidery thread in the needle and in the bobbin, both threads will show in the finished edging. The weight of the thread will determine the finished weight of the edging. Heavier thread will look more like crochet, lighter weight thread will look more like tatting.

3. Cut strips of the iron-off stabilizer approximately 1¹/₂" - 2" wide; the actual width will depend on the width of the finished edging. The stabilizer must be wide enough to extend underneath the edge of the ruffle and support the width of the edging.

4. Place a strip of the stabilizer under the edge of the fabric; the fabric may be basted in place but it is not necessary.

5. Choose a stitch such as a straight-stitch scallop or a three-step zigzag. The needle will catch the fabric edge only on the left-hand stitch of the first row of stitching; the other rows will be stitched over the stabilizer only. It may be necessary to mirror the stitch from side to side to make the left swing of the needle enter the fabric edge, which will be on the left (**fig. 1 and 2**).

6. Use a foot that provides good visibility of the stitching area, such as an open-toe appliqué foot or a clear decorative stitch foot.

7. Sew the first row of stitching so that the left-hand stitch of the design enters the fabric edge and the rest of the stitch design is formed on the stabilizer only. Stitch all the way across the first row (**fig. 2**).

8. Begin the second row of stitching with the first left-hand stitch entering the center of one design on the previous row. In other words, the designs for the second row will be staggered with the designs of the first row. The second row will be stitched on the stabilizer only and will not be attached to the fabric edge (**fig. 3**).

9. Sew as many rows as needed to make the edging the correct width, alternating the designs of each row with the previous row (**fig. 4**).

NOTE: It is very important that water or steam does not come into contact with the project while the stabilizer is attached to it. The liquid can release chemicals into the project which will make it disintegrate when heated.

10. To remove the stabilizer, cover the ironing surface with a press cloth. Do not use steam, use a dry iron only! Place the edging on the press cloth, right side down. Press the stabilizer with a dry, hot iron until the stabilizer turns brown. Gently brush away the stabilizer with a toothbrush. ⬛

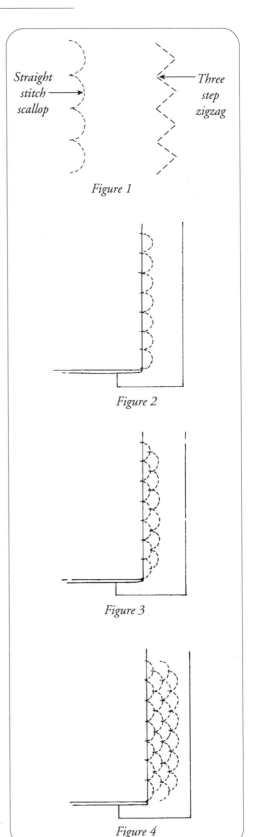

Straight stitch scallop

Three step zigzag

Figure 1

Figure 2

Figure 3

Figure 4

New Technique
Double Needle Edge Trim

The look of double piping is easily accomplished with this double needle trim. Using a double needle and a zigzag stitch allows two exactly parallel rows of stitching to be made at the same time. Depending on the width of the zigzag, there may be a tiny strip of fabric left between the two rows, or the stitches may butt together for a solid trim.

A double needle is really two needles attached to a single shank. The first number denotes the distance between the needles, the second number indicates the size of the needles. Use a 1.6, 2.0 or 2.5 double needle for this technique, in sizes 70 or 80. Some of the newer machines will use wider needles for this technique, but be sure to do a sample to check the zigzag width. Be sure that the zigzag width will allow the needles to clear the throat plate without hitting the edges and breaking.

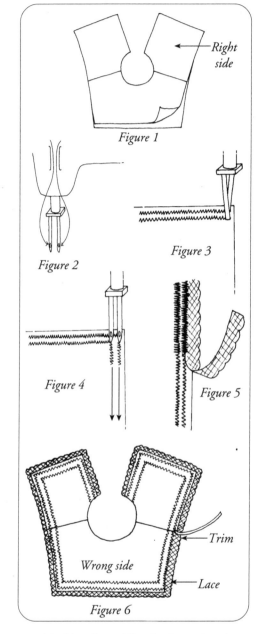

Figure 1

Figure 2

Figure 3

Figure 4

Figure 5

Wrong side

Trim

Lace

Figure 6

Supplies

✳ Double needle
✳ Machine embroidery thread
✳ Paper or water-soluble stabilizer

Directions

1. Work through all layers of the section to be trimmed. For example, on a lined collar, place the lining and the collar piece with wrong sides together and work through both layers (**fig. 1**). Note: You will stitch around the collar two times, one on top of the other.

2. Thread the double needle with decorative machine embroidery thread, using two colors for the most effective look. When threading the double needle, remember to run each thread separately, one on each side of the tension disk, and thread the needle that is on the same side of the tension disk (**fig. 2**).

3. The bobbin should be filled with cotton machine embroidery thread that is the same color as the fabric. Loosen the top tension slightly and make a practice piece before starting the actual project and use an open-toe or plastic foot for good visibility. Refer to the machine manual if further adjustments are needed. For some machines, it may be necessary to run both threads through the same side of the tension disk, and the tension may be adjusted differently.

4. For the first row of stitching (which will go all the way around the collar), set the machine for a narrow zigzag and short length, but not a satin stitch. Stitch with the outer needle on the stitching line. When a corner is reached, stop with the needles in the fabric and very carefully turn the work to the new direction (**fig. 3**).

5. Slowly raise the needles, they will pop back into a straight position, and continue stitching along the next side (**fig. 4**).

6. For the second row of stitching around the collar, set the zigzag a little wider (so that there is no empty space between the colored threads) and stitch around the line again with a satin stitch length; stitch over the satin stitches of the previous row. While stitching this second row, butt the edge of the lace (optional) to the edge of the stitching and catch the lace edge in the stitches (**fig. 5**).

7. After stitching the entire edge, trim away any excess fabric outside the stitching line from the wrong side. Be careful not to cut into the stitching (**fig. 6**).

Tips: When working the practice sample, check for these problems.

a. If the fabric "tunnels" under the stitches, the zigzag is too wide. Either narrow the stitch width or place a stabilizer underneath the fabric.

b. It may also be necessary to place a stabilizer under the edge while working the second stitch row.

c. If the edge of the fabric ripples, try running a row of straight stitches along the stitching line before working the zigzag rows. ▨

Shadow Sandwich Technique

This technique must be worked using two layers of fabric in order to create the sandwich. If the design will go at the hem, it will be placed between the two hem layers. If the design will be placed on the collar, sleeves, bodice, etc., that area of the garment must be lined.

Supplies

* Lightweight, light colored fabric for top layer
* Broadcloth or other tightly woven fabric for shadow color
* Machine embroidery thread to match the shadow color and the top fabric color
* Machine embroidery needle, size 70 or 80
* Lightweight paper-backed fusible web for sewing machine work, not craft weight

Directions

1. Trace the shadow design onto the paper side of the fusible web. Remember that if the design has a definite left and right side, it must be traced in reverse (**fig.** 1).

2. Cut out the design and set it aside.

3. If the design goes behind a hem, press the hem in place to create the facing, then open the hem out flat. If the design goes behind a collar or sleeve, trace the collar or sleeve onto the lining. Mark the placement for the design onto the lining or hem facing (**see fig.** 2).

4. Peel the paper backing away from the cut out designs. Place the designs on the lining or facing pieces. The designs must be placed on the side of the fabric that will face the wrong side of the top layer. Fuse the designs in place according to the instructions for the fusible web. When the designs are fused in place, they will face in the correct direction (**fig.** 2).

5. Fold the hem facing into place or place the top garment layer over the lining. If the design is in the hem area, hem the garment at this point. Pin the pieces together well to prevent slipping during construction (**fig.** 3).

6. Thread the machine needle with the thread to match the shadow and wind the bobbin with the thread that matches the lining or top layer. Slightly lower the top tension.

7. Set the machine for a short straight stitch, 1.5 to 2.0. Stitch through both layers along the outline of the shadow design. Be careful to stitch right along the outline; if the stitches are on the design, it will look like it wasn't trimmed well; if the stitches are on the top layer, a gap will show between the design and the stitches (**fig.** 4).

8. When the stitching is complete, do not backstitch. Pull the thread tails to the back side and tie into a knot before clipping the thread tails. ▨

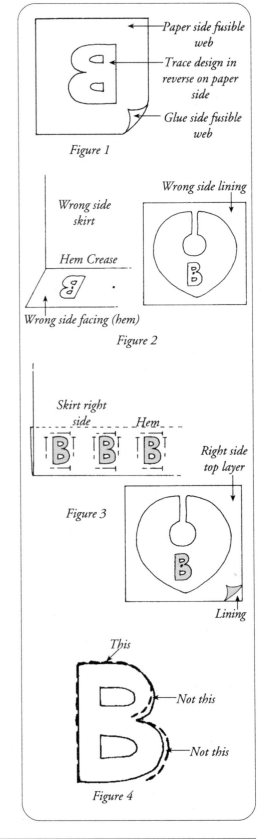

Paper side fusible web

Trace design in reverse on paper side

Glue side fusible web

Figure 1

Wrong side skirt

Hem Crease

Wrong side facing (hem)

Wrong side lining

Figure 2

Skirt right side

Hem

Right side top layer

Figure 3

Lining

This

Not this

Not this

Figure 4

Built-In Machine Embroidery on Heirloom Clothing

With the embroidery features on today's machines, any garment can have an elegant handmade look. For a handmade garment, the embroidery can be added during construction, making a one-of-a-kind original design. If the garment is purchased, the addition of machine embroidery can add a touch of elegance that will make an ordinary garment look like a designer original. Use the tips below for successful embroidery.

Directions

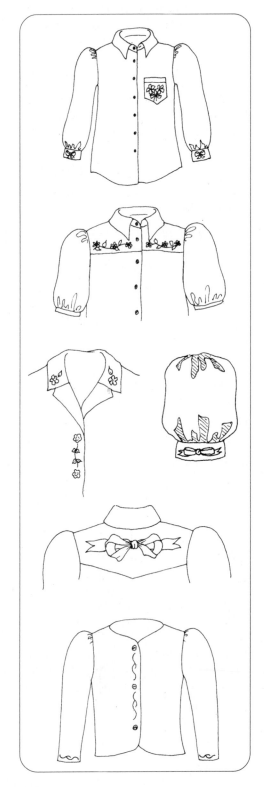

1. Follow the embroidery instructions for each particular machine to ensure good results.

2. When working with heirloom fabrics, be sure to stabilize the delicate fabric before adding embroidery. Spray starch works well on natural fibers. If more stability is needed, try a water-soluble or crisp paper tear-away stabilizer. Iron-off stabilizers are also available; they should be used primarily on fabrics which will not be washed and then ironed.

3. If a design is small, a hoop may provide enough stability. Be sure to use a padded hoop to prevent marks in the fabric.

4. The best way to secure thread tails is to pull them to the back and tie in a knot. A drop of seam sealant may be added to the knot for further security.

5. Placement of embroidery designs can be critical to the look of a garment. If possible, try on the garment before placing the embroidery. If the garment is being constructed, it is worth the time it takes to baste the major pieces together and try it on to mark placement on bodices or jackets.

6. For purchased garments, the pockets can often be removed, then reattached after the embroidery is complete. Try a crest or floral spray on a pocket. Bows are also good choices. Other good areas for embroidery are on collars, cuffs, front plackets, yokes and hems.

7. Another way to enhance the look of purchased garments is to replace the original buttons with new ones that coordinate with the embroidery. Try a vine design between front buttonholes, then add flower buttons. A scroll design between buttonholes looks great with tailored buttons.

8. Make sure that the embroidery threads and buttons used can be cared for by the same methods as the garment fabric. Finished embroidery should be pressed from the wrong side on a padded surface, with a press cloth. ▨

Decorative Serged Seams

Decorative serging is a quick way to dress up a project. It also makes construction go very quickly if the decorative seams are used as construction seams. The decorative threads can go in the upper and/or lower looper, and lightweight decorative threads can be used in the needle; the seams may be serged with two or three threads. Follow the instructions in the serger manual for the most effective settings. The following guidelines are tips that may make decorative serging easier and more fun.

Supplies

* Serger set for two- or three-thread decorative serging
* Decorative threads for one or both loopers
* Matching or coordinating thread for the needle

Directions

1. Decorative serged seams may be left raised, or they may be pressed to one side and top-stitched in place.

   a. If the seam will be left raised, use decorative thread in the upper and lower loopers. The needle may be threaded with lightweight thread to match or coordinate with the decorative looper threads (**fig. 1**).

   b. If the seam will be stitched down, the decorative thread may be used in the upper looper only, with the needle thread matching or coordinating with the decorative looper thread (**fig. 2**).

2. Make several sample pieces using different tension settings. Try to use the same fabrics as in the finished project.

3. The stitch length will vary with the weight of the decorative thread. Lightweight threads will require a closer stitch length than heavier threads.

4. Remember that with exposed seams, the seams will be sewn with the wrong sides together. Most seams will look better if a little fabric is cut away as the seam is made.

5. Make sure that the threads used can be cared for in the same way as the fabric.

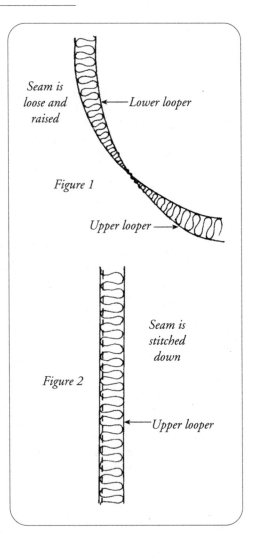

Seam is loose and raised — Lower looper

Upper looper

Figure 1

Seam is stitched down

Figure 2

Upper looper

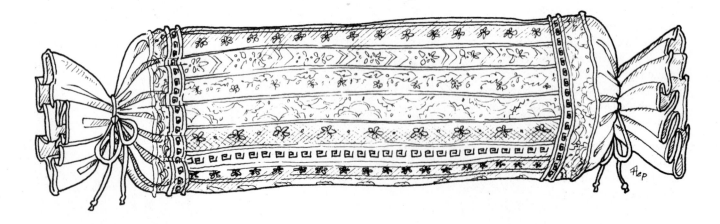

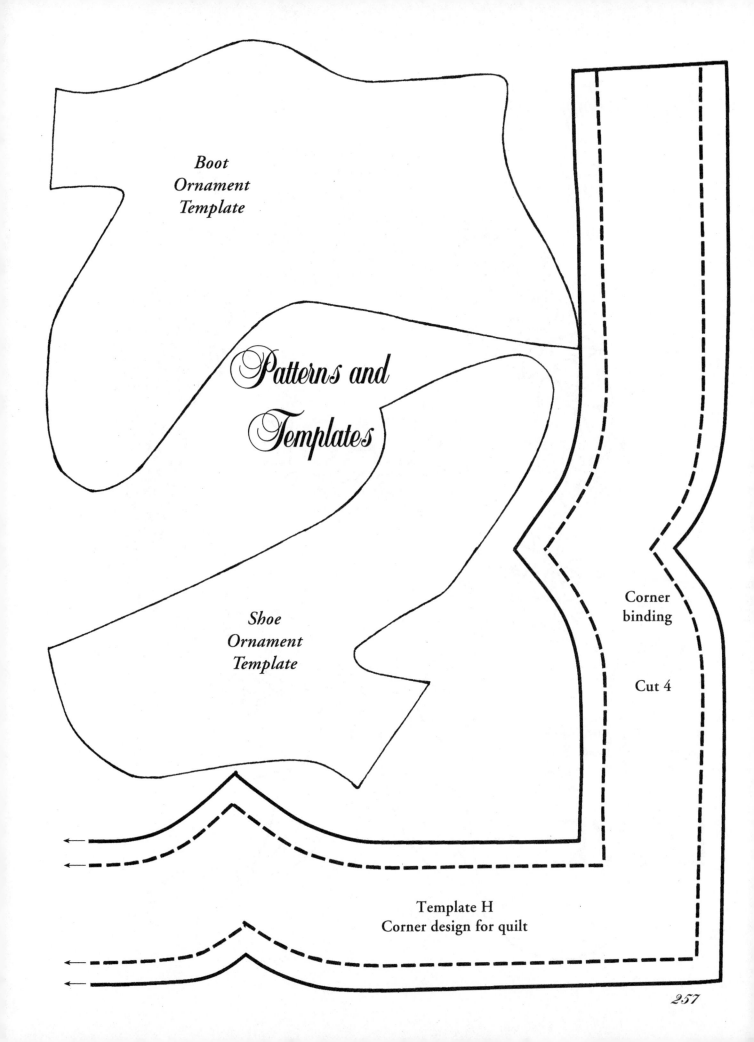

Boot
Ornament
Template

Patterns and
Templates

Shoe
Ornament
Template

Corner
binding

Cut 4

Template H
Corner design for quilt

Wreath Block 1,3,7 and 9
Template A

PEACE

JOY

HOPE

LOVE

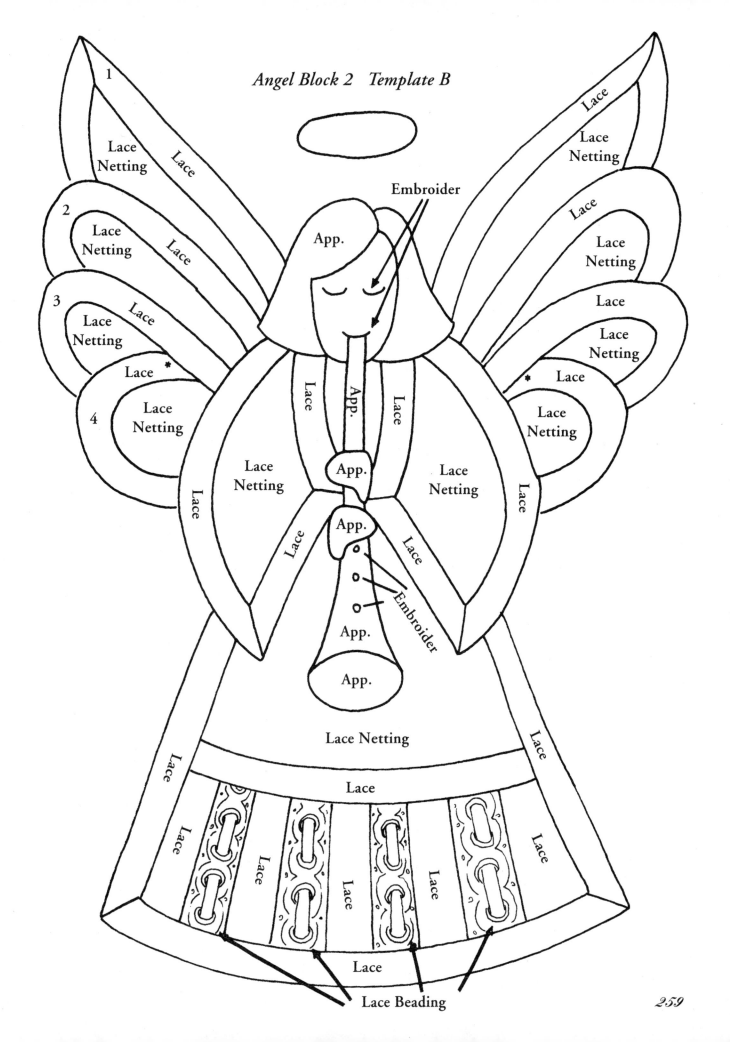

Angel Block 2 Template B

259

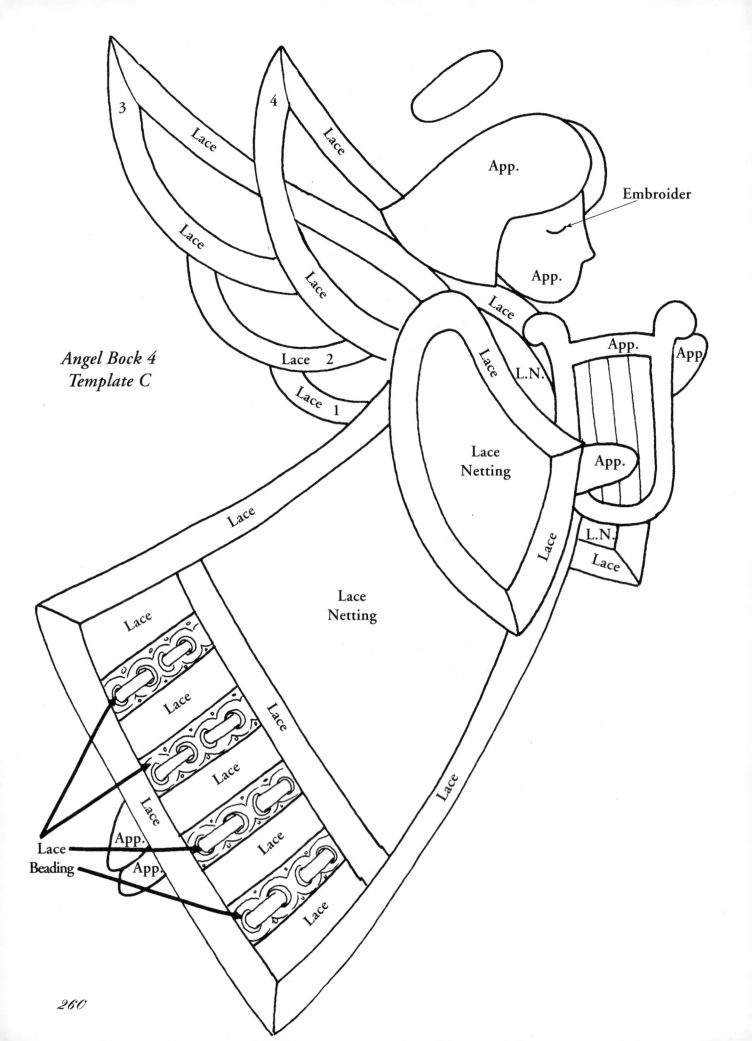

Angel Bock 4
Template C

260

Center Design
Block 5
Template D

My
Angels
watch over
Me

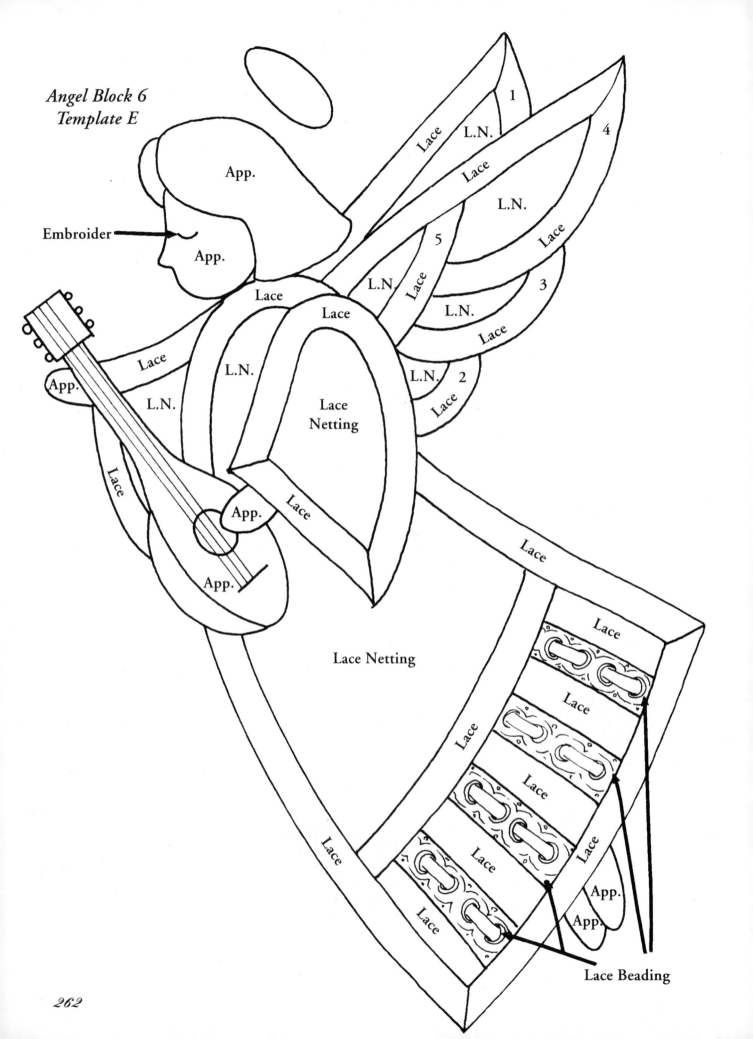

Angel Block 6
Template E

Embroider

App.

App.

App.

Lace

L.N.

Lace

1

L.N.

Lace

L.N.

4

Lace

5

L.N.

Lace

L.N.

3

L.N.

Lace

Lace
Netting

Lace

App.

App.

App.

L.N.

Lace

L.N.

2

Lace

Lace

Lace

Lace Netting

Lace

Lace

Lace

Lace

Lace

Lace

Lace

App.

App.

Lace Beading

262

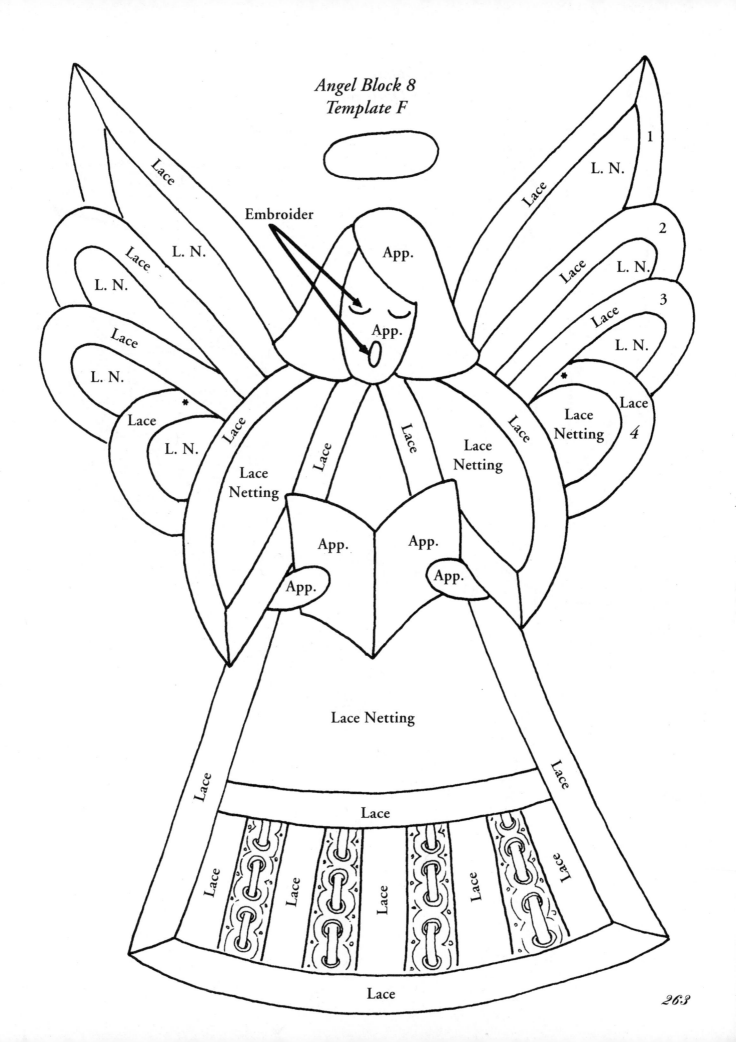

Angel Block 8
Template F

263

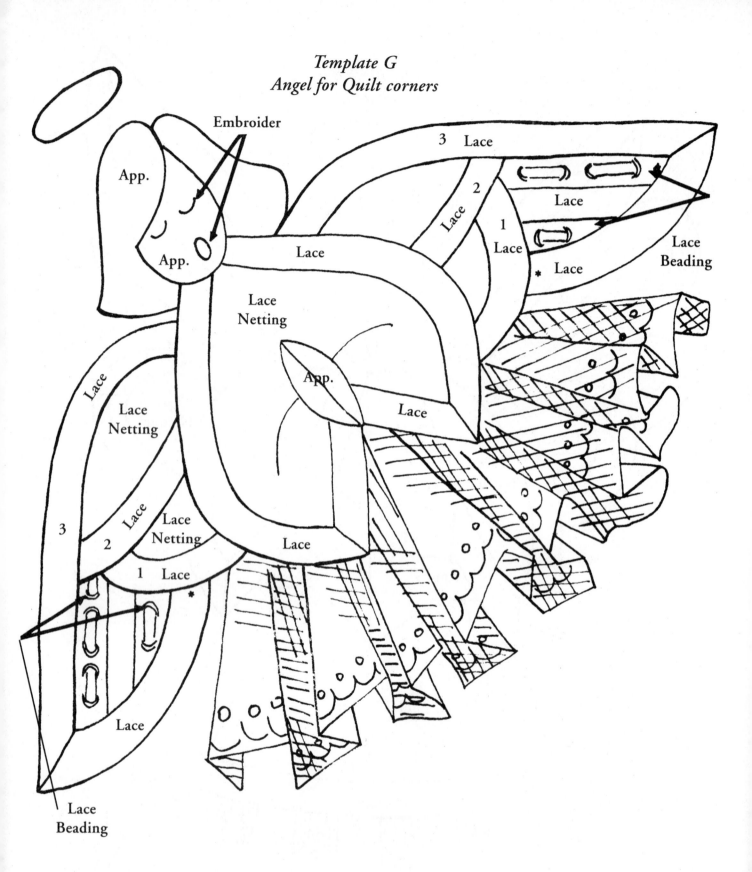

Template G
Angel for Quilt corners

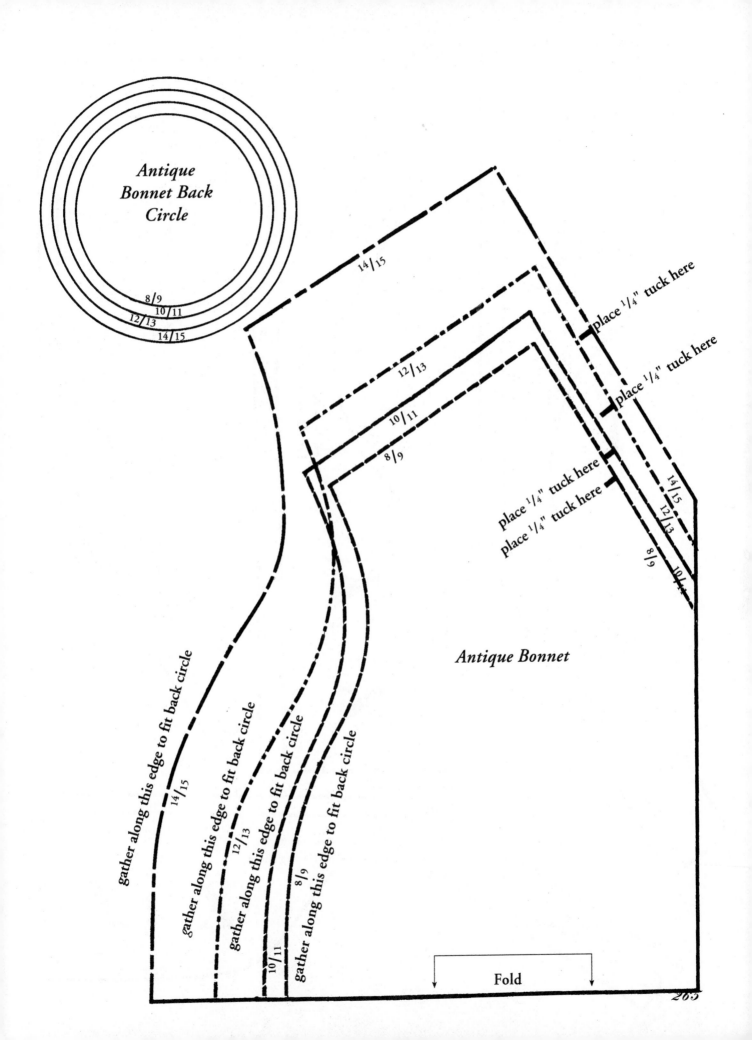

Antique Bonnet Back Circle

8/9
10/11
12/13
14/15

14/15

12/13

10/11

8/9

place ¼" tuck here

place ¼" tuck here

place ¼" tuck here

place ¼" tuck here

14/15

12/13

8/9

10/11

Antique Bonnet

gather along this edge to fit back circle — 14/15

gather along this edge to fit back circle — 12/13

gather along this edge to fit back circle — 10/11

gather along this edge to fit back circle — 8/9

Fold

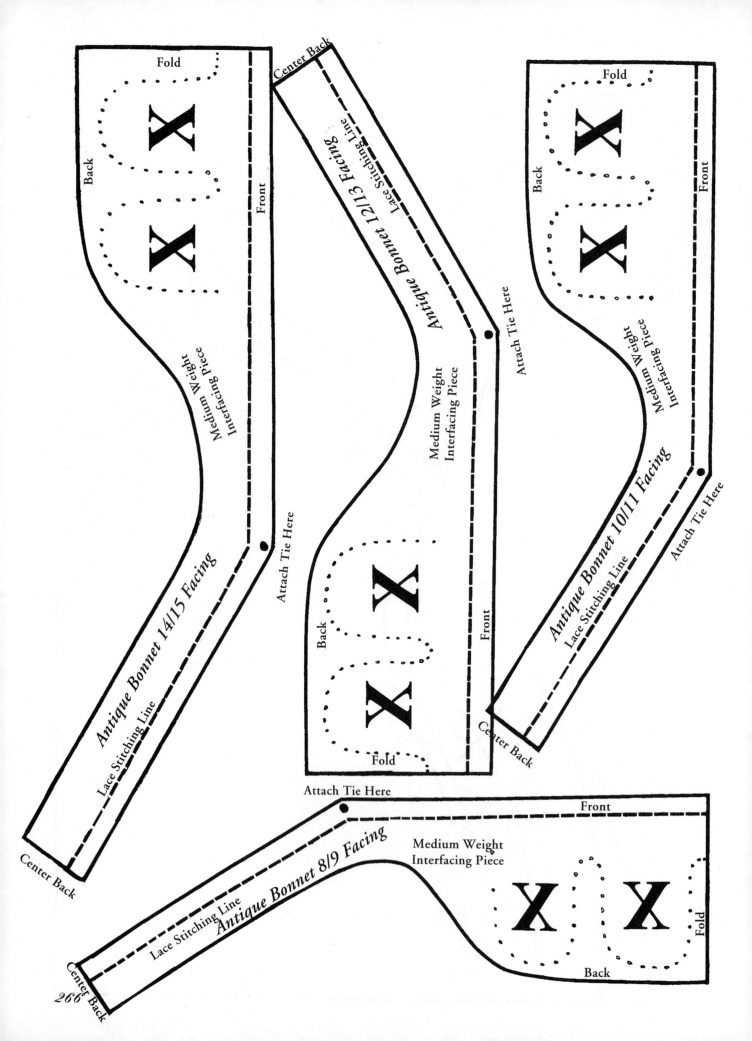

Fold

Back

Front

Medium Weight Interfacing Piece

Antique Bonnet 14/15 Facing

Lace Stitching Line

Attach Tie Here

Center Back

Center Back

Antique Bonnet 12/13 Facing

Lace Stitching Line

Medium Weight Interfacing Piece

Back

Fold

Attach Tie Here

Attach Tie Here

Fold

Back

Front

Medium Weight Interfacing Piece

Antique Bonnet 10/11 Facing

Lace Stitching Line

Attach Tie Here

Center Back

Attach Tie Here

Front

Medium Weight Interfacing Piece

Center Back

Center Back

Antique Bonnet 8/9 Facing

Lace Stitching Line

Back

Fold

266

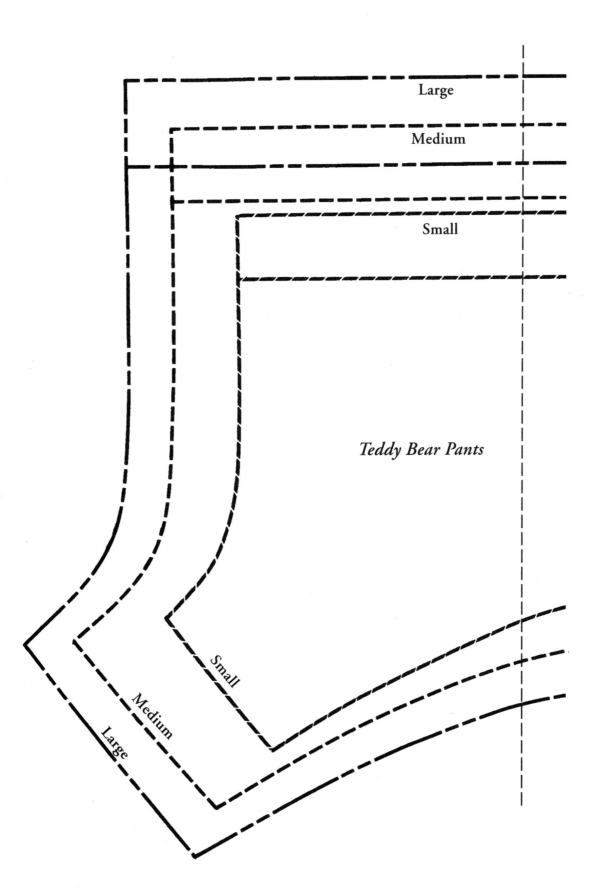

Large

Medium

Small

Teddy Bear Pants

Small

Medium

Large

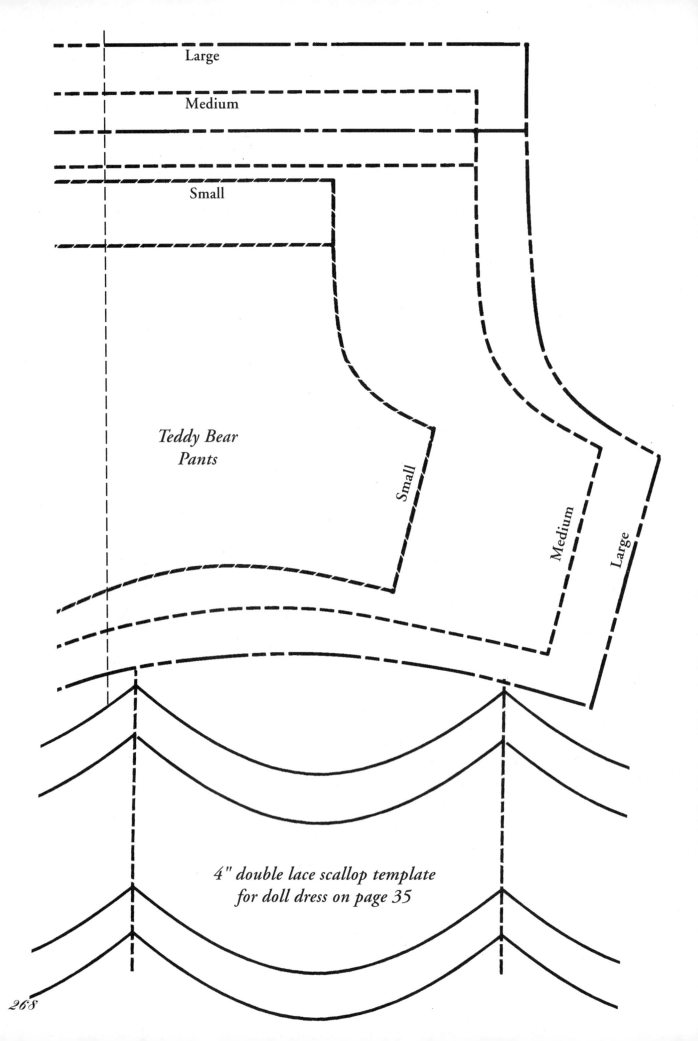

Large

Medium

Small

*Teddy Bear
Pants*

Small

Medium

Large

*4" double lace scallop template
for doll dress on page 35*

268

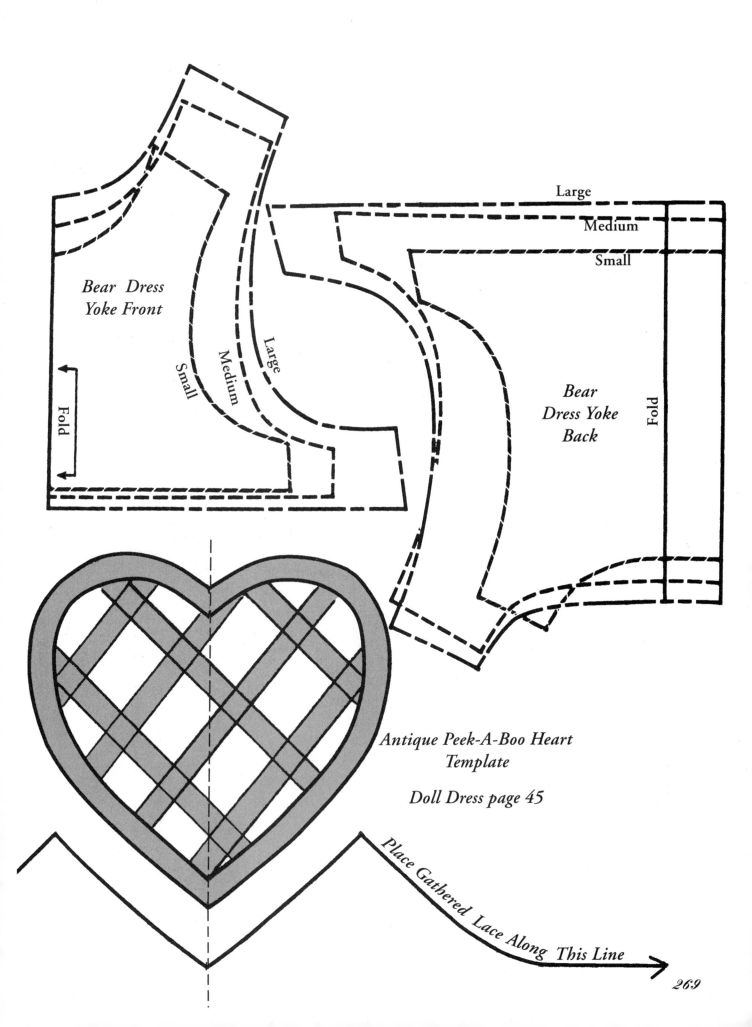

*Bear Dress
Yoke Front*

Fold

Small

Medium

Large

Large

Medium

Small

*Bear
Dress Yoke
Back*

Fold

*Antique Peek-A-Boo Heart
Template*

Doll Dress page 45

Place Gathered Lace Along This Line

269

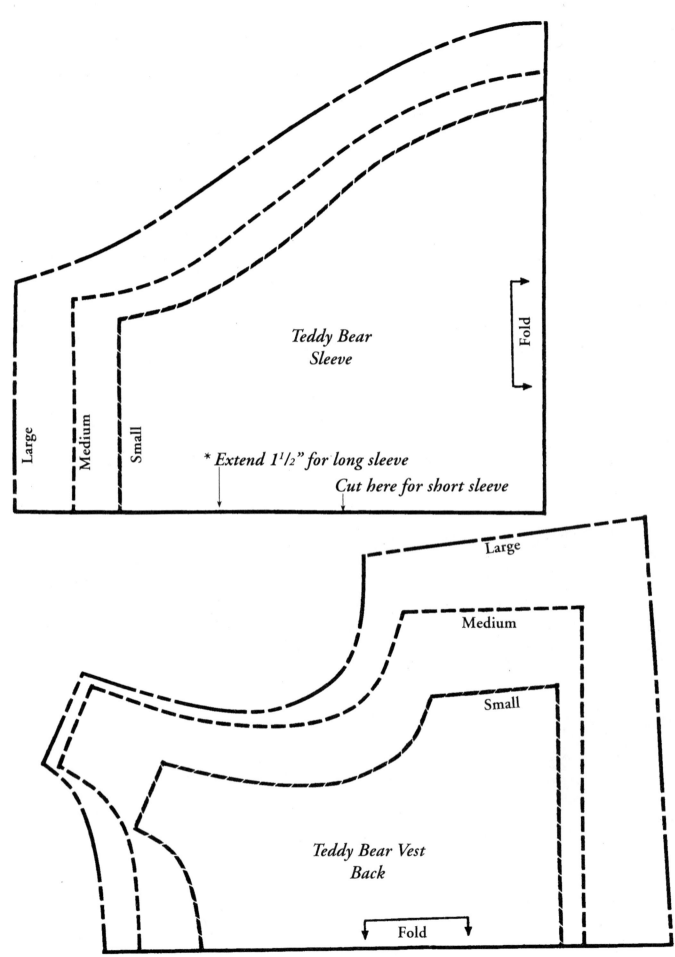

*Teddy Bear
Sleeve*

Fold

Large

Medium

Small

* *Extend 1¹/₂" for long sleeve*

Cut here for short sleeve

Large

Medium

Small

*Teddy Bear Vest
Back*

Fold

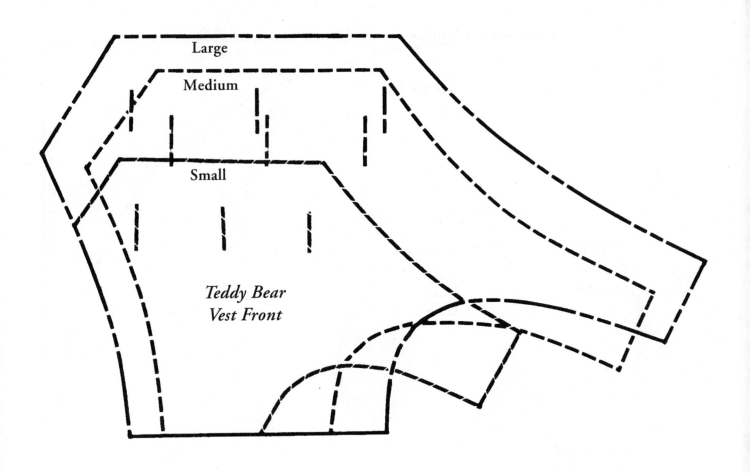

Large

Medium

Small

Teddy Bear
Vest Front

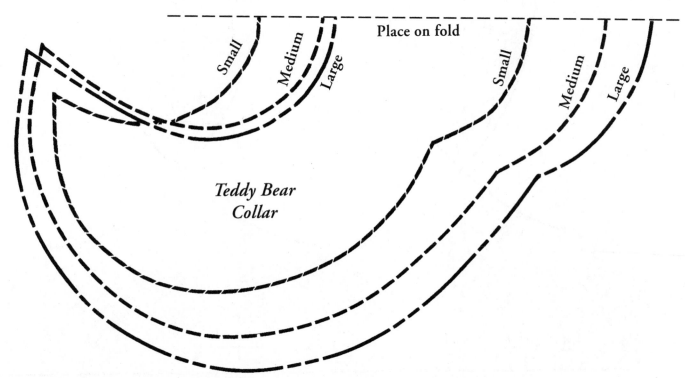

Place on fold

Small Medium Large Small Medium Large

Teddy Bear
Collar

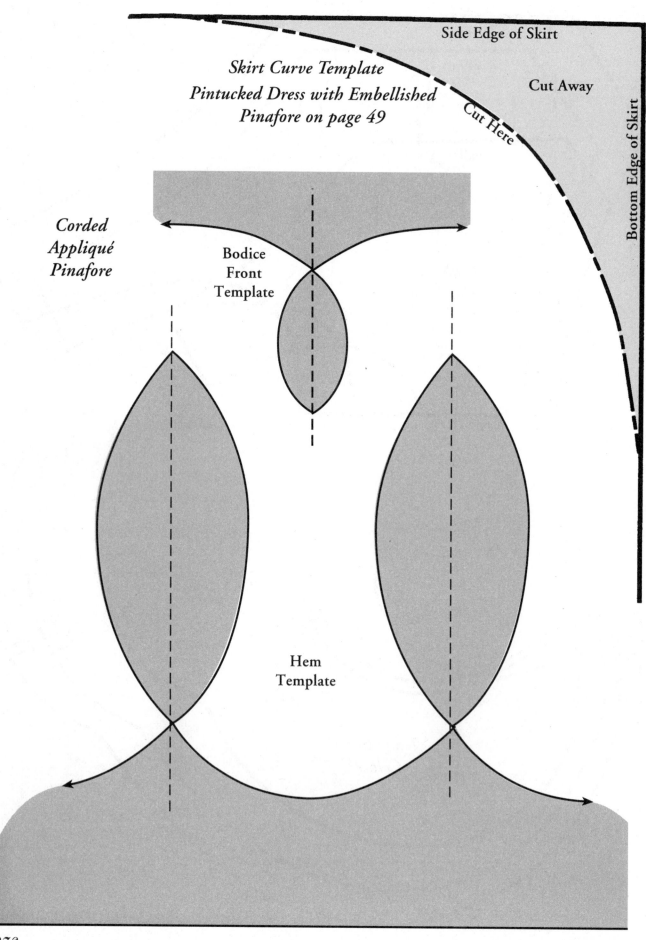

Skirt Curve Template
Pintucked Dress with Embellished
Pinafore on page 49

Side Edge of Skirt

Cut Away

Cut Here

Bottom Edge of Skirt

Corded
Appliqué
Pinafore

Bodice
Front
Template

Hem
Template

Index

About The Author

Martha Campbell Pullen, a native of Scottsboro, Alabama, is an internationally-known lecturer and author in the heirloom sewing field. After graduating with a degree in speech and English from the University of Alabama, she taught those subjects at almost every level of middle school and high school. Later, her studies led to receiving a Ph.D. in educational administration and management from the University of Alabama.

Her love of sewing and children's clothing encouraged the opening of Martha Pullen's Heirloom Shop in Huntsville, Alabama, August 1, 1981. Two months later, she opened Martha Pullen Company, Inc., the wholesale division. She has served on the board of directors of the Smocking Arts Guild of America and has presented workshops on French sewing by machine throughout the United States, Canada, Australia, England and New Zealand. Books she has written and published include *French Hand Sewing by Machine, A Beginner's Guide; Heirloom Doll Clothes; Bearly Beginning Smocking; Shadow Work Embroidery; French Sewing by Machine: The Second Book; Antique Clothing: French Sewing by Machine; Grandmother's Hope Chest; Appliqué, Martha's Favorites; Heirloom Sewing For Women; Joy of Smocking; Martha's Sewing Room; Victorian Sewing And Crafts; Martha's Heirloom Magic; Martha's Attic; Silk Ribbon Treasures; Heirloom Doll Clothes For Götz; Sewing Inspirations From Yesteryear, A Christmas to Remember* and *Madeira Appliqué by Machine.*

Martha is also the founder and publisher of a best-selling magazine, *Sew Beautiful,* which is dedicated to heirloom sewing. The publication charms more than 80,000 readers worldwide. She has just completed a television series for public television entitled, "Martha's Sewing Room." A second magazine, *Martha Pullen's Fancywork,* will premier August 1, 1997. Several times each year she conducts the Martha Pullen School of Art Fashion in Huntsville.

She is the wife of Joseph Ross Pullen, an implant dentist, mother of five of the most wonderful children in the world, and grandmother of the seven most beautiful, intelligent, precious and most adorable grandchildren in the world. She participates in many civic activities including the Rotary Club, and is an active member of her church. She also volunteers with the Southern Baptist Foreign Mission Board. In 1995 she was named Huntsville/Madison Chamber of Commerce Executive of the Year, becoming the second woman in the history of the award to receive this honor. ▨